Emanuel Deutsch

Literary remains of the late Emanuel Deutsch. With a brief memoir

Emanuel Deutsch

Literary remains of the late Emanuel Deutsch. With a brief memoir

ISBN/EAN: 9783337873639

Printed in Europe, USA, Canada, Australia, Japan

Cover: Foto ©ninafisch / pixelio.de

More available books at **www.hansebooks.com**

LITERARY REMAINS

OF THE LATE

EMANUEL DEUTSCH

WITH A BRIEF MEMOIR

NEW YORK
HENRY HOLT AND COMPANY
1874

CONTENTS.

MEMOIR.

EMANUEL OSCAR MENAHEM DEUTSCH was born at Neisse in Prussian Silesia on the 28th of October, 1829, of Jewish parents, whose family had been settled there for some generations.

In the atmosphere of his home he breathed a certain amount of intelligence and learning, but yet more of affection. There are perhaps no people on earth in whom the ties of relationship are so strong as among the Jews, and especially among the German Jews; the tenderness of the mother is scarcely equal even to the bond of close affection that usually exists between father and son. In the Deutsch family it was remarkably powerful, and continued so to the end. At the age of six, the young Emanuel entered the "Gymnasium" of Neisse, and remained in it for two years; but at the end of this time his father yielded to the entreaties of his uncle David Deutsch, then residing at Mislowitz, and gave up the boy's education into his hands. This uncle was a man of great learning: he was a Rabbi who had made the Talmud his especial study, and had written several scholarly works. The education was a severe one for so young a student. Winter and summer he had to rise at five o'clock, and to study without fire or food for one hour or two, until the time of the daily prayer had arrived, in which another hour was passed. The rest of the day, until 8 P.M., was passed in close application to his books, one quarter of an hour being the only time allowed for recreation, and about the same for exercise and fresh air. He used to look back to these years with painful self-pity, although his attachment to his uncle was profound and tender, and his gratitude to him unbounded.[1] On completing his thirteenth year Emanuel returned to Neisse, to celebrate his Bar-mitzva or religious majority, when it is the custom for Jewish lads to read publicly in the Synagogue a portion of the lesson from Scripture on the first following Sabbath. The sentence that fell to his share was this: "Get thee out of thy country, and from thy kindred and from thy father's house." (Gen. xii. 1.) He then resumed his studies at the Gymnasium, and notwithstanding his separation from his uncle, rejoiced to find himself again at Neisse, of which he was very fond.

The town is situated in a broad valley watered by the Neisse: it is a fortress of the second rank, garrisoned by about 5000 soldiers. Here is his own account of it :—

"In the most eastern part of Germany, in that corner where Russia, Prussia, and Austria meet, lies the province of Silesia. Very hardly contested by Maria Theresa, and hardly won by Frederick, it now forms the finest jewel in the crown of Prussia. The inhabitants are an industrious, intelligent, and above all, a merry people; there is a vivacity in them which has earned for them the epithet of the 'Frenchmen of Germany,' but their good-natured, childlike naïveté has also made them proverbial throughout the whole realm. Less rigid than the Prussians of the north, they have more of the Austrian volubility : except where, close to the boundaries of Russia, Sclavonic elements are so largely mixed with the populace as to make them 'stupid.'"

The contrasts that struck him day by day yet early in his youth, between the wit and wisdom he found in his Hebrew literature, and these "stupid" people made an impression upon him that he often referred to in after life; his sole amusement seems to have been watching the "rough, narrow-

[1] Dr. David Deutsch outlived his nephew only two months.

brained peasantry," bringing in provisions on most primitive carts to supply the garrison in the "much-respected fortress."

Stimulated by his love of learning, Emanuel entered the highest class of the Gymnasium against the wish of his parents, for, in the then unpleasant state of political affairs in Prussia, they not unnaturally opposed his embracing a learned profession, and would have preferred his devoting himself to the business of their house. But this was impossible to him. It is the custom in the "high schools" of Silesia for the pupils in the highest class to attend for two years; until that period is accomplished they are not permitted to go up for "Matriculation." In this case, before six months had elapsed, the masters found that Emanuel was capable of passing, and requested that he might do so: the higher authorities refused, on the ground that no exception to the rule could be made even for exceptional fitness; and it was not until petition after petition had been presented by the masters collectively, stating that they had nothing more to teach him, and representing the unfairness of keeping him at school, that they yielded to the pressure put upon them. He then proceeded to the University of Berlin, where he devoted himself at first chiefly to the study of Theology, without, however, relinquishing those Talmudic studies to which so much of his life had already been devoted. The enormous mass of transcriptions and translations from the Talmud which was found after his death,—beginning in the handwriting of a child, and continued up to within a very few years ago,—almost seemed in itself the work of an ordinary lifetime.

He was now just sixteen; and from this time forth, like many another German student, he supported himself entirely, paying his board, lodging, and fees by giving lessons. A year or two after, some Judaic stories and poems published in magazines—written with great elegance and full of interest—had earned him florins enough for his first excursion towards "Father Rhine" beyond his own land.

During his stay in Berlin he had thoroughly mastered English, and had made extensive studies in English literature. In 1855 Mr. Albert Cohen, of the firm of Asher and Co., in Berlin, was commissioned by the British Museum to recommend an assistant for the library department: Emanuel Deutsch had long been desirous of some means of visiting England, and when the appointment was offered to him he accepted it joyfully. He had then very little idea that it would be more than a temporary employment. He knew no one in the country, and little enough of English ways and habits. But he was considered by others, and he knew himself to be more than fit for the office.

A fragment concerning his studies, written in 1872, may be here inserted:

" *In magnis voluisse*—is it enough? who among us has not at some time or other striven for some high thing? and the preparation for the task . . . it would seem as if this had been, not rough hewn, but shaped with all the wise deliberation of a kindest Fate. Before I knew how to read and write the language of the land wherein I was born, my lips were taught to stammer the Aleph-Beth, and to recite my prayers in the tongue of David. As I grew up, Homer and Virgil stood side by side on my boyish bookshelf with the Mishnah and the Midrash. And before I was inured in the Akademe of Plato and his friends, it was deemed well to steep my soul for a time absolutely in that ocean called the Talmud: and to teach me fierce dialectics in the discussions of Rabina and Rab Ashi before I learnt to contrast the fierce lightnings that shook the rafters of Sura and Pumbeditha with the mild, serene, ironically smiling lips of Sokrates. And while Hengstenberg insisted with stentorian voice on every word of Scripture being verbally inspired, and the Hyksos being the sons of Jacob, Vatke, next door to him, represented the furthest steps of the non-Mosaic origin and authorship even of the Ten Commandments.

"Then leaving these theological arenas I found myself at the feet of Boeckh, who, with Attic grace opened up the arena of classic Hellas, making the *cistæ mysticæ* become clear revelations; under his guidance I saw that favoured branch of mankind at their play, in their earnestness, in the house and the market-place, in war and peace, their slaves, their women and children, their seers and priests, their poets and poetesses : and this while Meineke taught me Horace by the light of Herman and Heine.

"And to open my eyes for the greater features of human strivings, how out of barbarism grew the light and glory of the Renaissance and thence to the presence of our own day—and to show the bright germs of those goodly trees of freedom under whose shadows the peoples of Europe now dwell—was there not Ranke : while Ritter took us "from Greenland's icy mountains to Sah'ra's burning sands," and spoke of all plants, from the cedars of Lebanon to the hyssop that grows in the ruins of Vizagapatam ? To enable me better to understand the British Museum, the treatises on the Mine and Thine, and the Gate of the Trover, was there not Stahl, the brilliant and erudite German Disraeli, who defended Throne and State and a faith not that of his fathers, and interpreted to us the Pandects and the Institutes ?

"Enough of those days and the feasts spread before me : feasts of erudition, wisdom, and grace, within which, as the Talmud has it, the mother of the calf was yet more anxious to give suck than was the calf always to drink. The evenings passed, while the mind was too overwrought for midnight study, in sitting entranced before the noblest sons and daughters of Goethe, Schiller, Shakespeare, and Sophocles ; or Beethoven and Mendelssohn lulled the soul to blissful unconsciousness, or roused it to glow and enthusiasm unspoken.

"Then for nigh twenty years it was my privilege to dwell in the very midst of that Pantheon called the British Museum, the treasures whereof, be they Egyptian, Homeric, palimpsest or Babylonian cuneiforms, the mutilated glories of the Parthenon, or the Etruscan mysterious grotesqueness, were all at my beck and call, all days, all hours—Alexandria, Rome, Carthage, Jerusalem, Sidon, Tyre, Athens . . . ."

Here the fragment abruptly ends, without having mentioned v. Hagen who was his teacher in old German poetry and the "folk-lore" in which he delighted : and Bencke his teacher in psychology.

He had joined the British Museum in 1855. For fifteen years with mighty ardour and magnificent industry he studied and wrote, wrote and studied ; enjoying life among his friends, yet more among his books : shedding sunshine wherever he went, attracting and attaching not a few. It is impossible now to collect all his works, for he wrote lavishly and gave away prodigally, while looking onwards with eyes fixed on the *magnum opus* that was to be the work of his life—a treatise on the Talmud, to be followed by other

expositions of ancient Jewish literature. But 190 essays.
and articles written for 'Chambers's Encyclopedia' form in
themselves a goodly show, besides the articles from 'Smith's
Dictionary of the Bible,' and 'Kitto's Cyclopedia of Biblical
Literature,' which, by the special kindness of the editors, are
reprinted in this volume. In October 1867 the brief article
in the 'Quarterly Review,' sent forth as an *avant-courrier*,
excited so much attention both in England and on the Con-
tinent, that he was at once launched, as it were, from the
obscurity of a student into a rather unenviable notoriety :
and his time was a good deal cut up by the endless applica-
tions for lectures, articles, &c., with which he was besieged.
Encouraged, elated, he certainly was; but he worked on
steadily and had made considerable advances before illness
overtook him.

A proposal was made to him at the commencement of the
Abyssinian war to accompany our army into that country, as it
was thought that some valuable manuscripts and other
important antiquities might have rewarded the researches
of a scholar. For this his knowledge of Amharic and its cognate languages would have peculiarly fitted him. Fortunately
he yielded to the advice of one or two of his friends, and
declined an appointment that would have sadly wasted his
valuable time. Experience justified the prudence of their
counsels, since nothing of the slightest importance was found
in the country.

But this proposal, and a special invitation, unsought by
him, from Nubar Pasha, to witness the opening of the Suez
Canal, had presented the thoughts of travel in the East so
closely to him, that all the natural and old yearnings of his
heart were too completely awakened to slumber again. An

---

[1] This article was within a year translated into German, French, Swedish,
Russian, Danish and Dutch.

official commission from the British Museum, for the examination of certain localities in Cyprus and other places, had been suggested, and he was keen to go: he therefore earnestly requested the authorities to extend his annual leave from four weeks to eight, by uniting the leave of two years, to enable him to visit the Holy Land, even offering to forego his salary if necessary. He obtained ten weeks leave, and started 7th March 1869, returning 10th May. Unhappily the journey was too rapid and fatiguing even for his strength: with but little money at his command he underwent many hardships, and it is believed that he there laid the foundation of the disease of which he died. But in spite of these he enjoyed it all: "the sights and sounds of the real East—the full splendours of the days and nights—the trees and flowers, the holy stones, the wild fragrances"—worked up his ardent nature into an enthusiasm in which all the lofty patriotism of his race, all the passionate love of his fervid Oriental nature, and all the poetry of his artist heart, found vent. He dated his first letter from the shores of Palestine "The East: all my wild yearnings fulfilled at last!" Indeed, he was himself astonished at the emotion that choked him when he found himself among his own people at the Wailing-place in Jerusalem, and he could seldom speak of it afterwards without tears. "And I, too, in Phœnicia!" Fatigue and pain vanished when he beheld the Phœnician mason's marks, some of which his eyes were the first to distinguish on the walls of Sidon and Jerusalem.

But the very intensity of his enjoyment helped to wear him out. On his return he drew up a valuable and most interesting report of his journey for the Trustees of the British Museum, and delivered at least a dozen lectures, chiefly on the subject of Phœnicia, in various parts of the country. Early in the autumn he fell into a state of deep depression, partly from the fatigue of great overwork,[1] partly from the loss of very dear friends, and partly from the approach of illness of which he was then unconscious, but of which one premonitory symptom (almost entire sleeplessness) had come upon him. In December he wrote thus:

" . . . . . if it was not for this, I think I should long ago have given up the strife, and betaken myself to some quiet corner to wait in patience and meekness for what the voice would say. And if it found me an unworthy vessel, I should at least have peace within and peace without. . . . But—I have certain words in my possession which have been given me that they might be said to others, few or many. There is within me the whole terrible sum of throes and woes which made Rebecca, I believe, cry out against her double blessing. I know also that I shall not find peace or rest until I have said my whole say. And yet I cannot do it. And I yearn for things which I see, and which might have been mine, and would have been blessing and sunshine, and the cooling dew to the small germs within me;—and yet! and yet! I know that I ought not to look to the right or to the left; that I ought to be resigned; that I ought to fight down manfully every tear that wells up in my lonely heart, and that I ought to look but to the distant stars and work on ;—but I break down occasionally, and I want to know the Reason Why. And if a goodly flame shoots up, there are also so many ashes rolling down besides. And the ashes last longer than the flame—so much longer! It is not merely the results of hard and tedious dryasdusty investigations which I carry about with me and write into books, but those certain human problems which underlie them and give them tone and colour, and have begotten all those ancient matters, and which are so wondrously like the problems with which we do battle and are worsted. It is the continuity and solidarity of refined mankind which I have in my mind, and the sameness of its achievements, of its loves and hatreds, and prayers and curses, and conceptions of what is good and evil, and godly, positive and negative ; and reflecting upon all this, I find that I have nothing more to say—and ought to lay down a pen, which properly speaking I have never taken up. But all this is so confused and wild. . . . and I cannot take comfort in the thought of death,—I want to live—there is so much life, hot, full life within—that it shrinks from darkness and deadness. I envy those who can fly on the mind's wings to this harbour of refuge; I cannot follow, but keep tossing outside in my broken craft, through foam, and rock, and mist."

---

[1] Just at this time he brought out the article on "Islam" in the 'Quarterly Review,' and the letters on the Œcumenical Council in the *Times*.

And again:

"I work hard: but often I am on the brink of giving up. To resuscitate a time which perhaps after all had better remain dead, is a rash task. Who knows? perhaps after all I may be only and really in a dream, while I fancy I see golden towers and palaces gleaming in the dark blue depths, streets and market-places crowded with a motley crew—Roman, Greek, Byzantine, Jewish, Indian, and the rest—hearing the vague, wild hum of strange dead voices, and seeing above all the weird strained look in their eyes which prays and implores unceasingly—Redeem us! You remember the "Doctor, sind Sie des Teufels?" with which the captain caught hold of Heine's boots as he was leaning over the 'Schiffsrand,' looking downwards! But then he espied Her who had run away from him some hundred years before, and kept hiding down below. Whom am I looking for? And what will it avail anybody when I have proved to ocular demonstration that they had wisdom, and prowess, and honesty, and wit and humour (which is more), and passions and love in those buried days? For, after all, *this* is the end of all investigation into history or art: they were even as we are. Why therefore not be satisfied with this general result?"

And a little later :—

"For a long time now I have been frozen in every way. There is more struggle, more despair, more yearning, and more of helpless, hopeless, blind and dumb crying out, than even you have ever conceived. . . . As I am pondering over the fates of that creed of which I have traced the germs, Islam, and tried to see, to show the man who begot it visibly—as I work on with my metaphysical Talmud-developments, and see how wasted all that grace, and keenness, and catholicity of the minority has been on the majority, and *what* things of it all have become the heirlooms of 'Humanity,' and what others have been chilled into everlasting monuments of ice, seen and marvelled at by a few when the sun rises or sets, but otherwise useless,—as further I contemplated what kind of thing it is under which mankind feels happiest (for there never were such glorious times for the world at large), then my heart grows sad and sadder within me—and I feel what many a braver, stouter heart has felt: the futility of my own self-sacrifice. For it is that. I might be a thousand times more useful to my immediate friends by not giving myself up thus utterly to labours which, taken all in all, will amount to but very, very little, in the long run. I may prove and bring out a few details: I may teach a few—and these generally don't need to be taught this—that man is *not* bad from beginning, and certainly not because he does not happen to dress and eat quite in the approved fashion. But after all: what is the having done this compared to a real, good, active, useful life, when days mean days, and nights mean nights: a life not a prey to all kinds of haunting things, and one which has a real—not a so-called ideal—aim and purpose?"

In the spring of 1870 the frightful struggle of his naturally robust constitution began against the advancing disease.

It is not very easy to sketch the character of Mr. Deutsch, but we would fain draw some kind of portrait of him. He was of the Oriental type of Jews: eyes and hair of the darkest, with the flexible, ever-varying, expressive mouth of the Israelite; a face the reverse of handsome, but one that lighted up under the glow of an enthusiastic nature with a brightness that won the sympathies of the coldest listener. He was very small of stature, but sturdy and strong in make; and, until the last three years of his life, blessed with robust health and spirits that no work seemed to tire, no trials to exhaust. Unfortunately abundant health often induces entire indifference to the commonest rules of prudence or hygiene. With insatiable thirst for knowledge and vast energy in acquiring it, he lacked only that grand self-control which enables a man to live; without which the finer the power, the briefer its tenure. Except when induced to dine out, he seldom " found time " to dine at all; and the few hours of sleep he permitted himself to take were insufficient to restore the waste of the day. Possibly he might have struggled through these physical difficulties, had he had rest within; but his sensitive nature gave him no real repose, and a certain loneliness of heart that frequently hangs round the transplanted Jew, helped to wear out the apparently stout material of which he was made. Mr. Deutsch was absolutely free from all sentimentality and mental hysteria: his mind was cast in a manly and cheerful mould: he was brimming over with humour and playfulness which continued almost to the very end; but with all this, the tinge of melancholy which overshadows nearly all true Orientals, cast a thin veil over him that naturally darkened with the loss of health and the beginning of a terrible disease. Very proud by nature, his circumstances in England made him suffer painfully. He felt his attainments to be far beyond his position, and the galling official restrictions, petty rules, and annoying humiliations to which he was subjected, kept him during his last few years in a state of constant irritation, and unquestionably hastened his end. A little more bodily ease and the comforts due to men in the prime of life, no longer schoolboys: a little more freedom from care, and worthy consideration by the high powers of the country he had adopted, bestowed in time, would, without any doubt, have saved to us that mine of exceptional knowledge, that rare combination of gifts whose premature loss we now, too late, deplore.

Perhaps his chief external characteristic was brightness. As long as health was granted to him, no amount of work or fatigue ever troubled his *gaieté de cœur*, or dimmed the sparkling brightness of his society. He readily threw himself into the interests and occupations of others, with helpful hearty kindness, of which many and many reaped the full advantage; for, as his studies had been in some degree peculiar, he was continually applied to for information. Though sensitive to a fault he was not easily offended, but when once he had made a friend it was rare for him to lose him. During the commencement of his illness this sensitiveness increased upon him, and caused him not only to magnify slights and to fret over them with intense bitterness, but also to fancy them where none were intended. Shrinking from all around him, and rigidly determined to bear his pain alone and in secret, he could not be persuaded to see that some motive must be attributed to explain his withdrawal from his friends; and, while he resolutely concealed himself from them, he sorrowed bitterly over their neglect of him. But all this was only the not unnatural result of disease and pain, and his heart never wavered in loyalty to those who had loved, or been true friends to, him. Ambitious he certainly was: but it was not the poor ambition of personal prominence; it was only the ardent aspiration of a noble nature for the attainment of a lofty ideal; and in the very worst of his sufferings his keenest pang and bitterest trial was the despair of accomplishing the work he had laid out for himself,—the object of his whole life, and the idol of his heart.

We have said that he was a proud man. Enjoying a noble pride in his own gifts, he suffered also from the very foolish pride of not confessing to physical weakness. To the very last he kept from all but two or three—not more—of his most intimate friends, even from his daily companions in office, the knowledge of his failure of health. Attacked by a disease[1] that entailed agonies of pain, he yet bore it with a fortitude very rarely equalled: and not only dragged himself to his daily work at the Museum, but endured the terrible tortures arising from the necessarily active life there, with an heroic fortitude that was the unceasing amazement of his surgeon and nurse. Without any private means, and frequently denying himself in order to send assistance to the old family at home, giving up work meant living on the kindness of his friends: a suffering more painful to him to endure than his bodily illness; and it was exquisite pain to him to accept enough to carry him at last to the warmer climate he had longed so earnestly when in health to see. Through the one fault, so common in the noblest natures, he was just too proud to be able to take willingly even from those who

---

[1] Cancer; but this disease was never suspected during his life, and only discovered in a post-mortem examination. He had been treated for other almost equally painful diseases, and endured several operations.

loved him; he had lived too much alone and in exile to enjoy fully the happiness of being grateful to others for everything.

It will be readily seen even from this brief sketch what an immeasurable power of industry he possessed. He worked as almost only a German can work. Studying, labouring on all sides, what he acquired was really marvellous. He was extraordinarily well acquainted with English literature in all its varied styles and periods, enjoying it with fine taste and judgment. But his chief study was of Indo-European and Shemitic languages—Sanskrit, Chaldaic, Aramaic, and others. The study of his heart was Phœnician, and had his life been spared he would have concentrated all his energies upon that and Cuneiform. For this study, his un-failing natural accuracy—the backbone of a true scholar—peculiarly adapted him. It was truly said of him, "There is probably no one in England who possesses, to an equal degree, the varied knowledge combined with the intense sympathy for art, nature, and humanity that distinguished the deceased scholar." Neither did "the society which admired him understand the deep thought that underlaid his light sarcasms, the tremendous labour that resulted in his least writings, and the wealth of knowledge of which his chief work showed but a glimpse."

He had the fervid temperament of a poet, the tender heart of a woman, and a certain simplicity of nature that broke out occasionally as in a child. Intense in everything, he carried out a purity of life that showed no common self-restraint in one so ardent and so warm of heart; religiously blameless to the last. He was reverent without superstition, and free from prejudice notwithstanding his earnest, pas-sionate attachment to his country and to his people.

In the autumn of 1872 a despairing longing for warmth

and sunshine came upon him; "he would die happy if he could only once more hear the hum of the East:" he "almost thought a draught of the Nile would cure the incurable!" Means were found through the kindness of his many friends, and collected unknown to him; six months' leave was granted by the Trustees of the British Museum: and on the 18th of December he left England with a careful attendant for Italy.

And Italy seemed to bring him a sort of resurrection; the Egyptian gallery at Turin was enjoyed with delight: then came "Florence, the Andante to the vast second and third movements of Rome, while Naples was the final Cantabile— if there be such a thing in this symphony of glory, Italy. Verily," he wrote, "I live again, albeit stricken yet, but filled with a great happiness." He could see but little; but that little he saw with his usual intensity, and fell to copying inscriptions and taking notes as if a new life was going to begin for him. He left Brindisi on the 6th of January, and arrived at Alexandria on the 10th. Unfortunately the winter in Egypt was exceptionally damp and cold: Cairo was all in wild confusion, overcrowded with visitors for the Viceroy's *fêtes* on the marriages of his sons and daughters, and no accommodation was possible for an invalid. He wrote of the "piercing cold" under which he was "shivering," and said that the "ray of hope" which had shone so brightly on him in Italy was now almost extinguished; adding, "I sometimes cannot and will not realise the terrible truth: there is so immensely much of life within me yet, and my will is so savagely strong at times, and there is oh! so much, so much for me to do in all directions—surely it cannot be that all this is the last flicker!"

At length, after many delays, he got a place in a crowded

steamer, where he suffered terribly from the dirt and dis-
comfort. Yet, although his spirits had now almost completely failed him, he wrote with enjoyment of the passing
scenes " on the Nile—palm-groves, black Nubians, pelicans
on alternate legs, barren hills fringed with green embroidery,
castellated mud dwellings, big sugar-cane stretches : this on
both sides. Under me the river rolling its yellow mystic
waters, and around me there waves such a stream of life."
At Luxsor he found comfortable quarters in the house of
the Austrian Consul, from whom he received the utmost
kindness. But here he grew rapidly worse, and his
strength declined day by day, until he became unable to
leave his bed. " Yet all this while," he wrote, in nearly his
last letter, " my brain is teeming with work—work that
seems cut out as by special primæval arrangement for me
and me only. The tragical irony of my failure of life cuts
me to pieces. A whole flood of thoughts old and new—of
suggestions, facts, and conceits storm in upon me with every
breath I draw here, at every stone I stumble over, at every
single sign and token of this boundless tomb-world wherein
lie hidden how many civilizations ? the very door of my
house is formed out of a mummy-case inscribed with part of
the Ritual of the Dead in fading hieroglyphics ! oh, the
vast accumulation that has come into my brain from all I
see around me !—alas ! they are but day-dreams now —
golden visions wherewith my too vivid imagination beguiles
the long drawn-out days and nights of keen distress."

He got back to Cairo on the 30th of March, but after
three weeks of intense suffering removed to the Prussian
Deaconesses' Hospital at Alexandria, where a comfortable
apartment was provided for him, and where he had the
society of one kind friend as well as the careful watching of
the good Sisters. He still hoped to reach England again,

and had a berth engaged for him in the P. and O. steamer for the 7th of May. But when that day came he was already sinking rapidly, and early on the morning of the 12th of May, 1873, he died.

" I only wish for peace," were nearly his last words.

He was buried on the following morning in the Jewish cemetery at Alexandria.

A stone of polished red granite now covers his last resting-place, bearing four inscriptions. The Hebrew one was written by Dr. Hermann Adler, Rabbi, and is as follows, literally translated :

> Here is entombed the well-beloved—whose heart was burning with good things, and whose pen was the pen of a ready writer—Menahem, son of Abraham Deutsch, whom the Lord preserve ! He was born at Neisse, on the 1st Marheshvan, 5590 A.M., and departed from this world in Alexandria, on Monday the 9th Iyar, in the year ' Arise, shine; for thy light is come.' May his soul be bound up in the bond of life !

To explain the quotation here given, it will be remembered that every letter in the Hebrew alphabet has its numerical as well as its lingual value; dates are therefore almost always written upon tombstones embodied in some text of Scripture conveying the corresponding numerals in a chrono-grammatic form. In this case the date of Menahem Deutsch's death happens to form the above text from Isaiah lx. 1—an apt quotation which touchingly describes in the language of his own people that ardent aspiration after light which characterized his whole life.

The English inscription, literally translated also into German and Arabic, says :

> Here lie the earthly remains
> of the beloved
> EMANUEL OSCAR MENAHEM DEUTSCH,
> for eighteen years employed in the British Museum.
> Born at Neisse October 28, 1829.
> Died at Alexandria, May 12, 1873.

I.

THE TALMUD.[1]

WHAT is the Talmud?

What is the nature of that strange production of which the name, imperceptibly almost, is beginning to take its place among the household words of Europe? Turn where we may in the realms of modern learning, we seem to be haunted by it. We meet with it in theology, in science, even in general literature, in their highways and in their byeways. There is not a handbook to all or any of the many departments of biblical lore, sacred geography, history, chronology, numismatics, and the rest, but its pages contain references to the Talmud. The advocates of all religious opinions appeal to its dicta. Nay, not only the scientific investigators of Judaism and Christianity, but those of Mohammedanism and Zoroastrianism, turn to it in their dissections of dogma and legend and ceremony. If, again, we take up any recent volume of archæological or philological transactions, whether we light on a dissertation on a Phœnician altar, or a cuneiform tablet, Babylonian weights, or Sassanian coins, we are certain to find this mysterious word. Nor is it merely the restorers of the lost idioms of Canaan and Assyria, of Himyar and Zoroastrian Persia, that appeal to the Talmud for assistance; but the modern schools of Greek and Latin philology are beginning to avail themselves of the classical and postclassical materials that lie scattered through it. Jurisprudence, in its turn, has been roused to the fact that, apart from the bearing of the Talmud on the study of the Pandects and the Institutes, there are also some of those very laws of the Medes and Persians—hitherto but a vague

---

[1] This article appeared in the 'Quarterly Review' for October, 1867, vol. cxxiii., No. 246.

sound—hidden away in its labyrinths. And so too with medicine, astronomy, mathematics, and the rest. The history of these sciences, during that period over which the composition of the Talmud ranges—and it ranges over about a thousand years—can no longer be written without some reference to the items preserved, as in a vast buried city, in this cyclopean work. Yet, apart from the facts that belong emphatically to these respective branches, it contains other facts, of larger moment still: facts bearing upon human culture in its widest sense. Day by day there are excavated from these mounds pictures of many countries and many periods. Pictures of Hellas and Byzantium, Egypt and Rome, Persia and Palestine; of the temple and the forum, war and peace, joy and mourning; pictures teeming with life, glowing with colour.

These are, indeed, signs of the times. A mighty change has come over us. We, children of this latter age, are, above all things, utilitarian. We do not read the Koran, the Zend Avesta, the Vedas, with the sole view of refuting them. We look upon all literature, religious, legal, and otherwise, whensoever and wheresoever produced, as part and parcel of humanity. We, in a manner, feel a kind of responsibility for it. We seek to understand the phase of culture which begot these items of our inheritance, the spirit that moves upon their face. And while we bury that which is dead in them, we rejoice in that which lives in them. We enrich our stores of knowledge from theirs, we are stirred by their poetry, we are moved to high and holy thoughts when they touch the divine chord in our hearts.

In the same human spirit we now speak of the Talmud. There is even danger at hand that this chivalresque feeling— one of the most touching characteristics of our times—which is evermore prompting us to offer holocausts to the Manes of those whom former generations are thought to have wronged, may lead to its being extolled somewhat beyond its merit. As these ever new testimonies to its value crowd upon us, we might be led into exaggerating its importance for the history of mankind. Yet an old adage of its own says:

"Above all things, study. Whether for the sake of learning or for any other reason, study. For, whatever the motives that impel you at first, you will very soon love study for its own sake." And thus even exaggerated expectations of the treasure-trove in the Talmud will have their value, if they lead to the study of the work itself.

For, let us say it at once, these tokens of its existence, that appear in many a new publication, are, for the most part, but will-o'-the-wisps. At first sight one would fancy that there never was a book more popular, or that formed more exclusively the mental centre of modern scholars, Orientalists, theologians, or jurists. What is the real truth? Paradoxical as it may seem, there never was a book at once more universally neglected and more universally talked of. Well may we forgive Heine, when we read the glowing description of the Talmud contained in his "Romancero," for never having even seen the subject of his panegyrics. Like his countryman Schiller, who, pining vainly for one glimpse of the Alps, produced the most glowing and faithful picture of them, so he, with the poet's unerring instinct, gathered truth from hearsay and description. But how many of these ubiquitous learned quotations really flow from the fountain-head? Too often and too palpably it is merely—to use Samson's agricultural simile—those ancient and well-worked heifers, the "Tela ignea Satanæ," the "Abgezogener Schlangenbalg," and all their venomous kindred, which are once more being dragged to the plough by some of the learned. We say the learned: for as to the people at large, often as they hear the word now, we firmly believe that numbers of them still hold, with that erudite Capucin friar, Henricus Seynensis, that the Talmud is not a book, *but a man.* "Ut narrat Rabbinus Talmud"—"As says Rabbi Talmud"— cries he, and triumphantly clinches his argument!

And of those who know that it is not a Rabbi, how many are there to whom it conveys any but the vaguest of notions? Who wrote it? What is its bulk? Its date? Its contents? Its birthplace? A contemporary lately called it "a sphinx, towards which all men's eyes are directed at this hour, some with eager curiosity, some with vague anxiety." But why not force open its lips? How much longer are we to live by quotations alone, quotations a thousand times used, a thousand times abused?

Where, however, are we to look even for primary instruction? Where learn the story of the book, its place in literature, its meaning and purport, and, above all, its relation to ourselves?

If we turn to the time-honoured "Authorities," we shall mostly find that, in their eagerness to serve some cause, they have torn a few pieces off that gigantic living body; and they have presented to us these ghastly anatomical preparations, twisted and mutilated out of all shape and semblance, saying, Behold, this is the book! Or they have done worse. They have not garbled their samples, but have given them exactly as they found them; and then stood aside, pointing at them with jeering countenance. For their samples were ludicrous and grotesque beyond expression. But these wise and pious investigators unfortunately mistook the gurgoyles, those grinning stone caricatures that mount their thousand years' guard over our cathedrals, for the gleaming statues of the Saints within; and, holding them up to mockery and derision, they cried, These be thy gods, O Israel!

Let us not be misunderstood. When we complain of the lack of guides to the Talmud, we do not wish to be ungrateful to those great and earnest scholars whose names are familiar to every student, and whose labours have been ever present to our mind. For, though in the whole realm of learning there is scarcely a single branch of study to be compared for its difficulty to the Talmud, yet, if a man had time, and patience, and knowledge, there is absolutely no reason why he should not, up and down ancient and modern libraries, gather most excellent hints from essays and treatises, monographs and sketches, in books and periodicals without number, by dint of which, aided by the study of the work itself, he might arrive at some conclusion as to its essence and tendencies, its origin and its development. Yet, so far as we know, that work, every step of which, it must be confessed, is beset with fatal pitfalls, has not yet been done for the world at large. It is for a very good reason that we have placed nothing but the name of the Talmud itself at the head of our paper. We have sought far and near for some one special book on the subject, which we might make the theme of our observations—a book which should not merely be a garbled translation of a certain twelfth century "Introduction," interspersed with vituperations and supplemented with blunders, but which from the platform of modern culture should pronounce impartially upon a production which, if for no other reason, claims respect through its age,—a book that would lead us through the stupendous labyrinths of fact, and thought, and fancy, of which the Talmud consists, that would rejoice even in hieroglyphical fairy-lore, in abstruse propositions and syllogisms, that could forgive wild outbursts of passion, and not judge harshly and hastily of things, the real meaning of which may have had to be hidden under the fool's cap and bells.

We have not found such a book, nor anything approaching to it. But closely connected with that circumstance is this other, that we were fain to quote the first editions of this Talmud, though scores have been printed since, and about a dozen are in the press at this very moment. Even this first edition was printed in hot haste, and without due care ; and every succeeding one, with one or two insignificant exceptions, presents a sadder spectacle. In the Basle edition of 1578—the third in point of time, which has remained the standard edition almost ever since—that amazing creature, the Censor, stepped in. In his anxiety to protect the "Faith" from all and every danger—for the Talmud was supposed to hide bitter things against Christianity under the most innocent-looking words and phrases—this official did very wonderful things. When he, for example, found some ancient Roman in the book swearing by the Capitol or by Jupiter "of Rome," his mind instantly misgave him. Surely this Roman must be a Christian, the Capitol the Vatican, Jupiter the Pope. And forthwith he struck out Rome and substituted any other place he could think of. A

favourite spot seems to have been Persia, sometimes it was
Aram or Babel. So that this worthy Roman may be found
unto this day swearing by the Capitol of Persia or by the
Jupiter of Aram and Babel. But whenever the word
"Gentile" occurred, the Censor was seized with the most
frantic terrors. A "Gentile" could not possibly be aught but
a Christian; whether he lived in India or in Athens, in
Rome or in Canaan; whether he was a good Gentile—and
there are many such in the Talmud—or a wicked one.
Instantly he christened him; and christened him, as fancy
moved him, an "Egyptian," an "Aramæan," an "Amalekite,"
an "Arab," a "Negro;" sometimes a whole "people." We
are speaking strictly to the letter. All this is extant in our
very last editions.

Once or twice attempts were made to clear the text from
its foulest blemishes. There was even, about two years ago,
a beginning made of a "critical" edition, such as not merely
Greek and Roman, Sanscrit and Persian classics, but the
veriest trash written in those languages would have had ever
so long ago. And there is—M. Renan's unfortunate remark
to the contrary notwithstanding [1]—no lack of Talmudical
MSS., however fragmentary they be for the most part.
There are innumerable variations, additions, and corrections
to be gleaned from the Codices at the Bodleian and the
Vatican, in the Libraries of Odessa, Munich, and Florence,
Hamburg and Heidelberg, Paris and Parma. But an evil
eye seems to be upon this book. This corrected edition
remains a torso, like the two first volumes of translations of
the Talmud, commenced at different periods, the second
volumes of which never saw the light. It therefore seemed
advisable to refer to the Editio Princeps, as the one that
is at least free from the blemishes, censorial or typographical,
of later ages.

Well does the Talmud supplement the Horatian "Habent
sua fata libelli," by the words "even the sacred scrolls in the

---

[1] "On sait qu'il ne reste aucun manuscrit du Talmud pour contrôle
les éditions imprimées."—*Les Apôtres*, p. 262.

Tabernacle." We really do not wonder that the good Capucin of whom we spoke mistook it for a man. Ever since it existed—almost before it existed in a palpable shape—it has been treated much like a human being. It has been proscribed, and imprisoned, and burnt, a hundred times over. From Justinian, who, as early as 553 A.D., honoured it by a special interdictory Novella,[1] down to Clement VIII. and later—a space of over a thousand years—both the secular and the spiritual powers, kings and emperors, popes and anti-popes, vied with each other in hurling anathemas and bulls and edicts of wholesale confiscation and conflagration against this luckless book. Thus, within a period of less than fifty years—and these forming the latter half of the sixteenth century—it was publicly burnt no less than six different times, and that not in single copies, but wholesale, by the waggon-load. Julius III. issued · his proclamation against what he grotesquely calls the " Gemaroth Thalmud," in 1553 and 1555, Paul IV. in 1559, Pius V. in 1566, Clement VIII. in 1592 and 1599. The fear of it was great indeed. Even Pius IV., in giving permission for a new edition, stipulated expressly that it should appear without the name Talmud. "Si tamen prodierit sine nomine Thalmud tolerari deberet." It almost seems to have been a kind of Shibboleth, by which every new potentate had to prove the rigour of his faith. And very rigorous it must have been, to judge by the language which even the highest dignitaries of the Church did not disdain to use at times. Thus Honorius IV. writes to the Archbishop of Canterbury in 1286 anent that "damnable book" (*liber damnabilis*), admonishing him gravely and desiring him "vehemently" to see that it be not read by anybody, since " all other evils flow out of it."—Verily these documents are sad reading, only relieved occasionally by some wild blunder that lights up as with one flash the abyss of ignorance regarding this object of wrath.

We remember but one sensible exception in this Babel of

[1] *Novella* 146, Περὶ Ἑβραίων (addressed to the Præfectus Prætorio Areobiudus).

manifestoes. Clement V., in 1307, before condemning the book, wished to know something of it, and there was no one to tell him. Whereupon he proposed—but in language so obscure that it left the door open for many interpretations— that three chairs be founded, for Hebrew, Chaldee, and Arabic, as the three tongues nearest to the idiom of the Talmud. The spots chosen by him were the Universities of Paris, Salamanca, Bologna, and Oxford. In time, he hoped, one of these Universities might be able to produce a translation of this mysterious book. Need we say that this consummation never came to pass? The more expeditious process of destruction was resorted to again and again and again, not merely in the single cities of Italy and France, but throughout the entire Holy Roman Empire.

At length a change took place in Germany. One Pfefferkorn, a miserable creature enough, began, in the time of the Emperor Maximilian, to agitate for a new decree for the extermination of the Talmud. The Emperor lay with his hosts before Pavia, when the evil-tongued messenger arrived in the camp, furnished with goodly letters by Kunigunde, the Emperor's beautiful sister. Maximilian, wearied and unsuspecting, renewed that time-honoured decree for a confiscation, to be duly followed by a conflagration, readily enough. The confiscation was conscientiously carried out, for Pfefferkorn knew well enough where his former co-religionists kept their books. But a conflagration of a very different kind ensued. Step by step, hour by hour, the German Reformation was drawing nearer. Reuchlin, the most eminent Hellenist and Hebraist of his time, had been nominated to sit on the Committee which was to lend its learned authority to the Emperor's decree. But he did not relish this task. "He did not like the look of Pfefferkorn," he says. Besides which, he was a learned and an honest man, and, having been the restorer of classical Greek in Germany, he did not care to participate in the wholesale murder of a book "written by Christ's nearest relations." Perhaps he saw the cunningly-laid trap. He had long been a thorn in the flesh of many of his contemporaries. His

Hebrew labours had been looked upon with bitter jealousy, if not fear. Nothing less was contemplated in those days— the theological Faculty of Mayence demanded it openly— than a total "Revision and Correction" of the Hebrew Bible, "inasmuch as it differed from the Vulgate." Reuchlin, on his part, never lost an opportunity of proclaiming the high importance of the "Hebrew Truth," as he emphatically called it. His enemies thought that one of two things would follow. By officially pronouncing upon the Talmud, he was sure either to commit himself dangerously—and then a speedy end would be made of him—or to set at naught, to a certain extent, his own previous judgments in favour of these studies. He declined the proposal, saying, honestly enough, that he knew nothing of the book, and that he was not aware of the existence of many who knew anything of it. Least of all did its detractors know it. But, he continued, even if it should contain attacks on Christianity, would it not be preferable to reply to them? "Burning is but a ruffianly argument (*Bacchanten-Argument*)." Whereupon a wild outcry was raised against him as a Jew, a Judaizer, a bribed renegade, and so on. Reuchlin, nothing daunted, set to work upon the book in his patient hard-working manner. Next he wrote a brilliant defence of it. When the Emperor asked his opinion, he repeated Clement's proposal to found Talmudical chairs. At each German university there should be two professors, specially appointed for the sole purpose of enabling students to become acquainted with this book. "As to burning it," he continues, in the famous Memorial addressed to the Emperor, "if some fool came and said, Most mighty Emperor! your Majesty should really suppress and burn the books of alchymy [a fine *argumentum ad hominem*] because they contain blasphemous, wicked, and absurd things against our faith, what should his Imperial Majesty reply to such a buffalo or ass but this: Thou art a ninny, rather to be laughed at than followed? Now because his feeble head cannot enter into the depths of a science, and cannot conceive it, and does understand things otherwise than they really are, would you deem it fit to burn such books?"

Fiercer and fiercer waxed the howl, and Reuchlin, the peaceful student, from a witness became a delinquent. What he suffered for and through the Talmud cannot be told here. Far and wide, all over Europe, the contest raged. A whole literature of pamphlets, flying sheets, caricatures, sprang up. University after university was appealed to against him. No less than forty-seven sittings were held by the theological Faculty of Paris, which ended by their formal condemnation of Reuchlin. But he was not left to fight alone. Around him rallied, one by one, Duke Ulrich of Würtemberg, the Elector Frederick of Saxony, Ulrich von Hutten, Franz von Sickingen—he who finally made the Colognians pay their costs in the Reuchlin trial— Erasmus of Rotterdam, and that whole brilliant phalanx of the "Knights of the Holy Ghost," the "Hosts of Pallas Athene," the "*Talmutphili,*" as the documents of the period variously style them : they whom we call the Humanists.

And their palladium and their war-cry was—oh ! wondrous ways of History—the Talmud ! To stand up for Reuchlin meant, to them, to stand up for "the Law;" to fight for the Talmud was to *fight for the Church !* "Non te," writes Egidio de Viterbo to Reuchlin, "sed Legem: *non Thalmud, sed Ecclesiam !*"

The rest of the story is written in the "Epistolæ Obscurorum Virorum," and in the early pages of the German Reformation. The Talmud was not burnt this time. On the contrary, its first complete edition was printed. And in that same year of Grace 1520 A.D., when this first edition went through the press at Venice, Martin Luther burnt the Pope's bull at Wittenberg.

What is the Talmud ?

Again the question rises before us in its whole formidable shape; a question which no one has yet answered satisfactorily. And we labour in this place under more than one disadvantage. For, quite apart from the difficulties of explaining a work so utterly Eastern, antique, and thoroughly *sui generis,* to our modern Western readers, in

the space of a few pages, we labour under the further
disability of not being able to refer to the work itself.
Would it not indeed be mere affectation to presuppose more
than the vaguest acquaintance with its language or even its
name in many of our readers? And while we would fain
enlarge upon such points as a comparison between the
law laid down in it with ours, or with the contemporary
Greek, Roman, and Persian laws, or those of Islam, or even
with its own fundamental Code, the Mosaic: while we would
trace a number of its ethical, ceremonial, and doctrinal
points in Zoroastrianism, in Christianity, in Mohammedanism; a vast deal of its metaphysics and philosophy in Plato,
Aristotle, the Pythagoreans, the Neoplatonists, and the
Gnostics—not to mention Spinoza and the Schellings of our
own day; much of its medicine in Hippocrates and Galen,
and the Paracelsuses of but a few centuries ago—we shall
scarcely be able to do more than to lay a few *disjecta
membra* of these things before our readers. We cannot even
sketch, in all its bearings, that singular mental movement
which caused the best spirits of an entire nation to con-
centrate, in spite of opposition, all their energies for a
thousand years upon the writing, and for another thousand
years upon the commenting, of this one book. Omitting
all detail, which it has cost much to gather, and more to
suppress, we shall merely tell of its development, of the
schools in which it grew, of the tribunals which judged by it,
of some of the men that set their seal on it. We shall also
introduce a summary of its law, speak of its metaphysics,
of its moral philosophy, and quote many of its proverbs and
saws—the truest of all gauges of a time.

We shall, perhaps, be obliged occasionally to appeal to
some of the extraneous topics just mentioned. The Talmud,
like every other phenomenon, in order to become compre-
hensible, should be considered only in connection with things
of a similar kind: a fact almost entirely overlooked to this
day. Being emphatically a Corpus Juris, an encyclopædia of
law, civil and penal, ecclesiastical and international, human
and divine, it may best be judged by analogy and com-

parison with other legal codes, more especially with the
Justinian Code and its Commentaries. What the uninitiated
have taken for exceptional "Rabbinical" subtleties, or, in
matters relating to the sexes, for gross offences against
modern taste, will then cause the Talmud to stand rather
favourably than otherwise. The Pandects and the Institutes,
the Novellæ and the Responsa Prudentium should thus be
constantly consulted and compared. No less should our
English law, as laid down in Blackstone, wherein we may see
how the most varied views of right and wrong have been
finally blended and harmonised with the spirit of our times.
But the Talmud is more than a book of laws. It is a microcosm, embracing, even as does the Bible, heaven and earth.
It is as if all the prose and the poetry, the science, the faith
and speculation of the Old World were, though only in faint
reflections, bound up in it *in nuce*. Comprising the time
from the rise to the fall of antiquity, and a good deal of its
after-glow, the history and culture of antiquity have to be
considered in their various stages. But, above all, it is necessary to transport ourselves, following Goethe's advice, to its
birthplace—Palestine and Babylon—the gorgeous East itself,
where all things glow in brighter colours, and grow into
more fantastic shapes :—

> " Willst den Dichter du verstehen,
>   Musst in Dichter's Lande gehen."

The origin of the Talmud is coeval with the return from
the Babylonish captivity. One of the most mysterious and
momentous periods in the history of humanity is that brief
space of the Exile. What were the influences brought to
bear upon the captives during that time, we know not. But
this we know, that from a reckless, lawless, godless populace,
they returned transformed into a band of Puritans. The
religion of Zerdusht, though it has left its traces in Judaism,
fails to account for that change. Nor does the Exile itself
account for it. Many and intense as are the reminiscences
of its bitterness, and of yearning for home, that have survived
in prayer and in song, yet we know that when the hour of

liberty struck, the forced colonists were loth to return to the
land of their fathers. Yet the change is there, palpable,
unmistakeable—a change which we may regard as almost
miraculous. Scarcely aware before of the existence of their
glorious national literature, the people now began to press
round these brands plucked from the fire—the scanty records
of their faith and history—with a fierce and passionate love,
a love stronger even than that of wife and child. These
same documents, as they were gradually formed into a canon,
became the immutable centre of their lives, their actions,
their thoughts, their very dreams. From that time forth,
with scarcely any intermission, the keenest as well as the
most poetical minds of the nation remained fixed upon them.
"Turn it and turn it again," says the Talmud, with regard
to the Bible, "for everything is in it." "*Search* the Scriptures," is the distinct utterance of the New Testament.

The natural consequence ensued. Gradually, imperceptibly
almost, from a mere expounding and investigation for purposes of edification or instruction on some special point, this
activity begot a science, a science that assumed the very
widest dimensions. Its technical name is already contained
in the Book of Chronicles. It is "Midrash" (from *darash*,
to study, expound)—a term which the Authorised Version
renders by "Story."[1]

There is scarcely a more fruitful source of misconceptions
upon this subject than the liquid nature, so to speak, of its
technical terms. They mean anything and everything, at
once most general and most special. Nearly all of them
signify in the first instance simply "study." Next they are
used for some one very special branch of this study. Then
they indicate, at times a peculiar method, at others the
works which have grown out of these either general or special
mental labours. Thus Midrash, from the abstract "expounding," came to be applied, first to the "exposition" itself—even
as our terms "work, investigation, enquiry," imply both process and product; and finally, as a special branch of exposition

---

[1] See 2 Chron. xiii. 22, xxiv. 27.

—the legendary—was more popular than the rest, to this one branch only and to the books that chiefly represented it.

For there had sprung up almost innumerable modes of "searching the Scriptures." In the quaintly ingenious manner of the times, four of the chief methods were found in the Persian word Paradise, spelt in vowelless Semitic fashion, PRDS. Each one of these mysterious letters was taken, mnemonically, as the initial of some technical word that indicated one of these four methods. The one called P [*peshat*] aimed at the simple understanding of words and things, in accordance with the primary exegetical law of the Talmud, "that no verse of the scripture ever practically travelled beyond its literal meaning"—though it might be explained, homiletically and otherwise, in innumerable new ways. The second, R [*remes*], means Hint, *i.e.* the discovery of the indications contained in certain seemingly superfluous letters and signs in Scripture. These were taken to refer to laws not distinctly mentioned, but either existing traditionally or newly promulgated. This method, when more generally applied, begot a kind of *memoria technica*, a stenography akin to the "Notarikon" of the Romans. Points and notes were added to the margins of scriptural MSS., and the foundation of the Massorah, or diplomatic preservation of the text, was thus laid. The third, D [*derush*], was homiletic application of that which had been to that which was and would be of prophetical and historical dicta to the actual condition of things. It was a peculiar kind of sermon, with all the aids of dialectics and poetry, of parable, gnome, proverb, legend, and the rest, exactly as we find it in the New Testament. The fourth, S, stood for *sôd*, secret, mystery. This was the Secret Science, into which but few were initiated. It was theosophy, metaphysics, angelology, a host of wild and glowing visions of things beyond earth. Faint echoes of this science survive in Neoplatonism, in Gnosticism, in the Kabbalah, in "Hermes Trismegistus." But few were initiated into these things of "The Creation" and of "The Chariot," as it was also called, in allusion to Ezekiel's vision. Yet here again the power of the vague and myste-

rious was so strong, that the word Paradise gradually
indicated this last branch, the secret science only. Later, in
Gnosticism, it came to mean the "Spiritual Christ."

There is a weird story in the Talmud, which has given rise
to the wildest explanations, but which will become intelligible by the foregoing lines. "Four men," it says, "entered
Paradise. One beheld and died. One beheld and lost his
senses. One destroyed the young plants. One only entered
in peace and came out in peace."—The names of all four are
given. They are all exalted masters of the law. The last
but one, he who destroyed the young plants, is Elisha ben
Abuyah, the Faust of the Talmud, who, while sitting in the
academy, at the feet of his teachers, to study the law, kept
the "profane books"—of "Homeros," to wit, hidden in his
garment, and from whose mouth "Greek song" never ceased
to flow. How he, notwithstanding his early scepticism,
rapidly rises to eminence in that same law," finally falls away
and becomes a traitor and an outcast, and his very name a
thing of unutterable horror—how, one day (it was the great
day of atonement) he passes the ruins of the temple, and
hears a voice within "murmuring like a dove"—"all men
shall be forgiven this day save Elisha ben Abuyah, who, knowing me, has betrayed me"—how, after his death the flames
will not cease to hover over his grave, until his one faithful
disciple, the "Light of the Law," Meïr, throws himself over
it, swearing a holy oath that he will not partake of the joys
of the world to come without his beloved master, and that he
will not move from that spot until his master's soul shall
have found grace and salvation before the Throne of Mercy—
all this and a number of other incidents form one of the
most stirring poetical pictures of the whole Talmud. The
last of the four is Akiba, the most exalted, most romantic,
and most heroic character perhaps in that vast gallery of the
learned of his time; he who, in the last revolt under Trajan
and Hadrian, expiated his patriotic rashness at the hands of
the Roman executioners, and—the legend adds—whose soul
fled just when, in his last agony, his mouth cried out the last

word of the confession of God's unity:—"Hear, O Israel, the Lord our God is *One*."

The Talmud is the storehouse of "Midrash," in its widest sense, and in all its branches. What we said of the fluctuation of terms applies emphatically also to this word Talmud. It means in the first instance nothing but "study," "learning," from *lamad*, to learn; next indicating a special method of "learning" or rather arguing, it finally became the name of the great Corpus Juris of Judaism.

When we speak of the Talmud as a legal code, we trust we shall not be understood too literally. It resembles about as much what we generally understand by that name as a primeval forest resembles a Dutch garden.

Nothing indeed can equal the state of utter amazement into which the modern investigator finds himself plunged at the first sight of these luxuriant Talmudical wildernesses. Schooled in the harmonising, methodising systems of the West—systems that condense, and arrange, and classify, and give everything its fitting place and its fitting position in that place—he feels almost stupefied here. The language, the style, the method, the very sequence of things (a sequence that often appears as logical as our dreams), the amazingly varied nature of these things—everything seems tangled, confused, chaotic. It is only after a time that the student learns to distinguish between two mighty currents in the book—currents that at times flow parallel, at times seem to work upon each other, and to impede each other's action: the one emanating from the brain, the other from the heart —the one prose, the other poetry—the one carrying with it all those mental faculties that manifest themselves in arguing, investigating, comparing, developing, bringing a thousand points to bear upon one and one upon a thousand; the other springing from the realms of fancy, of imagination, feeling, humour, and above all from that precious combination of still, almost sad, pensiveness with quick catholic sympathies, which in German is called *Gemüth*. These two currents the Midrash, in its various aspects, had caused to set in the direction of the Bible, and they soon found in it two vast fields for the display of all their power and energy. The logical faculties turned to the legal portions in Exodus, Leviticus, Deuteronomy—developing, seeking, and solving a thousand real or apparent difficulties and contradictions with what, as tradition, had been living in the hearts and mouths of the people from time immemorial. The other—the imaginative faculties—took possession of the prophetical, ethical, historical, and, quaintly enough, sometimes even of the legal portions of the Bible, and transformed the whole into a vast series of themes almost musical in their wonderful and capricious variations. The first-named is called "Halachah" (*Rule, Norm*), a term applied both to the process of evolving legal enactments and the enactments themselves. The other, "Haggadah" (*Legend, Saga*) not so much in our modern sense of the word, though a great part of its contents comes under that head, but because it was only a "saying," a thing without authority, a play of fancy, an allegory, a parable, a tale, that pointed a moral and illustrated a question, that smoothed the billows of fierce debate, roused the slumbering attention, and was generally—to use its own phrase—a "comfort and a blessing."

The Talmud, which is composed of these two elements, the legal and the legendary, is divided into MISHNAH and GEMARA: two terms again of uncertain, shifting meaning. Originally indicating, like the technical words mentioned already, "study," they both became terms for special studies, and indicated special works. The Mishnah, from *shanah* (*tana*), to learn, to repeat, has been of old translated δευτέρωσις, second law. But this derivation, correct as it seems literally, is incorrect in the first instance. It simply means "Learning," like Gemara, which, besides, indicates "complement" to the Mishnah—itself a complement to the Mosaic code, but in such a manner that in developing and enlarging, it supersedes it. The Mishnah, on its own part again, forms a kind of text to which the Gemara is not so much a scholion as a critical expansion. The Pentateuch remains in all cases the background and latent source of the Mishnah. But it is

c

the business of the Gemara to examine into the legitimacy and correctness of this Mishnic development in single instances. The Pentateuch remained under all circumstances the immutable, divinely given constitution, the *written* law: in contradistinction to it, the Mishnah, together with the Gemara, was called the oral, or "Unwritten" law, not unlike the unwritten Greek 'Ρήτραι, the Roman "Lex Non Scripta," the Sunnah, or our own common law.

There are few chapters in the whole History of Jurisprudence more obscure than the origin, development, and completion of this "Oral Law." There must have existed from the very beginning of the Mosaic law a number of corollary laws, which explained in detail most of the rules broadly laid down in it. Apart from these, it was but natural that the enactments of that primitive Council of the Desert, the Elders, and their successors in each period, together with the verdicts issued by the later "judges within the gates," to whom the Pentateuch distinctly refers, should have become precedents, and been handed down as such. Apocryphal writings—notably the fourth book of Ezra—not to mention Philo and the Church Fathers, speak of fabulous numbers of books that had been given to Moses together with the Pentateuch: thus indicating the common belief in the divine origin of the supplementary laws that had existed among the people from time immemorial. Jewish tradition traces the bulk of the oral injunctions, through a chain of distinctly-named authorities, to "Sinai" itself. It mentions in detail how Moses communicated those minutiæ of his legislation, in which he had been instructed during the mysterious forty days and nights on the Mount, to the chosen guides of the people, in such a manner that they should for ever remain engraven on the tablets of their hearts.

A long space intervenes between the Mosaic period and that of the Mishnah. The ever growing wants of the ever disturbed commonwealth necessitated new laws and regulations at every turn. A difficulty, however, arose, unknown to other legislations. In despotic states a decree is issued, promulgating the new law. In constitutional states a Bill is brought in. The supreme authority, if it finds it meet and right to make this new law, makes it. The case was different in the Jewish commonwealth of the post-exilian times. Among the things that were irredeemably lost with the first temple were the " Urim and Thummim " of the high-priest —the oracle. With Malachi the last prophet had died. Both for the promulgation of a new law and the abrogation of an old one, a higher sanction was requisite than a mere majority of the legislative council. The new act must be proved, directly or indirectly, from the " Word of God "— proved to have been promulgated by the Supreme King— hidden and bound up, as it were, in its very letters from the beginning. This was not easy in all cases; especially when a certain number of hermeneutical rules, not unlike those used in the Roman schools (inferences, conclusions from the minor to the major and *vice versâ*, analogies of ideas or objects, general and special statements, &c.), had come to be laid down.

Apart from the new laws requisite at sudden emergencies, there were many of those old traditional ones, for which the *point d'appui* had to be found, when, as established legal matters, they came before the critical eye of the schools. And these schools themselves, in their ever restless activity, evolved new laws, according to their logical rules, even when they were not practically wanted nor likely ever to come into practical use—simply as a matter of science. Hence there is a double action perceptible in this legal development. Either the scriptural verse forms the terminus *a quo*, or the terminus *ad quem*. It is either the starting-point for a discussion which ends in the production of some new enact- ment; or some new enactment, or one never before investi- gated, is traced back to the divine source by an outward " hint," however insignificant.

This process of evolving new precepts from old ones by " signs,"—a word curiously enough used also by Blackstone in his "development" of the law—may in some instances have been applied with too much freedom. Yet, while the Talmudical Code practically differs from the Mosaic as much

as our Digest will some day differ from the laws of the time
of Canute, and as the Justinian Code differs from the Twelve
Tables, it cannot be denied that these fundamental laws have
in all cases been consulted, carefully and impartially as to
their spirit, their letter being often but the vessel or outer
symbol. The often uncompromising severity of the Pentateuch, especially in the province of the penal law, had
certainly become much softened down under the milder
influences of the culture of later days. Several of its injunctions, which had become impracticable, were circumscribed, or almost constitutionally abrogated, by the introduction of exceptional formalities. Some of its branches
also had developed in a direction other than what at first
sight seems to have been anticipated. But the power vested
in the "judge of those days" was in general most sparingly
and conscientiously applied.

This whole process of the development of the "Law" was
in the hands of the "Scribes," who, according to the New
Testament, "sit in the seat of Moses." We shall speak
presently of the "Pharisees" with whom the word is often
coupled. Here, meantime, we must once more distinguish
between the different meanings of the word "Scribe" at
different periods. For there are three stages in the oral
compilation of the Talmudical Code, each of which is named
after a special class of doctors.

The task of the first class of these masters—the "Scribes"
by way of eminence, whose time ranges from the return from
Babylon down to the Greco-Syrian persecutions (220 B.C.)—
was above all to preserve the sacred Text, as it had survived
after many mishaps. They "enumerated" not merely the
precepts, but the words, the letters, the signs of the Scripture,
thereby guarding it from all future interpolations and corruptions. They had further to explain these precepts, in
accordance with the collateral tradition of which they were
the guardians. They had to instruct the people, to preach
in the synagogues, to teach in the schools. They further, on
their own authority, erected certain "Fences," i.e. such new
injunctions as they deemed necessary merely for the better

keeping of the old precepts. The whole work of these men ("Men of the Great Synagogue") is well summed up in their adage: "Have a care in legal decisions, send forth many disciples, and make a fence around the law." More pregnant still is the motto of their last representative—the only one whose name, besides those of Ezra and Nehemiah, the supposed founders of this body, has survived—Simon the Just: "On three things stands the world: on law, on worship, and on charity."

After the "Scribes"—κατ' ἐξοχήν—come the "Learners," or "Repeaters," also called Banaïm, "Master-builders"—from 220 B.C. to 220 A.D. In this period falls the Maccabean Revolution, the birth of Christ, the destruction of the temple by Titus, the revolt of Bar-Cochba under Hadrian, the final destruction of Jerusalem, and the total expatriation of the Jews. During this time Palestine was ruled successively by Persians, Egyptians, Syrians, and Romans. But the legal labours that belong to this period were never seriously interrupted. However dread the events, the schools continued their studies. The masters were martyred time after time, the academies were razed to the ground, the practical and the theoretical occupation with the law was proscribed on pain of death—yet in no instance is the chain of the living tradition broken. With their last breath the dying masters appointed and ordained their successors; for one academy that was reduced to a heap of ashes in Palestine, three sprang up in Babylonia, and the Law flowed on, and was perpetuated in the face of a thousand deaths.

The chief bearers and representatives of these divine legal studies were the President (called Nasi, Prince), and the Vice-President (Ab-Beth-Din = Father of the House of Judgment) of the highest legal assembly, the Synedrion, aramaised into *Sanhedrin*. There were three Sanhedrins: one "Great Sanhedrin," two "lesser" ones. Whenever the New Testament mentions the "Priests, the Elders, and the Scribes" together, it means the Great Sanhedrin. This constituted the highest ecclesiastical and civil tribunal. It consisted of seventy-one members, chosen from the foremost priests, the heads of

tribes and families, and from the "Learned," *i. e.* the "Scribes"
or Lawyers. It was no easy task to be elected a member of
this Supreme Council. The candidate had to be a superior
man, both mentally and bodily. He was not to be either too
young or too old. Above all, he was to be an adept both in
the "Law" and in Science.

When people read of "law," "masters" or "doctors of the
law," they do not, it seems to us, always fully realise what
that word "law" means in Old or rather New Testament
language. It should be remembered that, as we have already
indicated, it stands for all and every knowledge, since all and
every knowledge was requisite for the understanding of it.
The Mosaic code has injunctions about the sabbatical journey;
the distance had to be measured and calculated, and mathematics were called into play. Seeds, plants, and animals had
to be studied in connection with the many precepts regarding
them, and natural history had to be appealed to. Then
there were the purely hygienic paragraphs, which necessitated
for their precision a knowledge of all the medical science of
the time. The "seasons" and the feast-days were regulated
by the phases of the moon; and astronomy—if only in its
elements—had to be studied. And—as the commonwealth
successively came in contact, however much against its will
at first, with Greece and Rome,—their history, geography,
and language came to be added as a matter of instruction to
those of Persia and Babylon. It was only a handful of well-
meaning but narrow-minded men, like the Essenes, who
would not, for their own part, listen to the repeal of certain
temporary "Decrees of Danger." When Hellenic scepticism
in its most seductive form had, during the Syrian troubles,
begun to seek its victims even in the midst of the "Sacred
Vineyard," and threatened to undermine all patriotism and
all independence, a curse was pronounced upon Hellenism:
much as German patriots, at the beginning of this century,
loathed the very sound of the French language; or as, not so
very long ago, all things "foreign" were regarded with a
certain suspicion in England. But, the danger over, the
Greek language and culture were restored to their previous

high position in both the school and the house, as indeed the union of Hebrew and Greek, "the Talith and the Pallium," "Shem and Japheth, who had been blessed together by Noah, and who would always be blessed in union," was strongly insisted upon. We shall return to the polyglott character of those days, the common language of which was an odd mixture of Greek, Aramaic, Latin, Syriac, Hebrew; but the member of the Sanhedrin had to be a good linguist. He was not to be dependent on the possibly tinged version of an interpreter. But not only was science, in its widest sense, required in him, but even an acquaintance with its fantastic shadows, such as astrology, magic, and the rest, in order that he, as both lawgiver and judge, should be able to enter also into the popular feeling about these wide-spread "Arts." Proselytes, eunuchs, freedmen, were rigidly excluded from the Assembly. So were those who could not prove themselves the legitimate offspring of priests, Levites, or Israelites. And so, further, were gamblers, betting-men, money-lenders, and dealers in illegal produce. To the provision about the age, viz., that the senator should be neither too far advanced in age "lest his judgment might be enfeebled," nor too young "lest it might be immature and hasty;" and to the proofs required of his vast theoretical and practical knowledge—for he was only by slow degrees promoted from an obscure judgeship in his native hamlet to the senatorial dignity—there came to be added also that wonderfully fine rule, that he must be a married man and have children of his own. Deep miseries of families would be laid bare before him, and he should bring with him a heart full of sympathy.

Of the practical administration of justice by the Sanhedrin we have yet to speak when we come to the Corpus Juris itself. It now behoves us to pause a moment at those "schools and academies" of which we have repeatedly made mention, and of which the Sanhedrin formed, as it were, the crown and the highest consummation.

Eighty years before Christ, schools flourished throughout the length and the breadth of the land;—education had been made compulsory. While there is not a single term for

"school" to be found before the Captivity, there were by that
time about a dozen in common usage.[1] Here are a few of
the innumerable popular sayings of the period, betokening
the paramount importance which public instruction had
assumed in the life of the nation: "Jerusalem was destroyed
because the instruction of the young was neglected." "The
world is only saved by the breath of the school-children."
"Even for the rebuilding of the Temple the schools must not
be interrupted." "Study is more meritorious than sacrifice."
"A scholar is greater than a prophet." "You should revere
the teacher even more than your father. The latter only
brought you into this world, the former indicates the way
into the next. But blessed is the son who has learnt from
his father: he shall revere him both as his father and
his master; and blessed is the father who has instructed his
son."

The "High Colleges" or "Kallahs"[2] only met during
some months in the year. Three weeks before the term the
Dean prepared the students for the lectures to be delivered
by the Rector, and so arduous became the task, as the
number of the disciples increased, that in time no less than
seven Deans had to be appointed. Yet the mode of teaching
was not that of our modern universities. The professors did
not deliver lectures, which the disciples, like the Student in
"Faust," could "comfortably take home in black and white."
Here all was life, movement, debate; question was met by
counter-question, answers were given wrapped up in allegories
or parables, the inquirer was led to deduce the questionable

---

[1] Some of these terms are Greek,
like ἄλσος, λαός: some, belonging to
the pellucid idiom of the people, the
Aramaic, poetically indicated at times
the special arrangement of the small
and big scholars, e. g. "Array," "Vineyard" ("where they sat in rows as
stands the blooming vine"): while
others are of so uncertain a derivation,
that they may belong to either language. The technical term for the
highest school, for instance, has long
formed a crux for etymologists. It
is *Kallah*. This may be either the
Hebrew word for "Bride," a well-
known allegorical expression for
science, "assiduously to be courted,
not lightly to be won, and easily
estranged;" or it may be the slightly
mutilated Greek σχολή, or it may
literally be our own word *University*,
from *Kol*, all, universus: an all-embracing institution of all branches of
learning.

[2] See preceding note.

point for himself by analogy—the nearest approach to the Socratic method. The New Testament furnishes many specimens of this contemporary method of instruction.

The highest rank in the estimation of the people was not reserved for the "Priests," about whose real position some extraordinary notions seem still afloat—nor for the "Nobles" —but for these Masters of the Law, the "Wise," the "Disciples of the Wise." There is something almost German in the profound reverence uniformly shown to these representatives of science and learning, however poor and insignificant in person and rank. Many of the most eminent "Doctors" were but humble tradesmen. They were tentmakers, sandalmakers, weavers, carpenters, tanners, bakers, cooks. A newly-elected President was found by his predecessor, who had been ignominiously deposed for his overbearing manner, all grimy in the midst of his charcoal mounds. Of all things the most hated were idleness and asceticism; piety and learning themselves only received their proper estimation when joined to healthy bodily work. "It is well to add a trade to your studies; you will then be free from sin."—"The tradesman at his work need not rise before the greatest Doctor."—"Greater is he who derives his livelihood from work than he who fears God"—are some of the most common dicta of the period.

The exalted place thus given to Work, as on the one hand it prevented an abject worship of Learning, so on the other it kept all ascetic eccentricities from the body of the people. And there was always some danger of them at hand. When the Temple lay in ashes, men would no longer eat meat or drink wine. A Sage remonstrated with them, but they replied, weeping: "Once the flesh of sacrifices was burnt upon the Altar of God. The altar is thrown down. Once libations of wine were poured out. They are no more." "But you eat bread; there were bread-offerings." "You are right, Master, we shall eat fruit only." "But the first fruits were offered up." "We shall refrain from them." "But you drink water, and there were libations of water." And they knew not what to reply. Then he comforted them by the assurance that He who had destroyed Jerusalem had promised to rebuild it, and that proper mourning was right and meet, but that it must not be of a nature to weaken the body for work.

Another most striking story is that of the Sage who, walking in a market-place crowded with people, suddenly encountered the prophet Elijah, and asked him who, out of that vast multitude, would be saved. Whereupon the Prophet first pointed out a weird-looking creature, a turnkey, "because he was merciful to his prisoners;" and next two common-looking tradesmen, who came walking through the crowd, pleasantly chatting. The Sage instantly rushed towards them, and asked them what were their saving works. But they, much puzzled, replied: "We are but poor workmen who live by our trade. All that can be said for us is that we are always of good cheer, and are good-natured. When we meet anybody who seems sad we join him, and we talk to him, and cheer him, so long that he must forget his grief. And if we know of two people who have quarrelled, we talk to them and persuade them, until we have made them friends again. This is our whole life." . . . .

Before leaving this period of Mishnic development, we have yet to speak of one or two things. This period is the one in which Christianity arose; and it may be as well to touch here upon the relation between Christianity and the Talmud—a subject much discussed of late. Were not the whole of our general views on the difference between Judaism and Christianity greatly confused, people would certainly not be so very much surprised at the striking parallels of dogma and parable, of allegory and proverb, exhibited by the Gospel and the Talmudical writings. The New Testament, written, as Lightfoot has it, "among Jews, by Jews, for Jews," cannot but speak the language of the time, both as to form and, broadly speaking, as to contents. There are many more vital points of contact between the New Testament and the Talmud than divines yet seem fully to realise; for such terms as "Redemption," "Baptism," "Grace," "Faith," "Salvation," "Regeneration," "Son of Man," "Son of God,"

"Kingdom of Heaven," were not, as we are apt to think, invented by Christianity, but were household words of Talmudical Judaism. No less loud and bitter in the Talmud are the protests against "lip-serving," against "making the law a burden to the people," against "laws that hang on hairs," against "Priests and Pharisees." The fundamental mysteries of the new Faith are matters totally apart; but the Ethics in both are, in their broad outlines, identical. That grand dictum, "Do unto others as thou wouldst be done by," against which Kant declared himself energetically from a philosophical point of view, is quoted by Hillel, the President, at whose death Jesus was ten years of age, not as anything new, but as an old and well-known dictum "that comprised the whole Law." The most monstrous mistake has ever been our mixing up, in the first instance, single individuals, or classes, with a whole people, and next our confounding the Judaism of the time of Christ with that of the time of the Wilderness, of the Judges, or even of Abraham, Isaac, and Jacob. The Judaism of the time of Christ (to which that of our days, owing principally to the Talmud, stands very near), and that of the Pentateuch, are as like each other as our England is like that of William Rufus, or the Greece of Plato that of the Argonauts. It is the glory of Christianity to have carried those golden germs, hidden in the schools and among the "silent community" of the learned, into the market of Humanity. It has communicated that "Kingdom of Heaven," of which the Talmud is full from the first page to the last, to the herd, even to the lepers. The fruits that have sprung from this through the wide world we need not here consider. But the misconception, as if to a God of Vengeance had suddenly succeeded a God of Love, cannot be too often protested against. "Thou shalt love thy neighbour as thyself" is a precept of the Old Testament, as Christ himself taught his disciples. The "Law," as we have seen and shall further see, was developed to a marvellously and perhaps oppressively minute pitch; but only as a regulator of outward actions. The "faith of the heart"—the dogma prominently dwelt upon by Paul—was a thing that stood much higher with the Pharisees than this outward law. It was a thing, they said, not to be commanded by any ordinance; yet was greater than all. "Everything," is one of their adages, "is in the hands of Heaven, save the fear of Heaven."

"Six hundred and thirteen injunctions," says the Talmud, "was Moses instructed to give to the people. David reduced them all to eleven, in the fifteenth Psalm : Lord, who shall abide in Thy tabernacle, who shall dwell on Thy holy hill ? He that walketh uprightly," &c.

"The Prophet Isaiah reduced them to six (xxxiii. 15):—He that walketh righteously," &c.

"The Prophet Micah reduced them to three (vi. 8) : What doth the Lord require of thee but to do justly, and to love mercy, and to walk humbly with thy God?

"Isaiah once more reduced them to two (lvi. 1):—Keep ye judgment and do justice.

"Amos (v. 4) reduced them all to one :—Seek ye me and ye shall live.

"But lest it might be supposed from this that God could be found in the fulfilment of his whole law only, Habakkuk said (ii. 4):—'The just shall live by his Faith.'"

Regarding these "Pharisees" or "Separatists" themselves, no greater or more antiquated mistake exists than that of their being a mere "sect" hated by Christ and the Apostles. They were not a sect,—any more than Roman Catholics form a "sect" in Rome, or Protestants a "sect" in England, —and they were not hated so indiscriminately by Christ and the Apostles as would at first sight appear from some sweeping passages in the New Testament. For the "Pharisees," as such, were at that time—Josephus notwithstanding— simply *the* people, in contradistinction to the "leaven of Herod." Those "upper classes" of free-thinking Sadducees who, in opposition to the Pharisees, insisted on the paramount importance of sacrifices and tithes, of which they were the receivers, but denied the Immortality of the Soul, are barely mentioned in the New Testament. The wholesale denunciations of "Scribes and Pharisees" have been greatly misunderstood. There can be absolutely no question on this point, that there were among the genuine Pharisees the most patriotic, the most noble minded, the most advanced leaders

of the Party of Progress. The development of the Law itself
was nothing in their hands but a means to keep the Spirit as
opposed to the Word—the outward frame—in full life and
flame, and to vindicate for each time its own right to interpret
the temporal ordinances according to its own necessities and
requirements. But that there were very many black sheep
in their flock—many who traded on the high reputation of
the whole body—is matter of reiterated denunciation in the
whole contemporary literature. The Talmud inveighs even
more bitterly and caustically than the New Testament against
what it calls the "Plague of Pharisaism," "the dyed ones,"
"who do evil deeds like Zimri, and require a goodly reward
like Phinehas," "they who preach beautifully, but do not act
beautifully." Parodying their exaggerated logical arrange-
ments, their scrupulous divisions and subdivisions, the Talmud
distinguishes seven classes of Pharisees, one of whom only is
worthy of that name. These are—1, those who do the will
of God from earthly motives; 2, they who make small steps,
or say, just wait a while for me; I have just one more good
work to perform; 3, they who knock their heads against walls
in avoiding the sight of a woman; 4, saints in office; 5, they
who implore you to mention some more duties which they
might perform; 6, they who are pious because they *fear* God.
The real and only Pharisee is he "who does the will of his
father which is in Heaven *because he loves Him*." Among
those chiefly "Pharisaic" masters of the Mishnic period,
whose names and fragments of whose lives have come down
to us, are some of the most illustrious men, men at whose
feet the first Christians sat, whose sayings—household words
in the mouths of the people—prove them to have been
endowed with no common wisdom, piety, kindness, and high
and noble courage: a courage and a piety they had often
enough occasion to seal with their lives.

From this hasty outline of the mental atmosphere of the
time when the Mishnah was gradually built up, we now turn
to this Code itself. The bulk of ordinances, injunctions, prohibitions, precepts,—the old and new, traditional, derived, or
enacted on the spur of the moment,—had, after about eight

hundred years, risen to gigantic proportions, proportions no
longer to be mastered in their scattered, and be it remembered, chiefly unwritten, form.   Thrice, at different periods,
the work of reducing them to system and order was undertaken by three eminent masters; the third alone succeeded.
First by Hillel I., under whose presidency Christ was born.
This Hillel, also called the second Ezra, was born in Babylon.
Thirst for knowledge drove him to Jerusalem.   He was so
poor, the legend tells us, that once, when he had not money
enough to fee the porter of the academy, he climbed up the
window-sill one bitter winter's night.   As he lay there listening,
the cold gradually made him insensible, and the snow
covered him up.   The darkness of the room first called the
attention of those inside to the motionless form without.
He was restored to life.   Be it observed, by the way, that
this was on a Sabbath, as, according to the Talmud, danger
always supersedes the Sabbath.   Even for the sake of the
tiniest babe it must be broken without the slightest hesitation, "for the babe will," it is added, "keep many a
Sabbath yet for that one that was broken for it."

And here we cannot refrain from entering an emphatic
protest against the vulgar notion of the "Jewish Sabbath"
being a thing of grim austerity.   It was precisely the contrary, a "day of joy and delight," a "feast day," honoured
by fine garments, by the best cheer, by wine, lights, spice,
and other joys of pre-eminently bodily import: and the
highest expression of the feeling of self-reliance and independence is contained in the adage, "Rather live on your
Sabbath as you would on a week day, than be dependent on
others."   But this only by the way.

About 30 B.C. Hillel became President.   Of his meekness,
his piety, his benevolence, the Talmudical records are full.
A few of his sayings will characterise him better than any
sketch of ours could do.   "Be a disciple of Aaron, a friend
of peace, a promoter of peace, a friend of all men, and draw
them near unto the law."   "Do not believe in thyself till
the day of thy death."   "Do not judge thy neighbour until
thou hast stood in his place."   "Whosoever does not increase

in knowledge decreases." " Whosoever tries to make gain by the crown of learning perishes." Immediately after the lecture he used to hurry home. Once asked by his disciples what caused him to hasten away, he replied he had to look after his guest. When they pressed him for the name of his guest, he said that he meant his soul, which was here to-day and there to-morrow. One day a heathen went to Shammai, the head of the rival academy, and asked him mockingly to convert him to the law while he stood on one leg. The irate master turned him from his door. He then went to Hillel, who received him kindly and gave him that reply—since so widely propagated—" Do not unto another what thou wouldest not have another do unto thee. This is the whole Law, the rest is mere commentary." Very characteristic is also his answer to one of those " wits " who used to plague him with their silly questions. " How many laws are there ?" he asked Hillel. " Two," Hillel replied, " one written and one oral." Whereupon the other, " I believe in the first, but I do not see why I should believe in the second." " Sit down," Hillel said. And he wrote down the Hebrew alphabet. " What letter is this ?" he then asked, pointing to the first. " This is an Aleph." " Good, the next ?" " Beth." " Good again. But how do you know that this is an Aleph and this a Beth ?". " Thus," the other replied, " we have learnt from our ancestors." " Well," Hillel said, " as you have accepted this in good faith, accept also the other." To his mind the necessity of arranging and simplifying that monstrous bulk of oral traditions seems to have presented itself first with all its force. There were no less than some six hundred vaguely floating sections of it in existence by that time. He tried to reduce them to six. But he died, and the work commenced by him was left untouched for another century. Akiba, the poor shepherd who fell in love with the daughter of the richest and proudest man in all Jerusalem, and, through his love, from a clown became one of the most eminent doctors of his generation, nay "a second Moses," came next. But he too was unsuccessful. His legal labours were cut short by the Roman executioner. Yet the

day of his martyrdom is said to have been the day of
the birth of him who, at last, did carry out the work,—
Jehuda, the Saint, also called " Rabbi " by way of eminence.
About 200 A.D. the redaction of the whole unwritten law
into a code, though still unwritten, was completed after the
immense efforts, not of one school, but of all, not through
one, but many methods of collection, comparison, and con-
densation.

When the Code was drawn up, it was already obsolete
in many of its parts. More than a generation before the
Destruction of the Temple, Rome had taken the penal jurisdiction from the Sanhedrin. The innumerable injunctions
regarding the temple-service, the sacrifices, and the rest, had
but an ideal value. The agrarian laws for the most part
applied only to Palestine, and but an insignificant fraction
of the people had remained faithful to the desecrated land.
Nevertheless the whole Code was eagerly received as their
text-book by the many academies both in Palestine and in
Babylonia, not merely as a record of past enactments, but
as laws that at some time or other, with the restoration of
the commonwealth, would come into full practice as of yore.

The Mishnah is divided into six sections. These are sub-
divided again into 11, 12, 7, 9 (or 10), 11, and 12 chapters
respectively, which are further broken up into 524 paragraphs. We shall briefly describe their contents :—

"Section I., *Seeds* : of Agrarian Laws, commencing with a chapter
on Prayers. In this section the various tithes and donations due to the
Priests, the Levites, and the poor, from the products of the lands, and
further the Sabbatical year, and the prohibited mixtures in plants, animals,
and garments, are treated of.

"Section II., *Feasts* : of Sabbaths, Feast and Fast days, the work
prohibited, the ceremonies ordained, the sacrifices to be offered, on them.
Special chapters are devoted to the Feast of the Exodus from Egypt, to the
New Year's Day, to the Day of Atonement (one of the most impressive
portions of the whole book), to the Feast of Tabernacles, and to that of
Haman.

"Section III., *Women* : of betrothal, marriage, divorce, &c. : also of
vows.

"Section IV., *Damages* : including a great part of the civil and criminal
law. It treats of the law of trover, of buying and selling, and the ordinary

monetary transactions. Further, of the greatest crime known to the law, viz., idolatry. Next of witnesses, of oaths, of legal punishments, and of the Sanhedrin itself. This section concludes with the so-called 'Sentences of the Fathers,' containing some of the sublimest ethical dicta known in the history of religious philosophy.

"Section V., *Sacred Things*: of sacrifices, the first-born, &c.; also of the measurements of the Temple (Middoth).

"Section VI., *Purifications*: of the various levitical and other hygienic laws, of impure things and persons, their purification, &c."

There is, it cannot be denied, more symmetry and method in the Mishnah than in the Pandects; although we have not found that minute logical sequence in its arrangement which Maimonides and others have discovered. In fact, we do not believe that we have it in its original shape. But, as far as the single treatises are concerned, the Mishnah is for the most part free from the blemishes of the Roman Code. There are, unquestionably, fewer contradictory laws, fewer repetitions, fewer interpolations, than in the Digests, which, notwithstanding Tribonian's efforts, abound with so-called "Geminationes," "Leges fugitivæ," "errativæ," and so forth; and, as regards a certain outspokenness in bodily things, it has at last been acknowledged by all competent authorities that its language is infinitely purer than that, for instance, of the medieval casuists.

The regulations contained in these six treatises are of very different kinds. They are apparently important and unimportant, intended to be permanent or temporary. They are either clear expansions of Scriptural precepts, or independent traditions, linked to Scripture only hermeneutically. They are "decisions," "fences," "injunctions," "ordinances," or simply "Mosaic Halachah from Sinai"—much as the Roman laws consist of "Senatusconsulta," "Plebiscita," "Edicta," "Responsa Prudentium," and the rest. Save in points of dispute, the Mishnah does not say when and how a special law was made. Only exceptionally do we read the introductory formula " N. N. has borne witness," "I have heard from N. N.," &c.; for nothing was admitted into the Code but that which was well authenticated first. There is no difference made between great laws and little laws—

D

between ancient and new Halachah. Every precept traditionally received or passed by the majority becomes, in a
manner, a religious, divinely sanctioned one, although it was
always open to the subsequent authorities to reconsider and
to abrogate; as, indeed, one of the chief reasons against the
writing down of the Code, even after its redaction, was just
this, that it should never become fixed and immutable. That
the Mishnah was appealed to for all practical purposes, in
preference to the "Mosaic" law, seems clear and natural.
Do we generally appeal in our law-courts to the Magna
Charta?

This uniform reverence for all the manifold contents of
the Mishnah is best expressed in the redactor's own words—
the motto to the whole collection—"Be equally consci-
entious in small as in great precepts, for ye know not their
individual rewards. Compute the earthly loss sustained by
the fulfilment of a law by the heavenly reward derived
through it; and the gain derived from a transgression by
the punishment that is to follow it. Also contemplate three
things, and ye shall not fall into sin: Know what is above
ye—an eye that seeth, an ear that heareth, and all your
works are written in a book."

The tone and tenor of the Mishnah is, except in the one
special division devoted to Ethics, emphatically practical.
It does not concern itself with Metaphysics, but aims at
being merely a civil code. Yet it never misses an opportunity of inculcating those higher ethical principles which
lie beyond the strict letter of the law. It looks more to
the "intention" in the fulfilment of a precept than to the
fulfilment itself. He who claims certain advantages by the
letter of the law, though the spirit of humanity should urge
him not to insist upon them, is not "beloved by God and
man." On the other hand, he who makes good by his own
free will demands which the law could not have enforced;
he, in fact, who does not stop short at the "Gate of Justice,"
but proceeds within the "line of mercy," in him the "spirit
of the wise" has pleasure. Certain duties bring fruits (interest) in this world; but the real reward, the "capital," is

paid back in the world to come : such as reverence for father and mother, charity, early application to study, hospitality, doing the last honour to the dead, promoting peace between man and his neighbour. The Mishnah knows nothing of " Hell." For all and any transgressions there were only the fixed legal punishments, or a mysterious sudden " visitation of God "—the scriptural " rooting out." Death atones for all sins. Minor transgressions are redeemed by repentance, charity, sacrifice, and the day of atonement. Sins committed against man are only forgiven when the injured man has had full amends made and declares himself reconciled. The highest virtue lies in the study of the law. It is not only the badge of high culture (as was of old the case in England), but there is a special merit bound up in it that will assist man both in this and in the world to come. Even a bastard who is learned in it is more honoured than a high-priest who is not.

To discuss these laws, their spirit, and their details, in this place, we cannot undertake. But this much we may say, that it has always been the unanimous opinion of both friends and foes that their general character is humane in the extreme: in spite of certain harsh and exceptional laws, issued in times of danger and misery, of revolution and reaction; laws, moreover, which for the most part never were and never could be carried into practice. There is an almost modern liberality of view regarding the "fulfilment of the Law" itself, expressed by such frequent adages as "The Scripture says: 'he shall live by them'—that means, he shall not *die through them*. They shall not be made pitfalls or burdens to him, that shall make him hate life.' 'He who carries out these precepts to the full is declared to be nothing less than a Saint.'" "The law has been given to men, and not to angels."

Respecting the practical administration of justice, a sharp distinction is drawn by the Mishnah between the civil and criminal law. In both the most careful investigation and scrutiny is required; but while in the former three judges are competent, a tribunal of no less than twenty-three is required for the latter. The first duty of the civil judges is always—however clear the case—to urge an agreement. "When," says the Talmud, " do justice and goodwill meet? When the contending parties are made to agree peaceably." There were both special local magistrates and casual "justices of peace," chosen *ad hoc* by the parties. Payment received for a decision annuls the decision. Loss of time only was allowed to be made good in case of tradesmen-judges. The plaintiff, if proved to have asked more than his due, with a view of thus obtaining his due more readily, was nonsuited. Three partners in an action must not divide themselves into one plaintiff and two witnesses. The Judge must see that both parties are pretty equally dressed, *i.e.* not one in fine garments, the others in rags; and he is further particularly cautioned not to be biassed *in favour of the poor against the rich*. The Judge must not hear anything of the case, save in the presence of both parties. Many and striking are also the admonitions regarding the Judge. " He who unjustly hands over one man's goods to another, he shall pay God for it with his own soul." " In the hour when the Judge sits in judgment over his fellow-men, he shall feel, as it were, a sword pointed at his own heart." "Woe unto the Judge who, convinced in his mind of the unrighteousness of a cause, tries to throw the blame on the witnesses. From *him* God will ask an account." " When the parties stand before you, look upon both as guilty; but when they are dismissed, let them both be innocent in thine eyes, for the decree has gone forth."

It would not be easy to find a more humane, almost refined, penal legislation, from the days of the old world to our own. While in civil cases—whenever larger tribunals (juries) had to be called in—a majority of one is sufficient for either acquittal or condemnation; in criminal cases a majority of one acquits, but a majority of two is requisite for condemnation. All men are accepted in the former as witnesses—always except gamblers (κυβεία—dice-players), betting-men (" pigeon-flyers"), usurers, dealers in illegal (seventh year's) produce, and slaves, who were disqualified

from "judging and bearing witness"—either for the plaintiff
or the defendant; but it is only for the defence that everybody, indiscriminately, is heard in criminal cases. The
cross-examination of the witnesses was exceedingly strict.
The formula (containing at once a whole breviary for the
Judge himself), with which the witnesses were admonished
in criminal cases was of so awful and striking a nature, that
"swearing a man's life away" became an almost unheard-of
occurrence :—

"How is one," says the Mishnah, "to awe the witnesses who are called
to testify in matters of life and death? When they are brought into Court,
they are charged thus : Perchance you would speak from conjecture or
rumour, as a witness from another witness—having heard it from 'some
trustworthy man'—or perchance you are not aware that we shall proceed
to search and to try you with close questions and searching scrutiny.
Know ye that not like trials about money are trials over life and death.
In trials of money a man may redeem his guilt by money, and he may be
forgiven. In trials of life, the blood not only of him who has been falsely
condemned will hang over the false witness, but also that of the seed of his
seed, even unto the end of the world; for thus we find that when Cain
killed his brother, it is said, 'The voice of thy brother's blood is crying to
me from the ground.' The word blood stands there in the plural number,
to indicate to you that the blood of him, together with that of his seed, has
been shed. Adam was created alone, to show you that he who destroys
one single life will be called to account for it, as if he had destroyed a
whole world. . . . . But, on the other hand, ye might say to yourselves,
What have we to do with all this misery here? Remember, then, that
Holy Writ has said (Lev. v. 1), 'If a witness hath seen or known, if he
do not utter, he shall bear his iniquity.' But perchance ye might say,
Why shall we be guilty of this man's blood? Remember, then, what
is said in Proverbs (xi. 10), 'In the destruction of the wicked there
is joy.'"

The "Lex Talionis" is unknown to the Talmud. Paying
"measure for measure," it says, "is in God's hand only."
Bodily injuries inflicted are to be redeemed by money; and
here again the Pharisees had carried the day against the
Sadducees, who insisted upon the literal interpretation of
the "eye for eye." The extreme punishments, "flagellation"
and "death," as ordained in the Mosaic Code, were inflicted
in a humane manner unknown, as we have said, not only to
the contemporary courts of antiquity, but even to those of

Europe up to within the last generation. Thirty-nine was the utmost number of strokes to be inflicted: but—the "loving one's neighbour like oneself" being constantly urged by the Penal Code itself, even with regard to criminals— if the life of the culprit was in the least degree endangered this number was at once reduced. However numerous the delinquent's transgressions, but one punishment could be decreed for them all. Not even a fine and flagellation could be pronounced on the same occasion.

The care taken of human life was extreme indeed. The judges of capital offences had to fast all day, nor was the sentence executed on the day of the verdict, but it was once more subjected to scrutiny by the Sanhedrin the next day. Even to the last some favourable circumstance that might turn the scale in the prisoner's favour was looked for. The place of execution was at some distance from the Court, in order that time might be given to a witness or the accused himself for naming any fresh fact in his favour. A man was stationed at the entrance to the Court, with a flag in his hand, and at some distance another man, on horseback, was stationed, in order to stop the execution instantly if any favourable circumstance should still come to light. The culprit himself was allowed to stop four or five times, and to be brought back before the judges, if he had still something to urge in his defence. Before him marched a herald, crying, "The man N. N., son of N. N., is being led to execution for having committed such and such a crime; such and such are the witnesses against him; whosoever knows aught to his favour, let him come and proclaim it." Ten yards from the place of execution they said to him, "Confess thy sins; every one who confesses has part in the world to come; for thus it is written of Achan, to whom Joshua said, My son, give now glory to the God of Israel." If he "could not" offer any formal confession, he need only say, "May my death be a redemption for all my sins." To the last the culprit was supported by marks of profound and awful sympathy. The ladies of Jerusalem formed a society which provided a beverage of mixed myrrh and vinegar, that, like an opiate, benumbed the man when he was being carried to execution.

There were four kinds of capital punishment,— stoning, burning, slaying with the sword, and strangling. Crucifixion is utterly unknown to the Jewish law. "The house of stoning" was two stories high, "stoning" in the Mishnah being merely a term for breaking the culprit's neck. It was the part of the chief witness to precipitate the criminal with his own hand. If he fell on his breast he was turned on his back; if the fall had not killed him on the spot, the second witness had to cast a stone on his heart; if he still survived, then and then only, the whole people hastened his death by casting stones upon him. The modes of strangling and burning were almost identical: in both cases the culprit was immersed to his waist in soft mud, and two men by tightening a cord *wrapped in a soft cloth* round his neck, caused instantaneous suffocation. In the "burning" a lighted wick was thrown down his throat when he opened his mouth at his last breath. The corpse was buried in a special place appropriated to criminals. After a time, however, the bones were gathered together and transferred to the burial place of the culprit's kin. The relations then visited the judges and the witnesses, "as much as to say, we bear no malice against you, for a righteous judgment have ye judged." The ordinary ceremonies of outer mourning were not observed in such cases, but lamentation was not prohibited during the first period of grief—"for sorrow is from the heart." There was no confiscation of the culprit's goods.

Practically, capital punishment was abrogated even before the Romans had taken it out of the hands of the Sanhedrin. Here again the humanising influences of the "Traditions" had been at work, commuting the severe Mosaic Code. The examination of witnesses had been made so rigorous that a sentence of capital punishment became almost impossible. When the guilt had, notwithstanding all these difficulties, been absolutely brought home, some formal flaw was sure to be found, and the sentence was commuted to imprisonment for life. The doctors of a later period, notably Akiba, who, in the midst of his revolutionary dreams of a new Independence, kept his eye steadily on a reform of the whole jurisdiction, did not hesitate to pronounce openly for the abolition of capital punishment. A Court which had pronounced one sentence of death in seven, or even seventy years, received the name of " Court of Murderers."

So far the Mishnah, that brief abstract of about eight hundred years' legal production. Jehudah, the "Redactor," had excluded all but the best authenticated traditions, as well as all discussion and exegesis, unless where particularly necessary. The vast mass of these materials was now also collected, as a sort of apocryphal oral code. We have, dating from a few generations after the redaction of the official Mishnah, a so-called external Mishnah (Boraita); further the discussions and additions belonging by rights to the Mishnah, called Tosefta (Supplement); and, finally, the exegesis and methodology of the Halacha (Sifri, Sifra, Mechilta), much of which was afterwards embodied in the Talmud.

The Mishnah, being formed into a code, became in its turn what the Scripture had been, a basis of development and discussion. It had to be linked to the Bible, it became impregnated with and obscured by speculations, new traditions sprang up, new methods were invented, casuistry assumed its sway—as it did in the legal schools that flourished at that period at Rome, at Alexandria, at Berytus,—and the Gemara ensued. A double Gemara: one, the expression of the schools in Palestine, called that of Jerusalem, redacted at Tiberias (not at Jerusalem) about 390 A.D., and written in what may be called "East Aramæan;" the other, redacted at Syra in Babylonia, edited by R. Ashe (365-427 A.D.). The final close of this codex, however, the collecting and sifting of which took just sixty years, is due to the school of the "Saboraim" at the end of the fifth century A.D. The Babylonian Gemara is the expression of the academies of Syra, Nehardea, Pum-Veditha, Mahusa, and other places, during six or seven generations of continuous development. This "Babylonian" Talmud is couched in "Western Aramæan."

Neither of the two codes was written down at first, and neither has survived in its completeness. Whether there ever was a double Gemara to all the six or even the first five divisions of the Mishnah (the sixth having early fallen into disuse), is at least very doubtful. Much however that existed has been lost. The Babylonian Talmud is about four times as large as that of Jerusalem. Its thirty-six treatises now cover, in our editions, printed with the most prominent commentaries (Rashi and Tosafoth), exactly 2947 folio leaves in twelve folio volumes, the pagination of which is kept uniform in almost all editions. If, however, the extraneous portions are subtracted, it is only about ten or eleven times as large as the Mishnah, which was redacted just as many generations before the Talmud.

How the Talmud itself became by degrees what the Mishnah had been to the Gemara, and what the Scripture had been to the early Scribes, viz. a Text; how the "Amoraim" (speakers), "Saboraim," and "Gaonim," those Epigoni of the "Scribes," made it the centre of their activity for centuries; what endless commentaries, dissertations, expositions, responses, novellæ, abstracts, &c., grew out of it, we cannot here tell. Only this much we will add, that the Talmud, as such, was never formally accepted by the nation, by either General or Special Council. Its legal decisions, as derived from the highest authorities, certainly formed the basis of the religious law, the norm of all future decisions: as undoubtedly the Talmud is the most trustworthy canon of Jewish tradition. But its popularity is much more due to an extraneous cause. During the persecutions against the Jews in the Persian empire, under Jesdegerd II., Firuz, and Kobad, the schools were closed for about eighty years. The living development of the law being stopped, the book obtained a supreme authority, such as had probably never been dreamt of by its authors. Need we add that what authority was silently vested in it belonged exclusively to its legal portions? The other, the "haggadistic" or legendary portion, was "poetry," a thing beloved by women and children and by those still and pensive minds which delight in flowers and in the song of wild birds. The "Authorities" themselves often enough set their faces against it, repudiated it and explained it away. But the people clung to it, and in course of time gave to it and it alone the encyclopædic name of "Midrash."

We have now to say a few words respecting the language in which these documents are couched, as furnishing an additional key to the mode of life and thoughts of the period.

The language of the Mishnah is as pure a Hebrew as can be expected in those days. The people themselves spoke, as we mentioned above, a corrupt Chaldee or Aramaic, mixed with Greek and Latin. Many prayers of the period, the Targums, the Gemaras, are conceived in that idiom. Even the Mishnah itself could not exclude these all-pervading foreign elements. Many legal terms, many names of products, of heathen feasts, of household furniture, of meat and drink, of fruits and garments, are borrowed from the classical languages. Here is a curious addition to the curious history of words! The bread which the Semites had cast upon the waters, in the archaic Phœnician times, came back to them after many days. If they had given to the early Greeks the names for weights and measures,[1] for spice and aromas,[2] every one of which is Hebrew: if they had imported the "sapphire, jasper, emerald," the fine materials for garments,[3] and the garments themselves—as indeed the well-known χιτών is but the Hebrew name for Joseph's coat in the Bible —if the musical instruments,[4] the plants, vessels, writing materials, and last, not least, the "alphabet" itself, came from the Semites: the Greek and Latin idioms repaid them in the Talmudical period with full interest, to the great distress of the later scholiasts and lexicographers. The Aramaic itself was, as we said, the language of the common people. It was, in itself, a most pellucid and picturesque idiom, lending itself admirably not only to the epigrammatic terseness of the Gemara, but also to those profoundly poetical

---

[1] μνᾶ, κάδος, δραχμή.
[2] μύρρα, κιννάμωμον, κασία, νάρδος, βάλσαμον, ἀλόη, κρόκος, &c.
[3] βύσσος, κάρπασος, σινδών.
[4] νάβλα, κινύρα, σαμβύκη, &c.

conceptions of the daily phenomena, which had penetrated even into the cry of the watchmen, the password of the temple-guards, and the routine-formula of the levitical functionary. Unfortunately, it was too poetical at times. Matters of a purely metaphysical nature, which afterwards grew into dogmas through its vague phraseology, assumed very monstrous shapes indeed. But it had become in the hands of the people a mongrel idiom; and, though gifted with a fine feeling for the distinguishing characters of each of the languages then in common use ("Aramaic lends itself best to elegies, Greek to hymns, Hebrew to prayer, Roman to martial compositions," as a common saying has it), they yet mixed them all up, somewhat in the manner of the Pennsylvanians of to-day. After all, it was but the faithful reflex of those who made this idiom an enduring language. These "Masters of the Law" formed the most mixed assembly in the world. There were not only natives of all the parts of the world-wide Roman empire among them, but also denizens of Arabia and India; a fact which accounts for many phenomena in the Talmud. But there is hardly anything of domestic or public purport, which was not called either by its Greek or Latin name, or by both, and generally in so questionable a shape, and in such obsolete forms, that both classical and Semitic scholars have often need to go through a whole course of archæology and antiquities before unravelling it.[1] Save only one province, that of agriculture. This alone, together with some other trades, had retained the old homely Semitic words: thereby indicating, not, as

---

[1] Greek or Latin, or both, were the terms commonly employed by them for the table (τραπέζα, tabula, τρισκελής, τρίπους), the chair, the bench, the cushion (subsellium, accubitum), the room in which they lived and slept (κοίτων, εὐνή, ἔξεδρα), the cup (cyathus, phiala potoria) out of which they drank, the eating and drinking itself (œnogarum, collyra, παροψίς, γλεῦκος, acraton, opsonium, &c.). Of their dress we have the στολή, sagum, dalmatica, braccœ, chirodota. On their head they wore a pileus, and they girded themselves with a ζώνη. The words sandalium, solea, soleus, talaria, impilia, indicate the footgear. Ladies adorned themselves with the catella, cochlear, πόρπη, and other sorts of rings and bracelets, and in general whatever appertained to a Greek or Roman lady's fine apparel. Among the arms which the men wore are mentioned the λόγχη, the spear, the μάχαιρα (a word found in Genesis), the pugio.

ignorance might be led to conclude, that the nation was
averse to it, but exactly the contrary: that from the early
days of Joshua they had never ceased to cherish the thought
of sitting under their own vine and fig-tree. We refer for
this point to the idyllic picture given in the Mishnah of the
procession that went up to Jerusalem with the first-fruits,
accompanied by the sound of the flute, the sacrificial bull
with gilt horns and an olive-garland round his head proudly
marching in front.

The Talmud does, indeed, offer us a perfect picture of the
cosmopolitanism and luxury of those final days of Rome,
such as but few classical or postclassical writings contain.
We find mention made of Spanish fish, of Cretan apples,
Bithynian cheese, Egyptian lentils and beans, Greek and
Egyptian pumpkins, Italian wine, Median beer, Egyptian
Zyphus: garments were imported from Pelusium and India,
shirts from Cilicia, and veils from Arabia. To the Arabic,
Persian, and Indian materials contained, in addition to these,
in the Gemara, a bare allusion may suffice. So much we
venture to predict, that when once archæological and linguistic science shall turn to this field, they will not leave it
again soon.

We had long pondered over the best way of illustrating to
our readers the extraordinary manner in which the "Haggadah," that second current of the Talmud, of which we
spoke in the introduction, suddenly interrupts the course of
the "Halacha,"—when we bethought ourselves of the device
of an old master. It was a hot Eastern afternoon, and while
he was expounding some intricate subtlety of the law, his
hearers quietly fell away in drowsy slumbers. All of a
sudden he burst out: "There was once a woman in Egypt
who brought forth at one birth six hundred thousand men."
And our readers may fancy how his audience started up at
this remarkable tale of the prolific Egyptian woman. Her
name, the master calmly proceeded, was Jochebed, and she
was the mother of Moses, who was worth as much as all
those six hundred thousand armed men together who went
up from Egypt. The Professor then, after a brief legendary

digression, proceeded with his legal intricacies, and his hearers slept no more that afternoon. An Eastern mind seems peculiarly constituted. Its passionate love for things wise and witty, for stories and tales, for parables and apologues, does not leave it even in its most severe studies. They are constantly needed, it would appear, to keep the current of its thoughts in motion; they are the playthings of the grown-up children of the Orient. The Haggadah, too, has an exegesis, a system, a method of its own. They are peculiar, fantastic things. We would rather not follow too. closely its learned divisions into homiletical, ethical, historical, general and special Haggadah.

The Haggadah in general transforms Scripture, as we said, into a thousand themes for its variations. Everything being bound up in the Bible—the beginning and the end—there must be an answer in it to all questions. Find the key, and all the riddles in it are solved. The persons of the Bible— the kings and the patriarchs, the heroes and the prophets, the women and the children, what they did and suffered, their happiness and their doom, their words and their lives —became, apart from their presupposed historical reality, a symbol and an allegory. And what the narrative had omitted, the Haggadah supplied in many variations. It filled up these gaps, as a prophet looking into the past might do; it explained the motives; it enlarged the story; it found connections between the remotest countries, ages, and people, often with a startling realism; it drew sublime morals from the most commonplace facts. Yet it did all this by quick and sudden motions, to us most foreign; and hence the frequent misunderstanding of its strange and wayward moods.

Passing strange, indeed, are the ways of this Prophetess of the Exile, who appears wherever and whenever she listeth, and disappears as suddenly. Well can we understand the distress of mind in a medieval divine, or even in a modern *savant*, who, bent upon following the most subtle windings of some scientific debate in the Talmudical pages—geometrical, botanical, financial, or otherwise—as it revolves round the Sabbath journey, the raising of seeds, the computation of tithes and taxes—feels, as it were, the ground suddenly give way. The loud voices grow thin, the doors and walls of the school-room vanish before his eyes, and in their place uprises Rome the Great, the Urbs et Orbis, and her million-voiced life. Or the blooming vineyards round that other City of Hills, Jerusalem the Golden herself, are seen, and white-clad virgins move dreamily among them. Snatches of their songs are heard, the rhythm of their choric dances rises and falls: it is the most dread Day of Atonement itself, which, in poetical contrast, was chosen by the "Rose of Sharon" as a day of rejoicing to walk among those waving lily-fields and vine-clad slopes. Or the clarion of rebellion rings high and shrill through the complicated debate, and Belshazzar, the story of whose ghastly banquet is told with all the additions of maddening horror, is doing service for Nero the bloody; or Nebuchadnezzar, the Babylonian tyrant, and all his hosts, are cursed with a yelling curse—à propos of some utterly inappropriate legal point; while to the initiated he stands for Titus the—at last exploded—"Delight of Humanity." The symbols and hieroglyphs of the Haggadah, when fully explained some day, will indeed form a very curious contribution to the unwritten history of man. Often—far too often for the interests of study and the glory of the human race—does the steady tramp of the Roman cohort, the pass-word of the revolution, the shriek and clangour of the bloody field, interrupt these debates, and the arguing masters and disciples don their arms, and, with the cry "Jerusalem and Liberty," rush to the fray.

Those who look with an eye of disfavour upon all these extraneous matters as represented by the Haggadah in the Talmud—the fairy tales and the jests, the stories and the parables, and all that strange agglomeration of foreign things crystallized around the legal kernel—should remember, above all, one fact. As this tangled mass lies before us, it represents at best a series of photographic slides, half broken, mutilated and faded: though what remains of them is startlingly faithful to the original. As the disciple had retained, in his memory or his quick notes, the tenor of the single debates, interspersed with the thousand allusions, reminiscences, *aperçus*, facts, quotations, and the rest, so he perpetuated it—sometimes well, sometimes ill. If well, we have a feeling as if, after a long spell of musings or ponderings, we were trying to retrace the course of our ideas—and the most incongruous things spring up and disappear, apparently without rhyme or reason. And yet there is a deep significance and connection in them. Creeping or flying, melodious or grating, they carry us on; and there is just this difference in the Talmudical wanderings, that they never lose themselves. Suddenly, when least expected, the original question is repeated, together with the answer, distilled as it were out of these thousand foreign things of which we did not always see the drift. If ill reported, the page becomes like a broken dream, a half-transparent palimpsest. Would it perhaps have been better if a wise discretion had guided the hands of the first redactors? We think not. The most childish of trifles, found in an Assyrian mound, is of value to him who understands such things, and who from them may deduce a number of surprisingly important results.

We shall devote the brief space that remains, to this Haggadah. And for a general picture of it we shall refer to Bunyan, who, speaking of his own book, which—*mutatis mutandis*—is very Haggadistic, unknowingly describes the Haggadah as accurately as can be :—

" . . . . Would'st thou divert thyself from melancholy ?
Would'st thou be pleasant, yet be far from folly ?
Would'st thou read riddles and their explanation ?
Or else be drowned in thy contemplation ?
Dost thou love picking meat ? Or would'st thou see
A man i' the clouds, and hear him speak to thee ?
Would'st thou be in a dream, and yet not sleep ?
Or, would'st thou in a moment laugh and weep ?
Would'st lose thyself, and catch no harm ?
And find thyself again without a charm ?
Would'st read thyself, and read thou know'st not what ?
And yet know whether thou art blest or not
By reading the same lines ? O then come hither,
And lay this book, thy head and heart together. . . . . "

We would not reproach those who, often with the best intentions in the world, have brought almost the entire Haggadistic province into disrepute. We really do not wonder that the so-called "rabbinical stories," that have from time to time been brought before the English public, have not met with the most flattering reception. The Talmud, which has a drastic word for every occasion, says, "They dived into an ocean, and brought up a potsherd." First of all, these stories form only a small item in the vast mass of allegories, parables, and the like, that make up the Haggadah. And they were partly ill-chosen, partly badly rendered, and partly did not even belong to the Talmud, but to some recent Jewish story-book. Herder—to name the most eminent judge of the "Poetry of Peoples,"—has extolled what he saw of the genuine specimens, in transcendental terms. And, in truth, not only is the entire world of pious biblical legend which Islam has said and sung in its many tongues, to the delight of the wise and simple for twelve centuries, now to be found either in embryo or fully developed in the Haggadah, but much that is familiar among ourselves in the circles of medieval sagas, in Dante, in Boccaccio, in Cervantes, in Milton, in Bunyan, has consciously or unconsciously flowed out of this wondrous realm, the Haggadah. That much of it is overstrained, even according to Eastern notions, we do not deny. But there are feeble passages even in Homer and Shakspeare, and there are always people with a happy instinct of picking out the weakest portions of a work; while even the best pages of Shakspeare and Homer are apt to be spoiled by awkward manipulation. At the same time we are far from advising a wholesale translation of these Haggadistic productions. Nothing could be more tedious than a continuous course of such reading, though choice bits from them would satisfy even the most fastidious critic. And such bits, scattered through the Talmud, are delightfully refreshing.

It is, unfortunately, not in our power to indicate any specimens of its strikingly keen interpretations, of its gorgeous dreams, its—

" Beautiful old stories,
 Tales of angels, fairy legends,
 Stilly histories of martyrs,
 Festal songs and words of wisdom ;
 Hyperboles, most quaint it may be,
 Yet replete with strength, and fire,
 And faith—how they gleam,
 And glow and glitter ! . . ."

as Heine has it.

It seems of more moment to call attention to an entirely new branch of investigation, namely, Talmudical metaphysics and ethics, such as may be gleaned from the Haggadah, of which we shall now take a brief glance.

Beginning with the Creation, we find the gradual development of the Cosmos fully developed by the Talmud. It assumes destruction after destruction, stage after stage. And in their quaintly ingenious manner the Masters refer to the verse in Genesis, " And God saw all that he had made, and behold it was very good," and to that other in Eccles. iii. 11, " God created everything in its proper season ;" and argue " He created worlds upon worlds, and destroyed them one after the other, until He created this world. He then said, " This pleases me, the others did not ;"—" in its proper season "—" it was not meet to create *this* world until now."

The Talmud assumes some original substance, itself created by God, out of which the Universe was shaped. There is a perceptible leaning to the early Greek schools. " One or three things were before this world: Water, Fire, and Wind: Water begat the Darkness, Fire begat Light, and Wind begat the Spirit of Wisdom." The *How* of the creation was not even matter of speculation. The co-operation of angels, whose existence was warranted by Scripture, and a whole hierarchy of whom had been built up under Persian influences, was distinctly denied. In a discussion about the day of their creation it is agreed, on all hands, that there were no angels at first, " lest men might say ' Michael spanned out the firmament on the south, and Gabriel to the north.' " There is a distinct foreshadowing of the gnostic Demiurgos—that antique link between the Divine Spirit and the World of Matter—to be found in the Talmud. What with Plato were the Ideas, with Philo the Logos, with the Kabbalists the "World of Aziluth," what the Gnostics called more emphatically the wisdom (σοφία) or power (δύναμις), and Plotinus the νοῦς, that the Talmudical Authors call Metatron.[1] The angels—whose names, according to the Talmud itself, the Jews brought back from Babylon—play, after the exile, a very different part from those before the exile. They are, in fact, more or less Persian : as are also for the most part all incantations, the magical cures, the sidereal influences, and the rest of the "heathen" elements contained in the Talmud. Even the number of the Angelic Princes is seven, like that of the *Amesha-Çpeñtas*, and their Hebrew names and their functions correspond, as nearly as can be, to those of their Persian prototypes, who, on their own part, have only at this moment been discovered to be merely allegorical names for God's supreme qualities. Much as the Talmudical authorities inveigh against those "heathen ways," sympathetic cures, the exorcisms of demons, the charms, and the rest, the working of miracles, very much in vogue in those days, yet they themselves were drawn into large concessions to angels and demons. Besides the seven Angel Princes, there are hosts of ministering angels—the Persian *Yazatas*—whose functions, besides that of being messengers, are twofold ; to praise God and to be guardians of man. In their first capacity they are daily created by God's breath out of a stream of fire that rolls its waves under the divine throne. As guardian angels (Persian *Fravashis*) two of them accompany every man, and for every new good deed man acquires a new guardian angel, who always watches over his steps. When the righteous dies, three hosts of angels meet him. One says (in the words of Scripture) "He shall go in peace," the second takes up the strain and says, "Who has walked in righteousness," and the third concludes, "Let him come in peace and rest upon his bed." If the wicked leaves the world, three hosts of wicked angels come to meet him.[2]

---

[1] This name is most probably nothing but Mithra.

[2] This science of angels and demons (*Shedim* = Pers. *Daevas*)—links between men and angels, or rather personified passions—which flourished very vigorously at the beginning of Christianity, is, altogether,

With regard to the providential guidance of the Universe, this was in God's hand alone. As He is the sole Creator and Legislator, so also is He the sole arbiter of destinies. "Every nation," the Talmud says, "has its special guardian angel, its horoscopes, its ruling planets and stars. But there is no planet for Israel. Israel shall look but to Him. There is no mediator between those who are called His children, and their Father which is in Heaven." The Jerusalem Talmud — written under the direct influence of Roman manners and customs, has the following parable: "A man has a patron. If some evil happens to him, he does not enter suddenly into the presence of this patron, but he goes and stands at the door of his house. He does not ask for the patron, but for his favourite slave, or his son, who then goes and tells the master inside: The man N. N. is standing at the gate of the hall, shall he come in or not?—Not so the Holy, praised be He. If misfortune comes upon a man, let him not cry to Michael and not to Gabriel, but unto Me let him cry, and I will answer him right speedily—as it is said, Every one who shall call on the name of the Lord shall be saved."

The end and aim of Creation is man, who, therefore, was created last, "when everything was ready for his reception." When he has reached the perfection of virtue "he is higher than the angels themselves."

Miracles are considered by the Talmud—much as Leibnitz regards all the movements of every limb of our body—as only possible through a sort of "prestabilitated harmony," i.e., the course of creation was not disturbed by them, but they were all primevally "existing," "pre-ordained." They were "created" at the end of all other things, in the gloaming of the sixth day. Among them, however, was— and this will interest our palæographers—also the art of writing: an invention considered beyond all arts: nothing short of a miracle. Creation, together with these so-called exceptions, once established, nothing could be altered in it.

---

one of the most interesting, particu- | Christianity, Islam, and Zoroastrian-
larly with regard to the striking | ism: but we forbear to enlarge upon
parallels it offers between Judaism, | it.

The Laws of Nature went on by their own immutable force, however much evil might spring therefrom. "These wicked ones not only vulgarize my coin," says the Haggadah with reference to the propagation of the evil-doers and their kin, bearing the human face divine, "but they actually make me impress base coin with my own stamp."

God's real name is ineffable; but there are many designations indicative of his qualities, such as the Merciful (Rachman, a name of frequent occurrence both in the Koran and in the Talmud), the Holy One, the Place, the Heavens, the Word, Our Father which is in Heaven, the Almighty, the Shechinah, or Sacred Presence.

The doctrine of the soul bears more the impress of the Platonic than of the Aristotelian school. It is held to be pre-existing. All souls that are ever to be united to bodies have been created once for all, and are hidden away from the first moment of creation. They, being creatures of the highest realms, are cognizant of all things, but, at the hour of their birth in a human body, an angel touches the mouth of the child, which causes it to forget all that has been. Very striking is the comparison between the soul and God, a comparison which has an almost pantheistic look. "As God fills the whole universe," says the Haggadah, "so the soul fills the whole body; as God sees and is not seen, so the soul sees and is not seen; as God nourishes the whole universe, so the soul nourishes the whole body; as God is pure, so the soul is pure." This purity is specially dwelt upon in contradistinction to the theory of hereditary sin, which is denied. "There is no death without individual sin, no pain without individual transgression. That same spirit that dictated in the Pentateuch: 'And parents shall not die for their children, nor the children for their parents,' has ordained that no one should be punished for another's transgressions." In the judgment on sin the *animus* is taken into consideration. The desire to commit the vice is held to be more wicked than the vice itself.

The fear of God, or a virtuous life, the whole aim and end of a man's existence, is entirely in man's hand. "Everything is in God's hand save the fear of God." But "one

hour of repentance is better than the whole world to come."
The fullest liberty is granted in this respect to every human
being, though the help of God is necessary for carrying it out.

The dogma of the Resurrection and of Immortality,
vaguely indicated in the various parts of the Old Testament,
has been fixed by the Talmud, and traced to several biblical
passages. Various are the similes by which the relation of
this world to the world to come is indicated. This world is
like unto a " Prosdora " to the next : " Prepare thyself in
the hall, that thou mayest be admitted into the palace :" or
" This world is like a roadside inn (hospitium), but the
world to come is like the real home." The righteous are
represented as perfecting themselves and developing all
their highest faculties even in the next world; " for the
righteous there is no rest, neither in this world nor in
the next, for they go, say the Scriptures, from host to host,
from striving to striving :—they will see God in Zion." How
all its deeds and the hour when they were committed are
unfolded to the sight of the departed soul, the terrors of the
grave, the rolling back to Jerusalem on the day of the great
trumpet, we need not here tell in detail. These half-meta-
physical half-mystical speculations are throughout in the
manner of the more poetical early Church fathers of old and
of Bunyan in our times. Only the glow of imagination
and the conciseness of language in which they are mostly
told in the Talmud contrast favourably with the verboseness
of later times. The Resurrection is to take place by the
mystic power of the " Dew of Life " in Jerusalem—on Mount
Olivet, add the Targums.

There is no everlasting damnation according to the
Talmud. There is only a temporary punishment even for
the worst sinners. " Generations upon generations " shall
last the damnation of idolaters, apostates, and traitors. But
there is a space of " only two fingers' breadth between Hell
and Heaven ;" the sinner has but to repent sincerely and the
gates to everlasting bliss will spring open. No human being
is excluded from the world to come. Every man, of whatever creed or nation, provided he be of the righteous, shall
be admitted into it. The punishment of the wicked is not

specified, as indeed all the descriptions of the next world are left vague, yet, with regard to Paradise, the idea of something inconceivably glorious is conveyed at every step. The passage, "Eye has not seen nor has ear heard," is applied to its unspeakable bliss. "In the next world there will be no eating, no drinking, no love and no labour, no envy, no hatred, no contest. The Righteous will sit with crowns on their heads, glorying in the Splendour of God's Majesty."

The essence of prophecy gives rise to some speculation. One decisive Talmudical dictum is, that God does not cause his spirit to rest upon any one but a strong, wise, rich, and humble man. Strong and rich are in the Mishnah explained in this wise: "Who is strong? He who subdues his passion. Who is rich? He who is satisfied with his lot." There are degrees among prophets. Moses saw everything clearly; the other prophets as in dark mirrors. "Ezekiel and Isaiah say the same things, but Isaiah like a town-bred man, Ezekiel like a villager." The prophet's word is to be obeyed in all things, save when he commands the worship of idolatry. The notion of either Elijah or Moses having in reality ascended "to Heaven" is utterly repudiated, as well as that of the Deity (Shechinah) having descended from Heaven "more than ten hands' breadth."

The "philosophy of religion" will be best comprehended by some of those "small coins," the popular and pithy sayings, gnomes, proverbs, and the rest, which, even better than street songs, characterise a time. With these we shall conclude. We have thought it preferable to give them at random as we found them, instead of building up from them a system of "Ethics" or "Duties of the Heart." We have naturally preferred the better and more characteristic ones that came in our way. We may add—a remark perhaps not quite superfluous—that the following specimens, as well as the quotations which we have given in the course of this article, have been all translated by us, as literally as possible, from the Talmud itself.[1]

---

[1] With regard to the striking parallels exhibited by them to some of the most sublime dicta of the Gospels, we disclaim any intention of having purposely selected them. It is utterly impossible to read a page of

"Be thou the cursed, not he who curses. Be of them that are persecuted, not of them that persecute. Look at Scripture : there is not a single bird more persecuted than the dove ; yet God has chosen her to be offered up on his altar. The bull is hunted by the lion, the sheep by the wolf, the goat by the tiger. And God said, 'Bring me a sacrifice, not from them that persecute, but from them that are persecuted.'—We read (Ex. xvii. 11) that while, in the contest with Amalek, Moses lifted up his arms, Israel prevailed. Did Moses's hands make war or break war ? But this is to tell you that as long as Israel are looking upwards and humbling their hearts before their Father which is in Heaven, they prevail ; if not, they fall. In the same way you find (Num. xxi. 9), 'And Moses made a serpent of brass, and put it upon a pole : and it came to pass, that if a serpent had bitten any man, when he beheld the serpent of brass, he lived.' Dost think that a serpent killeth or giveth life ? But as long as Israel are looking upwards to their Father which is in Heaven they will live ; if not, they will die.—'Has God pleasure in the meat and blood of sacrifices ?' asks the prophet. No ; He has not so much ordained as permitted them. It is for yourselves, he says, not for me that you offer. Like a king, who sees his son carousing daily with all manner of evil companions : You shall henceforth eat and drink entirely at your will at my own table, he says. They offered sacrifices to demons and devils, for they loved sacrificing, and could not do without it. And the Lord said, 'Bring your offerings to Me ; you shall then at least offer to the true God.'—Scripture ordains that the Hebrew slave who 'loves' his bondage, shall have his ear pierced against the door-post. Why ? because it is that ear which heard on Sinai, 'They are My servants, they shall not be sold as bondsmen :'—They are *My* servants, not servant's servants. And this man voluntarily throws away his precious freedom—'Pierce his ear !' —'He who sacrifices a whole offering, shall be rewarded for a whole offering ; he who offers a burnt-offering, shall have the reward of a burnt-offering ; but he who offers humility unto God and man, shall be rewarded with a reward as if he had offered all the sacrifices in the world.'—The child loves its mother more than its father. It fears its father more than its mother. See how the Scripture makes the father precede the mother in the injunction, 'Thou shalt love thy father and thy mother ;' and the mother, when it says, 'Honour thy mother and thy father.'—Bless God for the good as well as the evil. When you hear of a death say, 'Blessed is the righteous Judge.'—Even when the gates of heaven are shut to prayer, they are open to those of tears.—Prayer is Israel's only weapon, a weapon inherited from its fathers, a weapon tried in a thousand battles.— When the righteous dies, it is the earth that loses. The lost jewel will always

---

the Talmud and of the New Testament without coming upon innumerable instances of this kind, as indeed they constantly seem to supplement each other. We need not urge the priority of the Talmud to the New Testament, although the former was redacted at a later period. To assume that the Talmud has borrowed from the New Testament would be like assuming that Sanskrit sprang from Latin, or that French was developed from the Norman words found in English.

be a jewel, but the possessor who has lost it—well may he weep.—Life is a passing shadow, says the Scripture. Is it the shadow of a tower, of a tree? A shadow that prevails for a while? No, it is the shadow of a bird in his flight—away flies the bird and there is neither bird nor shadow.— Repent one day before thy death. There was a king who bade all his servants to a great repast, but did not indicate the hour: some went home and put on their best garments and stood at the door of the palace; others said, There is ample time, the king will let us know beforehand. But the king summoned them of a sudden; and those that came in their best garments were well received, but the foolish ones, who came in their slovenliness, were turned away in disgrace. Repent to-day, lest to-morrow ye might be summoned.—The aim and end of all wisdom are repentance and good works.—Even the most righteous shall not attain to so high a place in Heaven as the truly repentant.—The reward of good works is like dates: sweet and ripening late.—The dying benediction of a sage to his disciples was: I pray for you that the fear of Heaven may be as strong upon you as the fear of man. You avoid sin before the face of the latter: avoid it before the face of the All-seeing.—'If your God hates idolatry, why does he not destroy it?' a heathen asked. And they answered him: Behold, they worship the sun, the moon, the stars; would you have him destroy this beautiful world for the sake of the foolish?—If your God is a 'friend of the poor,' asked another, why does he not support them? Their case, a sage answered, is left in our hands, that we may thereby acquire merits and forgiveness of sin. But what a merit it is! the other replied; suppose I am angry with one of my slaves, and forbid him food and drink, and some one goes and gives it him furtively, shall I be much pleased? Not so, the other replied. Suppose you are wroth with your only son and imprison him without food, and some good man has pity on the child, and saves him from the pangs of hunger, would you be so very angry with the man? And we, if we are called servants of God, are also called his children.—He who has more learning than good works is like a tree with many branches but few roots, which the first wind throws on its face; whilst he whose works are greater than his knowledge is like a tree with many roots and fewer branches, but which all the winds of heaven cannot uproot.

"Love your wife like yourself, honour her more than yourself. Whosoever lives unmarried, lives without joy, without comfort, without blessing. Descend a step in choosing a wife. If thy wife is small, bend down to her and whisper into her ear. He who forsakes the love of his youth, God's altar weeps for him. He who sees his wife die before him has, as it were, been present at the destruction of the sanctuary itself— around him the world grows dark. It is woman alone through whom God's blessings are vouchsafed to a house. She teaches the children, speeds the husband to the place of worship and instruction, welcomes him when he returns, keeps the house godly and pure, and God's blessings rest upon all these things. He who marries for money, his children shall be a curse to him.—The house that does not open to the poor shall open to the physician. The birds in the air even despise the miser. He who gives charity in secret is greater than Moses himself. Honour the sons of the poor, it is they who bring science into splendour.—Let the honour of thy neighbour be to thee like thine own. Rather be thrown into a fiery furnace than bring any one to public shame.—Hospitality is the most important part of Divine worship. There are three crowns : of the law, the priesthood, the kingship ; but the crown of a good name is greater than them all.—Iron breaks the stone, fire melts iron, water extinguishes fire, the clouds drink up the water, a storm drives away the clouds, man withstands the storm, fear unmans man, wine dispels fear, sleep drives away wine, and death sweeps all away—even sleep. But Solomon the Wise says : Charity saves from Death.—How can you escape sin ? Think of three things : whence thou comest, whither thou goest, and to whom thou wilt have to account for all thy deeds : even to the King of Kings, the All Holy, praised be He.—Four shall not enter Paradise : the scoffer, the liar, the hypocrite, and the slanderer. To slander is to murder.—The cock and the owl both await the daylight. The light, says the cock, brings delight to me, but what are you waiting for ?—When the thief has no oppportunity for stealing, he considers himself an honest man.— If thy friends agree in calling thee an ass, go and get a halter around thee.—Thy friend has a friend, and thy friend's friend has a friend : be discreet.—The dog sticks to you on account of the crumbs in your pocket.—He in whose family there has been one hanged should not say to his neighbour, Pray hang this little fish up for me.—The camel wanted to have horns, and they took away his ears.—The soldiers fight, and the kings are the heroes.—The thief invokes God while he breaks into the house.—The woman of sixty will run after music like one of six.—After the thief runs the theft ; after the beggar, poverty.—While thy foot is shod, smash the thorn.—When the ox is down, many are the butchers.— Descend a step in choosing a wife, mount a step in choosing a friend.—If there is anything bad about you, say it yourself.—Luck makes rich, luck makes wise.—Beat the gods, and the priests will tremble. Were it not for the existence of passions, no one would build a house, marry a wife, beget children, or do any work.—The sun will go down all by himself, without your assistance.—The world could not well get on without perfumers and without tanners : but woe unto the tanner, well to the perfumer !—Fools are no proof.—No man is to be made responsible for words which he utters in his grief.—One eats, another says grace.—He who is ashamed will not easily commit sin. There is a great difference between him who is ashamed before his own self and him who is only ashamed before others. It is a good sign in man to be capable of being ashamed. One contrition in man's heart is better than many flagellations.— If our ancestors were like angels, we are like men ; if our ancestors were like men, we are like asses.—Do not live near a pious fool.—If you wish to hang yourself, choose a big tree.—Rather eat onions and sit in the shadow, and do not eat geese and poultry if it makes thy heart uneasy within thee.—A small stater (coin) in a large jar makes a big noise. A myrtle, even in a desert, remains a myrtle.—When the pitcher falls upon the stone, woe unto the pitcher ; when the stone falls upon the pitcher, woe unto the pitcher: whatever befalls, woe unto the pitcher.—Even if the bull have his head deep in his trough, hasten upon the roof, and drag the ladder after you.—Get your living by skinning carcases in the street, if you cannot otherwise, and do not say, I am a priest, I am a great man ; this work would not befit my dignity.—Youth is a garland of roses, age is a crown of thorns.—Use a noble vase even for one day—let it break to-morrow.—The last thief is hanged first.—Teach thy tongue to say, I do not know.—The heart of our first ancestors was as large as the largest gate of the Temple, that of the later ones like that of the next large one ; ours is like the eye of a needle.—Drink not, and you will not sin.—Not what you say about yourself, but what others say.—Not the place honours the man, but the man the place.—The cat and the rat make peace over a carcase.—A dog away from his native kennel dares not bark for seven years.—He who walks daily over his estates finds a little coin each time. —He who humiliates himself will be lifted up ; he who raises himself up will be humiliated. Whosoever runs after greatness, greatness runs away from him ; he who runs from greatness, greatness follows him.—He who curbs his wrath, his sins will be forgiven.—Whosoever does not persecute them that persecute him, whosoever takes an offence in silence, he who does good because of love, he who is cheerful under his sufferings—they are the friends of God, and of them the Scripture says, And they shall shine forth as does the sun at noonday.—Pride is like idolatry. Commit a sin twice, and you will think it perfectly allowable.—When the end of a man is come, everybody lords it over him.—While our love was strong, we lay on the edge of a sword ; now it is no longer strong, a sixty-yard-wide bed is too narrow for us.—A Galilean said : When the shepherd is angry with his flock, he appoints to it a blind bell-wether.—The day is short and the work is great ; but the labourers are idle, though the reward be great, and the master of the work presses. It is not incumbent upon thee to complete the work : but thou must not therefore cease from it. If thou hast worked much, great shall be thy reward : for the master who employed thee is faithful in his payment. But know that the true reward is not of this world." . . . .

Solemnly, as a warning and as a comfort, this adage strikes on our ear :—"And it is not incumbent upon thee to complete the work." When the Masters of the Law entered and left the academy they used to offer up a short but fervent prayer, in which we would fain join at this moment —a prayer of thanks that they had been able to carry out their task thus far ; and a prayer further " that no evil might arise at their hands, that they might not have fallen into error, that they might not declare pure that which was impure, impure that which was pure, and that their words might be pleasing and acceptable to God and to their fellow-men."

II.

ISLAM.[1]

THE Sinaitic Manifestation, as recorded in the Pentateuch, has become the theme of a thousand reflections in the Talmud and the Haggadah generally. Yet, however varied their nature—metaphysical, allegorical, ethical—one supreme thought runs through them all—the catholicity of Mono-theism, its mission to all mankind. Addressed, apparently, to a small horde of runaway slaves, the "Law," those funda-mental outlines of religious and social culture, revealed on Mount Sinai—"the lowliest of the range, to indicate that God's Spirit rests on them only that are meek of heart"—was indeed intended, the Masters say, for all the children of men. "Why," they ask, "was it given in the desert and not in any king's land?"—To show that even as the desert, God's own highway, is free, wide open to all, even so are His words a free gift to all; like the sun, the moon, and the stars. It was not given in the stillness and darkness of night, but in plain day, amidst thunders and lightnings. In-deed, it had been offered to all nations of the world before it came to the "chosen one." But they, one and all, had pointed to some special national bent or "mission" with which one or the other of these commandments would have interfered, and so they declined them all. And intensely characteristic are some of the ethnological pleas put into their mouths by the, at times, humorous Haggadah. As for those trembling waifs and strays who, worn out with

---

[1] This article appeared in the 'Quarterly Review' for October, 1869, vol. cxxvii., No. 254, p. 293, and re-viewed the following works:—1. 'The Koran.' 2. 'The Talmud.' 3. 'The Sunnah.' 4. 'The Midrash.' 5. 'Mohammad.' By Sprenger. Alla-habad, 1851. 8vo. Berlin, 3 vols., 1861–65. 8vo. 6. 'Life of Mahomet.' By William Muir. 4 vols. London, 1858–61. 8vo.

"anguish of spirit and cruel bondage," a short while since
would not even listen to the message of Liberty, and who
now, scared with terrors and wonders, cried "We will obey
and hear!"—obey, as the old commentators keenly point
out, unconditionally, whatever we may hear—to them no
choice had been left. Had they not accepted the "Law,"
that self-same mountain would have covered them up, and
that desert would have become their grave:—a dictum significantly echoed by the Koran.

But—the Legend continues—when this Law came to be
revealed to them in the fulness of time, it was not revealed
in their tongue alone, but in seventy: as many as there were
nations counted on earth—even as many fiery tongues leap
forth from the iron upon the anvil. . . . And as the voice
went and came, echoing from Orient to Occident, from heaven
to earth, all Creation lay hushed in awful silence. No bird
sang in the air, the winds were still, the Seraphim paused in
their three times "Holy!" "And all men," says Scripture,
"heard and saw." They "heard" the voice—and to each it
bore a different sound: to the men and the women, the
young and the old, the strong and the weak. It appeared
unto them like the voice of their fathers, their mothers, their
children, all those whom they loved with their holiest and
tenderest love. And they "saw." In that self-same hour
God's Majesty revealed Itself in its manifold moods and aspects: as Mercy and as Severity, as Justice and as Forgiveness, as Grace and Peace and Redemption. And through
the midst of all these ever-varying sounds and visions there
rolled forth the Divine word, "I am the everlasting, Jehovah,
thy God, *One* God!" . . . .

In these and similar strains the wide and all-embracing
nature of the Monotheistic creed and call is set forth in those
ancient documents to which we again venture to draw the
attention of our readers, and from a new point of view. If,
on a former occasion, we endeavoured to sketch out of themselves their own aim and purport, their poetry and their
prose, their law and their legend, we shall now endeavour to
show how they may be, and must be, utilised for the investi-

gation of phases of creed and thought apparently wide apart
in time and tendency and place; how far they form one of
the most important sources—the most important one, perhaps
—of Islam.

We are not about to enter here into any "Origines Islam-
ismi." This lies, at present, beyond our task. But those
who would adequately work out the whole problem of the
Talmud—as far as it lies within individual range—must
needs look somewhat deeply into the story of these phases.
And with regard to Islam, it seems as if the knowledge of
its beginning and progress, its tenets and its lore, were not
quite as familiar as they might be to the world at large,
notably England, which "holds the gorgeous East in fee."

But before we proceed with our subject, which we shall
treat with all the reverence and all the freedom which belong
to Science in these our days, let us look back—but a few
centuries—and see what, for instance, the great theologians
and scholars of the time of the Reformation thought and said
of Islam; of its doctrine and the preacher thereof.

Daniel's "Little Horn" betokens, according to Martin
Luther, Mohammed. But what are the Little Horn's Eyes?
The Little Horn's Eyes, says he, mean "Mohammed's Al-
koran, or Law, wherewith he ruleth. In the which Law
there is nought but sheer human reason (*eitel menschliche
Vernunft*)." . . . "For his Law," he reiterates, "teaches
nothing but that which human understanding and reason
may well like." . . . Wherefore—"Christ will come upon
him with fire and brimstone." When he wrote this—in his
"army sermon" against the Turks—in 1529, he had never
seen a Koran. "Brother Richard's" (Predigerordens) "Con-
futatio Alcoran," dated 1300, formed the exclusive basis of
his argument. But in Lent of 1540, he relates, a Latin
translation, though a very unsatisfactory one, fell into his
hands, and once more he returned to Brother Richard and
did his Refutation into German, supplementing his version
with brief but racy notes. This Brother Richard had, according to his own account, gone in quest of knowledge to
"Babylon, that beautiful city of the Sarassins," and at Baby-

lon he had learnt Arabic and been inured in the evil ways of
the Sarassins. When he had safely returned to his native
land, he set about combating the same. And this is his exordium : —"At the time of the Emperor Heraclius there
arose a man, yea, a Devil, and a firstborn child of Satan . . .
who wallowed in . . . and he was dealing in the Black Art,
and his name it was Machumet." . . . This work Luther
made known to his countrymen, by translating and commenting, prefacing and rounding it off by an epilogue. True
his notes amount to little more but an occasional " Oh fie,
for shame, yóu horrid Devil, you damned Mahomet ! " or,
" Oh Satan, Satan, you shall pay for that ! " or, " That's it,
Devils, Sarassins, Turks, it's all the same ! " or, " Here the
Devil smells a rat," or, briefly, " O pfui Dich, Teufel ! "—
except when he modestly, with a query, suggests whether
those Assassins, who, according to his text, are regularly
educated to go out into the world in order to kill and slay
all Worldly Powers, may not, perchance, be the Gypsies or
the " Tattern " (Tartars); or when he breaks down with a
" Hic nescio quid dicat translator." His epilogue, however,
is devoted to a special disquisition as to whether Mohammed
or the Pope be worse. And in the twenty-second chapter of
this disquisition he has arrived at the final conclusion that,
after all, the Pope is worse, and that he and not Mohammed
is the real " Endechrist." " *Wohlan*," he winds up, " God
grant us His grace, and punish both the Pope and Mohammed, together with their Devils. I have done my part as a
true prophet and teacher. Those who won't listen may leave
it alone." . . .

In similar strains speaks the learned and gentle Melanch-
thon. In an introductory epistle to a reprint of that same
Latin Koran which displeased Luther so much, he finds fault
with Mohammed, or rather, to use his own words, he thinks
that " Mohammed is inspired by Satan," because he " does
not explain what sin is," and further, since he " showeth not
the reason of human misery." He agrees with Luther about
the Little Horn :—though in another treatise he is rather
inclined to see in Mohammed both Gog and Magog. And

" Mohammed's sect," he says, " is altogether made up (*con-flata*) of blasphemy, robbery, and shameful lusts." Nor does it matter in the least what the Koran is all about. " Even if there were anything less scurrilous in the book, it need not concern us any more than the portents of the Egyptians, who invoked snakes and cats. . . . Were it not that partly this Mohammedan pest and partly the Pope's idolatry have long been leading us straight to wreck and ruin—may God have Mercy upon *some* of us ! " . . .

Thereupon Genebrard, on the Papal side, charged the German Reformers, chiefly Luther, with endeavouring to introduce Mohammedanism into the Christian world, and to take over the whole clergy to that faith. Maracci is of opinion that Mohammedanism and Lutheranism are not very dissimilar—witness the iconoclastic tendencies of both ! More systematically does Martinus Alphonsus Vivaldus marshal up exactly thirteen points to prove that there is not a shadow of difference between the two. Mohammed points to that which is written down—so do these heretics. He has altered the time of the fast—they abhor all fasts. He has changed Sunday into Friday—they observe no feast at all. He rejects the worship of the Saints—so do these Lutherans. Mohammed has no baptism—nor does Calvin consider such requisite. They both allow divorce—and so forth. Whereupon Reland—only 150 years ago—turns round, not without a smile on his eloquent lips, and wants to know how about the prayers for the dead, which both Mohammed and the Pope enjoin, the intercession of angels, likewise the visiting of the graves, the pilgrimages to the Holy Places, the fixed fasts, the merit of works, and the rest of it.

If there be any true gauge of an age or a nation, it is the manner in which such age or nation deals with religious phases beyond the pale. We shall not follow here the vicissitudes of that discussion of which we have indicated a few traits, nor the gradual change which came over European opinion with regard to Islam and its founder. How the silly curses of the Prideaux, and Spanheims, and D'Herbelots; how their " wicked impostors," and " dastardly liars " and "devils incarnate," and Behemoths and beasts and Korahs and six hundred and sixty-sixes, gave room, step by step almost, to more temperate protests, more civil names, less outrageous misrepresentations of both the faith and the man: until Goethe and Carlyle, on the one hand, and that modern phalanx of investigators, the Sprenger, and Amari, and Nöldeke, and Muir, and Dozy, on the other, have taught the world at large that Mohammedanism is a thing of vitality, fraught with a thousand fruitful germs; and that Mohammed, whatever view of his character (to use that vague word for once) be held, has earned a place in the golden book of Humanity.

There is, however, another view which, though more slowly, yet as surely, is gaining ground in the consciousness, if not of the world at large, yet of those who have looked somewhat more closely into this matter. It is this, that Mohammedanism owes more to Judaism than either to Heathenism or to Christianity. We would go a step further. It is not merely parallelisms, reminiscences, allusions, technical terms, and the like, of Judaism, its lore and dogma and ceremony, its Halacha and its Haggadah (words which we have explained at large elsewhere,[1] and which may most briefly be rendered by "Law" and "Legend"), which we find in the Koran;[2] but we think Islam neither more nor less than Judaism as adapted to Arabia—plus the apostleship of Jesus and Mohammed. Nay, we verily believe that a great deal of such Christianity as has found its way into the Koran, has found it through Jewish channels.

We shall speak of these things in due season. Meantime, we would turn for a moment to certain mediæval Jewish opinions both on Christianity and Islam, which will probably astonish our readers. They belong to very high authorities of the Judæo-Arabic Dispersion in Spain:—Maimuni, generally called Maimonides, and Jehuda Al-Hassan ben Halevi.

---

[1] See page 17.
[2] Several of these have been pointed out from Maracci, Reland, Mill, Sale, to Geiger (1833)—the *facile princeps* on this field—Muir, Nöldeke, Rodwell, &c.

The former, at the close of his great "Digest of the Jewish Law," fearlessly speaks of Christ and Mohammed as heralds of the final Messianic times. In filling the world with the message of the Messiah, with the words of Scripture and its precepts, they have, he says, caused these exalted notions and sacred words to spread to the furthest ends of the earth. The latter—sweet singer, as well as great philosopher—wrote a book, in Arabic, called "Kusari," wherein a Jew, a Christian, and a Mohammedan, are made to defend and to explain their respective creeds before the King of the Chazars—the king of the country now called the Crimea—who, in the tenth century of our era, had, together with his whole people, embraced Judaism. The Jewish speaker compares the religion founded by Moses to a seed-corn, which, apparently dissolved into its elements, is lost to sight; while in reality it assimilates the elements around and throws off its own husk. And in the glorious end, both it and the things around will grow up together even as *one* tree, whose fruit is the Messianic time. The concise description of Islam which the author puts into the mouth of the Mohammedan interlocutor is so fair and correct that it might stand at the beginning of a religious Mohammedan compendium.

But in this they were but the exponents of the real feeling of the Synagogue from the earliest times, on this matter. For, startling as it may seem, what we are wont to consider the emphatically *modern* idea of the "three Semitic creeds" —being by their fundamental unity on the one hand, and their varying supplementary dogmas on the other, apparently intended to bring all humanity within the pale of Monotheism—is found foreshadowed in those Talmudical oracles. They who composed them were truly called the Wise, the Disciples of the Wise. They did not prophesy; they would have shrunk with horror from a like notion; but with a heart full of poetry they often combined marvellous keenness of philosophical insight. And thus while they develop the minutest legal points with an incisive logical sharpness, while they keep our imagination spell-bound by their gorgeous lore, they at times amaze us with views apparently

wide apart from their subject; but views so large, so en-
lightened, so "advanced," that we have to read again
and again to believe:—even as the age of the Renaissance
was amazed and startled when the long-buried song and
wisdom of the Antique were made to open their divine lips
anew.

Parallel with those transparent allegories of all mankind
being addressed on Sinai; or those others of "God's name
being inscribed in seventy languages on Moses' wonder-
staff;" or of "Joshua engraving the Law in seventy stones
on the other side of the Jordan;" there runs the clear and
distinct idea of certain apostolic Monotheistic nations or
phases. They are three in number. These three are our
three "Semitic creeds."

We shall, out of the many Variants that in more or less
poetical guise embody this thought, echoed and re-echoed by
the highest authorities of the Synagogue, and as often used
and mis-used in fierce mediæval Judæo-Mohammedan controversy, select what we consider the very oldest. It is found
in the *Sifre*, a work, although of somewhat later redaction,
anterior to the Mishnah, and often quoted in the Talmud as
one of its own oldest sources.

A homiletic exposition of Numbers and Deuteronomy, it
lovingly tarries at the last chapter—Moses' parting blessing.
The Tanchuma introduces this chapter by the striking remark that while through all other blessings recorded in the
Pentateuch—of Noah, of Abraham, of Isaac, of Jacob—there
always rings some discord, some one harsh note, whereby the
bliss foretold is concentrated upon some special heads to the
exclusion of others, the dying song of Moses is one unbroken
strain of harmony. Its golden blessings flow for all alike,
and there is none to stand aside, weeping. And the *Sifre*,
in a kind of paraphrase of the special verses themselves,
literally continues as follows:—"'The Lord came from *Sinai*,'
that means:—the Law was given in *Hebrew*; 'and rose up
from *Seïr* unto them,' that means it was also given in *Greek*
(*Rumi*); 'and he shined forth from Mount *Paran*,' that
means in *Arabic*." . . .

There is a fourth language added, "'He came with the thousands of Saints,' and this means *Aramaic*.'" Even granting the typical nature of the three geographical names alluded to—and it is not to be denied that Sinai and Seïr are constantly used for Israel and Esau-Edom-Rome, while Faran plainly stands for Arabia, whether or not it be the name of the mountains round Mecca as contended—the connexion of the "thousands of Saints" with Aram, does not seem quite clear at first sight—unless it mean Ezra's puritans. What, however, is quite clear by this time is this, that "Aramaic" is typical of Judaism; that Judaism which has supplanted both Hebraism and Israelitism, and which, having passed through its most vital reformation under Aryan, notably Zoroastrian auspices, during the Exile, subsequently stood at the cradle both of Christianity and Mohammedanism. Aramaic represents that phase during and since the Babylonish captivity whose legitimate and final expression is the "Oral Law," the Talmud: that Talmud, which with one hand—like those Puritans—reared iron walls around the sacred precincts of Faith and Nationality, and with the other laid out those inmost precincts with flowery mazes, of exotic colours, of bewildering fragrance—"a sweet-smelling savour unto the Lord."

When the Talmud was completed (finally gathered in, we mean—not composed), the Koran was begun. *Post hoc— propter hoc.* We do not intend to convey the notion as if the Talmudical authors had foretold the Koran. On the contrary, had they known its nature they would scarcely have bestowed upon it the term of "Revelation." But here is the passage: a wondrous sign of their clear appreciation of the elements of culture represented by the nations and clans around them. Hellas-Rome and Arabia appeared to them the fittest preparatory mediums or preliminary stages of this great Sinaitic mission of Faith and Culture.

Post hoc—propter hoc. The Hebrew, the Greek, the Aramaic phases of Monotheism, the Old Testament, the New Testament, the Targum, and the Talmud, were each in their sphere fulfilling their behests. The times were ripe for the Arabic phase.[1]

In the year 571, was born Mohammed—or he, who, together with his mission, appears with that significant name of the "Praised," under which he was supposed to have been foretold in the Old and New Testament.[2] It was but a few years after the death of that Byzantine Louis XIV., Justinian, who had aimed at creating one State, one Law, one Church throughout the world; who had laid the first interdict upon the Talmud; who most significantly gathered building materials from all the famous "heathen" temples—of Baal of Baalbeck and Pallas of Athens, of "Isis and Osiris" of Heliopolis and the Great Diana of Ephesus, therewith to reconstruct the Hagia Sophia at Constantinople—the same Hagia Sophia wherein now the grave and learned doctors cease not to expound the Koran. In those days Arabia expected her own prophet. The Jews in Arabia are said to have watched for his appearance.

Few religions have been founded in plain day like Islam, which now counts its believers by more than a hundred millions, and which enlarges its domain from day to day, unaided. Most clearly and sharply does Mohammed stand out

---

[1] [We must protest against the construction put upon this passage by some of our contemporaries. The historical sequence of events is merely described; it was not our object to discuss the claims and authority of Judaism, Christianity, and Islamism; and it is a complete misrepresentation of our words to assert that we placed the three religions upon an equal footing.—Note by the Author to the SECOND EDITION.]

[2] There exist very grave doubts as to whether this really was the Prophet's name. Originally called Kothan, he is held to have first adopted the epithet of Mohammed, either together with his mission or, perhaps, not even before the Flight. It is not easy to fix upon the exact passages, either in the Old or New Testament, to which the Prophet himself alludes, as foretelling him by name: as Mo-

hammed in the Old, and as Ahmad, another form of the same name, in the New. Regarding the latter, probably John's Paraclete (amended by some into περικλυτός), which in Arabic might be Ahmad, is meant. As to the Old Testament, the Vulgate—that most faithful receptacle of Jewish tradition, as transmitted to Jerome by his Rabbis—will best help us. There is no doubt that, with that root *hamad* there is generally mixed up some kind of Messianic notion in the eyes of Targumists and Haggadists. And when in Haggai ii. 8, we find the word "Hemdah"=a precious thing, rendered, against grammar and context, by "*Desideratus—omnium gentium*," we may be sure that the Synagogue did look upon this passage as Messianic, though there be no very direct evidence extant.

against the horizon of history. Those who knew him, not for
hours, or days, or weeks, but from birth to death, almost
during his whole life, count not by units, or dozens, but by
thousands upon thousands, whose names and whose biographies have been collected; and his witnesses were men in
the fulness and ripeness of age and wisdom, some his bitterest
enemies. No religious code extant bears so emphatically and
clearly the marks and traces of one mind, from beginning to
end, as the Koran, though, as to materials and contents, there
is, as we have hinted already, a passing strange tale to tell.
It will therefore behove us, in order that we may better understand how Mohammed made these materials entirely his
own, how he moulded and shaped, and added unto them, to
try and realise first the man himself and the vicissitudes that
influenced his mind—its workings and its strugglings, its
despairs and its triumphs.

This shall be done very briefly. And, though it seems
next to impossible to separate the man from his book, we
shall yet attempt to separate them. True, the more than
twenty years which its composition occupied, are embalmed in
it with all their strange changes of fortune, with their terrors
and visions, their curses and their prayers, their bulletins
and their field-orders. The Koran does indeed illustrate and
explain its author's life so well that hitherto every biographer
(and there have been many and great ones) has suggested, in
accordance with his own views, a different arrangement of
that book. In its present shape a sheer chaos as regards
chronological or logical order of chapters and even verses,
it will lend itself admirably to all and any arrangement.
You may work it, as it were, backwards and forwards. Something is supposed to have happened at a certain time : here
is a verse looking like a vague allusion to it : therefore the
verse belongs to that period, and confirms the previously
doubtful fact. Here is a verse which alludes to some event
or other of which nothing is known, and the event is solemnly
registered, a fitting date is given to it, and the verse finds its
chronological place. But we have nothing to arrange, and
therefore, though it be less easy and less picturesque to

consider the author and the book as independently as may be, we do so at Mohammed's express desire as it were, and in bare justice to him. He wishes the Koran to be judged by its own contents. " Hic Rhodus, hic salta," he seems to cry. The Book is his sign, his miracle, his mission. His own story is another matter. And without preconceived opinions—either as panegyrist or as Advocatus Diaboli—shall we try to tell it and then be unfettered in our story of the Book. If we make use of the "Sunnah" for our purpose no one will blame us. This Midrash of Mohammedanism, as we should call those traditional records of the Prophet's doings and sayings, both in the legendary and juridical sense of the word, has, albeit in exalted tones and colours often, told us much of his outer and inner life. Used with the same patient care with which all documents are used by the impartial historian, it yields precious information.

We have reason to discard much of what has long been repeated about Mohammed's early life. All we know, or think we know now for certain, is that he lost his father before his birth, and his mother when he was six years of age. His grandfather who had adopted him died two years later, and his poor uncle Abu Tâlib then took charge of him. Though belonging to a good enough family, the Koreish, though sickly, subject to epilepsy, Mohammed had early to work for his living. He tended the flocks—even as Moses, David, and all prophets had done, he used to say. "Pick me out the blackest of these berries," he cried once at Medina, when prophet and king, he saw some people pass with berries of the wild shrub Arak. "Pick me out the blackest, for they are sweet—even such was I wont to gather when I tended the flocks of Mecca at Ajyâd." But by the Meccans tending of flocks was considered a very low occupation indeed. In his twenty-fourth year, a rich widow of Mecca, Chadija, about thirty-eight years of age, and twice before married, engaged his services. He accompanied her caravans on several journeys, probably as a camel-driver. Of a sudden she offered him her hand, and obtained the consent of her father by intoxicating him. She bore Mohammed two sons, one of whom he called after a popular idol, and four daughters. Both boys died early.

This is the whole story of Mohammed's outer life previous to the assumption of his mission. The ever-repeated tale of his having accidentally been chosen, in his thirty-fifth year, as arbiter in a quarrel about the replacing of the Black Stone in the Kaaba, is at least very questionable, as are his repeated travels in Syria with his uncles, to which we shall return anent a certain monk who appears in many aliases, and who proves to be more or less a myth.

Mohammed's personal appearance, a matter of some import, chiefly in a prophet, is almost feature by feature thus portrayed by the best authenticated traditionists:—

He was of middle height, rather thin, but broad of shoulders, wide of chest, strong of bone and muscle. His head was massive, strongly developed. Dark hair—slightly curled—flowed in a dense mass down almost to his shoulders. Even in advanced age it was sprinkled by only about twenty grey hairs—produced by the agonies of his "Revelations." His face was oval-shaped, slightly tawny of colour. Fine, long, arched eyebrows were divided by a vein which throbbed visibly in moments of passion. Great black restless eyes shone out from under long heavy eyelashes. His nose was large, slightly aquiline. His teeth, upon which he bestowed great care, were well set, dazzling white. A full beard framed his manly face. His skin was clear and soft, his complexion "red and white," his hands were as "silk and satin"—even as those of a woman. His step was quick and elastic, yet firm, and as that of one "who steps from a high to a low place." In turning his face he would also turn his full body. His whole gait and presence were dignified and imposing. His countenance was mild and pensive. His laugh was rarely more than a smile. "Oh, my little son!" reads one tradition, "hadst thou seen him thou wouldest have said thou hadst seen a sun rising." "I," says another witness, "saw him in a moonlight night, and sometimes I looked at his beauty and sometimes I looked at the moon, and his dress was striped with red, and he was brighter and more beautiful to me than the moon."

In his habits he was extremely simple, though he bestowed great care on his person. His eating and drinking, his dress and his furniture, retained, even when he had reached the fulness of power, their almost primitive nature. He made a point of giving away all "superfluities." The only luxuries he indulged in were, besides arms, which he highly prized, certain yellow boots, a present from the Negus of Abyssinia. Perfumes, however, he loved passionately, being most sensitive of smell. Strong drinks he abhorred.

His constitution was extremely delicate. He was nervously afraid of bodily pain, he would sob and roar under it. Eminently unpractical in all common things of life, he was gifted with mighty powers of imagination, elevation of mind, delicacy and refinement of feeling. "He is more modest than a virgin behind her curtain," it was said of him. He was most indulgent to his inferiors, and would never allow his awkward little page to be scolded, whatever he did. "Ten years," said Anas, his servant, "was I about the prophet, and he never said as much as "uff" to me." He was very affectionate towards his family. One of his boys died on his breast, in the smoky house of the nurse, a blacksmith's wife. He was very fond of children. He would stop them in the streets and pat their little cheeks. He never struck any one in his life. The worst expression he ever made use of in conversation was, "What has come to him?—may his forehead be darkened with mud!" When asked to curse some one, he replied, "I have not been sent to curse, but to be a mercy to mankind." "He visited the sick, followed any bier he met, accepted the invitation of a slave to dinner, mended his own clothes, milked his goats, and waited upon himself," relates summarily another tradition. He never first withdrew his hand out of another man's palm, and turned not before the other had turned. His hand, we read elsewhere — and traditions like these give a good index of what the Arabs expected their prophet to be—was the most generous, his breast the most courageous, his tongue the most truthful; he

was the most faithful protector of those he protected, the
sweetest and most agreeable in conversation; those who saw
him were suddenly filled with reverence, those who came
near him loved him, they who described him would say, " I
have never seen his like either before or after." He was of
great taciturnity, but when he spoke it was with emphasis
and deliberation, and no one could ever forget what he said.
He was, however, very nervous and restless withal, often low-
spirited, downcast as to heart and eyes. Yet he would at
times suddenly break through those broodings, become gay,
talkative, jocular, chiefly among his own. He would then
delight in telling amusing little stories, fairy tales, and the
like. He would romp with the children and play with their
toys—as, after his first wife's death, he was wont to play with
the dolls his new baby-wife had brought into his house.

The common cares of life had been taken from him by the
motherly hand of Chadija: but heavier cares seemed now to
darken his soul, to weigh down his whole being. As time
wore on, the gloom and misery of his heart became more and
more terrible. He neglected his household matters, and fled
all men. "Solitude became a passion to him," the traditions
record. He had now passed the meridian of his life. No
one seemed to heed the brooder, no one stretched out the
hand of sympathy to him. He had nothing in common with
the rest, and he was left to himself.

Much chronological discussion has arisen as to the date of
the event of which we are going to speak. So much, however, seems certain, that Mohammed was at least forty years
of age when he went, according to the custom of some of his
countrymen, to spend the Rajab, the month of universal
armistice among the ancient Arabs, on Mount Hirâ, an hour's
walk from Mecca. This mountain, now called Mount of
Light, consists of a huge barren rock, torn by cleft and
hollow ravine, standing out solitary in the full white glare of
the desert sun, shadowless, flowerless, without well or rill.
On this rock, in a small dark cave, Mohammed lived, alone,
and spent his days and his nights, according to unanimous
tradition, in " *Tahannoth.*"

The weary guesses that have been made from the days of these very traditions to our own, as to the meaning and derivation of this word, cannot be told. It has been put on the rack by lexicographers, grammarians, commentators, translators, investigators, of all hues and ages, and, we are sorry to add, with no satisfactory result. To the general meaning the context gave some cue, but the etymology of the word, and its technical signification, have remained a mystery, notwithstanding many various readings of its single letters suggested by sheer despair. One of the latest, and greatest, investigators, Sprenger, numbers it as of one the most "indigestible morsels" among the many strange and obsolete words that occur in connexion with Mohammed and the Koran.

We do not intend to do more than throw out suggestions —though very carefully weighed—for we must, to our regret, leave all our philological scaffoldings behind. Regarding this most mysterious word, we have a notion that it might be explained, like scores of other tough morsels in the Koran, by the Jewish, Hebrew, or Aramaic parlance of the period, as it is preserved most fortunately in the Talmud, the Targum, the Midrash. The word Tahannoth need not be emendated into *Tahannof*, or any other weird form, to agree with its traditional meaning, because we think that it is only the Hebrew word *Tehinnoth*, which occurs bodily in the Bible, and means "Prayers, Supplications." The change of vowels is exactly the same as that from the Hebrew *Gehinnom* (New Test. *Gehenna*) to the Koranic *Jahannam*. Among the Jews the word became technical for a certain class of devotional prayers, customary, together with fastings, throughout the month preceding the New Year's Day. It is known more generally as a term for private devotions throughout the year, chiefly for pious women.—This, however, only by the way.

To devotions and asceticism, then, Mohammed gave himself up in his wild solitude. And after a time there came to him dreams "resplendent like the rosy dawn." When he left his cave to walk about on his rocky fastness, the wild herbs that grew in the clefts would bend their heads, and the stones scattered in his way would cry, "Salâm! Hail, O Prophet of God." And horrified, not daring to look about him, he fled back into his cave. That same cave has now become a station for the Holy Pilgrimage, and on it that early predecessor of our Burckhardts and Burtons, " Hajj Joseph Pitts of Exon," the runaway sailor boy, delivered himself of the judgment that "he had been in the cave, and observed that it was not at all beautified, at which he admired."

Suddenly, in the middle of the night—the ". blessed night Al Kadar," as the Koran has it—" and who will make thee understand what the night Al Kadar is? That night Al Kadar, which is better than a thousand months . . . . which bringeth peace and blessings till the rosy dawn"—in the middle of that night, Mohammed woke from his sleep, and he heard a voice. Twice it called, urging, and twice he struggled and waived its call. But he was pressed sore, " as if a fearful weight had been laid upon him." He thought his last hour had come. And for the third time the voice called :—

" CRY ! "

And he said, " What shall I cry ? "

Came the answer : " CRY—in the name of thy Lord ! " . . .

And these, according to wellnigh unanimous tradition, followed by nearly every ancient and modern authority, are the first words of the Koran. Our readers will find them in the ninety-sixth chapter of that Book, to which they have been banished by the Redactors.

We hasten to add that when we said that the above sentence would be found in the ninety-sixth chapter of the Koran, we were not quite accurate. The word which we have ventured to translate *Cry* they will find rendered in as many different ways as there were translators, investigators, commentators, old and new. They will find Recite, Preach, Read, Proclaim, Call out, Read the Scriptures—namely of the Jews and Christians—and a weary variety of other meanings which certainly belong to the word, though the

greater part of them is of obviously later date and utterly
out of the question in this case.

Our reasons for deviating from these time-honoured versions were of various kinds. In the first place, the Arabic
root in question is *identical* with our own, and in this primitive root lie hidden all other significations. " Cry " is one
of those very few onomatopoetic words still common to both
Semitic and Indo-European. Its significations are indeed
manifold; from the vague sound given forth by bird or tree,
as in Sanskrit, to our English usage of silent weeping; from
the Hebrew " deep *crying* unto deep " to the technical
Aramaic " reading the Scriptures "—in contradistinction to
" reading the Mishnah "—from the weird German *Schrei* to
the Greek herald's solemn proclamation—it is always the
same fundamental root: biliteral or triliteral.

Secondly, because the principal words of this tradition are
startlingly identical—another fact not hitherto noticed, as far
as we are aware—with a certain passage in Isaiah: "The
Voice said Cry, and I said, What shall I cry ? "—a passage
in which no one has yet translated the leading verb by
Recite, Read, Read the Scriptures, though there was never a
doubt as to whether Isaiah knew the Scriptures and could
read, while Mohammed distinctly denied being a " Scholar."

And, thirdly, because from this root is also derived the
word *Koran*. Derived: for it was in the very special Jewish
sense of *Mikra*, Scripture, that Mohammed gave that name
to every single fragment of that book, until it became, even
as the word Mishnah, its collective and general name.

We now resume our recital of that first revelation and its
immediate consequences, as tradition has preserved it. It
is of moment.

When the voice had ceased to speak, telling how from
minutest beginnings man had been called into existence and
lifted up by understanding and knowledge of the Lord, who
is most beneficent, and who *by the pen* had revealed that
which men did not know, Mohammed woke from his trance
and felt as if " a book " had been written in his heart. A
great trembling came upon him so that his whole body

shook, and the perspiration ran down his body. He hastened home to his wife and said, "Oh, Chadija! what has happened to me!" He lay down, and she watched by him. When he recovered from his paroxysm he said, "Oh, Chadija! he, of whom one would not have believed it (meaning himself), has become either a soothsayer (Kahin[1]) or one possessed (by Djins)—mad." She replied, "God is my protection, O Abu-'l-Kasim! (a name of Mohammed derived from one of his boys), He will surely not let such a thing happen unto thee, for thou speakest the truth, dost not return evil for evil, keepest faith, art of a good life, and kind to thy relations and friends. And neither art thou a talker abroad in the bazaars. What has befallen thee? Hast thou seen aught terrible?" Mohammed replied, "Yes." And he told her what he had seen. Whereupon she answered and said, "Rejoice, O dear husband, and be of good cheer. He, in whose hands stands Chadija's life, is my witness that thou wilt be the prophet of this people." Then she arose and went to her cousin Waraka, who was old and blind, and "knew the Scriptures of the Jews and Christians." When she told him what she had heard, he cried out, "*Koddus, Koddus!*—Holy, Holy! Verily this is the *Namus* which came to Moses. He will be the prophet of his people. Tell him this. Bid him be of brave heart."

We must here interpose for a moment. This Waraka has given rise to much and angry discussion—chiefly as to his "conversion." He was long supposed to have been first an idolater, then a Jew, finally a Christian. It has been shown, however, by recent investigations, that whatever he was at first, he certainly lived and died a Jew. To our mind this one sentence goes a long way towards settling the point. *Koddus*—is simply the Arabicised Hebrew *Kadosh* (Holy). And while we need not prove that a Christian would scarcely have used this exclamation (any more than he would have

---

[1] The Hebrew "Cohen," priest, in a deteriorated sense like the German "Pfaffe." In the time of Mohammed it meant a low fortune-teller, an ever- ready interpreter of dreams, who had, like Daniel, to find out both the dreams and their solutions.

spoken of the "Namus"), we are reminded of the story in
the Midrash of the man whose heart was sore within him
for that he could neither read the Scripture nor the Mishnah.
And one day when he stood in the synagogue, and the precentor reached that part of the liturgy in which God's holy
name is sanctified, this man lifted up his voice aloud and
cried out with all his main : "*Kadosh! Kadosh! Kadosh!*"
(Holy! Holy! Holy!). And when they asked him what
made him cry out thus, he said, "I have not been deemed
worthy to read the Scriptures, or the Mishnah, and now the
moment has come when I may sanctify God, shall I not
lift up my voice aloud?"   "It did not last a year, or two,
or three," the legend adds, "but it so fell out that this man
became a great and mighty general, and a founder of a
colony within the Roman empire."

As to the "*Namus,*" it is a hermaphrodite in words. It is
Arabic, but also Greek. That it is Talmudical need we say
it?   It is in the first instance νόμος, Law, that which "by
custom and common consent" has become so. In Talmudical
phraseology it stands for the Thorah or Revealed Law. In
Arabic it further means one who communicates a secret
message. And all these different significations were conveyed by Waraka to Mohammed. The messenger and the
message, both divine, had come together, even as Moses
had been instructed in the Law by a special angel—not,
as former commentators, to save Waraka's Christianity, used
to explain, because to Mohammed, as to Moses, a new Law
was given, while Christ came to confirm what had been
given before.

Not long after this the two men met in the street of
Mecca. And Waraka said, "I swear by him in whose hand
Waraka's life is, God has chosen thee to be the prophet of
this people. The greatest *Namus* has come to thee. They
will call thee a liar; they will persecute thee, they will
banish thee, they will fight against thee. Oh that I could
live to those days! I would fight for thee." And he kissed
him on his forehead. The Prophet went home, and the words

he had heard were a great comfort to him and diminished
his anxiety.

After this Mohammed, in awe and trembling, waited for
other visions and revelations. But none came; and the old
horrible doubts and suspicions crept over his soul. He went
up to Mount Hirâ again—this time to commit suicide. But,
as often as he approached the precipice, lo, he beheld Gabriel
at the end of the horizon whithersoever he turned, who
said to him, "I am Gabriel, and thou art Mohammed, the
Prophet of God." And he stood as entranced, unable to
move backwards or forwards, until anxious Chadija sent out
men to seek him.

We must interrupt the course of the story for a moment
respecting this " Voice," which is called in the Koran, Gabriel,
or the Holy Ghost. We have on a previous occasion spoken
of the strange metamorphoses of Angels and Demons, as they
migrated from India to Babylonia, and from Babylonia to
Judæa.[1] Their further migration to Mecca did not produce
much change, since the process of Semitising them and making
them subservient to Monotheism had been wrought already
by the Talmud. Yet this strange identification of Gabriel
with the Holy Ghost which we find here is a problem not
fully to be solved, either by the Talmud or the Zend Avesta.

The Holy Ghost, an expression of most common occurrence in the Haggadah, is thus summarily explained by the
Talmud—as an emphatic answer probably to the popular
tendency of taking transcendental terms in a concrete sense.
" With ten names," says the Talmud, " is the Holy Ghost
named in Scripture. They are—Parable, Allegory, Enigma,
Speech, Sentence, Light, Command, Vision, Prophecy." In
the Angelic Hierarchy of the Talmud it is Michael (Vohu-
manô), and not Gabriel, who takes first rank. He stands
to the right of the Throne, Gabriel to the left; he represents
Grace; Gabriel, stern Justice: and though they are both
entrusted with watching over God's people, it is yet Michael

---

[1] See page 50.

who stands forth to fight for them, who brings them good
tidings, and who, as heavenly High Priest, "offers up the
souls of the righteous upon God's Altar." Yet he is often
accompanied by Gabriel, who is, be it observed, particularly
active in the life of Abraham. It is he who saves Abraham
from the fiery furnace into which Nimrod had cast him; in
the message of Isaac's birth he is one of the three ' men,' and
his place is to Michael's right hand. In all other respects, he
is the exact counterpart of the Persian Çraŏshŏ, and his principal office is that of revenging and punishing evil, while he
acts as a merciful genius to the good and elect. Hence, probably, he became in later Persian mythology, as well as in
the Talmud, the Divine Messenger. He is thus replete with
all knowledge, and—alone of all angels—is versed in all
human tongues. Islam has made a few transparently "ten-
dencious" changes. Gabriel here stands to the right hand
of the Throne, and Michael to the left, *i.e.* the former
becomes the Angel of Mercy, and the latter that of Punishment. Omar, it is said, once went into a Jewish Academy
and asked the Jews about Gabriel's office. He, they mockingly answered, is our enemy; he betrays all our secrets to
Mohammed, and he and Michael are always at war with
each other—an answer which, taken seriously by Omar, so
shocked him that he cried out, "Why, you are more unbe-
lieving than the Himyarites!" But might this strange identification of Gabriel and the Holy Ghost possibly be accounted
for by the fact that the mystic office with regard to the
birth of Christ, ascribed to the Holy Ghost by the Church,
is ascribed in Islam to Gabriel also, who, as in the New
Testament, announces the message to Mary, and that thus
the two have become fully identified in the minds of the
traditionists?

We have left Mohammed in the terror-stricken state of a
mind conscious of its mission, and vainly trying to struggle
against it. The grim lonely darkness within, the horrible
dread lest it all be but mockery and self-deception, or "the
Devil's prompting;" the inability of uttering, save in a few
wild rhapsodic sounds, that message which is silently and

agonizingly growing into shape—and Death seems the only
refuge and salvation—who shall describe it? It was through
these phases of a soul struggling between Heaven and Hell
that Mohammed went in those days, and the thought of
suicide came temptingly near. But, lo! Gabriel on the edge
of the horizon crying: I am Gabriel, and thou art Mohammed, God's Messenger. . . . Fear not!

It is not easy to say how long that state of doubt and
terror lasted. Tradition, wildly diverging here, is, of course,
of little use. Probably he was not quite free from it to the
day of his death. But, by degrees, and as he no longer had
to carry that dread burden in his lonely heart, he gathered
strength. His confidence in himself and in his mission rose.
No Demoniac, no contemptible soothsayer, no possessed
madman he—the voice within urged. And at times, a
blissful exultation took the place of the former horror. His
heart throbs with grateful joy. "By the midday splendour,
and by the stilly night," he cries, "the Lord does not reject
him, and will not forsake him, and the future shall be better
than the past. Has he not found him an orphan and given
him a home, found him astray and guided him into the
straight path, found him so poor and made him so rich?"
"Wherefore," he adds, "do not thou oppress the orphan,
neither repel thou him who asketh of thee—but declare
aloud the bounties of thy Lord!" . . . .

And the revelations now came one after the other without
intermission during a space of more than twenty years—
revelations, the central sun of which was the doctrine of
God's Unity, Monotheism, of which he, Mohammed, was the
bearer to his own people.

Yet these Revelations did not come in visions bright, transcendent, exalted. They came ghastly, weird, most horrible.
After long solitary broodings, a something used to move
Mohammed, all of a sudden, with frightful vehemence. He
"roared like a camel," his eyes rolled and glowed like red
coals, and on the coldest day terrible perspirations would
break out all over his body. When the terror ceased, it
seemed to him as if he had heard bells ringing, "the sound

whereof seemed to rend him to pieces "—as if he had heard
the voice of a man—as if he had seen Gabriel—or as if words
had been written in his heart. Such was the agony he endured, that some of the verses revealed to him well-nigh
made his hair turn white.

Mohammed was epileptic, and vast ingenuity and medical
knowledge have been lavished upon this point, as explanatory of Mohammed's mission and success. We, for our own
part, do not think that epilepsy ever made a man appear a
prophet to himself, or even to the people of the East; or, for
the matter of that, inspired him with the like heart-moving
words and glorious pictures. Quite the contrary. It was
taken as a sign of demons within—demons, " Devs," devils,
to whom all manner of diseases were ascribed throughout the
antique world, in Phœnicia, in Greece, in Rome, in Persia,
and among the lower classes of Judæa after the Babylonian
Exile. The Talmud, which denies a concrete Satan, or
rather resolves him rationally into " passion," " remorse,"
and " death,"—stages corresponding to his being " Seducer,"
" Accuser," and " Angel of Death "—speaks of these demons
as hobgoblins, or special diseases, and inveighs in terms of
contempt against the " exorcisms " in vogue[1] in Judæa about
the period of the birth of Christianity. Those " possessed "
loved solitary places, chiefly cemeteries; they tore their
garments, and were altogether beyond the pale. On the
special nature of the possessing demons, the "Shedim" of
the Talmud, the " Devils " of the New Testament, the Jin,
or Genii, of the Koran, as different from and yet alike to the
Devas, and as forming the intermediate beings between men
and angels, as in Plato (*Sympos.*), we may yet have to speak.

---

[1] True, Simon ben Yochai, the
fabulous author of the Zohar, to whose
rather badly kept shrine at Merom, a
few hours from Tiberias (where also
Shammai and Hillel are believed to
be buried), the Faithful of Palestine,
and even of Persia and India, make
their annual pilgrimage to this day,
did once, and apparently with the
approval of the Authorities, drive out
a devil from the Emperor's daughter
at Rome. But then this devil had
good-naturedly offered his services
himself, and the object of Simon's em-
bassy, the rescinding of an oppressive
decree, was considered so praiseworthy
in the main that these authorities
rather shut their eyes to the performance.

That they were all " pure, holy, everlasting angels from the beginning," and only came to be degraded (as were the Devas by " Zoroastrianism," and the gods of Hellas and Rome by Christianity) into wicked angels in the course of religious reformation or change,—is unquestionable, even if the Book of Enoch did not state it expressly. They are " fallen Angels "—fallen through pride, envy, lust. The two angels Shamchazai (Asai) and Azael (Uziel) of the Targum, the Midrash, and the Koran (Márut and Hárut), are thrown from heaven because of their desiring the daughters of man, even as Sammael himself loses his most high estate, because he seduces Adam and Eve. True, there is a peculiar something supposed to inhere in epilepsy. The Greeks called it a sacred disease. Bacchantic and chorybantic furor were God-inspired stages. The Pythia uttered her oracles under the most distressing signs. Symptoms of convulsion were even needed as a sign of the divine mania or inspiration. But Mohammed did not utter any of his sayings while the paroxysm lasted. Clearly, distinctly, most consciously, did he dictate to his scribe what had come to him—for he could not write, according to his own account. But it may well be, and it speaks for Mohammed's thorough honesty, that he himself believed, in the very first stages, to have been " inspired" during his fits by Jin. According to Zoroastro-talmudical notions, which had penetrated into Arabia, these Jin listened " behind the curtain" of Heaven and learnt the things of the future. These they were then believed to com-municate to the soothsayers and diviners. But it was dan-gerous eavesdropping enough. When the heavenly watchers perceived these curious goblins, they hurled arrows of fire at them : in which men saw falling stars. Mohammed soon, however, rejected this notion of " demoniac " inspiration: while from the Byzantines to Luther, and from Luther to Muir, it was the devil, who prompted the prophet. Muir has indeed instituted several minute comparisons between Satan tempting Christ and Mohammed. Whereat Sprenger somewhat irreverently observes, that since there be a Devil, he must needs have something to do.

G 2

Tempted as we feel, before we proceed to describe the
mental and religious atmosphere around Mohammed when
he came to proclaim "the faith of Abraham," that first
bearer of the emphatically Semitic mission, to enlarge upon
that great question of the day, the mission of the Semitic
races in general, we must confine ourselves to one or two
points touching their religious development. A brilliant
French *savant* has of late, in somewhat rash generalisation,
asserted that Monotheism is a Semitic instinct. On which
another, one of the most profound scholars—since, alas!
dead—observed that the assertion was perfectly correct, if
you exclude all the Semitic races save the Jews : and these,
it might be added, at a very late period indeed, notwithstanding all the teachings of Moses and the Prophets, not
after a thousand judgments had come upon them, all the
horrors of internecine war, misery, captivity, and exile. The
Phœnicians were idolaters, the Assyrians were idolaters, the
Babylonians were idolaters, and the Arabs were idolaters.
And yet perhaps the truth lies, as usual, in the middle. If,
according to Schelling, who goes much further, a vague
Monotheism is the basis of all religions, there certainly does
seem to be an abstract idea of absolute power of rule and
dominion hidden in the universal Semitic name of the All-
Powerful Supreme God, to whom all the other natural
Powers, in their personified mythic guises, are subject, and
in whom they, as it were, are absorbed. Baal, El, Elohim,
Allah, Elion, denote not merely the Light, the bright
Heaven, as Zeus, Jupiter (subject in his turn to Fate, or that
" which had once been spoken "), but Might, Almightiness—
absolute, despotic, that created and destroyed, did and undid
according to its own tremendous Will alone, and by the side
of which nothing else existed : while Jehovah-Jahve seems
to point to the other stage and side of absolute Existence,
the Being from all times and for all times, the *Ens*, the First
Cause. And what is especially characteristic of the Shemites
is this, that while, as Jewish and Arabic tradition has it, the
sons of Japhet (Indo-Germans) are kings, and those of Ham
slaves, the sons of Shem are prophets. A thousand times

lulled into sweet dreams of beauty, they are aroused a thousand times by the wild cry of the Prophet in their midst, who points heavenwards, "Behold who hath created all these!" But what is a Prophet?—In the Hebrew term, *Nabi*, which Islam adopted, there does not indeed appear to inhere that foretelling faculty, with which from the time of the Septuagint we are wont to connect it. For it is the Septuagint which first translates it by προφήτης, foreteller; while others render it by "Inspired," or simply "Orator." The manifold equivalents used in the Bible, such as watchman, seer, shepherd, messenger, one and all denote emphatically the office of watching over the events, and of lifting up the voice of warning, of reproving, of encouraging, before all the people at the proper hour. Hence the Haggadah has been called "the prophetess of the Exile," though no Haggadist was ever considered "inspired." The Prophet was above all things considered as the popular preacher and teacher, gifted with religious enthusiasm, with an intense love of his people, and with divine power of speech:— whence alone the possibility of prophetic schools. And most strikingly says the Midrash of Abraham that he was a Prophet, a *Nabi*, but not an "Astrologer," one whose calling it is not to forecast, but one who lifts men's minds heavenwards. In this sense—all transcendentalism apart—Mohammed might well be called a prophet even by Jews and Christians.

We can but guess at the state of Arab belief and worship before Mohammed? For though the Arabs enter the world's stage as long after the first joyous revelation of humanity in Hellenism, as the Assyrians and Babylonians, not to speak of the Phœnicians, had entered it before, they have left us but little record of their doings in the period of " Ignorance " —as with proud humility they called the time before Islam. From what broken light is shed by a few forlorn rays, we may conclude this, that they worshipped—to use that vague word—the Hosts of Heaven, and that with this worship there was combined a partial belief in resurrection among some clans. Others, however, seem to have ascribed everything to

"Nature," and to have denied a guiding Creator. We further
find traces of an adoration of fetishes: bodily representatives
of certain influences to be avoided, feared, and conciliated, or
to be loved, and gratefully acknowledged. The Sun and the
Moon, Jupiter and Venus, Canopus and Sirius and Mercury,
had their stony mementos, their temples, their priests, and,
be it well understood, the power of protecting those who fled
to their altars. Herodotus speaks of the Arabs as worshipping only Dionysos (whom Strabo changes into Jupiter)
and Urania, "whom they call" Orotal (probably Nur-Allah
= God's light), and Alilat—a feminine form of Allah, the
Phœnician Queen of Heaven, Tanith-Astarte. Of a worship
of heroes in the form of statues there are vague traces, but
so vague and so mythical that they cannot be counted
historical material. Trees and stones are further mentioned
as objects of primitive Arab worship, and on this point Maimonides has given, as is his wont, clear and transparent
explanations, into which we cannot, however, enter. Among
the latter the famous Black Stone of the Kaaba, that primeval temple ascribed to Abraham, stands foremost, next
we know of a White Stone (Al Lat), at Taïf, still seen by
Hamilton, and one or two more immovable tokens of some
great event, such as the Shemites were wont to erect,—
Jacob, among others, at Bethel (the general Phœnician term
for these stone erections)—mementos which the Pentateuch
emphatically protests against: "For *I* am Jehovah, your
God." Vaguer still are the records of the Oracle-Trees, one
of which stood near Mecca, while the other, dedicated to
Uzza, the Mighty Goddess, the Queen of Heaven, seems
to have spread all over the land, with its due complement of
priests and soothsayers, male and female. That there were
the usual accompaniment of Lares and Penates, more or less
coarse and bodily, such as always have been necessary for
the herd, need not be added. Thus, it is recorded of one
tribe that they worshipped a piece of dough, which, compelled by hunger, they cheerfully ate up. Some, we said,
did not believe in the resurrection. Some did; and therefore they tied a camel to a man's sepulchre, without pro-

viding it with any food. If it ran away, that man was ever-lastingly damned—and, be it observed here, that the Jews alone among the Shemites protested against everlasting damnation—if not, its blackened bones would, on the Day of Judgment, form a handy and honourable conveyance to the abode of his bliss. The Phantoms of the Desert, the Fata Morgana, Angels and Demons, and the rest of embodied ideas or ideals, formed other objects of pious consideration, but only as intermediators with the great Allah. Long before Mohammed, the people were wont, in their distress, to pray at their pilgrimages to him alone, in this wise: "At thy service, O Allah! There is no Being like unto Thee, and if there be one, it is Thou and not it that reigneth;" and when asked what was the office of their idols, they would answer that they were intermediators—much as Roman Catholics in the lower strata revere Saints and their emblems. Let it not be forgotten also that the perpetuation of this pre-Islamic idolatry, if so we call it, was due to a great extent to political reasons. The manifold Sanctuaries and their incomes belonged to certain noble families and clans.

So much for the Heathenism. We have now to consider the two other popularly assumed agents in that religious phase to which Mohammed has given its name, and which has changed the face of the world: Christianity and Judaism.

It has long been the fashion to ascribe whatever was "good" in Mohammedanism to Christianity. We fear this theory is not compatible with the results of honest investigation. For of Arabian Christianity, at the time of Mohammed, the less said perhaps the better. By the side of it, as seen in the Koran—and this book alone shows it to us authentically as Mohammed saw it—even modern Amharic Christianity, of which we possess such astounding accounts, appears pure and exalted. And as, moreover, the monk Bahira-Sergius-Georgius-Nestor, who is said to have instructed Mohammed, is a very intangible personage indeed, if he be not, as there is reason to believe, actually a Jew; and as the several Syrian travels during which Mohammed is supposed to have been further inured into Christianity, have to be taken *cum grano*, nothing remains but his contact with a few freed Greek and Abyssinian slaves, who, having lived all their life among Arabians, could hardly boast of a very profound knowledge of the tenets and history of Christianity. We shall, therefore, not be surprised to see the Koran polemising against some such extraordinary notions as that of Mary-Maryam, "the daughter of Imran, the sister of Harun," being not only the mother of God, but forming a person in the Trinity; or, on the other hand, to meet with the extraordinary legends from the apocryphal Gospel of the Infancy, and from the "Assumption" of Mary, ascribed to John the Apostle himself. Or, again, to see it adopt the heretical view of certain early Christian sects that it was not Christ, but Judas, who was executed, and that Christ had to allow the "hallucination" as a punishment for having suffered people to call him God. But that fundamental tenet of Christianity, viz. the Sonship, Mohammed fought against with unswerving consistency; and never grew tired of repeating, in the most emphatic terms which he, the master of speech, could find, his abhorrence against that notion, at which "the Heavens might tear open, and the earth cleave asunder." There is a brief chapter in the Koran, the "Confession of God's Unity," which is considered tantamount to the third part of the whole Koran, though it only consists of these words—"Say, God is one: the Everlasting God. *He begetteth not, and He is not begotten*, and there is none like unto Him." Still more distinctly is this notion expressed in another place:—"The Christians say Christ is the Son of God. May God resist them . . . how are they infatuated!" And, again:—"They are certainly infidels who say God is One of Three." . . . "Believe in God and His Apostle, but speak not of a Trinity. There is but One God. Far be it from Him that he should have a son." . . . "Christ the Son of Mary is no more than an Apostle." . . . "It is not fit for Allah that He should have a son. Praise to him!" (*i.e.* far be it from Him!)

Jesus, according to Mohammed, is only one of the six

Apostles, who are specially chosen out of three hundred and thirteen, to proclaim new dispensations, in confirmation of previous ones. These are Adam, Noah, Abraham, Moses, Jesus, and Mohammed.—But this point must come under further consideration under the tenets of Islam.

We now turn to Judaism, which, as we have hinted before, forms *the* kernel of Mohammedanism, both general and special. Here merely the preliminary observation that when we spoke of the Talmud as a source of Islam, we did not imply that Mohammed knew it, or, for the matter of that, had ever heard its very name; but it seems as if he had breathed from his childhood almost the air of contemporary Judaism, such Judaism as is found by us crystallised in the Talmud, the Targum, the Midrash.

Indeed, the geographical and ethnographical notices of Arabia in Scripture are to so astounding a degree in accordance with the very latest researches, that we cannot but assume the connection between Palestine and Arabia to have been close from the earliest periods. The Ishmaelites of the Arabian midland are, in the earliest documents, carefully distinguished from the Yoctanites and Kushites of Mahrah in the south: not to speak of the minute information revealed by the later documents. At what time Jews first went to Arabia is a problem which we shall not endeavour to settle. Of Abraham and Ishmael, and the halo of legends that surrounds these national heroes, hereafter. But even rejecting, as we must do, the hallucinations of two most eminent scholars regarding the immigration of an entire Simeonitic regiment in the time of Saul, who having fought a battle near Mecca—hence called Makkah Rabbah (Great Defeat)—settled as Gorhoms or Gerim (Strangers), and so forth—we cannot shut our eyes to the fact that Jews, " worshippers of the invisible God of Abraham," existed, though in small numbers, in Arabia, at a very primitive period indeed. Bokht-Nasar, as Nebuchadnezzar is called in early Arabic documents, caused many others to seek refuge in Arabia. The Hasmoneans forced a whole tribe of Northern Arabia to adopt Judaism; a Jewish king of Arabs fights against

Pompey. The Talmud shows a rather unexpected familiarity
with Arab manners and customs, and — to indicate one
curious point—the prophet Elijah, who appears there as a
kind of immortal tutelary genius—goes about in the guise of
an Arab (the Khidhr of Mohammedan legend). The angels
that appear to Abraham "look like Arabs"—not to speak of
Job and his three friends, the Queen of Sheba, and other
like Arab reminiscences. Centuries before Mohammed,
Kheibar, five days from Medina, and Yemen, in South
Arabia, were in the hands of the Jews. Dhu Nowas, the
last Jewish king of Yemen, falls by the hands of the Abyssinian Negus. The question for us remains, what phase of
faith these Jews represented.

It has been supposed that, though combined among themselves for purposes of war, they held little intercommuni-
cation with their brethren either in Palestine or even in
Arabia, and therefore were ignorant of the development of
"The Law" that went rolling on in Judæa and Babylonia.
The chief proof for this was found in the absence of Judæo-
Arabic literature before Mohammed. To us, this circumstance affords absolutely no proof. None, at least, that
would not perhaps rather confirm our view to the exact
contrary. We know how literatures may be and have been
stamped out; or had the Phœnicians, the Chaldæans, the
Etruscans, never any literature? We happen to know the
contrary, though nothing, not to say worse than nothing,
because more or less corrupt reminiscences, has remained of
it all. And, further, we have distinct proof in the very
Koran that not only did they keep *au courant* with regard
to Haggadah—witness all the legends of Islam—but even
Halachah. Mohammed literally quotes a passage from the
Mishnah,[1] and, further, gives special injunctions taken from
the Gemara, such as the purification with sand in default of
water, the shortening of the prayer in the moment of danger,

---

[1] Notably the judge's admonition
to the witnesses, that he who wan-
tonly destroys one single human life
will be considered as guilty as if he
had destroyed a whole world.

&c.[1] There is an academy, or Bethhamidrash, at Medina ; and Akiba, when on his revolutionary mission, is consulted by the Arab Jews about one of the most minute and intricate points of the Oral Law.

In truth, these Jews stood not merely on the heights of contemporary culture, but far above their Arab brethren. They represented, in fact, the Culture of Arabia. They could all read and write, whilst the Arabs had occasionally to capture some foreign scholars and promise them their liberty on condition that they should teach their boys the elements of reading and writing. The Jews—nay, the Jewesses, as Mohammed had to learn to his grief—were specially gifted with the poetic vein, as we shall see further on ; and poetry in Arabia was at the time of Mohammed the one great accomplishment. There was a certain fair held annually, where, as at the Olympic Games, the productions of the last twelve months were read and received prizes. The beautiful tale of the hanging up of the prize poems in the Kaaba, whence they were called Moallakat, is unfortunately a myth, since Moallakat does not betoken suspended ones, but (pearls) loosely strung together. But, undoubtedly, to have made the best poem of the season was a great distinction, not merely for the individual poet, but for his entire clan.

These Jewish tribes, some of whom derived their genealogy from priestly families (Al-Kahinani), lived scattered all over Arabia, but chiefly in the south, in Yeman (Himyar), "the dust of which was like unto gold, and where men never died." They lived, as did the other Arabs, either the life of roving Bedouins, or cultivated the land, or inhabited cities, such as Yathrib, the later Medina or City, by way of eminence—of the Prophet, to wit. Outwardly they had completely merged in the great Arabic family. Conversions of entire clans to Judaism, intermarriages, and the immense

---

[1] "Thy will be done in Heaven; grant peace to them that fear Thee on Earth; and whatever pleaseth Thee, do. Blessed art Thou, O Lord, who hearest Prayer"—is the formula suggested by the Talmud for the hours of mental distraction or peril.

family-likeness, so to speak, of the two descendants of Abraham—for the derivation of the Arabs from Ishmael, whatever may be alleged to the contrary, seems unquestionably
an ante-Mohammedan notion—facilitated the levelling work
of Jewish cosmopolitanism.   Acquainted, as we said, with
both Halachah and Haggadah, they seemed, under the
peculiar story-loving influence of their countrymen, to have
cultivated more particularly the latter with all its gorgeous
hues and colours.   Valiant with the sword, which they not
rarely turned against their own kinsmen, they never omitted
the fulfilment of their greatest religious duty—the release of
their captives, though these might be their adversaries; and
further, like their fathers, from of old, they kept the Sabbath
holy even in war, though the prohibition had been repealed.
They waited for the Messiah, and they turned their faces
towards Jerusalem.[1]   They fasted, they prayed, and they
scattered around them the seeds of such high culture as was
contained in their literature.   And Arabia called them the
People of the "Book;" even as Hegel has called them the
People of the "Geist."   These seeds, though some fell on
stones, and some on the desert sand, had borne fruit a
thousandfold.   Of generally practical, nay vital, institutions
which they had introduced, long before Mohammed, into the
land of their adoption, may be mentioned the Calendar; and
the intercalary month was by the Arabs called, in grateful
acknowledgment *Nassi* (Prince), the title of the Babylonian
head of the Jewish Diaspora.   The Kaaba and the Pilgrimage,
Yoctan and Ishmael, Zemzem and Hagar, received their
colouring from Jewish Arabs.   They were altogether looked
up to with much reverence, and their superiority would also

---

[1] The synagogues were generally
built in the form of a theatre, the
portal due west, so that the worship-
per's face was turned to the east, even
to the Holy of Holies of the Temple
of Jerusalem, in pious allusion to the
words (1 Kings viii. 29), "That their
eyes may be open towards this house
night and day . . . that thou mayest
hearken to the prayers which thy servant shall make *towards this place*."
Daniel prayed towards Jerusalem
and "the tower of David, builded for
an armoury" of the Song of Songs, is
taken allegorically as an allusion to
that enduring and mighty Holiness
that ever belonged to the spot, once
hallowed by the presence of the Shechinah. And the early Church followed also in this respect.

politically have stood them in very good stead, when Mohammed subsequently turned against them; had they known what
united action meant.

When we said that there were distinguished poets among
them, we meant poets not Jewish, but purely Arabic. Their
poems are all of intensely national Arabic type. Among
others we have fragments by Assamael (Samuel), "the faithful," a great chief, who dwelt in a strong castle, and who,
rather than betray his friend's confidence, saw his boy cut in
twain before his eyes. What has survived of his songs
breathes noble pride and loftiness of soul, tempered at times
by a strange sadness: joy of life and love of conviviality; as
indeed one of his poems opens with the mournful question
whether the women would lament him after his death, and
how? Both his son Garid, and his grandson Suba were poets;
so were Arrabi, whose sons fought against Mohammed; and
Aus, by whom we have a kind of characteristic, yet mild,
protest against his wife's change of creed. "We live," he
sings, "according to the Law (Thora) and Faith of Moses,
but Mohammed's Faith is also good. Each of us thinks
himself in the right path." Then there is Suraih, who
"would drink from the cup of those that are of noble heart,
even if there be twofold poison therein;" and about four or
five more, who sing of love and wine, the sword and faithfulness, hospitality and the horse. There were also Jewish
poetesses, whose poems, as we already mentioned, were "bitterer to Mohammed than arrows," and who did not escape his
vengeance.

We had to tarry somewhat on this out-of-the-way field of
the circumstances and position of Arabian Jews—not a little
of which would, but for Islam, never have been known. Of
their tenets and ceremonies, their legends and dogmas, as
transferred to Islam, we have to treat separately. And such
was Arabia as to difference of creeds when Mohammed arose.
We left him at the moment when he began to become aware
of his "Mission." But he was not without special predecessors. These were the *Hanifs*, literally in Talmudical
parlance—"hypocrites." "Four shall not see God," says the

Talmud, "the scoffers, the *Hanifs*" ("who are to be exposed at all hazards," while generally it is considered better "to be thrown into a fiery furnace than bring any one to public shame"[1]), "the liars, the slanderers." These Hanifs form a very curious and most important phase of Arabian faith before Mohammed—a phase of Jewish Christianity or Christian Judaism. They loved to style themselves also "Abrahamitic Sabians," and Mohammed, at the outset, called himself one of them. They were, to all intents and purposes, "heretics." They believed in One God. They had the Law and the Gospel, and further certain "Rolls of Abraham and Moses," called *Ashmaat*, to which Mohammed at first appeals. This word *Ashmaat*, or *Shamaata*, has likewise given rise to most hazardous conjectures. To us it appears very simply the Talmudical *Shemaata*, which is identical with Halachah or legal tradition. In Arabia it seems to have assumed the signification of Midrash in general, chiefly as regards its Haggadistic or legendary part.[2] These mysterious Rolls, about which endless discussions have arisen, thus seem, to our mind, to have been neither more nor less than certain collections of Midrash, beginning, as is its wont, with stern Halachah, ending, as is still more its wont, with gorgeous dreams of fancy, woven round the sainted heads of the Patriarchs, with transcendental allegories,— "tales of angels, fairy legends, festal songs, and words of wisdom." Nor does it much matter what were the original names of these rolls or collections in question (there must have been scores upon scores of them), since there is, as far as we can gather their probable contents, but little in them which has not survived in one form or the other in our extant Midrash-books.

There were some very prominent men among this sect, if sect it may be called. Foremost among them stands one Omayya, a highly-gifted and most versatile poet, who never

---

[1] *See* page 57.
[2] We have noticed the same process with regard to the word Midrash it-self in Palestine and Babylonia. *See* page 13.

would acknowledge Mohammed, and ceased not to write satires upon him; more especially as it had been his intention to proclaim himself prophet. Besides him there are recorded four special men (all relations of the Prophet, Waraka among them), who, disgusted with the fetishism into which their countrymen had sunk, once met at the Kaaba, during the annual feast, and thus expressed their secret opinion to each other. "Shall we encompass a stone which neither heareth nor seeth, neither helpeth nor hurteth? Let us seek a better faith" they said. And they went abroad to seek and to find the Hanifite creed—the "religion of Abraham."

This religion of Abraham, Mohammed came to re-establish, Mohammed the Hanifite, who succeeded where the others failed. He used the arguments, the doctrine, occasionally the very words of these his predecessors,—though we have here to be doubly on our guard against the possible colouring of later Mohammedan tradition—chiefly of Zaid, who refrained from eating blood and that which had been killed for idolatry —two things pointing emphatically to Jewish teaching.[1] Zaid, it is reported, also abhorred the barbarous burying alive of children, then customary among the Arabian savages, and "worshipped the God of Abraham." Also, did he say, "O Lord, if I knew what form of worship Thou desirest, I would adopt it. But I know it not." And when his nephew after his death asked the Prophet to pray for him, Mohammed said, "Verily I will: he will form a Church of his own on the Day of Judgment." Nay more, Zaid had actually taught at Mecca, and Mohammed openly declared himself his pupil.

We shall return to this "Religion of Abraham," which is the clue to Islam—and the mystery of which the Midrash alone solves satisfactorily. At this stage it behoves us to follow out the vicissitudes of Mohammed's career as briefly as we may: for without these we could never fully comprehend that religion, whereof he is the corner-stone and the pinnacle.

And first as to his early miracles, which nearly proved his

---

[1] Foremost among the seven fundamental "Laws of the Sons of Noah."

ruin. The Jews required a sign, says the New Testament.
The desire to see the Prophet, the chosen and gifted person,
perform things apparently contrary to what is called nature—
sights and sounds to wonder at, things by which to prove his
intimate communication with and the command over the
more or less personified powers of the Cosmos, of which
ancient and mediæval times had so vague a notion—is very
easily understood; and both the Old and New Testament
are replete with extraordinary manifestations. The Talmud,
while representing, to a certain extent, what is called the
"advanced" opinion of the time, certainly contains views
somewhat different from the popular one. "Esther's Miracle,"
it says, "was the last—*the end of all miracles.*" And she is
called, in allusion to the well-known Psalm-heading, "Hind of
the Dawn"—'*because with her it first became Light.*" And
since there is nothing in the whole story of Esther which
resembles in the faintest degree a "supernatural" act; and
since, moreover, the name of God does not even appear in
the book from beginning to end, this Talmudic parlance of
"miracles" is very like the modern use of the word "prophet," of which it was remarked the other day that "many
living writers, having first stripped the word of its ancient
meaning, bestow it freely upon anybody." Furthermore the
Mishnah had distinctly declared that miracles were "created"
from the very beginning, in the gloaming of the sixth day.
"God," says the Talmud, still more explicitly "made it a
condition upon the sea, when He created it, to open itself
before the Israelites; the fire to leave the three martyrs
unscathed; the heavens to open to the voice of Hezekiah,"
&c.[1] No less clearly is the meaning of the Masters further
expressed in such sentences as these: "The healing of a sick
person often is a greater miracle than that which happened
to the men in the pit. Those that have been saved from
flagrant sin may consider that a miracle has happened to
them. Do not reckon upon a miracle—they do not happen
every day. Those to whom a miracle happens often know

---

[1] *See* page 51.

it not themselves," &c. &c. But the old craving for wonders
was either still strong among them, or they wished to vex
Mohammed's soul—as they did in a thousand bitter little
ways—when they found themselves disappointed in him, and
so incited people to ask him for some miraculous performance.
He is asked, he complains, to cause wells and rivers to gush
forth, to bring down the heaven in pieces, to remove mountains, to have a house of gold, to ascend to heaven by a ladder,
to cause the dead to speak, and to make Allah and his Angels
testify to him—and he indignantly bursts out, "My Lord be
praised! Am I more than a man sent as an apostle? . . .
Angels do not commonly walk the earth, or God would have
despatched an angel to preach His truth to you;" and, he
says, when they do see a sign—even the moon splitting—
these unbelievers but turn aside, saying: "This is a well-
devised trick, a sleight of hand."

How well he had entered into the meaning of those Talmudical notions on miracles—"Esther's being the last"—
and how positively he spoke upon that point, though in vain,
is best shown by his protest that "the miracles of all prophets were confined to their own times. My miracle is *the
Koran* which shall remain for ever, and I am hopeful of
having more followers than any of the other prophets."
"Former prophets," he also used to say (and this is one of
the most momentous dicta) "were sent to their own sects. I
was sent to all. I have been sent for one thing only: to
make straight the crooked paths, *to unite the strayed tribes,*
and to teach that 'There is no God but God by whom the
eyes of the blind and the ears of the deaf shall be opened,
and the hearts of those who know nothing.'" And over and
over again he points to those much greater signs "in Heaven
and on Earth" than any wondrous manifestation that had
ever been wrought by prophets—the sun, and the moon, and
the stars, the day and the night, the structure of men's
bodies, the mountains which steady the earth, the water that
comes from on high to slake the thirst of man, and cattle,
and plant, and tree: even the olive-tree, and the palm-tree,
and the vine—and he speaks to these desert folk of the sea

H

upon which walk the great ships. Are not all these things
made for man's use and service, even while they serve Allah?
. . . "I never said that Allah's treasures are in my hands,
that I knew the hidden things, or that I was an Angel. . . .
I, who cannot even help or trust myself, unless Allah willeth.
Will ye not reflect a little?" . . . . Did they perceive the
flashes of lightning and the thunderous rolls? Allah would
show them His miracles in good time—even the yawning
mouth of Hell. Then they would indeed believe, even as
those people of the Cities of the Plain had believed, when it
was too late. Had their caravans passed the Dead Sea—
even Sodom and Gomorrha? Did they know how Thamud
and Ad were destroyed by a terrible cry from Heaven, or
what had become of Pharaoh? "These are the signs of
Allah. . . . He giveth Life, and He giveth Death, and unto
Him ye must return." . . . And to leave no doubt as to
what his own signs and wonders really consist of, the single
verses of the Koran are called *Ayat* = Hebr. *Ot:—letter, sign,
wonder.*

But all these protests availed nought. Miracles there must
be, and miracles there were. Three—and that is all—are
hinted at in the Koran. First, Mohammed's seeing Gabriel
"in the open horizon," when despair drove him to attempt
self-destruction: "One mighty in power, endued with understanding," revealed himself to him, then "on the highest
part of the horizon, at two bows' length." And again he
appears to him under a certain tree, "the Tree of the Limit"
—a lotos-tree: covered with myriads of angels, near the
Garden of Repose. This second vision, however, is probably
connected with the *Miraj*, or Mohammed's Night-journey.
The Jews had told the Arabians that no prophet ever arose
out of the Holy Land, and that Moses had gone up to
Heaven. What they did not tell them probably was that
other significant saying, that, since the destruction of Jerusalem, the gift of prophecy had fallen to fools and babes—a
dictum we have often enough felt inclined to quote of our
own days. And further, that the Talmud states, as expressly
as can be, that "Moses never went up to Heaven,"—even as

it is written, "The Heavens are Jehovah's, and the Earth hath He given to the children of man."[1]

It was therefore absolutely necessary that the Prophet should have been in the Holy Land, nay, in Jerusalem. And the *Miraj* happened, the transfiguration, the ascension, the real consummation of Mohammed's mission, and the centre of Islamic transcendental legend and creed. A whole volume of traditions exists on this one single point.

"'Praise be unto Him,' says the Koran, 'who transported His servant by night from the temple Al Harâm (Mecca) to the remotest temple (of Jerusalem), the circuit of which we have blessed, that we might show Him some of our signs. Verily He, that heareth, that seeth!'" . . .

And in verse sixty-two of that same chapter, this journey is emphatically declared to be a "Vision"—"a dream"—"a trial for men."

And these are its brief outlines, though Mohammed's own account was probably still more briefly and soberly conceived as compared with the worlds of golden dreams in which the later legend revels.[2]

In the middle of the night Gabriel appeared to Mohammed, and told him that the Lord had intended to bestow honour upon him such as He had not bestowed upon any born being yet, such as had never come into any man's heart. He arose, and they went to the Kaaba, which they encompassed seven times. Gabriel then took out Mohammed's heart, washed it in the well Zemzem, filled it with faith and knowledge, and put it back in its place. He was then clothed in a robe of light, and was covered with a turban of light, in which, in thousandfold rays of light gleamed the words, "Mohammed is God's Prophet; Mohammed is God's Friend." Then, surrounded by myriads of angels, he bestrode the

---

[1] *See* page 54.

[2] We may have occasion to trace some of the gorgeous features of this Vision in the latter Haggadah, when we speak of Mohammed's Heaven and Hell. Exceedingly characteristic are the differences on some points: among other things, the entire omission in the Mohammedan legend of that fifth Heaven of the Midrash "Gan Eden," which is reserved for the souls of noble women—Pharaoh's daughter, who so tenderly took pity on the child Moses, occupying the first place in the first circle.

Borak—which only means Lightning—who had the face of
a man; his red chest was as a ruby, and his back like a
white pearl. His wings reached from the eastern point of the
horizon to the western, and at every step he went as far as
eye could see. Thrice Mohammed prayed while he flew: at
Medina, at Madyan, at Bethlehem. Sweet voices were calling—to the left, to the right, before him, behind him:
beautiful women flitted around: he heeded nought. And
the angel told him that had he listened to the first voice, his
followers would have become Jews; to the second, Christians;
to the third, they would have given up Paradise for the pleasures of this world. At Jerusalem he entered, greeted by
new hosts of angels, the Temple (and the ring by which the
Borak was fastened has no doubt been seen by many of our
readers near the " Dome of the Rock "); and here all the
prophets, Christ among them, were assembled; and very
striking are the likenesses given of them. Abraham resembled Mohammed most of all.

Prayers were said, and Mohammed acted as Priest Precentor. Most of the prophets then held a brief discourse in
praise of God, and descriptive of their own individual mission on earth. Mohammed, having spoken last, ascended
Jacob's ladder, standing upon *the* Rock, the same which
forms, according to the Midrash, the foundation stone of the
earth. And a very strange-looking rock it is, rising a few
feet above the marble around, scarcely touched with the
chisel, and at its south-western corner there is seen the " foot-
print of the Prophet," and next to it the " handprint of
Gabriel," who held down the rock as it tried to rise heavenwards with God's Messenger. The ladder on which Mohammed mounted into the regions of light is the same which
Jacob saw in his dream: it reaches from Heaven to Earth,
and on it the souls of the departed return to God. It is
made of ruby and emerald, of gold and silver, and of precious
stones.

Having passed the angel who held the seven earths and
the seven heavenly spheres, and the blue abyss in which
float all ideal prototypes of things sublunary, he and Gabriel

arrived at the Gates of the first Heaven of the World, where myriads of new angels held watch. Both he and Gabriel entered and found other myriads praising God in the postures of Muslim prayer. On a magnificent throne sat Adam, dressed in light, the human souls arrayed by his sides—to his right the good souls, to his left the wicked ones. Further on were Paradise and Hell. Punishments were wrought here according to earthly deeds. The miserly souls were naked, and hungry, and thirsty; thieves and swindlers sat at tables filled with gorgeous things, of which they were not allowed to participate; and scoffers and slanderers carried heavy spiked logs of wood that tore their flesh, even as they had wounded the hearts of their fellow-men. Thus they passed heaven after heaven. In the second they found Christ and John the Baptist; in the third, Joseph and David; in the fourth, Enoch; in the fifth, Aaron; in the sixth, Moses, who wept because Mohammed was to be more exalted than he had been. In the highest heaven they found Abraham. Above the seventh heaven they came to a tree of vast leaves and fruits. In it is Gabriel's dwelling-place, on one branch of untold expanse; in another, myriads of angels are reading the Pentateuch; in another, other myriads of angels read the Gospel; yet in another, they sing the Psalms; and in another, they chant the Koran, from eternity to eternity. Four rivers flow forth from this region, one of which is the *river of Mercy*. There is also a House of Prayer there, right above the Kaaba.[1] Near it a tank of light, from which, when Gabriel's light approaches it, seventy-thousand angels spring into existence—which will remind our readers of the river of fire that rolls its flames under the Divine throne, and out of which rise ever new myriads of angels, who praise God and sink back into nought.[2] They approach the temple, singing praises unto God; and each time, when their voices resound, a new angel is born. " Not a drop of water is in

---

[1] In accordance with the Haggadistic notion of the "Jerusalem above," and the "heavenly Jerusalem" of the New Testament.
[2] *See* page 50.

the sea, not a leaf on a tree, not a span of space in the heavens
that is not guarded by an angel." And to this day all these
gorgeous transcendentalisms and day-dreams survive bodily
in certain Jewish mystic liturgical poems (Piut), into which
the golden rivers of the Haggadah have been turned by
Poets or "Paitanas" at an early period.[1]

A space further, a little space, after the Tree of the Limit,
Mohammed found himself of a sudden alone. Neither Gabriel nor Borak dared go beyond it; and he heard a voice
calling "Approach." And he passed on, and curtain after
curtain, and veil after veil was drawn up before him and fell
behind him. When the last curtain rose, he stood within
two bow-shots from the Throne; and here—says the Koran—
"he saw the greatest of the signs of his Lord." No pen dared
to say more. "There was a great stillness, and nothing was
heard except the silent sound of the reed, wherewith the
decrees of God are inscribed upon the tablets of Fate." . . .

It would indeed be a labour of love, and not without its reward, to follow this Miraj-Saga through all its stages, down
to the Persian and Turkish cycles. But it is not our task.
All we have to add here is that Mohammed is not to be
made responsible for some of his enthusiastic admirers when
they transformed this Vision—a vision as grand as any in the
whole Divine Comedy (which indeed has unconsciously borrowed some of its richest plumage from it), but which Mohammed, until he was sick of it, insisted on calling a *Dream*
—into insipidity and drivel.

One feature more deserves mention. When Zaid asked
the Prophet after his little daughter who had died, he
answered that she was in Paradise and happy. And Zaid
wept bitterly.

Remains, as of traditional miracles, the last one of the two
Angels who took out Mohammed's heart when he was a boy,.
purified it in snow, then weighed it, and found it weightier
than all the thousands they put into the other scale:—a

---

[1] In Western Europe this part of the Jewish Liturgy, as too mystical
for the weaker brethren, has now mostly been abrogated.

parable equally transparent, and hardly a "miracle" in the
conventional sense of the word.

Only one command was given to Mohammed on that occasion of the Ascension :—that his faithful should pray fifty
times daily. And when he returned to where Moses waited
for him, and told him this, Moses made him return to pray
God to reduce the number. And it was made forty. "This is
still too much," Moses said; "I know that the faithful will
not be able to do even thus much." And again and again was
the number reduced till it came to five, and Mohammed
no longer dared return to God, though Moses urged him
to do so.

Very strikingly indeed does the Haggadah manifest her constant presence, not merely throughout this whole Vision, but
even in such minute features as this last, of God's instructing
Mohammed about prayer.[1] For when the Pentateuch records that extraordinary manifestation of God to Moses on the
rock, where the glory of the Lord passeth by and proclaims :
"Jehovah, Jehovah, God, merciful and gracious, long suffering, and abundant of goodness and truth, and keeping mercy
for thousands, forgiving iniquity, and transgression and sin"
. . . the Talmud first of all introduces this passage, as is its
wont in the like anthropomorphistic passages, with the awe-
stricken, half-trembling words that, If Holy Writ had not
said this, no man would dare to speak of a like manifestation;
and, next, proceeds to explain that "*God showed Moses how
that men should pray.*"—"Let them invoke my Mercy and
my Long-suffering. I will forgive them. Jehovah—twice
repeated—means, It is Jehovah, even I, before man sinneth,
and I, the selfsame Jehovah, after he has sinned and repented."

It is time that we should now return, after these many indispensable little monographs, to the founder of Islam himself, as a historical personage. Ere we proceed to his book
and faith, we must sum up the events that led first to his
Flight, that event with which not only he, but Arabia, enters

---

[1] For the shortening of it see above, p. 91, note.

history, an event fraught with intense importance for all mankind.

When Mohammed had become clear as to his mission he sought converts. And his first convert was his faithful motherly Chadija; his second, the freed slave Zaid, probably a Christian, whom he adopted; and his third, his small cousin Ali, ten years of age. Chadija, his good angel, Tradition reports,

"believed in Mohammed and believed in the truth of the Revelation, and fortified him in his aims. She was the first who believed in God, in His messenger, and in the Revelation. Thereby God had sent him comfort, for as often as he heard aught disagreeable, contradictory, or how he was shown to be a liar, she was sad about it. God comforted him through her when he returned to her, in rousing him up again and making his burden more light to him, assuring him of her own faith in him, and representing to him the futility of men's babble."

And, in truth, when she died, not merely he but Islam lost much of their fervour, much of their purity. He would not be comforted, though he married many wives after her; and the handsomest and youngest of his wives would never cease being jealous of that "dead, toothless old woman." Abu Bakr, a wealthy merchant, energetic, prudent, and honest, joined at once. He had probably been a fellow-disciple of Mohammed at the feet of Zaid the Skeptic and was his confidant and bosom friend throughout his life—the only one who unhesitatingly joined, "who tarried not, neither was he perplexed," Mohammed said of him. It was he who stood at the head of the twelve chosen Apostles who subsequently rallied round the Prophet, among whom we find Hamza, the Lion of God, Othman, Omar, and the rest, men of energy, talent and wealth, and long before adverse to Paganism. Those twelve were his principal advisers while he lived, and after his death they founded an empire greater than that of Alexander of Rome. As to Abu Bakr, he was but two years younger than the Prophet, not a man of genius, but of calm, clear, impartial judgment, and yet of so tender and sympathetic a heart that he used to be called "the Sighing." He was not only one of the most popular men, but also rich and

generous, and thus his influence cannot well be overrated.
It is his adherence to Mohammed throughout, which, even by
those who most depreciate the Prophet, is taken as one of
the highest guarantees of the latter's sincerity. Nay, he is
said to have done more for Islam than Mohammed himself—
not to mention that, with his extensive knowledge of genealogy, one of the most important sciences of the period, he
was able at the Prophet's desire, to supply Hassan, the poet
of the Faith, with matter for satires against the inimical
Koreish.

Most of Mohammed's relations seemed to have treated his
teachings with scorn. "There he goes," they used to say;
"he is going to speak to the world about the Heavens now."
Abu Lahab, in open family council, called him a fool,
instantly upon which followed that characteristic Surah,
"Perish shall the hands of Abu Lahab. May he perish. . . .
And his wife shall carry fuel for his hell fire." The other
Meccans treated the whole story of his mission, his revelations, and dreams, with something like pitying contempt, as
long as he kept to generalities, though the number of uninflu-
ential adherents grew apace. But when he spoke of their
gods, which they naïvely enough would call Thagût (Error),
the technical Jewish word for Idols,[1] as Idols, they waxed
wroth, and combined against him, until the stir both he and
they made, spread more and more rapidly and dangerously,
and with it rose his own courage. He felt committed. All
hesitations, and doubts, and fears, and reconciliations, he
cast behind him now. He openly set the proud Meccans at
defiance. He cursed those who reviled him with burning
curses. He cursed their fathers in their graves; nay, his
own father would undergo eternal punishment in hell, for
that he had been an idolater. "There is no God but Allah!"
He cried it aloud, day and night, and the echoes became more
and more frequent.

His life was in jeopardy now, and his uncle Abu Talib,
under whose protection he had fallen when a youth, stood

---

[1] See *Targums*, page 319, *post*.

forth against the whole clan. He would protect him if they all combined against him. Did he believe in his Mission? Not in the least. He remained steadfast in his own creed or skepticism to the day of his death. But he was an Arab, a Shemite. He had adopted him, and promised to protect him; and nothing, absolutely nothing, could cause him to break that holiest of engagements. He received the deputations of his kinsfolk, listened to their speeches, " how that Mohammed blasphemed their gods, called the living fools and the dead denizens of hell fire, that he was mad, brought disgrace upon their family and the whole clan, that he ought to be extinguished somehow—anyhow ; " and he shook his head, saying nothing,' or next to nothing. Again they returned and again, and, at last, demanded that the Possessed Man should be given up to them to be dealt with according to their judgment. If not—" We are determined no longer to bear his blasphemy towards our gods, nor his insults towards ourselves. If thou givest him protection, we will fight both him and thee, until one of us shall have been extinguished."

Abu Talib sent for Mohammed and told him what had happened, representing to him the position of affairs, and spoke to him about the danger he had brought upon their good old tribe. And very characteristic, not merely for the dramatis personæ, but for Arab feeling, is the further story of the interview. Mohammed, though fully believing now that even his uncle was about to abandon him to the mercies of his kinsfolk, replied—"By Allah, uncle, if they put the sun to my right hand, and the moon to my left, I will not give up the course which I am pursuing until Allah gives me success or I perish." And the tears starting to his eyes, he turned to depart. Then Abu Talib cried out aloud, " Son of my brother, come back !" And he returned. And Abu Talib said: " Depart in peace, O my nephew! Say whatever thou desirest, for, by Allah, I will in no wise abandon thee, for ever."

Fanaticism, here baffled, sought an outlet elsewhere. As usual the weak and the unprotected became the first victims

and martyrs to their faith, whilst others apostatised, until
Mohammed himself advised his converts to go to Abyssinia,
where there ruled a pious and just king, and where they
would find protection. Here also, when Meccan ambassadors
pursued them, and tried to obtain their extradition, they
declared their creed to the Negus in these words:—

"We lived in ignorance, in idolatry, and unchastity, the strong oppressed
the weak, we spoke untruth, we violated the duties of hospitality. Then
a prophet arose, one whom we knew from our youth, with whose descent,
and conduct, and good faith, and morality we are all well acquainted. He
told us to worship one God, to speak the truth, to keep good faith, to
assist our relations, to fulfil the rights of hospitality, to abstain from all
things impure, ungodly, unrighteous. And he ordered us to say prayers,
give alms, and to fast. We believed in him, we followed him. But
our countrymen persecuted us, tortured us, and tried to cause us to forsake our religion, and now we throw ourselves upon your protection with
confidence."

They then read him the nineteenth chapter of the Koran,
which speaks of Christ and John the Baptist, and they all
wept, and the King dismissed the Meccan messengers, re-
fusing to give up the refugees. As to the nature of Christ
they gave him a somewhat vague account, with which the
King, however, agreed—to his later discomfiture.

This nineteenth chapter, which so moved them all, contains the story both of the Annunciation of John's birth to
Zacharias, and that of Christ's birth to the Virgin. It is
here where Maryam = Mary, "the daughter of Amrán, the
sister of Harún," is described, as in the Gospel of the Infancy,
as leaning on a barren trunk of a palm-tree when the throes
come upon her, and she cries, "Would to God that I had
been dead and forgotten before this." . . . . And a voice
came from within, "Grieve not." And a rivulet gushed
forth at her feet, and the erst withered palm glistened with
luscious dates. Then, taunted by the people for having
borne a child—"her father not being a bad man, nor her
mother disreputable"—the child itself, even Christ, to whom
she mutely points, answers to everybody's wonderment, out
of his cradle, in this wise: "I am a servant of Allah. He
has given me the Book, and He has appointed me as a

Prophet." And a few verses further on, a new rhyme indicates the commencement of a new episode, which reads as follows: "This is Jesus, the son of Maryam, according to the true doctrine" (not "the words of truth," as often translated), "which they doubt. It is not fit for God that He should have a son. Praise to Him!" (*i.e.*, far be it from Him). And finally at the end of this same chapter,—

"They say God has begotten a son. In this ye utter a blasphemy; and but little is wanting but the Heavens should tear open, and the earth cleave asunder, and the mountains fall down, for that they attribute children to the Merciful, whereas it is not meet for God to have children. No one in Heaven and on Earth shall approach the Merciful otherwise than as His servant." [1] . . .

This is the first *Hejrah*, the first triumph of the Faith. But meanwhile Mohammed himself had recanted, apostatised —twice. While the small band were proclaiming the purity of his Revelation before the Negus of Abyssinia, Mohammed had gone to the Kaaba and in his sorely embittered state of mind, finding himself alienated from everybody, in the midst of an absolutely hopeless, almost single-handed struggle, invoked, before the assembled Koreish, their three popular idols—" the sublime swans," whose intercession might be sought. The Assembly were delighted, and, though they despised his feebleness, they yet wished to put an end to the unseemly strife, and forthwith declared their readiness to believe in his doctrine, since it embraced the worship of their ancient gods. But on the day following Mohammed publicly rescinded that declaration. " The devil had prompted him," he declared boldly, and bitterer waxed the feud than before. But his mind was, as we said, in a sorely vexed state at that time. He was low spirited, nervous, full of fear, and he was still ready to make concessions. To escape abuse he at about the same period declared that he had been commanded to permit the continuation of sacrifices to the idols; and then he repented again, and verses expressive of his contrition at his momentary weakness came and comforted

---

[1] Compare above, p. 88.

him in the midst of the new troubles caused by his recanta-
tion. At that time it was also that great comfort came to
him in the conversion of those two: Hamza, called the Lion
of God, and Omar, the Paul of Islam, whilom Mohammed's
bitterest adversary, who had entered the house of Mohammed
girded with his sword, resolved on slaying him, and who
returned a Muslim, the most zealous apostle of the faith,.
its most valiant defender and mainstay. Among the twelve
of whom we spoke, Abu Bakr and Hamza became the principal heads and mainsprings of young Islam.

And now the breach in the clan was completed. The
whole family of Mohammed, the Hashimites, were excommunicated. Great hardships ensued for both sides for the
space of three years, until when both were anxious to remove
the excommunication, the document itself was found to have
been destroyed by worms—all but the name of God with
which it commenced. While thus, on the one hand, Mohammed's star seemed in the ascendant, he having forced,
if not recognition, at any rate toleration, a bitter grief befel
him. Chadija, sixty-five years of age, died; shortly after
his protector, Abu Talib: and, as if to fill the cup of his
misery, he now became aware also that he was a beggar.
As long as Chadija lived she provided for him, leaving him
to believe in his prosperity. For he was chiefly occupied
with his Revelations, and with going about preaching to the
caravans, the pilgrims, the people, at the fairs. And behind
him went his other uncle, like a grim shadow, and when he
exhorted the people to repeat after him: "There is no God
but Allah," and promised that they would all be kings if
they did—as indeed they became; Abu Lahab "the squinter,"
with his two black side-curls, would mock at him, call him
a liar and a Sabian. And the people mocked after him,
and drove him away, and said "Surely your own kinsfolk
must know best what sort of a prophet you be." This Abu
Lahab now had to stand forward, and as kinsman to take
upon himself the galling charge of protecting Mohammed,
whom he loathed. Abu Talib had resisted on his death-bed
the entreaties both of Mohammed and of the Koreish—the

one trying to induce him to embrace Islam, the others to
give up his nephew. He did neither, and thus left the
matter where it was. But Mohammed felt the awkwardness
and danger of his position as the protected of his great foe
very keenly, and he resolved to turn away from the place of
his birth, even as Abraham had done, and Moses, and other
prophets, and try to gain a hearing elsewhere. He accordingly went to Tayif, within three days' journey of Mecca, but
he was unsuccessful. They hinted that his life would not be
safe among them. The rabble hooted and pelted him with
stones. He returned with a sad heart. On his road he
stopped, and preached. And as whilom the stones had said
Amen to the blind Saint's sermon, so now, legend says, the
Jin listened to his words, as men would not hear him. And
when Zaid, who went with him, asked him how he dared to
return to the Koreish, he replied, " God will find means
to protect His religion and His prophet."

And in the midst of these vicissitudes the event happened
without which Mohammedanism would never have been heard
of, save as one of the thousand outbreaks of sectarianism.

Medina, then Yathrib, was inhabited by a great number
of Jews. They had, as mentioned before, an academy, where
both Halachah and Haggadah were expounded, though very
unostentatiously. They lived in peace and friendship with
their neighbours, but had often religious conversations with
them, in which the idolaters fared badly enough. With
keenness of intellect, with sudden sparks of *esprit*, with all
the arts of casuistry, they showed them the inanity of their
form of belief. They further, as the keepers of holy books,
told them such legends and tales about their common ancestor Abraham, their common kinsman Ishmael, and all
that befel those before, and those after them, that their
imagination was kindled, their heart moved, their intellect
fired, and that secretly they could not but agree to the mental
and religious superiority of these their neighbours. But their
Arab pride would not yield; and when they openly denied
this superiority of Faith, the Jews would tell them that their
Messiah would come and punish them for their unbelief,

even as the unbelief of the legendary aborigines who had lived there before them had been punished.

When the few pilgrims who had patiently listened to Mohammed, at his many preachings, brought back the strange tidings to Medina that a certain man of good family had publicly renounced the old gods, and had spoken of the God of Abraham, and of his mission to convert his brethren to him, not a Jew, not preaching Judaism, but an Arab, a Gentile like themselves, a man of their own kith and kin, a man who had gradually acquired a certain position and following in spite of all attacks and hindrances, it struck some of the advanced and far-seeing men of that city, that this was an opportunity not to be lost. If their people, "in whom more dissension was to be found than in any other on the face of the earth," could be united by one pure faith, which was emphatically their own, and which, though acknowledging some of the fundamental truths of Judaism, did not acknowledge Judaism itself, it would be a vast achievement; and if, further, they would acknowledge the coming man, the Messiah, with whom they had been threatened by the Jews, before even these knew of him, they would gain a doubly brilliant victory. And they went to Mohammed secretly as a deputation, and told him that if he were capable of creating that union, religious and political, which was needed, they would acknowledge him to be the foretold prophet, and "the greatest man that ever lived."

Mohammed then recited to them a brief summary of the commandments—to worship but One God, not to steal, not to commit adultery, not to kill their children, not to slander, and to obey his authority in things "right and just," which they repeated after him. This is called the women's vow, because the same points were afterwards repeated for the benefit of the women in the Koran, and because there was no mention of fighting for the faith in this formula.

Shortly after this a solemn and secret compact was entered into between another influential deputation from Medina and himself: in the stillness of night, "so that the sleeper should not be awakened, and the absent not be waited for." Here he more fully declared his faith. There are, he told them, many forms of Islam or Monotheism; and each takes a different kind of worship or outer garment. The real points consist of the belief in the Resurrection, in the Day of Judgment, and, above all, unconditional faith in one only God, Allah, unto whom utter submission is due, and who alone is to be feared and worshipped. Other essential points are consistency in misfortune, prayer, and charity.

Whereupon they swore allegiance into his hands. This over, he selected twelve men among them—Jesus had chosen twelve Apostles, and Moses his elders of the tribes of Israel, he said — and exhorted those who had not been chosen, not to be angry in their hearts, inasmuch as not he but Gabriel had determined the choice. These were the twelve "Bishops" (Nakib), while the other men of Medina are called "Aids" (Ansár).

Secretly as these things had been done, they soon became known in Mecca, and now not a moment was to be lost. The Koreish could no longer brook this; Mohammed's folly had become dangerous. About one hundred families of influence in Mecca, who believed in the Prophet, silently disappeared, by twos, and threes, and fours, and went to Medina, where they were received with enthusiasm. Entire quarters of the city thus became deserted, and Otba, at the sight of these vacant abodes, once teeming with life, "sighed heavily," and recited the old verse: "Every dwelling-place, even if it have been blessed 'ever so long, at last will become a prey to wind and woe." . . . "And," he bitterly added, "all this is the work of our noble nephew, who hath scattered our assemblies, ruined our affairs, and created dissension among us." The position now grew day by day more embarrassing. A blow had to be struck. Still Mohammed was in Mecca, he, Ali, and Abu Bakr. An assembly of the Koreish met in all despatch at the town-hall, and some chiefs of other clans were invited to attend. The matter had become a question for the commonwealth, not for a tribe.—And the Devil also came, according to the legend, in the guise of a venerable sheikh. Stormy was the meeting, for the men began to be afraid. Imprisonment for life, perpetual exile, and finally. death, were proposed. It is for this that Satan is wanted by the legend. No Arab would have counselled death for Mohammed. The last proposal was accepted; its execution deferred to the first dark night. A number of noble youths were to do the bloody deed. Meanwhile they watched his house to prevent his escape.

But meanwhile, also, "the angel Gabriel" had told Mohammed what his enemies had planned against him. And he put his own green garment upon Ali, bade him lie on his own bed, and escaped, as David had escaped, through the window. A price was set upon his head. Abu Bakr, the "sole companion," was with him. They hid in a cave in the direction opposite from that leading to Medina, on Mount Thaur. A spider wove his web over the mouth of the cave, relate the traditions. Be it observed, by the way, that even this spider and web belong to the Haggadah, and are found in the Targum to the ninety-fifth Psalm, where David is, by these means, hidden from his enemies. Two wild pigeons laid their eggs at the entrance of the cave, so that the pursuers were convinced that none could have entered it for many a long day; and the pigeons were blessed ever after and made sacred within the Holy Territory. Once or twice danger was nigh, and Abu Bakr began to fear. "They were but two," he said. "Nay," Mohammed said, "we are three; God is with us." And He was with them. It was a hot day in September, 622, when Mohammed entered Yathrib, from that time forth honoured by the name of *Medinat An-Nabi*, the City of the Prophet, at noon:—ten, thirteen, or fifteen years (the traditions vary) after his assumption of the sacred office. This is the Hejrah, or Mohammedan Era, which dates from the first month of the first lunar year after the Prophet's entry into the city. A Jew watching on a tower espied him first, in order that there might be fulfilled the words of the Koran, "The Jews know him better than they know their own children." Before entering the gate he alighted from his camel and prayed.

From that time forth Mohammed's life, hitherto obscure

I

and dark, stands out in its minutest details. He now is
judge, lawgiver, king; even to the day of his death. We
shall leave our readers to follow out the minutiæ of his life
in any of the biographies at their hand, which, from this
period forth, no longer differ in any essential point.

But here we turn at once to that period of his open dissensions with the Jews, who, as we said already, formed a
very influential section at Medina. He had by degrees come
to sanction and adopt as much of their dogmas, their legends,.
their ceremonies, as ever was compatible with his mission as
a Prophet of the Arabs, and one who, barring the fundamental dogma of the Sonship, wished to conciliate also the
Christians. He constantly refers to the testimony of the
Jews, calls them the first receivers of the Law, and not
merely in such matters as turning in prayer towards Jerusalem, instead of the national sanctuary, the Kaaba, he had
followed them—nay, at Medina he even adopted the Day of
Atonement, date, name, and all. All he wanted in return
was that they should acknowledge him as *the* Prophet of the
Gentiles (*Ummi*), and testify to his mission. But the veil
had suddenly been torn from the eyes of these Jews. If they
had thought him a meet instrument to convert all Arabia to
Judaism, and had eagerly fostered and encouraged him, had
instructed him in law and legend, and had caused him to
believe in himself and his mission, they of a sudden became
aware that their supposed tool had become a thing of ever-
growing power; and they had recourse to the most dangerous arms imaginable for laying that ghost which they had
helped to raise. They laughed at him publicly. They told
stories of how he came by his "Revelations." They who had
been so anxious to inure him into the Midrash, challenged
him by silly questions on Haggadistic lore,—to which he was
imprudent enough to give serious replies,—to prove his Mes-
siahship, with which they unceasingly taunted him. They
produced the Bible, and showed how different the tales he
told of the patriarchs and others were from those contained
in that book: they who had begotten this Haggadistic guise
themselves. Of course the stories did not agree, and even

Christians (Omayyah and others) testified to that fact. What remained for Mohammed but to declare that, in those instances, both Jews and Christians had falsified their books? or that they did not understand them—applying to them the rabbinical designation of certain scholars: that though they had the books, they were but " as asses laden with them," and comprehended not their contents; or that they gave out foolish stories to be *the* Book itself. He now declared that, " of all men, Jews and Idolaters hate the Muslims most." And, in truth, when asked whether they preferred Mohammed's teaching or Idolatry, they would reply—as their ancestors had done centuries before—" Idolatry :—since idolaters did not know any better, whilst there were those who knowingly perverted the pure doctrine, and sowed strife and dissension between Israel and their Father which is in Heaven." Some Jewish fanatics even attempted his life— one, innocently enough, by witchcraft; another, by the more earnest missile of a stone. They wrote satires and squibs upon him, men and women. There was no end to their provocations. They mispronounced his Koranic words—" twisting their tongues "—so as to give them an offensive meaning. Their " look down upon us," sounded like "O our wicked one." For " forgiveness " they said " sin ;" for " peace upon thee " —" contempt upon thee," and the like. They mocked at his expression of " giving God a good loan "—" we being rich and He poor !" they said—evidently forgetting the similar expressions of the Mishnah itself, which speaks of certain good deeds[1] as bringing interest in this world, while the capital is reserved for the next. And the inevitable happened. The breach came to pass, and there was hatred even unto death on both sides. It was too late to substitute another faith, other doctrines, other legends, even had they been at hand. But as much as could be done without endangering the whole structure, to show the irreconcilable breach, was done now.

---

[1] Such as reverence for father and mother, charity, early application to study, hospitality, doing the last honours to the dead, promoting peace between man and his neighbour. *See* page 34.

The faithful were no longer to turn their faces towards Jerusalem, but towards Mecca. Friday was made the day of rest, and the call to prayer was introduced as a supposed protest against the trumpet of the synagogue, though the trumpet was scarcely ever used for the purpose of the call to prayer. The Jews were not to be saluted in the streets; the faithful were to abstain from eating with them; they are declared beyond the pale—and bitterly had they to rue their lost game.

In the first year of the Hejrah Mohammed proclaimed war against the enemies of the faith. At Badr the Muslims first stood face to face with the Meccans, and routed them, though but 316 against 600. The Koreish and certain Jewish tribes were the next object of warfare. Six years after the Flight he proclaimed a general pilgrimage to Mecca. Its inhabitants though prohibiting this, concluded a peace with him, whereby he was recognised as a belligerent, and the pilgrimage was carried out the very next year. Next other Jewish tribes had to feel his iron rod, whilst he nearly lost his life at the hands of a Jewess, another Judith, who tried to poison him, and, when charged with the crime, said that she had only wished to see whether Mohammed really was a Prophet, and now she was convinced of it. She thus saved her own life; but the poison worked on, and in his dying hour Mohammed spoke of that poison "cutting his heart strings." His missionaries now sought a larger sphere than Arabia. Letters were sent by him to Heraclius, to the Governor of Egypt, to Abyssinia, to Chosroës II.., to Amra the Ghassanide. The latter resented this as an insult, executed the messenger, and the first war between Islam and Christianity broke out. Islam was beaten. Mecca at these news rose anew, threw off the mask of friendship, and broke the alliance. Whereupon Mohammed marched of a sudden 10,000 men strong upon them before they had time for any preparation, took Mecca by storm, and was publicly acknowledged chief and prophet. More strife and more, chiefly minor, contests followed, in which he was more or less victorious. In the year ten of the Hejrah he undertook his last solemn

pilgrimage to Mecca, with at least 40,000 Muslims, and
there on Mount Arafat blessed them, like Moses, and repeated his last exhortations; chiefly telling them to protect
the weak, the poor, and the women, and to abstain from
usury.

Once again he thought of war. He planned a huge expedition against the Greeks; but he felt death approaching.
One night, at midnight, he went to the cemetery of Medina,
and prayed and wept upon the tombs, and asked God's blessing for his "companions resting in peace." Next day he
went to the mosque as usual, ascended the pulpit, and commenced his exhortation with these words: "There was once
a servant unto whom God had given the option of whatever
worldly goods he would desire, or the rewards that are near
God; and he chose those-which are near God." And Abu
Bakr, hearing these words, wept and said, " May our fathers
and mothers, our lives and our goods, be a sacrifice for you,
O messenger of God." And the people marvelled at these
words. They wist not that the prophet spoke of his near
death, but Abu Bakr knew. For a few more days Mohammed went about as usual; but terrible headaches, accompanied by feverish symptoms, soon forced him to seek rest.
He chose Ayisha's house close to the mosque, and there took
part as long as he could in public prayers. For the last time
he addressed the faithful, asking them, like Moses, whether
he had wronged any one, or whether he owed aught to any
one. To round the story off right realistically, there was an
imbecile present who claimed certain unpaid pennies; which
were immediately refunded to him, though not without a
bitter word. He then read passages from the Koran pre-
paring them for his death, and exhorted them to keep peace
among themselves. Never after that hour did he ascend the
pulpit, says the tradition, "till the day of the Resurrection."
Whether he intended to appoint a successor—Mosaylima,
perhaps, the pseudo-prophet, as Sprenger suggests—or not,
must always remain a mystery. It is well known that the
writing-materials for which he had asked were not given to
him. Perhaps they did think him delirious, as they said.

Some medicine was given to him, accompanied by certain
superstitious rites and formulas. He protested with horror
when he became aware of this. He wandered; somewhat
of Heaven and Angels were his last words—"Denizens of
Heaven . . . Sons of Abraham . . . prophets . . . they fall
down, weeping, glorifying His Majesty. . . ." Ayisha, in
whose lap his head rested, felt it growing heavy and heavier:
she looked into his face, saw his eyes gazing upwards, and
heard him murmuring: "No, the companions above . . . in
Paradise." She then took his hand in hers, praying. When
she let it sink, it was cold and dead. This happened about
noon of Monday (12th or 11th) of the third month in the
11th year of the Hejrah (8th June, 632). Terrible was the
distress which the news of his death caused. Many of the
faithful refused to believe in it, and Omar confirmed them in
their doubt. But Abu Bakr sprang forth, saying, "Whosoever among you has believed in Mohammed, let him know
that Mohammed is dead; but he who has believed in Mohammed's God, let him continue to serve Him, for He is still
alive and never dies. . . ."

We have in this succinct review of the stages through
which Mohammed went, carefully abstained from pronouncing
upon him *ex cathedrá*, from accusing or defending him. All
this has been done, and public opinion is at rest on the point,
for instance, of his marrying many wives, or committing
wholesale slaughter when an example had to be made. Also
with regard to his " cunning," and " craftiness," and the rest
of it. There is, Mohammedans tell us now, polygamy and
massacre enough and to spare in the Bible, and its heroes are
in no wise exempt from human frailties. Moreover, "far-
sighted prudence and energetic action "—provided always
that they belong to the victorious camp—are not considered
very grave faults. But we have also abstained from adducing
many Koranic passages, however tempting it was to substitute for our own sober account the glowing words of " inspiration "—the cry out of the depths of an intensely human
heart in its sore agony—the wail over the peace that is lost
—the exultant bugle-call that proclaims the God-given tri-

umph—the yell of revenge, or the silent anguish, and the unheard, the unseen tear of a man. These things do indeed write a more faithful biography than the acutest historian will ever compile out of the infinite and infinitesimal mosaics at his disposal.

Mohammed has had many biographers, from the Byzantines who could not satisfy their souls with heaping up mountains of silly abuse from Maracci and Prideaux—the former of whom has, not without some show of reason, been accused of being a secret believer, while the latter wishes to stop by his biography, " the great prevailing infidelity in the present age," more especially as he has reason to fear that " wrath hath some time gone forth from the Lord," and that the " Wicked One may, by some other such instrument, overwhelm us with foulest delusions "—to those great authorities, Sprenger, Muir, Nöldeke, Weil, Amari. The work of the first of these we have placed at the head of our paper because it is the most comprehensive, the most exhaustive, the most learned of all, because, more than any of the others, it does, by bringing all the material bodily before the reader, enable him to form his own judgment. Next to him in fulness and genuineness of matter, though not in genius perhaps, stands, to our thinking, Muir; only that a certain preconceived notion anent Satan seems to have taken somewhat too firm a hold upon his mind. Both Muir and Sprenger have drunk out of the fulness of the East in the East, spending part of their lives in research on Indian and Mohammedan soil. Weil, Amari, Nöldeke,[1] have earned the first places among Koranic investigators in Europe, while Lane, that most illustrious master of Arab lexicography, has, both in his classical Notes on the "Arabian Nights" and in his "Modern Egyptians," thrown out most precious hints on the subject. And those that have written his life have all written it out of his book, the Koran, and its complement the Sunnah, and each has written it differently.

---

[1] We may on another occasion enter more fully upon the individual merits of their works, and those of many others in this large field: for the present, a bare reference to them must suffice.

The Koran is a wonderful book in many respects, but
chiefly in this, that it has no real beginning, middle, or end.
Mohammed's mind is best portrayed here. It was not a
well-regulated mind. Weil, in touching terms, almost appeals
to the shadow of Mohammed to come and enlighten him as
to what he said, when he said it, how he said it. He cannot
forgive him, he states at the commencement of his " Introduction," that he did not put everything clearly and properly
in order before his death—even as a man sends his " copy "
to the printers. From date-leaves and tablets of white stone,
from shoulder-bones and bits of parchment, thrown promiscu-
ously into a box, and from " the breasts of men," was the first
edition of the Koran prepared, one year after the prophet's
death, and the single chapters were arranged *according to
their respective lengths:* organ-pipe fashion—and not even
that accurately. And Mohammed's book is not even as the
Pentateuch, according to the Documentary Theory. There
are not several accounts of the same or different events
vaguely put together. Nor is it even like the Talmud, which,
though apparently leading us by the Ariadne-thread of the
Mishnah through its labyrinths, yet every now and then
plunges us into pathless wildernesses of cave and vault;
through which ever and anon streams in the golden light
of day, showing the wise aim and plan of their tortuous
windings. But in the Koranic structure there is no cunning,
no special purpose, and, indeed, you may begin at every page
and end at every page. Unless one should prefer to read it
from beginning to end—and we warrant that, as it now
stands, no one will easily perform that feat, unless he be a
pious Muslim, or, perchance, makes it his Arabic text-book.
Hence also not one of these *savans* agrees about the succession of the Chapters. There is certainly a vast amount of
truth or probability on the side of some suggestions; and
Sprenger has, to our mind, come nearest, because he was the
least fettered by conventionalities of view, but, son of the
Alps and of the Desert, he set authority at defiance and
sought out his path for himself. Yet with him, too, it is
difficult to agree at times, according to the greater or less

sympathy one feels with his stand-point and the view he takes of the Prophet himself.

Broadly speaking, three principal divisions may, with psychological truth, be established; the first, corresponding to the period of early struggles, being marked by the higher poetical flight, by the deeper appreciation of the beauties of nature, in sudden, most passionate, lava-like outbursts, which seem scarcely to articulate themselves into words. The more prosaic and didactic tone warns us of the approach of man-hood, while the dogmatising, the sermonising, the reiteration, and the abandoning of all Scriptural and Haggadistic help-mates point to the secure possession of power, to the consum-mation and completion of the mission. But these divisions must not be relied upon too securely. There rings through what may fairly be considered some of the very last Revela-tions ever and anon the old wild cry of doubt and despair; the sermon turns abruptly into a glowing vision; a sudden rhapsody inappropriately follows a small dogmatic disqui-sition, or a curse fiery and yelling as any of the hottest days is hurled upon some unbeliever's doomed head; while the very first utterances at times exhibit the theorising, reflecting, arguing tendencies of ripe old age.

And it is exactly in these transitions, quick and sudden as lightning, that one of the great charms of the book, as it now stands, consists: well might Goethe say that "as often as we approach it, it always proves repulsive anew; gradually, however, it attracts, it astonishes, and, in the end, forces into admiration." The Koran, moreover, suffers more than any other book we could think of by a translation, however masterly. If anywhere, it is here that the *summum jus summa injuria* holds good. What makes the Talmud so particularly delightful is this peculiar fact, that whenever jurisprudence with its thousand technicalities and uncouth terms is out of the question, it becomes easy, translucent, and clear to the merest beginner. The pathetic *naïveté* of its diction, and the evident pains it takes to make all its sayings household words, is something for which we cannot be too grateful. Hence also the fact that these words in

their wisdom and grace must needs find an echo in every
true heart, if told exactly as they stand, without attempt
to colour them. The grandeur of the Koran, on the other
hand, consists, its contents apart, in its diction. We cannot
explain the peculiarly dignified, impressive, sonorous nature
of Semitic sound and parlance; its *sesquipedalia verba*, with
their crowd of prefixes and affixes, each of them affirming
its own position, while consciously bearing upon and influ-
encing the central root—which they envelop like a garment
of many folds, or as chosen courtiers move round the anointed
person of the King.

May be, some stray reader remembers a certain thrill on
waking suddenly in the middle of his first night on Eastern
soil—waking, as it were, from dream into dream. For there
came a voice, solitary, sweet, sonorous, floating from on high
through the moonlight stillness — the voice of the blind
Mueddin, singing the Ulah, or first Call to Prayer. At the
sound whereof many a white figure would move silently on
the low roofs, and not merely, like the palms and cypresses
around, bow his head, but prostrate, and bend his knees. And
the sounds went and came, "Allahu Akbar . . . . Prayer
is better than sleep . . . . There is no God but He . . . .
He giveth life, and He dieth not . . . . Oh! thou Bountiful
. . . . Thy mercy ceaseth not . . . . My sins are great,
greater is Thy mercy . . . . I extol his perfection . . . .
Allahu Akbar!"—and this reader may have a vague notion
of Arabic and Koranic sound, one which he will never forget.

But the Koran is *sui generis*, though its contents be often
but the old wine in new bottles, and its form strikingly
resembling that of pre-Islamic poetry, which it condemns.
It is rhythmical, rhymed, condescends to word-plays, and
indulges — and in one place to an appalling degree — in
refrains. As usual, the rhyme — the swaddling clothes of
unborn thought — here too seems to run away at times, if
not with the sense, at all events with the numbers. Yet
not far; only that for the sake of the soft dual termination
certain gardens and fountains and fruits are doubled: whilst
on the other hand a lofty contempt for this thraldom is

shown by *m* being made to answer to *n*, *l* to *r*, and so forth.
Yet here, as in all these critical exoteric questions, we are
treading on very dangerous ground, and we shall content
ourselves with mentioning that there are at least three principal schools at variance on the very question whether the
Koran *is* rhymed throughout: one affirming it, the other
denying it, and the third taking a middle course.

We reserve all that we have to say on the ˜uter or critical
aspect of the Koran for the present; the scientific terms on
this field: rules, divisions, and subdivisions, most minute and
manifold, and the entire Masoretic apparatus, with all the
striking analogies with the corresponding Jewish labours
that reveal themselves at every step.

We turn, in preference, at once to the intrinsic portion of
this strange book — a book by the aid of which the Arabs
conquered a world greater than that of Alexander the Great,
greater than that of Rome, and in as many tens of years as
the latter had wanted hundreds to accomplish her conquests;
by the aid of which they, alone of all the Shemites, came
to Europe as kings, whither the Phœnicians had come as
tradesmen, and the Jews as fugitives or captives; came to
Europe to hold up, together with these fugitives, the light
to Humanity—they alone, while darkness lay around; to
raise up the wisdom and knowledge of Hellas from the dead,
to teach philosophy, medicine, astronomy, and the golden
art of song to the West as well as to the East, to stand at
the cradle of modern science, and to cause us late epigoni
for ever to weep over the day when Granada fell.

We said that there is a great likeness between pre-Islamic
poetry (even that of those inane " priests ") and the Koran.
If Mohammed wished to go straight to the heart of his people,
it could only be through the hallowed means of poetry—the
sole vehicle of all their "science," all tradition, all religion,
all love, and all hatred. And, indeed, what has remained of
fragments of that period of pre-Islamic poetry which immediately preceded Mohammed, broken, defaced, dimmed, as it
is, by fanaticism and pedantic ignorance, prove it sufficiently
to have been of all the brilliant periods of Arabic literature the

most brilliant. There arises out of the Hamasa, the Moalla-kat, the Kitab, Al-Aghani, nay, out of the very chips that lie embedded in later works, such a freshness, and glory, and bloom, of desert-song—even as out of Homer's epics rise the glowing spring-times of humanity and the deep blue heavens of Hellas—as has never again been the portion of Arab poetry. Wild, and vast, and monotonous as the yellow seas of its desert solitudes, it is withal tender, true, pathetic, soul-subduing; much more so than when in beauteous Andalus the great-grandchildren of these wild rovers sang of nightly boatings by torchlight, of the moon's rays trembling on the waves, of sweet meetings in the depths of rose-gardens, of Spain's golden cities and gleaming mosques, and the far away burning desert whence their fathers came. Those grand accents of joy and sorrow, of love, and valour, and passion, of which but faint echoes strike on our ears now, were full-toned at the time of Mohammed; and he had not merely to rival the illustrious of the illustrious, but to excel them; to appeal to the superiority of what he said and sang as a very sign and proof of his mission. And there were, at first, many and sinister tokens of rivalry and professional hatred visible, to which religious fanaticism carried fuel. Those that had fallen fighting against him were lamented over in the most heartrending and popular dirges. Poets of his time said even as Jehuda Al-Hassan-Halevi, that great Hebræo-Arabic minstrel, did hundreds of years after them, that they failed to see anything extraordinary in his verses. Nay, they called him names,—a fool, a madman, a ridiculous pretender and impostor; they laughed at the people of Medina for listening to "such an one." And these rival-poets formed a formidable power. Their squibs told, while the counter-satires he caused to be written fell flat. Not even "sudden visitations," by which some of the worst offenders were found struck to death, stopped the "press." Until there came a revelation—"Shall I declare unto you," he asks in the Surah called "the Poets," "on whom the Devils descend? They descend upon every lying and wicked person . . . most of them are liars. And those who err follow the steps of the poets. Seest thou not how they rove as bereft of their senses through every valley ? " . . . Which reminds us strikingly of Kutayir, a pre-Islamic poet, and the answer he gave to people asking him "How he managed when poetry became difficult to him?" and he said, " I walk through the deserted habitations and through the blooming greenswards; then the most perfect songs become easy, and the most beautiful ones flow naturally "—"roving bereft of his senses through every valley !" . . . .

Mohammed is said to have convinced a rival, Lebid, a poet-laureate of the period, of his mission, by reciting to him a portion of the now second Surah. Unquestionably it is one of the very grandest specimens of Koranic or Arabic diction, describing how hypocrites " are like unto those who kindle a fire without, and think themselves safe from darkness. But while it is at its biggest blaze, God sends a wind; the flame is extinguished, and they are shrouded in dense night. They are deaf, and dumb, and blind. . . . Or when in darkness, and amidst thunder and lightning, rain-filled clouds pour from heaven, they in terror of the crash thrust their fingers into their ears. . . . . But God compasseth the infidels around. . . . . The flash of the lightning blindeth their eyes—while it lights up all things, they walk in its light—then darkness closes in upon them, and they stand rooted to the ground."

But even descriptions of this kind, grand as they be in their own tongue, are not sufficient to kindle and preserve the enthusiasm and the faith and the hope of a nation like the Arabs, not for one generation, but for a thousand. Not the most passionate grandeur, not the most striking similes, not the legends, not the parables, not the sweet spell of rhyme-fall and the weaving of rhythmic melodies, and all the poet's cunning craft—but the kernel of it all, the doctrine, the positive, clear, distinct doctrine. And this doctrine Mohammed brought before them in a thousand, so to say, symphonic variations, modulated through the whole scale of human feeling. From prayer to curse, from despair to exultant joy, from argument, often casuistic, largely-spun-out argument, to vision, either in swift, and sudden, and terrible transition, or in repetitions and reiterations — monotonous and dreary and insufferably tedious to the outsider—but to him alone.

The poets before him had sung of love. One of the principal forms of pre-Islamic poetry was, indeed, the Kasida, which almost invariably commenced with a sorrowful remembrance of her who had gone none knew whither, and the very traces of whose tent, but yesterday gleaming afar in the midst of the wide solitudes, had disappeared overnight. Antara, himself the hero of the most famous novel, sings of the ruins, around which ever hover lovers' thoughts, of the dwelling of Abla, who is gone, and her dwelling-place knows her not; it is now desolate and silent. Amr Al Kais, "the standard-bearer of poets, but on the way to hell," as Mohammed called him, of all things praises his fortune with women, chiefly Oneisa, and in brilliant, often Heinesque, verse sings of the good things of this world; until his father banishes him on account of an adventure wherein he, as usual, had been too happy. And of a sudden, in the midst of a wild revel, he hears that his father has been slain, and not a word said he. But higher and louder waxed the revel, and he drank deep, and gamed till the grey dawn; when he arose of a sudden, and swore a holy oath that neither wine nor woman should soothe his senses until he had taken bloody vengeance for his father; and when consulting the oracle, he drew an arrow with the inscription "Defence," he threw it into the idol's face, saying, "Wretch, if thy father had been killed, thou wouldst have counselled Vengeance, not Defence."

They sang of valour and generosity, of love and strife, and revenge, of their noble tribe and ancestors, of beautiful women, "often even of those who did not exist, so that woman's noble fame should be spread abroad among kings and princes," as the unavoidable scholiast informs us; of the valiant sword, and the swift camel, and the darling horse, fleeter than the whirlwind's rush. Or of early graves, upon which weeps the morning's cloud, and the fleeting nature of life, which comes and goes as the waves of the desert-sand, and as the tents of a caravan, as a flower that shoots up and dies away—while the white stars will rise and set ever-lastingly, and the mountains will rear their heads heaven-wards, and never grow old. Or they shoot their bitter arrows of satire right into the enemy's own soul.

Mohammed sang none of those. No love-minstrelsy his, not the joys of this world, nor sword nor camel, nor jealousy or human vengeance, not the glories of tribe or ancestor, nor the unmeaning, swiftly and for ever extinguished existence of man, were his themes. He preached *Islam*.

And he preached it by rending the skies above and tearing open the ground below, by adjuring heaven and hell, the living and the dead. The Arabs have ever been pro-ficient in the art of swearing, but such swearing had never been heard in and out of Arabia. By the foaming waters and by the grim darkness, by the flaming sun and the setting stars, by Mount Sinai and by Him who spanned the firma-ment, by the human soul and the small voice, by the Kaaba and by the Book, by the Moon and the dawn and the angels, by the ten nights of dread mystery and by the day of judgment. That day of judgment, at the approach whereof the earth shaketh, and the mountains are scattered into dust, and the seas blaze up in fire, and the children's hair grows white with anguish, and like locust-swarms the souls arise out of their graves, and Allah cries to Hell, Art thou filled full ? and Hell cries to Allah, More, give me more, . . . while Paradise opens its blissful gates to the righteous, and glory ineffable awaits them—both men and women.

The kernel and doctrine of Islam Goethe has found in the second Surah, which begins as follows :—

"This is the Book. There is no doubt in the same. A *Guidance* to the righteous. Who believe in the *Unseen*, who observe the *Prayer*, and who give *Alms* of that which we have vouchsafed unto them. And who believe in that which has been sent down unto thee—(the *Revelation*) which had been sent down to those before thee, and who believe in the *Life to come*. They walk in the guidance of their Lord, and they are the blessed. As to them who believe not—it is indifferent to them whether thou exhortest them or not exhortest them. They will not

believe. Sealed hath Allah their hearts and their ears, and over their
eyes is darkness, and theirs will be a great punishment.—'And in this
wise,' Goethe continues, 'we have Surah after Surah. Belief and unbelief
are divided into upper and lower. Heaven and hell await the believers or
deniers. Detailed injunctions of things allowed and forbidden, legendary
stories of Jewish and Christian religion, amplifications of all kinds, boundless tautologies and repetitions, form the body of this sacred volume, which
to us, as often as we approach it, is repellent anew, next attracts us ever
anew, and fills us with admiration, and finally forces us into veneration.'"

Thus Goethe. And no doubt the passage adduced is as good
a summary as any other. Perhaps, if he had gone a little
further in this same chapter, he might have found one still
more explicit. When Mohammed at Medina told his
adherents no longer to turn in prayer towards Jerusalem,
but towards the Kaaba at Mecca, to which their fathers had
turned, and he was blamed for this innovation, he replied:—

"That is not righteousness: whether ye turn your faces towards East
or West, God's' is the East as well as the West. But verily righteousness
is his who believes in God, in the day of judgment, in the angels, in the
Book and the prophets; who bestows his wealth, for God's sake, upon
kindred, and orphans, and the poor, and the homeless, and all those who
ask; and also upon delivering the captives; he who is stedfast in prayer,
giveth alms, who stands firmly by his covenants, when he has once entered
into them; and who is patient in adversity, in hardship, and in times of
trial. These are the righteous, and these are the God-fearing."

Yet these and similar passages, characteristic as they be, do
not suffice. It behoves us to look somewhat deeper.

First of all, What is the literal meaning of Islam, the
religion of a Muslim? We find that name Muslim already
applied to those *Hanifs*, of whom we have spoken above,
who had renounced, though secretly, idolatry before Mohammed, and had gone out to seek the "religion of Abraham," which Mohammed finally undertook to re-establish.
The Semitic root of the word Muslim yields a variety of
meanings, and accordingly Muslim has had many interpretations. But in all these cases—even as is now becoming so
universally clear in the terms of the New Testament—it is
as useless to go back to the original root for the elucidation
of some special or technical, dogmatic, scientific, or other
term of a certain period, as it is to ask those for an explana-

tion who lived to use that same term long after it had assumed an utterly new, often the very opposite, meaning. *Salm*, the root of *Islam*, means, in the first instance, to be tranquil, at rest, to have done one's duty, to have paid up, to be at perfect peace, and, finally, to hand oneself over to Him with whom peace is made. The noun derived from it means peace, greeting, safety, salvation. And the Talmud contains both the term and the explanation of the term Muslim, which in its Chaldee meaning had become naturalised in Arabia. It indicates a "Righteous man." In a paraphrase of Proverbs xxiv. 16, where the original has *Zadik* (*Ziddik* in Koran), which is rightly translated by the Authorised Version, "Just Man," the Talmud has this very word. "Seven pits are laid for the 'Muslim,'" (*Shalmana*—Syr. *Msalmono*) it says, and "one for the wicked, but the wicked falls into his one, while the other escapes all seven." [1] The word thus implies absolute submission to God's will—as generally assumed— neither in the first instance, nor exclusively, but means, on the contrary, one who strives after righteousness with his own strength. Closely connected with the misapprehension of this part of Mohammed's original doctrine is also the popular notion on that supposed bane of Islam, Fatalism: but we must content ourselves here with the observation that, as far as Mohammed and the Koran are concerned, Fatalism is an utter and absolute invention. Not once, but repeatedly, and as if to guard against such an assumption, Mohammed denies it as distinctly as he can, and gives injunctions which show as indisputably as can be that nothing was further from his mind than that pious state of idle and hopeless inanity and stagnation. But to return to Islam. The real sum and substance of it is contained in Mohammed's words: "We have spoken unto thee by revelation:—*Follow the religion of Abraham.*" . . . .

---

[1] There is also the story in the Talmud of the Master whose name was *Shalman* (Solomon), and they said to him, "Thou art full of peace, and thy teaching is peace (perfect) and thou hast made peace between the disciples."

K

What did Mohammed and his contemporaries understand by this religion of Abraham? "Abraham," says the Koran, pointedly and pregnantly, "was neither a Jew nor a Christian, but he was pious and righteous, and no idolater." Have we not here the briefest and the most rationalistic doctrine ever preached? Curious and characteristic is the proof which the Koran finds it necessary to allege (partly found, by the way, in the Midrash) for this:—There *was* no Law (or Gospel) revealed then—there were, in fact, no divisions of Semitic creed, no special and distinctive dogmas in Abraham's time yet. The Haggadah, it is true, points out that, when Scripture says "he heard my voice," it meant that to him were given, by anticipation, all that the Law and the Prophets contain. And in order rightly to understand the drift of Mohammed's words, we must endeavour to gather the little mosaics as they lie scattered about in all directions in the Talmud and Midrash. Perchance a picture, anent Abraham's faith and works, may arise under our hands—a not unworthy ideal of Judaism, which formed it, and Mohammedanism, which adopted it; of Abraham, the righteous, the first, and the greatest Muslim. It may also further elucidate, by the way, the words of the Mishnah, "Be ye of the Disciples of Abraham." " The divine light lay hidden," says the Midrash, "until Abraham came and discovered it."

Again we have to turn—driven by absolute necessity—to one of those indigestible morsels, one of the many *cruces* of the exegetes of Orient and Occident. The word used in the Koran for the " Religion of Abraham " is generally *Milla*. Sprenger, after ridiculing the indeed absurd attempts made to derive it from an Arabic root, concludes that it must be a foreign word, introduced by the teachers of the " Milla of Abraham " into the Hejaz. He is perfectly right. Milla = Memra = Logos, are identical: being the Hebrew, Chaldee (Targum, Peshito in slightly varied spelling), and Greek terms respectively for " *Word*,"—that surrogate for the Divine Name used by the Targum, by Philo, by St. John. This Milla, or " Word," which Abraham proclaimed, he,

" who was not an astrologer, but a prophet "—teaches, according to the Haggadah, first of all, the existence of One God, the Creator of the Universe, who rules this Universe with mercy and lovingkindness.[1] He alone also, neither angel nor planet, guides the destinies of man. Idolatry, even when combined with the belief in Him, is utterly to be abhorred; He alone is to be worshipped; in Him alone trust is to be placed in adversity. He frees the persecuted and the oppressed. You must pray to Him and serve Him in love, and not murmur when He asks for your lives, or even for lives still dearer to you than your own. As to duties towards man, it teaches—" Lovingkindness and mercy are the tokens of the faith of Abraham." " He who is not merciful is not of the children of Abraham." " What is the distinguishing quality of Abraham's descendants? their compassion and their mercy." (Be it observed, by the way, that in all these Talmudical passages the word *Rachman* is used, which term for " Merciful" forms an emphatic mark in the Koran.) " Abraham not merely forgave Abimelech, but he prayed for him; " and this mercy, charity, and lovingkindness is to be extended to every being, without reference to " garment," birth, rank, creed, or nationality. Disinterestedness and unselfishness are self-understood duties. Though the whole land had been promised to Abraham by God, he *bought* the ground for Sarah's tomb. After the victorious campaign he took nothing, no, not even " from a thread to a shoe-latchet" from the enemy. Modesty and humility are other qualities enjoined by him. Rule yourself, he said, before you rule others. Eschew pride, which shortens life—modesty prolongs it. It purifies from all sins, and is the best weapon

---

[1] " God," says the Talmud, in boldest transcendental flight, " *prays*." And what is that prayer?—" Be it my will that my mercy overpower my justice." The Koran says :—" God has laid down for Himself the Law of Mercy."

God's Mercy, says the Midrash, was the only link that held the universe together before the " Law" came to be revealed to man. And very beautifully does the Haggadistic version of the manner in which the universe, which, spite of all, would not rest firmly, but kept swaying to and fro in space, " even as a great palace built of mortal man, the foundations whereof are not firmly laid," contrast from all those well-known wild heapings-up of monsters begotten for steadying purposes.—" The earth shook and trembled, and would not find rest until God created Repentance :—then it stood."

for conquest. His humility was shown even by the way in which he exercised his hospitality. He waited himself on his guests, and when they tried to thank him, he said, " Thank Him, the One, who nourisheth all, who ruleth in heaven and earth, who killeth and giveth life, who causeth the plants to grow, and who createth man according to His wisdom." He inaugurated the Morning Prayer—even as did Isaac that of the Evening, and Jacob that of the Night. He went, even in his old age, ever restless in doing good, to succour the oppressed, to teach and preach to all men. He " wore a jewel round his neck, the light of which raised up the bowed-down and healed the sick, and which, after his death, was placed among the stars." And see how he was chosen to be tempted with the bitterest trial, in order that mankind might see how steadfast he remained—" even as the potter proves the strength of his ware, not by that which is brittle, but by that which is strong." And when he died, he left to his children four guardian angels—" Justice and Mercy, Love and Charity."

Such are the floating outlines of the faith of Abraham to be gathered from the Haggadah; and these traits form the fundamental bases of Mohammed's doctrine—often in the very words, always in the sense, of these Jewish traditions. The most emphatic moment, however, we find laid upon the Unity of God, the absence of Intermediators, and the repudiation of any special, exclusive, " privileged " creed. This is a point on which the Talmud is very strong—not merely declaring its aversion to proselytism, but actually calling every righteous man, so that he be no idolater, a " Jew" to all intents and purposes. The tracing of the minutiæ of general human ethics is, comparatively speaking, of less import, considering that these, in their outlines, are wonderfully alike, in Hellas and India, and Rome and Persia and Japan; so that it would indeed be difficult to say who first invented the great law of goodwill towards fellow-creatures. But the manner and the words in which these things are inculcated, mark their birthplace and the stages of their journey clearly enough in the Semitic creeds.

And with the doctrines—if so we may call them—of Abraham, as we gathered them from the Jewish writings, Mohammed also introduced the whole legendary cycle that surrounds Abraham's head, like a halo, in these same writings. We have in the Koran, first of all, that wondrous Haggadistic explanation, how Abraham first came to worship, in the midst of idolaters, the One invisible God—how he first lifted up his eyes heavenwards and saw a brilliant star, and said, This is God. But when the star paled before the brightness of the moon, he said, This is God. And then the sun rose and Abraham saw God in the golden glory of the sun. But the sun, too, set, and Abraham said, " Then none of you is God ; but there is one above you who created both you and me. Him alone will I worship, the Maker of Heaven and Earth ! " How he then took an axe and destroyed all the idols and placed the axe in the hands of the biggest, accusing him of the deed ; how he is thrown into the fiery furnace, and God said to the fire, " Be thou cold ; " how he entertained the Angels, and how he brought his beloved son to the Altar, and an " excellent victim " (a ram from Paradise) was sacrificed in his stead; and so on. All this, though only sketched in its outlines in the Koran, is absolute Haggadah, with scarcely as much of alteration as would naturally be expected in the like fantastic matter, even as is the rest of that " entire world of pious biblical legend which Islam has said and sung in its many tongues, to the delight of the wise and simple, for twelve centuries now, to be found either in embryo or fully developed in the Haggadah." [1]

But here, in the midst of our discourse, we are compelled to break off, reserving its continuation : notably with regard to the theoretical and practical bearing of the religion of Mohammed, and the relation of its religious terms [2] and

---

[1] See page 48.

[2] *E.g.* Koran, Forkan (= Pirke, exposition of Halachah), Torah (Law), Shechinah (presence of God), Gan Eden (Paradise), Gehinnom (Hell), Haber (Master), Darash (search the Scriptures), Rabbi (teacher), Sabbath (day of rest), Mishnah (Oral Law), &c., all of which are bodily found in the Koran, as well as even such words as the Hebrew *Yam* (for Red Sea), &c.

individual tenets to those of Judaism; also its progress and
the changes wrought within the community by many and
most daring sects; and the present aspect of the Faith and
its general influence.   And this our Exordium we will sum
up with the beginning of the Surah, called the Assembly,
revealed at Medina :—

"In the name of God, the Merciful, the Compassionate.   Whatsoever is
in heaven and on earth praises God the King, the Holy One, the Almighty,
the Allwise.   It is He who out of the midst of the illiterate Arabs has
raised an Apostle to show unto them his signs, and to sanctify them, and
to teach them the Scripture and the Wisdom, them who before had been
in great darkness. . . . . This is God's free Grace, which He giveth unto
whomsoever He wills.   God is of great Mercy !"

III.

NOTES OF A LECTURE ON THE TALMUD.[1]

MR. DEUTSCH began his lecture by speaking of the various and contradictory ideas people had about the Talmud: some believing it to be almost divine: others that it was nothing but folly and childishness. Those who investigated the book were, he said, like those explorers sent by Moses into the Promised Land, the majority of whom returned with tales of iron walls and monstrous giants, while a few came back carrying a huge bunch of delicious grapes. Many were the striking and poetical similes suggested by that strange work, such as an ocean, or a buried city; but speaking of it strictly as a book, the nearest approach to it was Hansard. Like Hansard, it is a law-book: a miscellaneous collection of Parliamentary debates, of bills, motions, and resolutions; with this difference that in Hansard these propositions, bills, and motions, gradually grow into an Act: while in the Talmud the Act is the starting-point, and the debates its consequence. The disquisitions in the Talmud seek to evolve the reasons for the Act out of Scripture, of which itself is a development and an outgrowth; while at the same time, supplementary paragraphs are constantly drawn out of its own legal text. These bills or Acts are called the *Mishnah*, both collectively and individually; the discussions, *Gemara*; both together, Talmud.

The Talmud, however, contains a vast deal more than

---

[1] Delivered on Friday evening, May 15, 1868, at the Royal Institution of Great Britain, Albemarle Street.

Hansard: it is not confined to strictly legal matters. All
those manifold assemblies wherein a people's mental, social,
and religious life are considered and developed, are here
represented. Parliament, Convocation, Law-Courts, Academies, Colleges, the Temple and the Synagogue—even the
Lobby and the Common Room have left realistic traces
upon it. The authors of this book, who may be counted by
hundreds, were always the most prominent men of the people
in their respective generations; and thus undesignedly and
designedly show the fulness and the various phases of this
people's life and progress at every turn.

The Talmud, in this wise, contains besides the social,
criminal, international, human and divine Law, along with
abundant explanations of Laws not perfectly comprehended,
corollaries and inferences from the Law, that were handed
down with more or less religious reverence, an account also
of the education, the arts, the science, the history, and
religion of this people for about a thousand years: most
fully perhaps of the time immediately preceding and following the birth of Christianity. It shows us the teeming streets
of Jerusalem, the tradesman at his work, the women in their
domestic circle, even the children at play in the market-
place. The Priest and the Levite ministering in their holy
sites, the preacher on the hillside surrounded by the multitude, even the story-teller in the bazaar: they all live, move
and have their being in these pages. Nor is it Jerusalem or
even the hallowed soil of Judæa alone, but the whole antique
world that seems to lie embalmed in it: we find here the
most curious notices of the religion of Zoroaster—how it
gradually was restored to its original status; as if all things
which had dropped out of the records of antique humanity
had taken refuge in the Talmud.

Athens and Alexandria, Persia and Rome, their civilizations and religions old and new are represented at every
turn. That cosmopolitanism which for good or evil has ever
been the characteristic trait of the Jewish people, and which
was, in fact, the highest type of teaching, is most vividly
represented in this book. One of the most striking historical

points is their always coming in contact, generally against
their will, with the most prominent nations, exactly at the
moment when the latter seem to have reached the highest
point of culture in their own development. Passing over the
three different stages of the people as Hebrews, Israelites,
Jews—names which have a distinct significance—we find
them connected with Chaldea, Egypt, Phœnicia, Assyria,
Babylonia, Persia, Greece, Rome, Arabia. Yet that cosmopolitanism never for one moment interfered with the most
marked mental individuality. There always remained the
one central sun, the Bible: around this ever revolved that
great Cosmos, the Talmud—wild and vague, though it may
be—and from it, as shown in the *Gemara*, the *Mishnah* is
begotten.

The Talmud has been harshly dealt with, more owing to
the blunders of friends than of foes. Some people have
supposed that whatever any Jew wrote was a Talmud : others
have spoken of it as a revelation, and claimed inspiration for
it. The fact is, that what each of these men wrote was
purely his own : and no one of them would have claimed
more for them than that they were his own utterances. And
it was only because some of the laws or injunctions in it were
attributed to Moses on Mount Sinai, that any sort of divinity
was predicated of it.

As to its "dates," nothing can be more authentic than the
memory of the East. The Talmud has been preserved with
absolute authenticity in the memory of doctors and disciples,
in the same way as many Brahmins and Parsee priests can
repeat, without the variation of a single accent, entire Vedas
and other chapters of their sacred books, although without
the slightest conception of their contents, and wholly ignorant of their meaning. The same was true of the followers
of Zoroaster. At the same time, there is no doubt, that
much was written down by way of note by scribes, who yet
did not venture upon the work of redaction. What alterations
there are in the Talmud are owing to censors who changed
passages that were supposed to clash with Christianity, and
produced the most singular obscurities. The censor's work

was fruitless, for in reality there was nothing in the genuine Talmud to be taken out.

But indeed we have, apart from the clearest and most irrefutable evidences of witnesses, all the ordinary internal evidences of history. We have an array of carefully preserved historical names and dates from beginning to end; names and dates, the general faithfulness and truth of which have never yet been called into question. From the Great Synagogue down to the final completion of the Babylonian Gemara, we have the legal and philosophical development of the nation always embodied as it were in the successive principal schools and men of their times. Its chief importance for religious history is the manner in which it informs us of things and circumstances at the time of the birth of Christianity, among the Priests and Pharisees, of the education, synagogues, preaching, of women, of angels and demons, &c. It gives us the ethical sayings, the parables, gnomes, &c., which were the principal vehicle of the common Jewish teaching from an almost pre-historic period. These sayings were often tender, poetical, sublime: but they were not absolutely *new:* there was not one that was not substantially contained in the canonical and uncanonical writings of the Old Testament.

Here also, we find the first cry of separation between Church and State: the first antagonism or contest of ceremonialism and free investigation. The Priests were the representatives of a privileged class, and, it must always be remembered, of one family. The first revolt against this system we have in the story of Korah. It was doubtless good for the Jews at that time, and for centuries after that revolt was quelled: they could scarcely have got on without the Sacrifices, Temple, and all its concomitants; but after the Babylonian captivity when idolatry had died out, learning became of higher moment. The Priests had sadly deteriorated as a body, with some bright exceptions, since the days of the Maccabees, when they by an accident suddenly found themselves in political power. From being, as Moses intended them to be, the receivers of the people's free gifts,

their messengers—not mediators—and their teachers, they
had become, chiefly in the upper strata, an encroaching and
ignorant faction. The ordinary priests had mostly sunk into
mere local functionaries of the Temple, while many of the
High Priests, who in their later days *bought* their sacred
office from the ruling foreign power, had forgotten the very
elements of that Bible which they had been especially
appointed to teach. But a strong re-action set in. The
Pharisees, in view of the clouds that they saw gathering
round the Commonwealth, had but one cry — Education:
catholic, compulsory and gratuitous. The watchwords re-
sounding from one end of the Talmud to the other are the
words, "learn—teach; teach—learn." The Priesthood, the
Sacrifices, the Temple, as they all went 'down at one sudden
blow, seemed scarcely to leave. a gap in the religious life of
the nation. The Pharisees had long before undermined
these things, or rather transplanted them, into the people's
homes and heart. Every man in Israel, they said, is a
priest, every man's house a temple, every man's table an
altar, every man's prayer his sacrifice. Long before the
Temple fell, it had been virtually superseded by hundreds of
synagogues, schools, and colleges, where laymen read and
expounded the Law and the Prophets. The Priest as such,
or the Levite, played but a very insignificant part in the
synagogue and school. The function of pronouncing the
"Benediction" on certain occasions, and a kind of vague
"precedence" was all that the synagogue had preserved of
the former high estate of the sons of Aaron. Yet on the
other hand, many of these men, having lost their former
privileges, applied themselves all the more vigorously to
study, and to the great national work of Education. Nor
was there any real personal antagonism between the "pharisaical" or "popular" party, and the descendants of the
"sacred" tribe and family. There is on the contrary a
legend, one of the most cherished of all the legends (as
usual faithfully interpreting the people's real feeling), which
tells how, when the enemy entered the Holy of Holies, the

Priests and Levites, led by the venerable High Priest himself, bearing aloft the golden key of the sanctuary, were seen
ascending to the highest summit, and then precipitating
themselves, with all the tokens and emblems of their sacred
trust, into the blazing ruins of the Temple—rather than
deliver them up to the conquerors!

Strenuously and indefatigably, we have said, the Pharisees
advocated education; and by their unceasing efforts, hundreds
of synagogues, colleges, and schools arose, not only in Judæa,
but throughout the whole Roman Empire. Over Judæa,
after many unsuccessful attempts, education was made compulsory everywhere except in Galilee. Peculiar circumstances arising out of its geographical position behind
Samaria and Phœnicia, had reduced that beautiful country
to be the Bœotia of Palestine. The faulty pronunciation of
its inhabitants was the standing joke of the witty denizens
of the metropolis. After the fall of Jerusalem, however, this
was altered; and Galilee became in her turn, the seat of
some of the most exalted Academies.

The regulations and provisions for public instruction were
extremely strict and minute. The number of children allotted to one teacher, the school buildings and their sites,
the road even that led to them, everything was considered;
no less the age of the pupils and the duties of the parents
with regard to preliminary preparation and continuous
domestic supervision of their tasks. The subjects, the
method, the gradual weaning even of the pupil into a
teacher or helpmate of his fellow-pupils—all these things
are carefully exposed in the Talmud. Above all is the great
principle *Non multa sed multum*, the motto of all schooling
in the Talmud. Good fundamental grounding, elementary
maternal teaching, and constant repetition are some of the
chief principles laid down. The teachers, in most cases,
taught gratuitously: considering theirs a holy and godly
office, for which the reward would surely not fail them. The
relation between master and disciple was generally that of
father and child, or friend and friend. Next to Law, Ethics,

History, and Grammar—Languages were one of the principal subjects of study. We hear of Coptic, Aramaic, Persian, Median, Latin, but above all Greek. The terms in which this last language is spoken of verge indeed on the transcendental. This also is the only language which it seems to have been incumbent to teach even to girls. Medicine was another necessary subject of instruction: the hygienic laws and the anatomical knowledge (bound up with religion) transmitted to us in the book show indeed no small proficiency for its time. Mathematics and astronomy formed another part of instruction, and were indeed considered indispensable. We hear of men to whom the ways of the stars in the skies were as familiar as the streets of their native city, and others who could compute the number of drops in the ocean, who foretold the appearance of comets, &c. Next came Natural History, chiefly Botany and Zoology. The highest point, however, was reached in Jurisprudence, which formed the most extensive and thoroughly national study.

. The chief aim and end of all learning—the Talmud is never tired of repeating—is *doing*. All knowledge is but a step to "modesty and the fear of heaven;" and innumerable are the parables whereby this lesson is inculcated. After briefly adverting to Prayers and Sermons and the whole worship of Temple and Synagogue at the time of Christ, the speaker turned to the "political" portions of the "Law" under consideration, and having pointed out how almost the modern theory of constitutionalism was contained in, it, briefly touched upon the relationship between Royalty, State, and subjects, and the provisions for taxes, for war, the legislative and judicial powers, &c. Both this, the legal, and the other, the ethical part of the book—so closely intertwined that they can hardly be separated—may be said to grow out chiefly of one fundamental axiom of the Talmud, viz. the utter and absolute equality of all men and the obligation to " follow God," by imitating the mercy attributed to Him by Scripture. No book can possibly point out in stronger language than the Talmud does, the extreme sinfulness of sin.

Next the speaker alluded to the holy influence exercised by the women, of whom the Talmud not only records the noblest deeds, but whom, even as the angels themselves, it makes at times the bearers of most sublime thoughts. Regarding the latter, it was shown at some length how both they and their counterparts " the demons" were—though partly adopted from Persian or rather Zoroastrian metaphysics—made the vehicles of national Jewish doctrines. Indeed, all those pantheistic and dualistic principles which the people had gathered from the creed of other nations, were transformed under the skilful hand of the Talmudical masters into strictly monotheistic elements, by being either idealized into abstract notions of right and wrong, or surrounded by a poetical halo which deprived them of any real existence. Thus Satan (Sammael, the "Primeval Serpent"), though mythologically his functions are precisely similar to those of the Persian "Evil Spirit," *i.e.* those of Seducer, Accuser, and Angel of Death, is yet explained away philosophically as meaning merely "Passion," which seduces, produces remorse, and kills. The demons are said to have masks before their faces, which fall only when the sin is committed; it is then only that, as bitter self-reproaches, they surround the sinner on all sides. Another instance of this is the legend of Isaac, in which "Satan," as the Angel of Death, appears first as an accuser of Abraham (as of Job) before God, next as a seducer to Abraham in the garb of an old man, to Isaac in that of a youth, finally to Sarah, informing her of the danger in which her son had been placed. There is also the legend of the death of Moses, in which Satan, eager to vanquish the "divine man," is thwarted by God's Name even to the end.

In the same manner Asmodeus (the Persian Aêshma) "Lilith," and the rest of the demoniacal powers, as well as those allegorical monsters the "Leviathans," the "Cocks," the "Bulls," and the rest of the ever-repeated reproaches to the Talmud, have to play their instructive part. All these are taken almost bodily from the Zendavesta, which in itself represents more or less a protest against the Vedic faith. They are either reduced into their original meanings in the Talmud, or they are ridiculed and made to inculcate some moral lesson. On the other hand the famous "Sea Fairy Tales," taken from Vedic sources, are made into guises of political, if not religious satires. When the Persians broke off from the Indians, the good gods of the old system became the bad gods of the new, and *vice versâ*.

After dwelling on the causes of the obscurity of some of the matters found in the Talmud and their apparent want of dignity—occasioned partly by the circumstances and the manners of the period, and partly by the neglect of copyists, and the undying fanaticism which ever tried to "improve" this important record of humanity—the speaker instanced the various modes in which the Talmudical authors figured to themselves the Messianic times, and the utter and absolute freedom with which they expressed their opinion on this as on every other religious topic. Every sermon, every discourse that treated of holy things ended with the one comprehensive formula "And may to Sion come the Redeemer!" The opinions of the modes and objects of his coming are many and various; the Talmud records them all equally, faithfully, and without comment, save that to him who says the Messiah is no longer to be expected, it adds, "May God forgive him!"

Further remarks on the value of the Talmud as a "human study" in our days, and the scientific manner in which it should be treated, followed. It required, the speaker said, a certain system and method entirely of its own, being itself in almost every respect an exceptional work. Above all, however, the investigator should not only be armed with patience and perseverance such as is scarcely needed for any other branch of study, but he must leave all and every prejudice, religious and otherwise, behind him. Then, and then only, might he hope to gather in it some of the richest and most precious fruits of human thought and fancy.

The legend of Elijah standing on the mountains of Judæa three days before the appearance of the Messiah, proclaiming peace and redemption to all mankind, followed by the legendary vision of the final consummation of all things, and of the abolition of Hell and Death,—one of the grandest legends ever conceived,—formed the conclusion of the discourse.

IV.

A LECTURE

DELIVERED AT THE

MIDLAND INSTITUTE, BIRMINGHAM.

——•◦•——

DECEMBER 7, 1868.

DR. EMANUEL DEUTSCH explained that the Talmud is the work which embodies the civil and canonical law of the Jewish people; that it consists of the *Mishnah*, or text, and the commentary, or *Gemara*; that its contents have reference not merely to religion, but also to philosophy, medicine, history, jurisprudence, and the various branches of practical duty; that it is, in fact, a law civil and criminal, national and international, human and divine, forming a kind of supplement to the Pentateuch—a supplement such as it took 1000 years of a nation's life to produce; and that it is not merely a dull treatise, but it appeals to the imagination and the feelings, and to all that is noblest and purest; that between the rugged boulders of the law which bestrew the pass of the Talmud there grow the blue flowers of romance and poetry, in the most catholic and Eastern sense. Parable, tale, gnome, saga—its elements are taken from heaven and earth; but chiefly and most lovingly from the human heart and from Scripture, for every verse and every word in this latter became, as it were, a golden nail upon which it hung its gorgeous tapestries. But it would be a great mistake to suppose that the poet's cunning had been at work in the Talmud. It was only his heart. The chief feature and charm of its contents lay in their utter *naïveté*. Taken

L

up, as they appeared, at random, and told in their simple, inartistic, unconscious form, they touched the soul. But nothing could be much more distressing than to attempt to take them out of their antique garb and press them into some kind of modern fashionable dress; or worse still, to systematise and methodise them. It would be as well to attempt to systematise the songs of the bird in the wood, or a mother's parting blessing. He had, however, to endeavour to reproduce a portion of the contents of the Talmud, in their own vague sequence and phraseology; and he should confine himself almost to smaller productions, as parables, apophthegms, allegories, and the like minute things, which were most characteristic, and required little explanation.

The fundamental law of all human and social economy in the Talmud was the utter and absolute equality of man. It was pointed out that man was created alone—not more than one at different times, lest one should say to another, " I am of the better or earlier stock." And it failed not to mention that man was created on the last day, and that even the gnat was of more ancient lineage than man. In a discussion which arose among the doctors as to which was the most important passage in the whole Bible, one pointed to the verse, "And thou shalt love thy neighbour as thyself." The other contradicted him and pointed to the words, "And these are the generations of man "—not black, not white, not great, not small—but *man*.

Or, again, they pointed out the words, "And these are the ordinances by which men shall live "—not the priest, or the levite—but men. The law given on Mount Sinai, the masters said, though emphatically addressed to one people, belonged to all humanity. It was not given in any King's land, not in any city, or inhabited spot, lest the other nations might say, "We know nothing of it." It was given on God's own highway, in the desert—not in the darkness and stillness of night, but in plain day, amid thunder and lightning. And why was it given on Sinai? Because it is the lowliest and the meekest of the mountains—to show that God's spirit rests only upon them that are meek and lowly in their hearts. The Talmud taught that religion was not a thing of creed or dogma or faith merely, but of active goodness. Scripture said, "Ye shall *walk* in the words of the Lord." " But the Lord is a consuming fire—how can man walk in His way?" "By being," they answered, " as He is—merciful, loving, long-suffering. Mark how on the first page of the Pentateuch God clothed the naked—Adam; and on the last He buries the dead—Moses. He heals the sick, frees the captives, does good to His enemies, and He is merciful both to the living and to the dead."

In close connection with this stood the relationship of men to their neighbours—chiefly to those beyond the pale of creed or nationality. The Talmud distinctly and strongly set its face against proselytism, pronouncing it to be even dangerous to the commonwealth. There was no occasion, it said, for conversion to Judaism, as long as a man fulfilled the seven fundamental laws. Every man who did so was regarded as a believer to all intents and purposes. It even went so far as to call every righteous man an Israelite. Distinct injunctions were laid down with regard to proselytes. They were to be discouraged and warned off, and told that the miseries, privations, and persecutions which they wished to take upon themselves were unnecessary, inasmuch as all men were God's children, and might inherit the hereafter; but if they persisted, they were to be received, and were to be ever afterwards treated tenderly. They illustrated this by a beautiful parable of a deer coming from the forest among a flock of sheep, and being driven off at night and the gate shut against it, but being after many trials, at length received and treated with more tenderness than any of the sheep. Next stood reverence both for age and youth. They pointed out that not merely the tables of the law which Moses brought down the second time from Sinai, but also those which he broke in his rage, were carefully placed in God's tabernacle, though useless. Reverence old age. But all their most transcendental love was lavished on children. All the verses of Scripture that spoke of flowers and gardens were applied to children and schools. "Do not touch mine anointed ones, and do my prophets no harm." "Mine anointed ones" were school children, and "my prophets" their teachers.

The highest and most exalted title which they bestowed in their most poetical flights upon God himself was that of "Pedagogue of Man." There was drought and the most pious men prayed and wept for rain, but none came. An insignificant-looking person at length prayed to Him who caused the wind to blow and the rain to fall, and instantly the heavens covered themselves with clouds, and the rain fell. "Who are you," they cried, "whose prayers alone have prevailed?" And he answered, "I am a teacher of little children." When God intended to give the law to the people, He asked them whom they would offer as their guarantees that they would keep it holy, and they said Abraham. God said, "Abraham has sinned—Isaac, Jacob, Moses himself—they have all sinned; I cannot accept them." Then they said "May our children be our witnesses and our guarantees." "And God accepted them; even as it is written "From the mouths of the wee babes has He founded His empire." Indeed the relationship of man to God they could not express more pregnantly than by the most familiar words which occurred from one end of the Talmud to the other, "Our Father in Heaven."

Another simile was that of bride and bridegroom. There was once a man who betrothed himself to a beautiful maiden, and then went away, and the maiden waited and waited and he came not. Friends and rivals mocked her, and said "He will never come." She went into her room, and took out the letters in which he had promised to be ever faithful. Weeping she read them and was comforted. In time he returned, and enquiring how she had kept her faith so long, she showed him his letters. Israel in misery, in captivity, was mocked by the nations for her hopes of redemption; but Israel went into her schools and synagogues and took out the letters, and was comforted. God would in time redeem her, and say, "How could you alone among all the

mocking nations be faithful?" Then Israel would point to
the law and answer, "Had I not your promise here?"

Next to women, angels were the most frequent bearers of
some of the sublimest and most ideal notions in the Talmud.
"Underneath the wings of the seraphim," said the Talmud,
"are stretched the arms of the Divine mercy, ever ready to
receive sinners." Every word that emanated from God was
transformed into an angel, and every good deed of man
became a guardian angel to him. On Friday night, when
the Jew left the synagogue, a good angel and a bad angel
accompanied him. If, on entering the house, he found the
table spread, the lamp lighted, and his wife and children in
festive garments, ready to bless the holy day of rest, the
good angel said, "May the next Sabbath and all following
ones be like unto this; peace unto this dwelling—peace!"
and the bad angel, against his will, was compelled to say
"Amen." If, on the contrary, everything was in confusion,
the bad angel rejoiced, and said "May all your Sabbaths and
week days be like this;" while the good angel wept and said
"Amen." According to the Talmud, when God was about
to create man, great clamouring arose among the heavenly
host. Some said, "Create O God a being who shall praise
Thee on earth, even as we sing Thy glory in heaven."
Others said, "O God, create no more! Man will destroy the
glorious harmony which Thou hast set on earth, as in
heaven." Of a sudden, God turned to the contesting host
of heaven, and deep silence fell upon them all. Then before
the throne of glory there appeared bending the knee the
Angel of Mercy, and he prayed, "O Father, create man. He
will be Thine own noble image on earth. I will fill his heart
with heavenly pity and sympathy towards all creatures;
they will praise Thee through him." And there appeared
the Angel of Peace, and wept: "O God, man will disturb
Thine own peace. Blood will flow; he will invent war, confusion, horror. Thy place will be no longer in the midst of
all Thy earthly works." The Angel of Justice cried, "You
will judge him, God! He shall be subject to my law, and
peace shall again find a dwelling-place on earth." The

Angel of Truth said, "Father of Truth, cease! With man you create the lie." Out of the deep silence then was heard the divine word : "You shall go with him—you, mine own Seal, Truth; but you shall also remain a denizen of heaven —between heaven and earth you shall float, an everlasting link between both."

The question was asked in the Talmud, why children were born with their hands clenched, and men died with their hands wide open; and the answer was that on entering the world, man desired to grasp everything, but when he was leaving it all slipped away. Even as a fox, which saw a fine vineyard, and lusted after its grapes, but was too fat to get in through the only opening there was, until he had fasted three days. He then got in; but having fed, he could not get out, until he had fasted three days more. "Poor and naked man enters the world; poor and naked does he leave." To woman the Talmud ascribed all the blessings of the household. From her emanated everything noble, wise, and true. It had not words enough to impress man with the absolute necessity of getting married. Not only was he said to be bereaved of peace, joy, comfort, and faith without a wife, but he was not even called a man. "Who is best taught?" it asked; and the answer is, "He who has learned first from his mother."

Alexander the Great was repeatedly spoken of in the Talmud. In his travels in the East, one day he wandered to the gate of Paradise, and knocked. The guardian angel asked, "Who is there?" "Alexander." "Who is Alexander?" "Alexander, you know—*the* Alexander—Alexander the Great—Conqueror of the world." "We know him not —he cannot enter here. This is the Lord's gate; only the righteous enter here." Alexander begged something to show he had been there, and a small portion of a skull was given him. He took it away, and showed it contemptuously to his wise men, who brought a pair of scales and placing the bone in one, Alexander put some of his silver and gold against it in the other; but the silver and gold "kicked the beam." More and more silver and gold were put into the scale and at last all his Crown jewels and diadems were in, but they all flew upwards like feathers before the weight of the bone. Then one of the wise men took a grain of dust from the ground and placing it on the bone, the scale went up. The bone was that which surrounded the eye,—and nothing will ever satisfy the eye, until grains of dust and ashes are placed upon it, down in the grave.

In his travels Alexander came to Ethiopia, and a cause was decided in his presence by the king of that country. A man who had recently purchased land found a treasure upon it, which was claimed by the seller of the land. The king reconciled the rival claims by suggesting that the son of one of the men should marry the daughter of the other, and that the treasure should be given as the dowry. Alexander was moody, and the King of Ethiopia asked, " Are you dissatisfied with my judgment?" "Well," Alexander said, "I am not dissatisfied; I only know we should have judged differently in our country." "How?" "We should of course have taken the treasure at once into the King's exchequer, and both those men would have been beheaded on the spot." The King of Ethiopia said, "Allow me to ask a question. Does the sun ever shine in your country?" "Of course." "And does it ever rain?" "Certainly." "Have you any cattle?" "Yes." "Then that is the reason why the sun shines, and the rain rains—it can't be for you."

The lecturer concluded by remarking that what he had been able to bring before the audience proved as it were but a drop in a vast ocean of the Talmud—that strange, wild, weird ocean, with its leviathans, and its wrecks of golden argosies, and with its forlorn bells that send up their dreamy sounds ever and anon, while the fisherman bends upon his oar, and starts and listens, and perchance the tears may come into his eyes.

V.

NOTES OF A LECTURE ON SEMITIC PALÆOGRAPHY.[1]

CLOSELY connected as the sciences of Palæography and Epigraphy are with almost every province of historical, chronological, linguistic, and archæological studies, their Semitic branch was, Mr. Deutsch said, perhaps, of the greatest importance of all. It is only our own generation that seems to have become alive to the fact that our knowledge both of the East and the beginnings of the West must be sought, or at least complemented, in the East. Considering that most of those earliest Hellenic ornaments—vases and gems, vessels and garments, animals and vegetable substances, weights and measures, and even musical instruments, mentioned in the oldest remnants of Greek literature, the Homeric writings—were imported into Europe, together with their Semitic names, by Semites, it must indeed be evident at once how large must be the share of Semitism in the origin of modern civilization. Semite arts and sciences, gods and inhabitants, were grafted upon Indo-Germanic strata, and the peculiarly happy union of the two principal elements of culture produced the vast glory of the antique. He then traced the figures of our own alphabet (the very name of which but denotes the first two Semitic letters) through the dark stages of Etruscan, Old-Italic, Old-Hellenic, &c., back to the rude scrawls of pre-historic Phœnician stonecutters; and further, our own mode of writing

---

[1] From the 'Athenæum,' No. 2022, July 28, 1866. Re-printed by permission.

from left to right, through the boustrophedon, or writing both ways, as the ox ploughs, to the primitive manner of writing from right to left, in Semitic languages, and as those Eastern nations that have adopted the Arabic character still do. There was, Mr. Deutsch said, a strange kind of fascination connected with that peculiar study; it was, to a certain extent, like following the forms of the characters drawn by the hand of some great man, or some one peculiarly dear to us, from the stage of their full development and vigour to the first childish scribbles, through all the phases of intervening years with their many events. We should, probably, find them always different, yet always alike in their broad outline. The wide vista displayed to us by a retrospective glance at all the tribes and idioms that made use of this alphabet, which suddenly, as it were, found itself called upon, poor and vowelless as it was, to serve them all to its best abilities, is amazing. No less the extraordinary adaptability it proved in this emergency, and the infinite variety of shapes it subsequently had to assume, according to time and clime. These and a crowd of other speculations lifted the discipline which led to them almost out of the humble sphere of a philological handmaiden to that of a mistress of an immense domain; not only yielding much solid, substantial produce in the way of scientific results, but also giving full sway to those larger and deeper thoughts of the universal solidarity of humanity, which almost touch the realms of poetry.

Semitism, in its earliest and most widespread influence upon Europe, is chiefly represented by the Phœnicians. To their insignificant country alone it was given to do what neither Egypt nor Assyria, with all their perfection of industry and art, were able to do, viz. to supply the link between the East and the West. Communicating, by Arabia and the Persian Gulf, with India and the coast of Africa towards the Equator, and on the north, along the Euxine, with the borders of Scythia, beyond the Straits of Gibraltar, with Britannia, if not with the Baltic, they introduced the elements of culture to the remotest ends of the earth; everywhere planting colonies, erecting temples, and laying the foundations for a more humane life than the aborigines in most of those far-off lands had ever dreamt of. An outline of Phœnician commerce, Mr. Deutsch said, would comprise almost every conceivable object of home or foreign growth, or manufacture; but of Phœnician Art,—"in gold and silver, in brass and iron, in purple and in blue, in stone and in timber, in fine linen and precious stones,"—infinitely little has survived; and, touching on Phœnician religion,—a symbolical worship of natural phenomena, of abstract ideas, and of allegories and special Numina,—the complete identity of many deities thus created with classical deities was dwelt upon. A sketch of Phœnician literature, which must have been most extensive, and completely in accordance with their high state of cultivation and refinement, was then given. This literature consisted, first, of a vast number of theological, or rather theogonical works, whose authors were reputed to be the gods themselves, and which were only accessible to the priests or to those initiated in the mysteries. From the allegorical explanation of these writings sprang a vast cosmogony, insignificant fragments of which only have come down to us, mutilated and misinterpreted by their Greek reporters. Next to this sacred literature stands their didactic poetry, somewhat related to the Orphic. We further know of their erotic works, of works on history, geography, navigation, agriculture,—in short, of almost every modern branch of science and *belles-lettres*.

But all this wealth of literature has perished, and the scanty extracts that may have survived in foreign literatures cannot be looked upon as really authentic. For genuine and unadulterated "literature" we must look to the original monuments themselves; to inscriptions on coins and weights, on votive tablets, on sacrificial stones, on tombstones, and on sarcophagi. Broken utterances, faintest echoes though they be, out of them there might perhaps be reconstructed more of the life of that wonderful nation, that had so many things in common with the English, than has hitherto been dreamt of.

Before proceeding to speak of these monuments themselves, and principally of those most recently excavated, Mr. Deutsch alluded to a notion which seems to be still abroad, that the Phœnician, being a lost language, which is only now being recovered by degrees, offered the same amount of uncertainty in some of its decipherings as hieroglyphics, cuneiforms, &c., were supposed still to offer. The only difficulties that present themselves to the Phœnician decipherer consist either in the newness of terms met, which do not offer any Semitic analogies; or in their peculiar orthographical or grammatical forms; or, finally, in the similar shapes some of the characters (B, D and R principally) exhibit. But here, again, the difficulty is soon solved by the context; almost with the same ease with which the vowels are supplied in any Semitic language, or the sometimes missing diacritical points in any of the idioms written in Arabic characters.

Mr. Deutsch next enumerated the most important recent discoveries on the soil of Phœnicia (Sidon) and her numerous colonies, first giving an outline of the history of Phœnician investigation in Europe. Phœnician finds have been very frequent of late years. While up to the middle of the last century hardly anything was known of the existence of Phœnician inscriptions, there is scarcely a museum in Europe now which does not boast of one or two lapidary or numismatic monuments, that have to tell some tale or other in the aboriginal tongue of Canaan. Since Pococke's discovery of thirty-one inscriptions on the site of ancient Citium, Malta, Sardinia, Carthage, Algiers, Tripoli, Athens, Marseilles, and a host of other places, have given up a number of these eloquent contributions to the history of the Semites who once dwelt upon these spots. The most extensive find lately made consists of nearly a hundred inscriptions, excavated on the site of ancient Carthage,—all votive tablets, with but two exceptions. One of these exceptions is a precious sacrificial tariff, which complements in the happiest way a similar sacred document, found some years ago at Marseilles. The other is probably a tombstone, erected by a

father to his son. Another highly interesting monument
was excavated about 1863 in Sardinia, and consists of the
base of an altar, inscribed with a trilingual (Latin-Greek-
Phœnician) legend. A comparison of these three translations, or rather paraphrases, among themselves, leads to
most interesting results in many branches of Greek, Roman,
and Phœnician antiquities, and chiefly in comparative
hierology; while the Phœnician inscription itself, the
largest of the three, is perhaps one of the most curious
ever discovered, yielding a number of new linguistic, mytho-
logical and orthographical items. After dwelling upon other
bilingual, Assyro-Phœnician, Græco-Phœnician, &c., remnants, and upon the excavations by recent French explorers
and their results, Mr. Deutsch turned to the Himyaritic
inscriptions, lately embodied in the collections of the British
Museum, consisting of votive bronze tablets found in South
Arabia, and couched in a long-lost idiom, the nearest approach to which is traced in the present Amharic: allied to
Ethiopic and Hebrew. The numerous Hebrew inscriptions
which have of late been brought to light, the tombstones
from Aden (with several Himyaritic Alephs), the many
hundreds of tombstones copied in various parts of the
Crimea, some of which bore very remote dates indeed, the
inscription on the "Tomb of the Kings," with its double
(Syriac and Hebrew) characters, the family vault of the
"Bene Chezir," indicated by a Hebrew inscription in archaic
square characters on the "Tomb of St. James," with liga-
tures such as were only found on the so-called "Chaldeo-
Egyptian" Papyri, and the other minor epigraphs discovered
by Renan, De Saulcy, De Vogüé, and others, in their various
exploratory tours in the Holy Land, were briefly explained.
Finally, Mr. Deutsch described the photographs with Hebrew
and Samaritan inscriptions (see *Athenæum*, No. 2018), consisting chiefly of representations of the famous Samaritan
Scroll, inscriptions on synagogues in Galilee, and the probably most ancient Samaritan epigraph on a stone immured
in a wall of a mosque near Nablus,—the reading of which he
has been able fully to restore,—which were brought home

by the first expedition set on foot by the Exploration Fund. From the future activity of this association Mr. Deutsch expected valuable results also for those sciences which had formed the theme of his paper.

Mr. Deutsch concluded by briefly recapitulating the various points of interest connected with the pursuit of these studies, and the large gain derived from them for the varied disciplines of human knowledge. Semitic Palæography and Epigraphy supplied one of the strongest links in that chain which binds the remotest ages to our own; and visibly represent, as it were, the undying continuity and solidarity of civilized humanity.

VI.

NOTES OF THREE LECTURES ON
SEMITIC CULTURE.[1]

MAY 29, 1869.

Mr. DEUTSCH alluded first to his recent but hurried journey through the lands of Shem, and described with much vividness the ancient cities of Jerusalem, Damascus, Tyre and Sidon, now in sadness, but yet full of intensity of life and beauty: and spoke of the touching sight of the faces, with their thousand years of woe written in them, that lean against the wailing-place on the walls of Jerusalem. He then glanced very briefly at the intellectual work achieved by the nations conventionally called Shemites, and the influence exercised by them upon the life and thought of the ancient and modern world. The term, vaguely applied as it is to Assyrians, Chaldeans, Babylonians, Syrians, Ethiopians, Phœnicians, Hebrews, Arabs, and other kindred races, was, he said, an acknowledged misnomer, embracing certain descendants of Ham, such as the Phœnicians and Ethiopians, and excluding others, descendants of Shem, such as Elamites, Assyrians, and Babylonians, as enumerated in the genealogical table in Genesis. These peoples have ever been grouped together as speaking what were called the Oriental tongues; but at the end of the last century, the gigantic linguistic discoveries in the realms of Eastern philology—notably of Sanskrit and Zend—imperiously called for some clear and specific name to distinguish them from the Aryan or Sanskrit-speaking peoples. To each and every term some objection was raised, until the one that was on all hands

---

[1] Delivered at the Royal Institution, Albemarle Street.

allowed to be utterly and hopelessly wrong, the term Semitic, was unanimously received, and has been perpetuated to this day. All these, and particularly the Phœnicians, Hebrews, and Arabs, exhibit some most striking common features. Apart from their languages, which are identical as to fundamental elements and structure, there are found among them all certain traits of character, partly traceable to the very nature of the Semitic homesteads; such as pliability combined with iron fixedness of purpose, depth and force, yearning for dreamy ease, together with the capacity for hardest work, and the love of abstract thought. But of all their gifts the one that has told most upon humanity, and left upon it their impress for all times to come, touching upon its highest problems and fixing its noblest aims, is that to them, to the Shemites alone, we owe our spiritual conception of the Deity—monotheism. No Aryan, however elevated in mind, could have formed that idea of God which would seem to have been innate in the Semitic mind. Yet so far from this conception arising from an "instinct," as has been asserted, it is the product of a series of reflections, which, clad in legendary garb, still form one of the favourite topics of Semitic folk-lore. Yet, paradoxical though it may seem, this "instinct" did not prevent the Shemites, with one exception, from being "idolaters." And this one exception, the Jews, did not really cease to be idolaters until all the horrors of fire and sword, of war, exile, and the utter blotting out of political existence, had come upon them: punishments all of which are ascribed to this very deviation from monotheism. And yet a sharp distinction is visible between, for instance, the Indo-Germanic and the Semitic mythology, or rather conception of the Cosmos and its ruling spirits. There never was a real division of powers in the Semitic system, notwithstanding its apparent Dualism. Pantheism in the Greek sense is utterly unknown to the Shemites. Nature is nothing but that which has been begotten, and is ruled absolutely by the one Great Absolute Power. And only in the more or less abstract conception of this one Power are found what differences there do exist in the Semitic creeds in their respective stages. There is but one name for this

Being: Baal, El, Elohim, Allah, Elyon, Astarte-Tanis—
meaning one and all of them, Might, Almighty, Omnipotent,
the Divine Judge—while Jehovah denotes the mercy which
revokes and tears up the dread decree before it is carried into
execution. Abraham and his descendants were the first
apostles of conscious and absolute monotheism.

Semitic arts and sciences, though of the strongest possible
influence upon Europe, always remained inferior—or proportionately less developed—to those of the West, which
they had to a certain extent begotten; while their literature
in some instances stands absolutely foremost, and rules
supreme to this day. The Shemites, from some strange
idiosyncrasy, perpetuated by religious ordinances, abhorred,
all of them, at certain stages, the making visible pictures
of things they revered, loved, worshipped. And all the
intensity of their most intense souls, their loves and their
yearnings, took refuge in the realms of imagination. The
greatest charm of these tales and songs consists just in this,
that, however unearthly and ethereal are the beings introduced, they are always most thoroughly human, thus appealing to our best and most catholic sympathies. The great
storehouse, the Midrash, teems with gems that have been
scattered broadcast over not merely the whole Jewish and
Mohammedan, but over also the classical and Christian
world, together with all those other elements of civilisation
and refinement which the Shemites never ceased to impart
to our Western lands. A passing allusion was here made to
the strange, mysterious instinct, so to say, that has ever and
will ever draw both peoples and individuals to the Semitic
East, to seek some balm, or comfort, or light. The Crusades
were nothing more nor less than the outcome of one of these
wild yearnings eastwards that had spread over Europe; and
the only tangible results from them were certain beautiful
Saga-cycles, which we now call mediæval, which will be said
and sung as long as humanity endures. He then dwelt upon
the characteristics of the Shemitic language, where the consonants are everything and the vowels nothing: the poverty
of flexion and crudeness of syntax, as compared with the
Indo-Germanic languages.

Turning to the principal nations, mentioned individually, Mr. Deutsch first drew a sketch of Babylonian culture, such as it is revealed, however fragmentarily, by the semi-fabulous records said to be written by Berosus, the priest of Bel, and by such surviving ruins as the "Tower of Babel" with their cuneiform records, and pointed out how strong had been its influence upon those Shemites who lived in the full light of history. He touched upon the creed and the concomitant tenets and rites of the Babylonians, essentially a worship of the Hosts of Heaven, much inveighed against by the Prophets. Their chief worship was of Baal, Bel, the Sun, and of Mylitta or Astarte, the moon, the female principle: the planets, the stars, birds, fishes, &c. The result of this devotion to supernatural as well as natural objects was three-fold; it led to astrology, astronomy, and to the creation and maintenance of a kalendar of singular accuracy. The second of these was utilized by the seafaring Phœnicians.

The Phœnicians form, in some respects, the most important fraction of the whole group of antique nations, notwithstanding that they sprung from the most obscure and insignificant families: this fraction when settled, was constantly exposed to inroads by new tribes, was utterly conquered and sub-jected by utter strangers when it had taken a great place among nations, and yet by industry, by perseverance, by acuteness of intellect, by unscrupulousness and want of faith, by adaptability and pliability when necessary, and dogged defiance at other times, by total disregard of the rights of the weaker, they obtained the foremost place in the history of their times, and the highest reputation not only for the things they did, but for many that they did not. They were the first systematic traders, the first miners and metallur-gists, the greatest inventors (if we may apply such a term to those who kept an ever-watchful look-out for the inventions of others and immediately applied them to themselves with some grand improvements on the original idea); they were the boldest mariners, the greatest colonizers, who at one time held not only the gorgeous East but the whole of the then half-civilized West in fee—who could boast of a form of government approaching to constitutionalism; who of all nations of their time stood highest in practical arts and sciences, and into whose laps there flowed an unceasing stream of the world's entire riches, until the day came when they began to care for nothing else, and the enjoyment of material comforts and luxuries took the place of the thirst for and search after knowledge. Their piratical prowess and daring was undermined; their colonies, grown strong enough to stand alone, fell away from them, some after a hard fight, others in mutual agreement or silently: and the nations, in whose estimation and fear they had held the first place and been tributary to them, disdained them, ignored them, and finally struck them utterly out of the list of nations, till they dwindled away miserably, a warning to all who should come after them.

Of their powers of adaptation, we may take, for example, their adoption of the Babylonian system of weights and measures, which they transmitted through the Greeks to Europe; while in the matter of writing, they were in no sense the originators of the alphabet which we use to this day, for this they developed, or rather simplified, out of the so-called cuneiforms—an originally hieroglyphical or monogrammic kind of writing, which, by degrees, begot the most complicated systems, and still offers not inconsiderable difficulties; but their improvements and modifications of which have been spread over the whole world.

With all their defects, few, if any people, have left behind them so many impressions of their greatness, or, indeed, so remarkable a name. Thus we find the Phœnicians steering by the Pole-star—a discovery of the highest moment in Navigation—while the Greeks still clung to Ursa Major; and they sent out an expedition in the time of Necho which lasted three years, but which rounded the Cape at least 2000 years before Vasco da Gama.

Of their form of government we have few details, but it is certain that they practised or allowed an amount of freedom unknown among the nations around their earliest homes or among whom they settled as colonists; and there can be no doubt that on the whole their rule was beneficial and generally humane: the Greeks and Romans were indebted to them immeasurably, and we ourselves not a little. About the origin of their name there has been considerable doubt : some deriving it from *phoinix*, the date-palm, others connecting it directly with the legend of Cadmus, literally the "man from the East," who appears as their leader from Phœnicia to Europe.

The religion of the Phœnicians was a Pantheistic worship of Nature. No nation of antiquity, perhaps, possessed a more endless pandemonium than they did; a circumstance easily explained by their peculiar position and relations. They consisted originally of a variety of tribes, each of whom had their own special deities, and although the supreme Numenor, the principle of their chief deity, was probably the same with both, those Phœnicians who dwelt in the north had different names and attributes in some respects for their gods from those who dwelt in the south. Their one peculiarity is that they divided their conception of the divine essence more politically, or geographically, than philosophically. It was the local sanctuaries no less than the peculiar attributes that distinguish the different Baalim as to their names. Besides the supreme God of the whole country, there is Baal-Zur, Baal-Zidon, Baal-Hermon, &c., denoting so many geographical localities. Their Melkart is not a special deity, but merely means the king of the special city of that particular colony. Baal simply means *lord*, while Moloch means sacrifice. Some curious classical legends are clearly of Phœnician origin, *e. g.* that of the Minotaur or Moloch-worship in Crete; while one of their ancient festivals, that of the "wedding of the land and sea," is still performed every year at modern Tyre. The Phœnician form of government, with its king-high-priest, its senate and commons, resembled very closely modern constitutionalism: thus allowing the fullest development of industry and artistic manufactures—manufactures such as we meet with under their original Phœniko-Hebrew names in the Homeric poems. They were the inventors of the manufacture of glass and of vitreous pastes; and, for many centuries, after their name had been forgotten in their own land, ships, which we may well call Phœnician, conveyed their cargoes of sand from Mount Carmel to the glass-factories of mediæval Venice. In mining they excelled, the Lebanon supplying them with inexhaustible stores of iron ore: the realistic description of mining in the Book of Job may be remembered. Abundant remains are found of their engravings on copper and gems: while the mighty blocks of the recently excavated wall of the Temple at Jerusalem—doubtless the labour of Solomon by the hands of Hiram's men—the still-remaining ruins of Tyre and Aradus, and probably of Tiryns and Mykenæ, attest what they did in their days of grandeur and almost unlimited power.

The many-sided development of Phœnician literature, its science and its *belles-lettres*, its theology and its philosophy, whereof but very few and suspicious fragments survive, was sketched, and the only real and genuine utterances that do exist in lapidary inscriptions were specially enumerated. These — commencing with the inscriptions discovered at Citium by Pococke about a century ago, down to the most recent, in all about 150—are mostly votive or dedicatory to some god or goddess; there are, however, four remarkable exceptions: first, the two levitical or priestly tariffs, indicating the sum and the portions of the sacrifice belonging to the ministering functionaries, the one of which is in Marseilles, the other in the British Museum; further, the celebrated Ashmunazar tomb in the Louvre; and the trilingual (Phœniko-Greek-Latin) inscription of the altar found in Sardinia, now in the museum at Turin; the deciphering of these writings was shown to rest on as firm a basis as that of any Greek or Roman or English lapidary document. Tyre and Sidon, in their present condition, were then described.

JUNE 5.

The second lecture was devoted to the work of the most important representative branch of that family of nations whom we call Shemitic—a people of many fates, of many names. The Bible calls them "the people of God;" Mohammed, the "people of the Book;" Hegel calls them "the people of the Geist;" we know them by the terms

Hebrews, Israelites, or Jews,—terms the indiscriminate use of which Mr. Deutsch strongly deprecated, inasmuch as these terms formed distinct landmarks in the history of the people under consideration. From the dark beginnings of the Mesopotamian times down to the Egyptian bondage the word Hebrew—derived from *Ibri*, meaning from the other side of the Euphrates, or from *Eber* the great-grandson of Shem—points to that idyllic period, the records of which are more or less those of a family only. With the awakening of self-consciousness and nationality they assume the victory-boding and mysterious name of Israel, as the children of him who obtained it after the night-long struggle at Penuel; and from the time of Babylon and the Great Dispersion they are Jews (Yehudin), or descendants of Judah. The history of this last period is unparalleled in the annals of Humanity. It is among them that the Divine Oneness first grew into a dogma, absolute, uncompromising. And speaking of the period between the immigration from Mesopotamia and the emigration to Egypt, Mr. Deutsch pointed out the deeper signification of this emigration than has been usually recognized, since he considered that it represents the course of education by which this people has ever been systematically brought into contact with other nations at the very time of the highest development of the latter; that Egypt, to which they went as rude shepherds and huntsmen from the idyllic, simple, twilight life at home, was Egypt at the most brilliant stage, perhaps, of its culture, as proved by the literature, the arts and the sciences of the time. Yet, at this very period, it is to be remembered, the supreme unity of the Godhead was taught in Egypt to the initiated, although to the uninitiated it was veiled in a cloud of mystery, ceremony, and symbol. Nor are the points of contact between the Egyptian and the Mosaic ritual few. In the scrolls entombed with the dead in those days the name of God is never mentioned save in the guise of the phrase Nuk-pu-nuk, which means *I am that I am*. The Mosaic constitution, political and religious, was explained, as well as the literature begotten at different stages, reflecting the people's mental state from the time of Joshua to that of the establishment of monarchy and the contemporaneous elevation of priestly power and the spread of education. Yet even now they developed little or nothing of the arts and sciences : for these they were dependent upon other nations, chiefly the Phœnicians, to whom they owe most of their commerce. It was with them that they undertook that famous voyage of discovery from which they brought back those strange things, with their purely Sanskrit names, recorded in the Bible. One occupation only seems to have been after their own heart, the tilling of the soil.

The fall of the monarchies and the captivity, chiefly that of Babylon, begins the emphatically Jewish period, which is not ended yet. The story of the Exile remains still to be written, but it will be long before it is accomplished. It is one of the most momentous and problematic of all times. Glimpses are revealed to us of the state of culture of Persia and Babylonia at that period; but never until the contemporary literature is fully known will the relation between the Vedas and the Avesta, Zoroastrianism and the Talmud, be revealed. The analogies between the Persian creed of the time and the Judaism of the captives is so striking that we may fairly doubt which have most influenced the other; we only see clearly the extraordinary and radical change which, within the space of a few generations, came over the exiles under the influence of the civilization and religion of Persia.

To the Dispersion, which began with Babylon and lasts to this hour, is principally due that cosmopolitan element in Judaism which has added so vastly to its own strength and durability, and even, geographically, to the wonderfully rapid spread of Christianity in its beginnings. To this Babylonian exile must be traced some of the most important institutions of the Synagogue. In this same period all those fierce yearnings for a Deliverer, an Anointed, a Messiah— one of the highest and most ideal conceptions of Humanity —found their loudest and most glowing utterance. Then came also all the great basis of the further development of Judaism, the oral Law, which, under the guise of heaping ordinance upon ordinance, in reality, perhaps unconsciously, aimed at the highest mental liberty, the emancipation of the spirit from the letter. They returned to Judæa as brands plucked from the burning: they carried with them their writings, few and scanty in number, embodying their history and their poetry, their law and their legends, saved out of a vast multitude of writings which perished irredeemably, and is now only known to us in faint snatches and echoes. The work of re-organization was wrought by the "Men of the Great Synagogue": the collection of the Canon and the institution of the Targums, or translations, followed. In these popular Aramaic translations they were anxious to avoid all and everything that could mislead and puzzle even the least-prepared member of the community; all anthropomorphisms and things transcendentally or mysteriously worded in the Bible, or apt to give offence, were either omitted or paraphrased. The position of the Meturgeman, or interpretations, and the growth of Targumic literature, its reputed authors, and its influence upon all later versions,—were illustrated by numerous examples. Then came the Masorah, or diplomatic preservation of the Sacred Text, whose germs were also laid in those days, chiefly to check a too free handling of the Scriptural contents. Much was said of the Talmud, of its origin and growth, of its manner of teaching and preaching, its national and its foreign elements, and the influence these things have exercised upon Christianity and Mohammedanism, the latter of which grew out of Judaism at the moment when the great epoch of Talmudical development had been violently brought to an end. The worship in the Synagogue, with the voluntary prayers current at the time, when the simple supplications of old no longer satisfied the yearnings of the people, were explained; and it was shown how the mental progress or decay of the different periods were embodied in the enormous mass of liturgies in which the Jews delighted, every country and city composing their own. The rise of Mohammedanism, and the relation between Muslims and Jews, gave birth to one of the most brilliant epochs in Hebrew literature under the Moorish rule: the Jews and the Spanish-Arabs emulating each other in the renewal of Greek science. The new-born Arabs, carrying everything before them, and appropriating to themselves the learning of all the peoples they conquered in the East and West, made Jewish literature what it now is, kaleidoscopic, cosmopolitan. The period which commenced with Maimonides (whose great work, founded upon the broad principle that the Bible must be expounded in accordance with rational conclusions, became the text-book of the mediæval universities), and which ended with Moses Mendelssohn, was one less of original production than of scholastic, theologic, exegetic philosophy, overshadowed to a great extent by baneful mystic tendencies. But during this period the art of printing was invented; and while bigotry called it the Black Art and the work of the Devil, the Jews hailed it with rapture, and called it "a holy labour"; Jewish printing-presses at once sprung up throughout Europe. The new epoch, however, which commenced with Mendelssohn, is not closed yet. The once proscribed and detested Jews have ever since his day taken a prominent place in the public and scientific life of Europe, in art, in literature, in finance, in politics; they have been in truth the vanguard and missionaries of civilization. And their destiny is not yet fulfilled.

JUNE 12.

This Lecture was devoted to the third representative branch of the Shemites, the Arabs. The Phœnicians came to Europe as traders: the Jews as fugitives: or captives, the Arabs entered it as conquerors. They inaugurated a reign of science, of poetry, of learning, of culture, such as had not been seen since the golden days of Hellas: a culture which has left its traces upon Europe to this day, and which then shone, the only light in utter darkness, over a people brilliant in chivalry and song, full of noble courtesy and of simple piety. The Jews furthered the work of catholic human culture: the Arabs inaugurated modern science. The day of the fall of Granada was one of the saddest days in history. The origin of the primitive Arabs is a matter of the profoundest obscurity—an obscurity both natural and artificial, since with the commencement of Mohammedanism all that had been was declared unworthy of record, and its memorials were wilfully destroyed; thus the "time of ignorance," as that whole previous period was called, became, indeed, a true designation. Enough, however, remains to prove that Arab culture stood in high renown as early as the golden period of Hebrew literature; no higher praise could be bestowed upon the wisdom of Solomon than that it was like unto the wisdom of the Arabs. The Queen of Sheba was an Arab, Job's friends were Arabs, and many other instances: while the period shortly before Mohammed was certainly one of the most brilliant in Arabic literature, emphatically as regards poetry, though the tale of the Moallakat, as poems "suspended" (in the Kaaba), must be rejected.

The double aspect of the Deity which was noticed before as a general feature of early Semitic creeds is found among the heathen Arabs as Nur Allah—God's light—and Alilat the female El, corresponding to the Baal-faced Tanis or Astoreth of the Phœnicians. There are vague traces of a tree and stone worship; the veneration of certain personified divine attributes, and some singular fetishes, with good and evil demons, made up the early Arab religion, which Mohammed came to overthrow, putting Judaism, more or less Arabicized, in its stead. Yet long before Mohammed these things were, even by the herd, recognised as mere intermediators with the great Allah, and their worship would have been abrogated long before if strong interests of another kind had not been attached to their sanctuaries. Besides astrological, genealogical, and dream lore, poetry formed the chief part of ante-Mohammedan literature; and what little has come down of the latter almost outshines what has come later. The Kasida, the favourite poetical form, was devoted to love, valour, and wisdom, its imagery being derived from the desert solitudes around and the starry skies above. In the midst of a nation thus gifted and prepared, but widely scattered, and waiting, as it were, for some rallying-point, Mohammed was born. His early history is surrounded by a legend-cycle, yet the difficulties of arriving at a rational account are not so great as in other cases ; for the history of Islam requires only the discarding certain items, such as his travels in Syria, the monk Sergius, and the rest; because the notion of the influence of Christianity chiefly rests on these. But the influence of Christianity upon this new religion, "the Religion of Abraham," as Mohammed called it, is as scanty as that of heathenism. Indeed, the basis of dogmatic Christianity, viz. the Sonship of Christ, Mohammed inveighed against early and late.

It was Judaism, as developed under the influence of the oral law, which is principally represented in the Koran, not merely with regard to certain rabbinical terms, implying the most important dogmas and doctrines of Judaism, but even some of the most minute Talmudical ordinances are bodily transferred to the new code. The explanation of this phenomenon is found not in isolated personal communications, but in the general position of the Jews of Arabia, who represented the educated and most influential part of the community, and who had long prepared the way for the introduction of that religion of Abraham which Mohammed came to preach to his kin. Mr. Deutsch described the nature of the new revelation and the emphatic manner in which Mohammed protested against the idea that he was able to work miracles, adding that what were reported (such as the night journey) were declared to be visions. The contents of the Koran, the fundamental code of Islamism, were next considered; with the redaction and the masoretic labours bestowed upon it, as well as the style, varying with the periods of the Prophet's life—its whole tone and tenour, and the almost demoniacal influence the book has exercised since its appearance. The two chief divisions of Islam, the practical and the dogmatical, were then discussed; and the general spirit of the religion, as practised by the Koran, not as explained by some later commentators and exegetics, was broadly characterised as one of justice, truth, and mercy.

The Sunnah or oral traditions were then explained, and among the numerous sects which sprang up within Mohammedanism, the Mutazilites, the Sincere Brethren, the Ismailis, were singled out, and their bold speculations ending in the absolute discarding of all Revelation and Supranaturalism, were dwelt upon. Some of the secret fundamental rules of their respective organizations and their missionary canons, were things of no small influence upon mediæval and modern rationalism, producing a vast development of religious thought; they offer the best proof against the common assumption that Islam is identical with mental and religious petrifaction. Among the many points often repeated without being warranted by facts, is the absolute fallacy of the notion that Fatalism is a doctrine of the Koran: it teaches the very contrary doctrine. Mohammed's whole system is one of faith built on hope and fear. Nor did the word Islam originally betoken that absolute and blind submission which it afterwards came to mean, but rather the being at peace and living in accordance with God's words and commands, leading the life of a righteous man; in the sense in which the derivatives of the Semitic Salam occur in early Aramaic.

The Koran for a time seemed to stifle all literature; it was God's own word, and it was enough. But Arabic literature, quickened by the contact with Greek science and the enormous mental activity of the Jews, began to develop anew in Spain, and became encyclopædic. The one branch in which it now again excelled was poetry; yet here the old forms, so well suited to the desert, could no longer be used in luxurious city life; it soon, however, adapted itself to all this, retaining only a vague, undefinable yearning after the infinite that is strangely beautiful. Its influences upon European literature—Dante, Petrarch, Boccaccio—are easily traced; and not unnaturally, since studious youths flocked from all parts of the world to the schools and academies of Spain. It is thus that the Arabs, together with the Jews, stand, as it were at the cradle of modern science. Yet there is certainly now a pause, or rather retrogression in the mental life of that great people: its causes will, however, most surely be amended, and the Arab Shemite will once more take his share in the ruling of the world's destinies.

VII.

EGYPT, ANCIENT AND MODERN.[1]

Re-published by permission.

THIS book is another proof of the vast and wholesome change that is gradually taking place in the learned literature of Germany. Although treating of a most abstruse subject, it is yet not only fit for human reading, but is absolutely one of the most interesting works which we have seen for some time. It consists of a series of essays or lectures delivered before a select circle in Berlin, during the last nine years, by Dr. Brugsch, the eminent Egyptologist. On changing his professorial chair at the Prussian University for his new official post at Cairo, he has published these essays as a farewell gift to his friends in Europe. They are divided into two parts, the first of which contains sketches and reminiscences of his journeys on the Nile, through the desert, and in the streets of Cairo. Teeming as these picturesque descriptions are with valuable and interesting remarks, we refrain from dwelling upon them. We prefer to reserve our space for the second part, in which the latest results of hieroglyphic science are put before us in so lucid and fascinating a manner that we are apt to forget at times how enormous were the labours which produced them.

The first essay of the second part is entitled " An Ancient Egyptian Fairy Tale ; the Oldest Fairy Tale in the World." It is the first German, and altogether the first *complete*, version of the celebrated papyrus acquired by Mrs. D'Orbiney in 1852, which is now in the British Museum. Although,

---

[1] This article appeared in the 'Saturday Review' for December 9, 1865, and reviewed the following work :—'Aus dem Orient.' Von Heinrich Brugsch. Zwei Theile. Berlin: Grosse.

Dr. Brugsch says, the text has for years been before the learned world, nothing but extracts from it—of which we gave an account some time ago—have been translated as yet. And he adds quaintly, that this first version is not a philological trick nor altogether an offspring only of his own fancy. "My humble merit is confined simply and solely to the application to a given text of the rules of hieroglyphical grammar, which in these days have become the common property of science"—a statement of which the followers of Sir G. Cornewall Lewis will do well to make a note. This papyrus dates from the fourteenth century B.C., when Pharaoh Ramses Miamun, the founder of Pithom and Ramses, ruled at Thebes, and literature celebrated its highest triumphs at his brilliant court. Nine pre-eminent *savans* were attached to the person of this king, the contemporary of Moses. At their head stood, as " Master of the Rolls," a certain Kagabu, unrivalled in elegance of style and diction. It was he, probably, who officiated as Keeper at that vast Library at Thebes of which classical writers speak as having borne the inscription " ψυχῆς ἰατρεῖον "—somewhat similar to Frederic II.'s inscription over the Royal Library at Berlin, " Nutrimentum Spiritus." This hieroglyphic document is the only one hitherto known which belongs to the world of fiction. Hymns, exhortations, historical records, accounts of journeys, general essays, eulogies on kings, and *bills*, form the general staple of that very brittle literature. Written expressly "in usum Delphini "—namely, for the Crown Prince, Seti Menephta, son of Rameses II.—our papyrus bears the following critical note, or mark of official censorship :—" Found worthy to be wedded to the names of the Pharaonic Scribe Kagabu and the Scribe Hora and the Scribe Meremapu. Its author is the Scribe Annana, the proprietor of this scroll. May the God Toth guard all the words contained in this scroll from destruction !" In language and manner it resembles most of the productions of its classical period. It is lucid and clear, and though full of poetical fancy, yet simple and unaffected, reminding the reader occasionally of the grand simplicity in word and thought found in Scripture. It further resembles the latter in its occasional monotony and repetitions ; both, however, drawbacks common to nearly all the early documents of different literatures. The tale itself is rather a curious one to be selected for the special reading of a young prince. Its "motive" is the same as in the story of Joseph and Potiphar's wife. The chief persons are two brothers and the wife of the elder one, who brings a false accusation against her young brother-in-law. The latter saves himself from his brother's wrath, and goes, aided by the Sun-God, through a peculiar transformation. The wife meets her well-deserved fate, and the two brothers are in the end restored to each other's esteem and love, and the elder becomes regent of Egypt. Apart from the general literary interest attaching to this relic of more than three thousand years ago—which gains a peculiar significance from the fact that it was first written and read at the very Court of Ramses II. at which Moses was educated—it incidentally reveals so much of the manners and customs, the notions and views, of that peculiar era of ancient Egypt, that we cannot be too grateful for its almost miraculous preservation.

Of more vital interest, however, are those hieroglyphic discoveries which enable us to trace the sojourn of the Israelites in Egypt, in its monuments. Almost all recent investigators of this subject agree that the time between the immigration and the Exodus formed part of one of the most glorious epochs of Pharaonic rule—namely, that of the eighteenth dynasty. For twenty centuries Egyptian sovereigns had held all the country in undisturbed possession, when suddenly, pushed by the Assyrians, Shemitic hordes broke into the Eastern Delta and seized upon it, gradually extending their dominions so as to make even the kings of Upper Egypt tributary. For more than five hundred years the Egyptians bore the yoke of these foreign conquerors— called in the inscriptions either "Amu," *i. e.* "shepherds of oxen," or "Aadu," "detested, wicked ones"—whose kings held court at Tanis (Hauar, Avaris) in much prouder style than the Theban monarchs themselves. Who were the gallant and skilful generals who, by a few bold strokes, re-conquered the independence of Egypt, and expelled or utterly subdued the foreign population, is not known. But this reverse to the fortunes of the native Pharaohs happened, we know for certain, during that eighteenth Theban dynasty, and the three centuries that followed form the most flourish-ing period of Egyptian history. Egyptian armies penetrated into Palestine, marched along the royal road by Gaza and Megiddo to the banks of the Euphrates and Tigris, made Babylon and Nineveh tributary, and erected their last vic-torious columns on the borders of Armenia, where, as the hieroglyphic texts have it, Heaven rests on its four pillars. No doubt these conquests in Asia, and the thousands and thousands of Shemitic prisoners whom the conquerors carried home as slaves, were looked upon in the light of reprisals for the long period of Shemitic oppression. Endless are the processions of figures on the gigantic and apparently in-destructible temple walls erected by these wretched Asiatic prisoners, representing them in the act of carrying water to knead the mortar, forming bricks in wooden frames, spread-ing them out to dry in the sun, carrying them to the buildings in the course of erection, and the like; all this being done under the eye of Egyptian officials, lounging about armed with weighty sticks, while different inscriptions inform us of the nature of the special work done by these "prisoners whom the King has taken, that they might build temples to his gods."

About the middle of the fifteenth century before our era, there arose a new dynasty, the nineteenth, at the head of which stands Rameses I. It is under the long rule of his grandson, Rameses II., who mounted the throne at about 1400, that we meet with the first monumental hints re-garding the events recorded in Scripture. This Per-aa or Pher-ao—literally "High House"—who reigned sixty-six years, erected, so the hieroglyphical sources tell us, a chain of forts or fortified cities from Pelusium to Heliopolis, of which the two principal ones bore the names of "Rameses" and "Pachtum," our biblical "Pithom"; both situated in the present Wadi Tumilat, near the sweet-water canal that joined the Nile with the Red Sea. Papyri of the time of this "Pharaoh of the Exodus" give a glowing description of those new strongholds. In the Papyrus Anastasi (in the British Museum), the scribe Pinebsa reports to his superior, Amenenaput, how very "sweet" and "incomparable" life is in Rameses, how "its plains swarm with people, its fields with birds, and its ponds and canals with fishes; how the meadows glitter with balmy flowers, the fruits taste like unto honey, and the corn-houses and barns overflow with grain." This official further describes the splendid reception given to the king at his first entry (in the tenth year of his reign) into the new city, and how the people pressed forward to salute "him, great in victory." We even find the very name of the Hebrews recorded in the official reports of the day. A papyrus in the Museum of Leyden contains the following, addressed by the scribe Kauitsir to his superior, the scribe Bakenptah :—

"May my Lord find satisfaction in my having complied with the instruction my Lord gave me, saying, Distribute the rations among the soldiers, and likewise among the *Hebrews* (Apuru) who carry the stones to the great city of King Rameses-Miamun, the lover of truth; [and who are] under the orders of the Captain of the police-soldiers, Ameneman. I distribute the food among them monthly, according to the excellent instructions which my Lord has given me."

Similar distinct indications of the people and their state of serfdom are found in another Leyden papyrus, and even in the long rock-inscription of Hamamât. Joseph had never been at the court of an Egyptian Pharaoh, but at that of one of those Shemite kings of Avaris-Tanis; and when, after the expulsion of this foreign dynasty and the quick extinction of the one which overthrew it, Rameses had come to the throne, it was natural enough that "he knew not Joseph."

The Exodus took place under Menephtes, the successor of that second Rameses in the sixth year of whose reign Moses probably was born. In the twenty-first year of his rule, Rameses had concluded a treaty with the Hittites, the text

N

of which is found cut into a stone-wall at Thebes, and in
which occurs the following important passage :—" If the
subjects of King Rameses should come to the King of
the Hittites, the King of the Hittites is not to receive them,
but to force them to return to Rameses the King of Egypt."
This sufficiently explains the fear expressed by the biblical
Pharaoh, lest the people might " go up from the land." The
Shemitic population, subdued and enslaved as they were,
had one glowing desire only—to escape from Egypt, and
join their brethren at home in their wars against the
Pharaohs.

The name of Moses is now universally recognised to be of
Egyptian origin. It is the Mas or Massu of rather frequent
occurrence on the monuments, and means " child." A
certain connection of Egyptian ideas with the Mosaic legislation, its sacrifices, purifications, &c., is also no longer
questioned. But there is one most important monumental
testimony, which is not sufficiently recognised yet, and
which fully proves that to those far-famed Egyptian adepts
of priestly wisdom the sublime doctrine of the Unity of the
Deity was well known, and that the manifold forms of
the Egyptian Pantheon were nothing but religious masks, so
to speak—grotesque allegorical embodiments of that originally pure dogma communicated to the initiated in the
Mysteries. And the initiated took their sublime Confession
of Faith, inscribed upon a scroll, with them even into the
grave. The name of the One God, however, is not mentioned on it, but is expressed only in the circumlocution,
Nuk pu Nuk—" *I am he who I am.*" Who does not instantly
remember the awful " I am that I am " sounding from amid
the flames of the bush ?

We shall not further pursue these and similar points of
high importance touched upon in the essay inscribed "Moses
and the Monuments," but turn to a chapter quaintly entitled
" What the Stones are Saying." It is the vast and varied
number of stone inscriptions found in Egyptian tombs of
which Dr. Brugsch here treats. He finds the reason for the
people dwelling during their lifetime in tents of mud, but

erecting everlasting monuments for their corpses, in their firm conviction of the existence of another, an everlasting, world, to which this present one is merely the entrance-hall. While a general inscription on the walls of these tombs uniformly exhorts the living to praise the Deity gladly, to leave all earthly things behind when the parting moment arrives, and to pray for the dead, there are others upholding most characteristically the advantages and the high rank possessed by the *literatus* in comparison with all other ranks and professions. Thus many are found like the following :—

"What does all this talk about an officer being better off than a scholar amount to? Just look at an officer's life, and see how manifold are his miseries. While still young he is shut up in a military school. He is there punished until they make his head to bleed ; he is stretched out and beaten. After that, he is sent to the wars into Syria. He must wander on rocky heights, he has to carry his bread and drink suspended from his arm, like unto a beast of burden. The water he gets is foul. Then he is marched off to mount guard over the tent. After that, the enemy arrives and catches him, as in a mousetrap. Should he, however, be lucky enough to return to Egypt, he will only be like a worm-eaten block of wood. Should he be sick, he is put on a litter and carried on a donkey's back. His things, meanwhile, are stolen by thieves, and his attendants run away."

Truly a picture of an Egyptian soldier's life worthy of Joseph Bertha, *le Conscrit.* But other trades and professions fare no better when contrasted with the *savant's* noble state. There are similar caricatures from the farmer's or peasant's life, down to that of the barber, "who has to run from inn to inn to get customers." Out of this high opinion of, and eager desire for, literary education and refinement, there grew almost naturally an eminently high ethical and moral code of feeling. Take the following inscription over a tomb at El-Kalb, over four thousand years old :—" He loved his father, he honoured his mother, he loved his brother, and never left his house with an angry heart. A man of high position was never preferred by him to a humbler man." There are many traces even of that chivalrous deference to women which is always found in highly-cultivated nations. The names of the husbands are more often omitted in the genealogical tablets than those of the "Ladies of the House," whose principal ornament, the stones record, was their "love to their wedded lords." They are called in the inscriptions —not generally given to poetic phraseology—"the beautiful palms, whose fruit was tender love," and the most glorious present accorded to the favourites of the Gods is "the esteem of men and the love of women."

The last chapter in the book is a valuable contribution to comparative Indo-Germanic mythology, treating of certain Sagas found both in Firdusi and the Nibelungen, and of a number of mysterious customs and notions common to both Persians and Germans. Although this is no less replete with interesting facts and speculations than the foregoing essays, we cannot further enlarge upon it here. All we can do is once more to thank the eminent author, now dwelling in that land which already has revealed to him so many of its secrets, and to express the hope that, notwithstanding his many official and editorial occupations, he will find leisure again to speak to us thus pleasantly of Pharaonic scrolls and stones.

VIII.

HERMES TRISMEGISTUS.[1]

Re-published by permission.

———◆◇◆———

FEW figures in the Pantheon of the ancient world are as many-sided and mysterious as Hermes, the antique impersonation of Thought. It is he who institutes and practises all sciences, all arts, all professions. A god himself, he is also the Divine councillor and messenger, charioteer and cup-bearer. He is, further, an astronomer, a legislator, a priest, a physician. He plays the lyre, he boxes, he tends the cattle. He is the keeper of dreams, a merchant, a thief, and an author. With the profoundest wisdom and the most recondite lore, he combines the capability of playing cunning tricks and coarse practical jokes. As multifarious as his talents and his trades are also his emblems, his native countries, his parentages, and his names. In Egypt he is—albeit self-created—the son of the Nile and of Isis, and wears the head of an ibis. He presides over the moon, defends the good souls in Hades, and inscribes the names of the kings on the tree of life in Paradise. The wrigglings of a serpent have taught him the art of hieroglyphics, and his own name is first spelt in these new signs, whence perhaps its many variants—Toth, Teti, Teut, &c. In Phœnicia he is one of the eight mystic Kabiri, or mighty ones. His father is the Heaven, his mother the Day. He invents mining and metal-lurgy, medicine and the alphabet—the same, by the way, which we use in these days. His Phœnician name is Kadmus,

---

[1] This article appeared in the 'Saturday Review' for March 30, 1867, and reviewed the following work:— 'Hermès Trismegiste.' Traduction complète, précédée d'une étude sur l'origine des livres hermétiques, par L. Ménard. Ouvrage couronné de l'Institut. Paris: Didier et Cⁱᵉ.

the Primeval or Eastern; also Taaut. Passing over the many various denominations and occupations assigned to the great cosmopolitan by the Babylonians, Pelasgians, Etruscans, and other but vaguely-known peoples, we find him in Greece as the son of Zeus and Maia. How, but four hours old, he steals and eats two oxen of Apollo, and forthwith invents the lyre, whereby he soothes both him and Zeus, is well known. It is he also who chains Prometheus, kills Argus, liberates Io, conducts the goddesses before Paris, and does the thousand and one other things in which, under the guise of allegory, the myths seem to indicate various progressive stages of culture. In Rome, where his rude statue in the earliest days held a purse, his name was Mercury—from *mercari*, to traffic. Merchants used to dip laurel rods into a well near the Porta Capena sacred to him. What stages he and his mystic worship passed through there, until in the latter days he was identified with Anubis himself, we cannot tell. Equally characteristic, however, is the manner in which by slow degrees the archaic trunks or pillars that were intended to represent him were endowed with a bearded head, with a certain symbolic emblem—the removal of which caused Alcibiades' downfall—with the petasus, the caduceus, the palm-tree; and how every successive generation of artists added some new improvement, until at last he grew into that beautiful, half-dreamy, half-artful, beardless youth of glorious proportions, such as we know him in the Vatican and in the British Museum.

When the gods of Greece and Rome went into exile—either degraded into evil spirits or promoted into Christian saints—he returned to the East. Taaut-Kadmus-Hermes-Mercury-Anubis reappears in Arabic and Persian legends as Henoch or Idris, the Mahommedan Elijah. Pitiful is the way in which some Arabic writers try to spell his epithet of Trismegistus, and the elaborate manner in which they explain it. Three times, they say, was he born; in three different places—in Babylonia, in Egypt, in Greece; and three times did he go through life without sin. Further, he was king, philosopher, and priest; or was, did, or did not any three other different things. But the middle ages were as puzzled about this figure as was antiquity itself. Everything about Hermes seemed a mystery and an allegory.

To add to the bewilderment, he had also written Egyptian books. Clemens of Alexandria ascribes to him 42; Jamblichus, 20,000; Manetho the exact number of 36,525. Whether these are the years of a sacred' Egyptian cycle, or so many verses, distichs or hemistichs, or whether they are merely a round figure to express the enormous bulk of sacerdotal writings which Egypt produced, is of small importance here. Suffice it to notice that everything above and below earth and heaven was supposed to be treated in these books—from the most divine mysteries of cosmogony and the essence of God, to the discipline of kings and geography. But no profane eye had ever seen more than the outside of these sacred scrolls, which were carried about in procession on certain feasts, but the contents of which were never revealed to any one beyond the priestly pale. Certain scanty hieratic papyri, treating of medicine, and first deciphered in our days, are the only fragments of this literature extant.

When, in the latter days of Rome, Egypt came to be looked upon as the mother of all wisdom, the greatest curiosity began to be manifested anent these reputed works, the divine mysteries of which might, it was thought, renew the strength of a doomed world. But fire and sword had done their work on the Nile. Every trace of that redeeming literature seemed lost for ever, when all of a sudden, a number of books came to light, nobody knew exactly how, bearing the mighty name of Hermes Trismegistus. They treated, exactly as had been surmised, of the Soul, of God, of Nature, of Transmigration, of Immortality, and other theological and metaphysical questions. They were supposed to have been in Greek, translated from the original Egyptian, or, as was held till within the last two hundred years, from the *Arabic*. A more mysterious production, [and 'one more strangely reflecting the Proteus-like and ubiquitous nature of the God of Dreams, could certainly not be found. These fragments, such as they are now before us, are composed of the most

widely divergent elements under the sun, but withal cunningly woven into one harmonious whole. Most curious,
however, is the theology broached in them, which is Jewish,
Christian, and Platonic, or rather Alexandrian, and yet a
thing of itself. Monotheism, Polytheism, Pantheism, are all
equally represented, but none can call the work its own. In
the middle of the Egyptian Pantheon, with interlocutors
such as Isis, Horos, and Tat, we find the Logos, side by side
with the archaic myths of the Phœnician Cosmogony. The
Gnostic Demiurgos is plainly foreshadowed, and the arguments for immortality are borrowed from the early materialistic schools of Thales, Anaximander, and Anaximenes.
The language, corrupt though it be, at times rises to a grand
melodious eloquence, and in some portions it becomes quite
patent that we have to deal with an originally rhythmical
composition. The Midrash has furnished it with many a
favourite simile, and with many of its most gorgeous poetical
fancies. Altogether, these fragmentary writings seem a
kind of ancient most catholic microcosm, to which all creeds
and all systems have contributed their share, and in which
arguments may be found for and against every metaphysical
and speculative doctrine of East or West, archaic or recent,
that ever was conceived.

The Church Fathers did not know what to make of it all.
That these writings emanated from a heathen—god or man—
was clear enough: but then the dogma of the Trinity
appeared in them, and they call God "Divine Majesty" and
"Father." Some, like Lactantius, held the work to be the
echo of a primeval revelation which was much corrupted in
the course of time. Others, like Jamblichus, felt the strong
hand upon them, and unhesitatingly acknowledged the
transcendental nature of the book. "Truly," he says, "the
way that leads to God, Mercurius has taught and described."
But still, how this wily god should have become possessed of
the true knowledge was a sore puzzle—a puzzle that has
occupied many a generation since, but which the scholiasts,
after their usual manner, have got over by declaring Hermes
to be the Devil incarnate.

It would be interesting indeed to know who really wrote these kaleidoscopic books. There breathes a fervour in them that reminds us of the strange and strong exotic perfume which may cling to a vase during all the centuries of its entombment. A deep yearning for truth, for the under-standing of the great mystery of the Cosmos, makes itself felt in every line. The method is at times that of an adroit, brilliant, quick fencer, who espies every weak point; at times, again, it proceeds with a vague dreaminess, pointing to the stars or to the sea, and both thought and voice seem hushed. There are sudden outbursts of love and of faith, profoundly poetical and genuine. And through the whole there runs a deep bitter sadness, as over a world of beauty and joy which is about to sink back into chaos. That there is also to be found in these vilely mutilated and much "improved" fragments, longwindedness and clumsiness, feebleness and venom, will not astonish those who are accus-tomed to see the Censor rampant in ancient books which, according to his notion, did not quite agree with the true and orthodox faith of his own time. Perhaps, also, ancient palimpsest-manufacturers produced supplements to Mercury long before the goldmakers of the middle ages turned their attention to the production of Hermetic literature. But who wrote the Nibelungen, who the Vedas, who the Book of Job?

Much more useful, however, for the understanding of the book than the knowledge of its author's name, real or ficti-tious, is the time in which he wrote. And of that time we can just see the dim outlines. Of all the strange phases in the religious history of mankind, none is so strange, none so fraught with deep philosophical and psychological problems, as that which followed the introduction of Christianity into the ancient world. Rome had then well nigh completed her conquests. The barriers of East and West were broken down, and from the remotest corners of the empire philosophers and priests, scholars and teachers, flocked to Alexandria, to Athens, to Rome, the chief academies and the emporiums of thought. Here they discussed their respective creeds and

systems, and, however widely differing in the beginning, in
the end they had frequently exchanged and amalgamated
them, utterly unconscious of the process.   Eclecticism was
altogether the chief characteristic of that period.   Alexandria
had scholasticized, allegorized, and symbolized so long that
everything was at last explained to mean its very reverse.
Athens, or rather the educated classes of Greece, were votaries
of a Platonism identical with scepticism.   As for Rome herself, that acute policy of hers which so readily admitted the
gods of Egypt and Persia into her promiscuous pantheon had
begun to bear the bitter fruit of grovelling superstition and
unbridled licentiousness.   To all this there came the teachings of Judaism, which through its adherents had spread
over a great part of the ancient world.   The pure ethics of
that faith, even before they were brought out more prominently by Christianity, the rigorous austerity with which
the Jews clung to their strange symbolic tenets—nay, the
exclusive spirit of Judaism itself—had something awe-in-
spiring to the antique mind.   The irresistible manner in
which Christianity swept from the Euphrates to the Ganges,
and from the Nile to the Tiber, taking by storm a whole
world agitated to its lowest depths, and yearning for some
new and more human faith than any it had known before,
need not be dwelt upon.   But what concerns us here is the
fact that all the ancient creeds seemed of a sudden to unite
against this common enemy.   Polytheism, doomed to die,
would not surrender easily, but looked for allies even in the
camp of purest Monotheism.   It used every effort, marshalled
every argument, touched every string.   And when we read
Julian the Apostate's bitter and tearful elegy—for this seems
the only word for his celebrated pamphlet—when we hear
Libanius imploring the " ragged " priests and votaries of the
new faith to spare at least some of the temples, to leave a
few gold and silver treasures in the sanctuaries, and not to
break every one of the marble statues; when Symmachus in
the name of the senate prays that the one altar of Victoria,
by whose aid they had conquered the world, might be left
to the city—we cannot but feel a mournful sympathy with

these pleaders for the last remnants of the "springtime of humanity." In the foremost ranks of the advocates of Polytheism stood some of the very best men—philosophers, poets, writers, men of education, refinement, and of high social standing. They had but one word for Christianity—Atheism. They denounced it as an impious, weird, unpractical creed. They pointed to the golden splendour of Hellenism, to the arts and the sciences, the prose and the poetry, the men and the women it had begotten. They pointed to the victories which their ancient gods, who were now to be dethroned and degraded for the sake of the "pale Galilean," had won for them. The notions of the Christian Hell and Purgatory, of Satan and his angels of darkness, of the awful fundamental mysteries of the new faith, were repugnant to them beyond expression. The ethics, sublime and simple, human yet divine, which the New Testament teaches, were, they said, taken from Plato, or were simply Jewish. This open opposition, however, did not prevail. The current was too strong. The anti-Christian champions then bethought themselves of stratagems. Into the wild chaos of so-called pseudopigraphical writings—the missionary tracts of the early centuries, named, in order to carry conviction more easily, after all possible biblical personages—they threw their own gospel, cunningly adopting the enemy's own language. Thus in the midst of the thousand prophecies, revelations, epistles, evangels ascribed to everybody from Adam and Ham to Nebuchadnezzar and the three men in the fiery pit—and, as if there were not names enough in the Bible, fathered upon some fancy names, such as Pachor, Barkor, Balsemum, Abraxas, Armagil—there appears Hermes Trismegistus. On a would-be ancient Egyptian "platform," he pleads for anything and everything—Pantheism, Polytheism, or Judaism—against Christianity, but under so skilful a mask that pious Church Fathers actually used him in their charges to the faithful; and thus, unwittingly, have preserved some precious fragments that would otherwise have been lost.

The principal and most complete of these Hermetic books

is called *Poemander, i. e.* Shepherd of Men.   It is not unlikely
that this name was given to it in imitation of the well-known
Christian "Pastor Hermas," very popular in those days.   It
contains a cosmogony, made up of Greek philosophy and a
Hellenism that recalls both the joyful elasticity of Hellas
and the severe rationalism of Rome, of Jewish allegories, of
Egyptian legends, and even of Persian demonology, together
with Neoplatonic Christianity.   The first Essence—the
Intelligence—creates another creative power, the Logos,
which again produces seven ministers for the seven heavenly
spheres.   Man's soul is made by God, but his body is produced by himself, in a manner that reminds one of the story
of Narcissus.   One of the theories principally insisted upon
with regard to the whole Cosmos is its imperishable nature.
"Nothing is lost, and it is only by mistake that changes are
called death and destruction," is the theme of a whole
chapter.   There is also a "Sermon on the Mount," but it is
only the title that recalls that other "Sermon."   Among the
other fragmentary writings, such as the addresses from
Hermes to Tat, his son, to Asclepios, and to Ammon, those
of the "Sacred Book" are the most characteristic and
important.   Particularly fine is the description given here
of the creation of man out of certain unruly souls, and of the
arguments urged against it by the Elements, which foresee
the new being's wild and godless career.   The whole piece
is Haggadistic in its shape and partly in its contents, but it
is also largely indebted to Plato's Timæus.

The most striking portion of the whole work, however,
seems to us to be that grandly weird "burden" pronounced
upon Egypt, or rather the whole modern world, which is
contained in the "Asclepios," or discourse of Initiation.   It
is as if "der Menschheit ganzer Jammer" had been in the
mind of the man who wrote it.   Having spoken of the
triumph of Christianity and the consequent return of the
gods from earth to heaven, he continues :—

" . . . You weep, Asclepios ! I have still more mournful messages.
. . . Egypt herself will fall into apostasy. . . . And, full of the disgust
of all things, man will no longer admire and love. this world.   He will

turn away dismayed from this most perfect work, the best work of this and of all times. In the general weariness and vexation of souls, this vast universe will be disdained. This immutable work of God, this glorious and perfect construction, this manifold assembly of pictures, where the Divine Will, prodigious in miracles, has brought everything together into one unique harmony, ever worthy of veneration, praise, and love. . . . They will prefer darkness unto light; they will hold death better than life. . . . No one will look up to the heavens. The man of religion will be considered a fool, the impious a sage; fury will go for bravery; the worst will be called the best. The soul, and all the questions connected with it—whether it be born mortal, or whether it may aspire to immortality—everything that I have exposed to you here, they will only laugh at; they will see sheer vanity only in it. . . . *The Religion of Intelligence* will be persecuted; new laws, new rights will be established; not a word or thought that is holy, religious, worthy of heaven and heavenly things, will be tolerated. . . . Pitiful separation of gods and men! Nothing will remain but *Wicked Angels*; they will be mixed up with miserable humanity; their hand will be upon it; they will push it into all evil undertakings—into war, rapine, lies, into everything contrary to the nature of the souls. . . . The earth will no longer keep its balance, the sea will no longer be navigable, the regular course of the stars will be troubled in heaven. All Divine voices will be silent, the fruits of the land will be corrupted, the soil will no longer yield fruit, the air itself will be filled with dark torpor. Such will be the old age of the world, irreligion and disorder, confusion of all rules—of all that is good. . . ."

After all this corruption the regeneration of the world, "*the holy restoration of nature*," will be wrought by the "*Lord and Father*" in a marvellous manner.

It is strange how these books of Hermes—to which in the middle ages there were made many other spurious additions —have been neglected. Even Parthey's edition—the first critical one ever attempted—is not quite complete; and since "that learned divine Doctor Everard's" English translation of the "Divine Pymander" was edited by "J. F." in 1650, not the slightest notice seems to have been taken of that remarkable work, or any other remnant of Hermes, in England. In Germany the "Poemander" has been translated once or twice within the last hundred years, but save Baumgarten-Crusius (1827), no one seems to have paid any particular attention to it. In France, François de Foix translated and commented on it in 1579, and dedicated it to Marguerite of Navarre. Ever since it has slept in peace till

M. Ménard, at the instigation of the Academy, took it up again and retranslated both the Poemander and the other fragments. His version is, considering all the difficulties he has had to contend with, creditable on the whole. But we cannot bestow even that modicum of praise on the *étude* with which he prefaces it, and for which we presume the Academy has bestowed the prize upon him. We wonder what his competitors' essays must have been like. It certainly would require a being as learned, as acute, as prophetical perhaps as the divine Hermes himself to unravel all the different threads which Judaism, Hellenism, and Egyptianism have woven into this gorgeous fabric. But some approach to a clearing-up might have been made, not by vague references to MM. de Rougé and Vacherot, nor even by extracting them, but by earnest and patient working at the bulk, not only of early and late Hellenistic, but also of Haggadistic and hieroglyphical sources. M. Ménard seems to be as innocent of the one as he is of the other, but he quotes the Bhagavat-Gîtâ. Interesting and elaborate as the essay appears, considered as a contribution to general French literature, it is deplorably shallow and windy when judged by the depth and vast interest of the matter it pretends to treat of. None but those who, with weariness of heart and racking brains, have tried to penetrate through the learned deserts which surround the subject can fully appreciate the disappointment caused by this *étude*. There is a very good reason why the profoundest German scholars have avoided it. Where they feared to tread, M. Ménard has rushed in, and the result is his ponderous *feuilleton*. He evidently tries to imitate M. Renan. But M. Renan would have written much more fascinatingly, if not more learnedly.

IX.

JUDÆO-ARABIC METAPHYSICS.[1]

Re-published by permission.

—◦◦◦—

GIVEN that most complex and fragmentary body of literature, ranging from times beyond historic ken down to the fulness of Hellenic culture, which we call collectively the Old Testament; given further those mazes of legal enactments, gorgeous day-dreams, masked history, ill-disguised rationalism, and the rest which form the Talmud and the Midrash; given also the Kabbala, and, finally, Plato and Aristotle as developed by Jews and Mohammedans either on the basis of their fundamentally identical creed or independently—what was the attitude of the Synagogue towards all these elements, as far as they treated of the first problems of all religion and all philosophy? What was the process whereby the widely diverging statements and speculations on Creation, the Soul, the Hereafter, the nature of the Deity, contained in those authorities, were sought to be blended and harmonized so as to satisfy both Jewish faith and thought?—a faith fervent and passionate beyond measure, to which all visions and all transcendentalism and allegories were so many historical facts, for all of which death was sweet and holy—and a boldness of thought which, with all reverence, frankly said, as Socrates had said, "That divinely revealed wisdom of which you speak I deny not, inasmuch as I do not know it; I can only understand human reason." The everlasting battle between reason and blind belief in "that which is written" was fought with very grim seriousness in the early period of the middle ages

---

[1] This article appeared in the 'Saturday Review' for March 5, 1870, and reviewed the following work:—'Studien über jüdisch-arabische Religions - Philosophie.' Von Dr. A. Schmiedl. Wien: 1869.

within the bosom of the Jewish Church. And while we survey the history of that controversy as it was taken up and continued in the Christian Church, we blush to find, from the very days of Albertus Magnus, the Doctor Universalis, and Thomas Aquinas, the Doctor Angelicus, down to our own perfect nests of arguments both on the side of orthodoxy and of rationalism, unconsciously perhaps, but most unmistakably stolen from the mediæval successors of those same Rabbis to whom Jerome owed his Vulgate lore. To write a history of Jewish metaphysics would indeed be an undertaking worthy to rank with the highest, most difficult, most interesting and instructive tasks; especially if attempted as a contribution to the history of human rationalism. The religious development from, say Hillel the "freethinker," who calmly compressed all the Law and the Prophets into the familiar "Be good, my dear," to Maimonides, the "Great Eagle," who more explicitly and scientifically lays down the supreme axiom that every word of the Bible must either be in accordance with rational conclusions or be explained "metaphorically," and who totally denies an "individual" working of Providence; and on to Baruch Spinoza, in whom Goethe—how much of this nineteenth century besides?—lives and moves and has his being—this would indeed be goodly work for a whole lifetime.

Our author has not attempted anything so ambitious. Very far from it. He is satisfied with gathering a few mosaics from the discussions on these metaphysical topics in the Judæo-Arabic schools; and we are duly grateful. In the circumscribed field which he has chosen he has worked conscientiously, and on the whole very successfully. But the curse of wishing to write "popularly" has been upon him, and consequently, being bereft of that very special gift of enthusiasm which is akin to poetry, and which at times is found to lend a strange charm even to the most abstruse subjects, he has so far failed. The mere discarding of learned notes is not always sufficient to make a book either striking or pleasant. Nor has Dr. Schmiedl always been happy in the methodical arrangement of his subjects: whence spring repetitions of a needless and very tedious kind. There is also a looseness of style and language which a little care would have obviated. Having delivered our soul of these slight objections, we shall give a brief glance at the varied contents of the volume itself.

The first disquisition or chapter—the subject of which is taken up again in the second—treats of the Deity as conceived by Jewish philosophy. The existence of God is of course presupposed; or it would no longer be Jewish philosophy. But what about his attributes? Has He any? Scripture, literally taken, seems to affirm this. Yet, taken in a higher sense, as understood by the Alexandrines, the Targum, and the Talmud, it denies it. Philosophy, on its part, found a *contradicto in adjecto* in an absolute Being or Supreme Cause the sole essence of which is its Oneness and Uniqueness, being considered, either subjectively or objectively, as presenting qualities or *accidences*. This contest between the "Attributists" and "Nonattributists" was indeed one of the fiercest and bitterest, and each camp boasted of brilliant champions. But the latter carried the day, led by no meaner authorities than Ibn Ezra, Jehuda Halevi, and Maimonides. The last of these goes the length of calling the view of his antagonists anti-Jewish. "As well might you say at once that 'He is One but rather Three, besides being Three but rather One.' If you give attributes to a thing, you define this thing; and defining a thing means to bring it under some head, to compare it with something like it. God is sole of His kind. Determine Him, circumscribe Him, and you bring him down to the modes and categories of created things." The Talmud in its characteristic way relates the story of a precentor who heaped divine epithet upon epithet, and whom a master asked when he had finished—"And have you now quite exhausted God's good qualities?" The Psalms speak of "silence" as the best mode of praising God. Nor is the endeavour which goes through all postexilian literature, of finding a kind of medium between the Inconceivable and the world of matter, foreign to this notion. "Word," or "Holy Ghost," or "Shechinah," are the forms under which Judaism at that early

o

period tried in its speech and thought to approach that which itself, shrouded in the ineffable mystery of the Tetragrammaton, was beyond human thought or approach. Indeed, we should say that the whole Angelology, so strikingly simple before the exile, and so wonderfully complex after it, owes its quick development on Babylonian soil to the same awe-stricken desire which grows with growing culture, removing that inconceivable *Ens* further and further from human touch and ken. At the same time the Talmud protests against anything like the notion of angels interceding on the part of man. They are nought but messengers, created for the purpose of their message. More clearly still does Maimonides call every natural law, every being, animated or other, so that it fulfils a certain behest, an "Angel." Thus, he says, a prophet is an angel; the elements are angels; the stars are angels; and so are the sea, the winds, and the human intellect. When the Talmud speaks of God as having consulted the angels ("the Circle or Family above") in the fashioning of every part of the human organism, this, he says, shows that everything in creation is done in accordance with the manifold laws of nature, each ruling over its own sphere, and all coming more or less into play in the complicated human frame. Again, when the Talmud reduces the number of angels whom Jacob saw in his dream at Bethel to four, two mounting upwards and two descending downwards, it merely hints at the wondrous weaving and working in the Cosmos by the four fundamental elements—fire and air which strive upwards, and water and earth which tend downwards. And, as if to leave no doubt, the Talmud had further called thinking man superior to the angels. This dictum, however, was fiercely contested in the mediæval schools. Is man greater because he has a will and may struggle against evil, while the angel can only do what he is bidden? or because man is the centre of creation, even as the earth, according to the astronomy of the period, rests in the middle of the universe? And some schools unhesitatingly doubted and denied the very truth of this opinion enunciated by the Talmud. Is man greater than other creatures? And is he the aim and end of the creation, or merely the most perfect organism on earth? Saadia holds the former, Ibn Ezra and Maimonides hold the latter, view. Scripture, argues the first, calls angels "divine beings," and the stars (which the "angels" are supposed to be moving) "sons of God." But remember, Ibn Ezra says, how infinitely larger certain stars are than the whole earth, and do you think that the inconceivably vast host of the heavens can be meant for, and inferior to, the small dust-born human being? Still more sharply does Maimonides ridicule the very notion of "stars or angels" being made for the sake of man, who by the side of these "intelligences" sinks into utter insignificance. The practical consequence of this discussion was that the "honourable mention," not to say "invocation," of angels—which had been stamped out by the Talmud, and which had grown up again by stealth under foreign influences—now received its death blow. Even the minor masters call it rank idolatry. And the Kabbalists, to whom Angelology is almost the first condition of religious existence, are forced to plead that all those endless varieties of their holy names are but so many anagrams of divine and biblical epithets, and that it is God and not "Patrons" whom they invoke. To stretch the point to the utmost, it was distinctly denied that when Joshua prostrated himself before the angel, he intended to show the angel any reverence. He bowed down before Him who had deemed him worthy of a message—even as a man shows honour even to a dead piece of paper which comes from some one he reveres.

Among the many topics further touched upon in the book before us, such as prophecy, metempsychosis—the notion of which, we may passingly observe, Saadia calls "sheer insanity"—the resurrection, allegorism, &c., we would fain have dwelt somewhat more fully upon the Anthropomorphisms and Anthropopathisms in the Bible with which Judaism, properly so called, had from the beginning dealt unsparingly. From the Targum, which scrupulously effaces every term which might lead to the thought of a corporeal existence of God, to the Midrash, whose most daring protest against the human similes used even by the prophets Maimonides approvingly quotes; from the broad axiom of the Mishnah, that these things are not to be taken literally—" the Thorah speaking merely in a human way "—to the days when Yedaya Penini could say that at last this Anthropomorphistic absurdity had been finally driven even from the obscurest brains—we find one endless series of attempts to get rid of all materialistic interpretation of undoubtedly materialistic terminology. Rough, indeed, is the manner in which Maimonides disposes of the " Voice " on Sinai, or God's "descending thereon "—which the Talmud already declares to be but a figure of speech—and nothing can be more characteristic than the almost contemptuously good-natured manner in which he finally allows the hopelessly unthinking to do as they please about these things. " If some of the shortsighted will not rise to the step to which we endeavour to lift them, let them by all means imagine all such terms (Angels, &c.) to refer to something material—no great harm will come of it." It was indeed only the devotees of Kabbala and Karaism who still protested against these rationalizing Talmudistic views, and their end has been either petrifaction and death, or, worse still, coarse imposture and religious delirium.

We here take leave of our author grateful for his suggestive and learned " Studies," and hoping soon to meet him again on the same field. But let him not be afraid of bringing with him his whole apparatus next time, however bulky it may be.

X.

LES APÔTRES.[1]

" WITHOUT haste, without rest," M. Renan proceeds with his idyl of the Origins of Christianity. Two years and a half have now elapsed since the publication of his ' Life of Jesus' ; an interval during which he hopes "some of his readers will have learnt to look somewhat more calmly upon these problems." In accordance with the programme sketched out in that volume, the present instalment treats of the Apostles. But the author has thought fit to alter the original plan in so far that not the period from the death of Jesus to the end of the first century, but only the history of the twelve years 33—45 is contained in the present book. St. Paul's conversion, not his labour, is spoken of here ; he is to form the central figure of the next book, which will commence with his first mission.

We confess at once that a more seductive, but also more trying task than that of pronouncing upon this book has rarely fallen to our share. While we read it and read it again, it carries us away, swiftly, irresistibly. There is in it a pathos which stirs the mind to its inmost depths. The power of its diction is wondrous sweet and strong. Picture follows picture, musical cadence follows cadence, epigrammatic casuistry suddenly changes into broken accents of love, —the vast glory of the antique fades before a dark group of sainted women. Jerusalem the Golden rapidly nearing her supreme hour,—Antioch and all her marble gods,—the

---

[1] This article appeared in the ' Athenæum' of May 12, 1866, and reviewed the following work :—' Les Apôtres.' Par Ernest Renan. Paris, Lévy; London, Nutt. Re-printed by permission.

waving lily-fields of Galilee and the million-voiced life of the
Urbs et Orbis,—Paul, the proud, learned, passionate, refined
convert, and the lowly band of peasant-disciples, whose only
wisdom was to love their Master "jusqu'à la folie,"—psychological and physiological problems, and chiefly the working
of those mystic powers that move between light and darkness,
between life and death:—all these, and a thousand other
themes, are touched upon in rapid succession with cunning
hand; and through the whole there breathes a fervour strange
and strong as some heavy exotic perfume,—an ardent adoration of something indefinite, dreamy, ideal, which takes our
hearts and our senses captive, hushes the loud protest and
lulls our doubts into repose. We yield to the spell, and
"shut out thinking."

But when we wake from this trance and try to grasp the
argument, to realize the story, its divine heroes and heroines,
we seem to be trying to realize what we have heard and seen
in dreams. The landscape erst so sunny lies veiled in a mist,
the living men and women have become like unto shadows,
and when they speak their voice is thin. A thousand incon-
gruities and impossibilities become apparent at once. In this
book, perhaps even more than in the former, the gaps of
history are filled out by visions. Fact, or at least tradition,
is blended with fancies. And it is far from easy to separate
again what the hand of an artificer like M. Renan has welded
together, principally when, as is not rarely the case, he purposely seems to have avoided fathoming the real state of
things to the full, lest it might interfere with the more
picturesque or poetical conception.

When compared with the former volume, the present one
seems to be somewhat inferior in verve. Not that M.
Renan's style is less brilliant, his skill of grouping—posing,
we might say—less consummate, or his diction less like a
blending of Victor Hugo and Lamennais. But there is something pointedly conciliatory in his tone. His views about
miracles and the "supernatural" are certainly unchanged—
perhaps, if possible, more advanced still; but he states them
rather differently. He argues, he reasons, where before he

pronounced. He is exquisitely courteous, and always on his guard not to offend by the form of his utterance. But from this there springs at times a great uncertainty as to his meaning. When, after having utterly disproved a thing, he continues to speak of it as an existing reality, he reminds us slightly of a modern poet invoking Apollo and the Muses; only that a universal agreement about Apollo and the Muses being a glorious dream of the past may be taken for granted, while dogmas and miracles are to many people still something very real indeed. Science should never be vague; it should leave us no doubts as to the writer's own meaning; on all occasions it should use nothing but explicit, clear and decisive terms after the verdict has once gone forth. His eagerness not to vex leads M. Renan almost into flirting with orthodoxy *pur sang*, and, more characteristic still, with Imperialism—*Césarisme*, as he has it. He professes great admiration for the centralizing system of Rome, which not only gave her, in his opinion, the power over East and West but which also gave to the still and pensive minds, the votaries of science and art, the ease and the leisure for their solitary musings. No wonder if, as we hear, liberal France should have taken great offence at this new line of the late Professor of the Hebrew chair.

Another point, and one of the most vital, is the flagrant want of acquaintance displayed in this volume with certain sources which, in the Introduction to the first, were spoken of so hopefully and confidently. We mean those terrible mounds of "Chaldee" literature, to which of late our attention has been drawn more and more :—The Targums, the Talmuds, the Midrashim, even the Zohar, and the rest of late Kabbalistic lore. *Hic Rhodus, hic salta.* They, and nothing but they, we believe, can give us a real notion of the mental atmosphere, of the dogmas and doctrines, the ethics and ceremonies, the sagas and parables, the prose and the poetry, of the time when Christianity was born. It was far from sufficient to adduce, as the author has done in the first volume, some scanty fragments of legendary lore out of old collections, and try to verify them with foreign aid. Little is to be gained, after all, by tracing a few parallel instances of proverbial sentences. What was wanted now, and what we looked forward to in this book, was the proof of the existence, within the Jewish community, of such notions as the Logos, the Trinity, the working of the Holy Ghost, the suffering and redeeming Messiah. Further, what ideas terms like Son of God, Son of Man, Gift of Tongues, and the like, originally conveyed to the popular mind; what were the notions of the Schools about Redemption, Regeneration, Repentance, Confession of Sin, Baptism, Absolution, and a thousand other things current among the contemporary Jewish world, but utterly bewildering to the Gentiles, and, let us confess it, still far from clear to our own generation, after well-nigh two thousand years' working. The style, the idiom, the innumerable open and latent allusions, the form and substance, in fact, of the fundamental Books of Christianity contained in the New Testament, written, as Lightfoot has it, by Jews, among Jews, for Jews, (" à Judæis, atque inter et ad Judæos ") can only be properly appreciated and thoroughly understood by constant reference to the oral literature of the period.

We did not expect M. Renan to succeed where no one has succeeded before him. He is far from being able to grapple with a task like this. But he should at least have endeavoured to illustrate, from the materials already at hand, some of the most prominent and obvious points. Second-, nay, tenth-rate sources would have taught him to avoid flagrant errors like that of the " Regeneration " being an idea of which no one had ever heard before; while nothing can be more common than the adage that " a proselyte's mind becomes like that of a new-born child. " The Midrash even explains the passage in Genesis (xii. 5), " the souls they had *made* (gotten) in Haran," to refer to new converts, who were to be considered as newly born from the moment when they embraced the faith. He would have known that the voice from Sinai was said to have divided itself into seven, or seventy, fiery tongues—according to the supposed number of nations on earth—"just as the hammer strikes many sparks from the iron upon the anvil ;" and he should have used this

most popular notion in his explanation of the gift of tongues.
He would, if he had really looked into these matters, have
avoided that most fatal note (p. 262), "It is well known that
no manuscript of the Talmud remains by which the printed
editions could be checked,"—while scores and scores of
codices, for the most part fragmentary, but fully available
for a critical edition (such as is now in hand), are scattered
all over the public libraries of Europe, in Italy, in France, in
England, in Germany, in Russia, in Holland. The imperial
Library in Paris alone contains eight—oddly registered—
MSS., with almost unexamined fragments; and, no doubt,
the Mazarin Library counts some valuable portions among its
treasures,—only that its Catalogue must for Talmudical works
be consulted under "Hæretici," under which heading, as
Lebrecht says, "Rabbi Gamaliel and Calvin, Rabbi Akiba
and Luther, slumber peacefully together." It is this same
vagueness of information about the Talmud which recently
caused a writer in one of our Quarterlies to make an extraordinary computation about the probable size of this book.
Judging from a special edition of the Mishnah, in six folios,
he reckoned, if we remember rightly, that the Talmud must
needs fill ninety—unconscious, apparently, of the fact that it
has been printed times innumerable (there are five different
editions in the press at this moment), and that it is almost
invariably printed in twelve volumes. This state of things
reminds us very forcibly of our old friend the "Rabbinus
Talmud," and we think it high time that it should cease.

But to return. We know full well that a knowledge
requisite for such a history of the "Origins," in fact, for such
a Commentary on the New Testament, as we have it, ideally,
in our mind's eye,—a knowledge which should not only know
at what particular spot in these mounds it should excavate,
but, having excavated, would understand how to sift and use
these materials properly, with a profoundly pious and reverential mind,—a knowledge not narrow, sectarian, one-sided,
but catholic, human, large, one to which Homer and Horace
and Goethe and Tennyson should not be more foreign than
Church Fathers, and archæologists, palæographers and anti-

quaries,—a knowledge, above all, which, in awaking the long-buried past, should always remain mindful of the living present, its aspirations and its wants:—such a knowledge, we know, is not easily found or easily gotten. But an approach to the ideal might be striven after, and the task which we have indicated is one as high and noble as it is pressing.

It will not be necessary for us to enter into the general question of Renan's book, "theologically considered." This we must leave to the special theologians of the different schools. We shall only endeavour to give an idea of it as a work of science, as which he has sent it forth. His own standpoint is so well known that it would be utter waste of breath to reason upon it at this time of the day. As we said before, the present volume treats only of the first twelve years of the new creed. It is as well that these twelve years should occupy a special place; for it is that period which has decided the existence of a church that, starting without a name and without almost any distinguishing feature, save the belief in its founder,—a church which for a time was considered, and considered itself, neither more nor less than a small band of most orthodox and rigorous Jews, keeping the ceremonies more strictly than the " Pharisees" themselves,—has conquered and regenerated the world. During this period it was that dogmas the most vital, like the Resurrection, the influence of the Holy Ghost, and the rest, became christian dogmas. The organization of the Church of Jerusalem, its first trials and triumphs, how it spread to Antioch, and there first became conscious of being a thing distinct from Judaism, there also adopted for ever the name given to it by strangers in ignorance or derision,—how, above all, that most startling and, to the young community, most repulsive notion of opening the gates to the heathen sprang into being,—what were the nature and circumstances of these Gentiles, intellectually, politically, morally, socially, and theologically, and how their admission acted upon the faith of the community :—these are indeed topics which deserve a large space all their own.

St. Paul, as we have mentioned, is not included in this book

called "The Apostles." His conversion alone is recounted
as an event of the time, and its importance is duly dwelt
upon. But he is not an apostle, properly speaking, although
he assumes that name. He represents, the author says, the
travelling and the conquering Church; but he himself is,
withal, but " a labourer of the second hour, almost an
intruder." And here M. Renan takes the opportunity of
formally protesting against what he calls the fashionable
notion of our day—of looking upon Paul, rather than upon
Jesus, as the founder of Christianity. Not only is he not to
be compared to Jesus, but not even to the last of his
disciples. The only reason for his standing out so prominently in history he finds in the greater amount of written
information that has survived regarding him. Important
though he be, yet he had not tasted "of the ambrosia of the
Galilean preaching," but only of its "aftertaste." In fact,
the early Church looked upon him with great suspicion—nay,
as upon a "Simon Magus." The Church of Corinth, although
founded by him exclusively, pretended to be founded jointly
by Peter and him, in order to be able to boast of the former's
name and authority. Papias and Justin do not even mention
his name. The only difference was that " he had a theology,
Peter and Mary Magdalen had not"; and for this reason
Christian theology, when written documents took the place of
oral tradition, gave him a higher place on account of his
extensive writings.

Apropos of Simon Magus, we shall be glad to learn in the
next volume what M. Renan's exact notions of the independent existence of this mysterious figure are. It is well
known that Tübingen (Baur-Volkmar) looks upon him as a
mere fiction, a type of Paul, invented by the Anti-Gentile or
Judæo-Christians, and as whose bitterest adversary Peter
himself appears in the Clementines. But what we are most
eager to see solved in the next volume is the contradiction
between the author's emphatic protest against this "modern"
notion anent this Apostle—a notion as old, at least, as Toland
—at the beginning of the book and his own forcible arguments in favour of this same notion later on; for there he

distinctly and repeatedly argues that, without Paul, that is, without his energetic perseverance in admitting the Gentiles, and disregardiug the "Law,"—two things in which he holds him not only to have differed from the other disciples, but to have directly deviated from the intentions of Jesus himself,—the young sect would have disappeared very speedily, like fifty others of the time, without leaving a trace behind. He speaks of the other Apostles as " small, narrow-minded (*étroits*), ignorant, inexperienced, as much as they could possibly be." If Paul, he says, had known Jesus alive, it is doubtful whether he would have attached himself to Him. " His doctrine will be his own, not that of Jesus; the revelations of which he is so proud are the fruit of his own brain." "The Christ whom he had seen on the way to Damascus was not the Christ of Galilee, but the Christ of his own imagination, of his own individuality. Nay, he avoids contact with the disciples for a long time, lest he might be imbued with notions and doctrines they, who had " tasted of the ambrosia," had heard from their Master. At his conversion, sudden as it was, "he had nothing new to learn." This can only mean that Christianity, at its outset, had no doctrines or dogmas different from Judaism, " Pharisaical" Judaism to wit, save the belief that the Messiah had appeared in Jesus, which Judaism denied. " Pauline" Christianity, therefore, with its abrogation of the " Law," must, according to M. Renan, be considered as a thing totally different from the primitive Christianity of the disciples and the first Church. Thus, the author in the middle of the book, designates Paul virtually as the originator of that Christianity which lives, and is to us of much higher import than that original Christianity which died, and which was practically Judaism in all but one point —a point, moreover, by no means so vital, so fixed as is generally assumed. The opinions of the contemporary authorities were strangely divided on the Messiah question. Yet he loudly repudiates this notion in the Introduction. Surely he does not protest for the benefit of readers who go no further into the book? Or shall we assume that he has not fully made up his mind on the subject?—This, however, is but one of the many instances where vagueness of conception and the desire to hold an original ground of his own—while his arguments all go in favour of a common contemporary notion—lead him into dilemmas or make him obscure.

Highly characteristic is the manner in which he makes use of the opinions of investigators on the sources for this book, and chiefly on the Acts. These sources—considering that he virtually excludes all but those extant in Greek—lie in a very narrow compass. The Acts he, too, holds to be written by Luke: he dates them about 80, and from Rome; written there perhaps, he significantly adds, for Flavius Claudius,—"a powerful personage, whose official position required consideration,"—a circumstance which to him would explain many things. *Noblesse oblige.* We have not, indeed, to look for anything like what we should call historical truthfulness in this account; but then " it is only the sceptic who writes history *ad narrandum.*" " Le bon Luc," he thinks, is a very different being from his master, Paul. The latter is uncompromising, severe, "personal," heedless of anything save the doctrine he holds and the ideas he wants to disseminate—a " Protestant;" while Luke impresses him rather as a " good Catholic;" docile, optimist, calling every priest a " holy priest," every bishop a " great bishop " (how very like some other writers!); ready to embrace all kinds of fictions rather than to acknowledge that these holy priests and these great bishops quarrel and fight among themselves in rather an unholy fashion sometimes. But Luke is strongly impressed with the " ecclesiastical authority;" the " Church of Rome" seems already to have been present to his mind, and weighed upon it. He, the good Luke, could enter into the political and hierarchical spirit by which this Church, from the first centuries, was distinguished. He therefore writes history as an apologist of the Court of Rome would—" à toute outrance." He writes as an Ultramontane historian of the time of Clement the Fourteenth would have written, praising both the Pope and the Jesuits, or as that same personage will 200 years hence show that Antonelli and Merode loved each other like brethren.

With the exception of the "hierarchy," which seems to us to savour strangely of M. Renan's early training, the kernel of all this, viz., that the "Acts" is a work cunningly written so as to suit both the Gentile and the Judæo-Christians, is precisely what Schneckenberger, Schwegler, Baur, Zeller, nay, Michaelis, Paulus, and even De Wette, to some extent, have long urged. But no one has contrived to exculpate the author as M. Renan does. Craftiness and subtlety are the terms those rude German rationalists apply to a writer who, in their opinion, hacked and garbled and suppressed and added *in majorem fidei gloriam*. A more terrific blow has certainly never been aimed at the "système d'histoire ecclésiastique convenu" of which such writing as he represents it would be a specimen, than M. Renan's defence.

But M. Renan does not go the whole length of Tübingen. He does not think that the book is, for those reasons of intrinsic falsehood and systematic misrepresentations, to be rejected *en bloc*, even in its first chapters, which are most open to objections. He does not think that certain personages (the Eunuch, Tabitha, &c.) are entirely invented; but some popular tales concerning them he assumes to have been used skilfully to prove the two doctrines of the writer, viz., the legitimate call of the Gentiles and the *Divine Institution of the Hierarchy*.

We shall not pursue this point any further: firstly, because we are repeatedly referred to the next volume, in which the writer is going to speak fully on the authenticity of these writings, and to the new edition of the first volume, in which the author's opinions on the Fourth Gospel are to be further elucidated and defended; and, secondly, because there is, as far as we can see, nothing new in all that M. Renan brings forward on these things, save the peculiar colouring which he gives to the eclectic results of older investigations. We may, therefore, safely defer what we have to say on the subject until he brings forward his own original results. But before we pursue the course of the story itself, we must hear him speak once more on miracles, in reply to the objections urged against his arguments in the first volume.

The science of criticism, he says, can know nothing of miracles. They are impossibilities; and this is not a metaphysical theory, but simply a fact of observation, of experience. No miracle has ever been proved; but every miracle, when closely examined, has turned out to be either an imposture or a delusion. Catholicism, which still believes in the power of working miracles, has never produced one, except in out-of-the-way places. Let there be a miracle wrought in Paris, under the eyes of competent men of science, and there will be an end of all doubt. They have, without a single exception, never been wrought before those who were capable of discussing and investigating them properly. It is not, as some argue, for those who doubt them to disprove their reality, but for those who believe to prove them. If Buffon had been asked to give a place in his "Natural History" to centaurs and sirens, he would naturally have asked to be shown some specimens first. "But you must prove to us that they do not exist." "Nay," he would have replied, "you must prove that they do." Why, M. Renan asks, does no one really believe in angels or demons, although texts innumerable speak of them? Because, simply, the existence of an angel or demon has never been proved. The argument from the great phenomena of the universe is a simple fallacy. You cannot argue that because the nature of the sun is not yet sufficiently known to astronomers, therefore it is a miracle, and therefore all reported miracles are true. The creation is a grand marvel, but everything moves in it according to everlasting laws. God is in all things always, and to assume that sudden interferences are necessary would be derogatory to His work and to Himself; as if the universe, like a watch, wanted occasional mending. And miracles reported in historical times are not to be proved by a reference to pre-historic times. Nor is the "moral" miracle of any greater weight. True, the success of Christianity is one of the greatest facts in the religious history of the world; but it is not therefore a miracle. Buddhism, Babism, and Islamism use exactly the same arguments as Christianity. They had their miracles, their martyrs, their sudden and marvellous successes. And granting Christianity to be a unique fact,—what of Hellenism? Is not this the ideal perfection in Literature, Art, Philosophy? Does not Greek Art surpass all other arts as much as Christianity does all other religions? If Christianity is a prodigy of sanctity, Hellenism is a prodigy of beauty. A unique thing, however, is not a miraculous thing. God is, in different degrees, in everything beautiful, good and true. But in no instance is his divine presence in any religious or philosophical movement, a special privilege or an exception. "And if our Church rejects us," he continues, "let us not recriminate; thanks to our modern days, this kind of hatred is impotent. Let us take comfort in thinking of that invisible Church which embraces the excommunicated saints, the best souls of every time. Those whom one church has banished are always its elect; they are in advance of their time. The heretic of to-day is the orthodox of the future. And what, besides, is the excommunication of man? The Heavenly Father excommunicates only the dry spirits and the narrow hearts. If the priest refuses to admit us into his cemetery, let us forbid our families to protest. God judges. The earth is a good mother, that makes no distinctions; the body of a good man laid in the unconsecrated corner brings its own blessing with it."

It is one man's duty, he says, to speak, another's to be silent, although they may both think and feel alike. "The good Bishop Colenso has committed such an act of honesty as the Church has not seen since its origin, when he wrote down his doubts the moment they came into his mind. But the humble Catholic priest, in a country of a narrow and timid spirit, must be silent. Many and many a discreet tomb around village churches thus covers "les poétiques, réserves d'angéliques silences." Will the merit of those whose duty it was to speak be equal to that of those secrets which God alone knows?

At this point the author enters into what we cannot help describing as one of the most perfect personal explanations or *orationes pro domo* which we have ever seen. Jarring as many of its notes must be,—chiefly where he speaks of the future Church,—it will yet enlist a great deal of sympathy.

He replies to the many personal attacks made upon him with a calmness and moderation which are truly admirable. The truth, he says, will not be furthered by "so much agitation." The timid ought not to read what disturbs their faith. "Practical people," again, he says, have asked him what has been his real object in writing this book? "Eh, mon Dieu! le même qu'on se propose en écrivant toute histoire." To write a history, to investigate and to make known the grand events of the past as accurately as possible, and in a manner befitting them. "Had I to dispose of several lives, I should spend one in writing a history of Alexander; another, in writing a history of Athens; a third, in writing a history of the French Revolution, or of the order of Francis of Assisi. As to shaking anybody's faith, that thought has been a thousand miles away from me."

He most emphatically denies having had the slightest desire to combat established creeds. His is not the part of a controversialist, but another more obscure—more fruitful for science. So far from desiring to establish anything new, he exhorts his readers to remain in their respective churches, and to derive what good they can from them. He sees the times of Avignon and the counter-Popes coming back once more. The Catholic Church, he thinks, is about to pass through a new sixteenth century; but, notwithstanding its schisms and divisions, it will remain the Catholic Church: and in a hundred years, the proportion of Protestants, Catholics and Jews will be about the same, he holds, as it is now, only that there will be more in each community who will believe in the spirit rather than in the letter. The "pure Church" does not want to raise its standard against the old ones, for this would not accelerate, but retard, the general softening of dogmatism. Luther and Calvin created Loyola and Philip the Second. And, above all, Christianity must not be weakened, for what should we be without it?

When M. Renan speaks of Christianity he means something different from what is usually understood by this term.

P

Not the complex of dogmas and ethics, which we know by
that name, but brotherly love and charity, and the pure
adoration of the Supreme power, without any dogmatic
admixture, seems to be the ideal upon which he bestows this
name, or that other of the "Pure Church of the Future."
He concludes:—"Peace, then, 'au nom de Dieu!' Let the
different orders of humanity live side by side, not in falsifying
their own genius in order to make mutual concessions to
each other, but in mutually supporting each other. Nothing
should rule here below to the exclusion of its contrary; no
power should be able to suppress the others. The harmony
of humanity results from the free emission of the most dis-
cordant notes. Let orthodoxy succeed in killing science, we
know what will then happen; the Mohammedan world and
Spain are dying because they too conscientiously fulfilled
that task. Let rationalism try to rule the world without
regard for the religious wants of the soul, the experience of
the French Revolution is there to teach us the consequences
of such a mistake. The instinct of Art, carried to the
highest delicacies, but without honesty, made the Italy of
the Renaissance a cut-throat place. 'L'ennui, la sottise, la
médiocrité,' are the punishment of certain Protestant countries, where, under the pretext of good sense and Christian
spirit, Art has been suppressed, and Science reduced to
something ugly. Lucretius and St. Theresa, Aristophanes
and Socrates, Voltaire and Francis of Assisi, Raphael and
Vincent de Paul, have equally reason to be, and humanity
would be less if a single one of its component elements were
wanting."

Here we shall, for the present, leave this book, which, pre-
eminent neither for deep erudition nor original research, for
scientific precision nor logical consistency, with visionary
fancies instead of facts, and a thousand and one faults of
conception and detail, yet cannot but be considered one of
the most remarkable and characteristic contributions to the
question of all time.

XI.

FIVE LETTERS ON THE ŒCUMENICAL COUNCIL.[1]

———•◇•———

TUESDAY, SEPT. 14, 1869.

THE curtain is about to rise upon that great Council of
Rome which has long been casting its shadows before.
Sixth of the Lateran or first of the Vatican, it can only be
called Œcumenical at this time of the day by a stretch of
courtesy. Inasmuch as all " cardinals, patriarchs, primates,
archbishops, bishops, abbots with quasi-episcopal jurisdiction,
generals of orders, together with certain erudite men and
princely persons," are convoked, it is distinct from all other
kinds of Synods, national, provincial, and otherwise. But
Church historians do not agree as to the total number of
Œcumenical Councils hitherto held. The well-known mnemonic hexameter, " Ni Co E, Chal Co Co, Ni Co La, La La
La, Ly Ly Vi, Flo Tri," standing for Nicæa, Constantinople,
Ephesus, &c., which counts but seventeen, is not accepted
by all. When, for example, the Œcumenical Council of
Ephesus, in 449, had decided, not without the aid of "swords
and sticks and many monks' heels," that Eutyches' opinion
about the nature of Christ was the orthodox one, another
Œcumenical Council, held eleven years later at Chalcedon,
decided that the decision of its predecessor was null and
void, and that so far from being an Œcumenical Council,
it was a Council of Brigands—" *Latrocinium Ephesinum.*"

---

[1] From the 'Times' of Sept. 14th and 21st, Oct. 5th and 19th, and Nov.
12th, 1869. Re-printed by permission.

Even so the Council of Basle was called "*Basiliscorum spelunca dæmonumque caterva*," because it rebelled against the Pope, its master. It will, therefore only deserve the Œcumenical when all will have gone well, and the Synod that comes after shall have approved its doings.

Meanwhile there is much and loud knocking heard behind the stage. The works of St. Peter, we learn, have nearly reached their completion. Signor Sarti's plans having been rejected, the device of Vespignani has been adopted instead. The Papal throne stands at the end of the transept, the altar of the Council in the centre, the stalls for the fathers being grouped around, no longer, alas! in eleven, but owing probably to urgent affairs in their respective dioceses, in seven rows. The whole space, instead of being closed by an apse at the Confession, will be shut in by a curtain, which can be drawn aside so that the assembled multitudes may, as time serves, behold the grand scene. The stenographers chosen from the different nations, so that they may not stumble over any foreign—say British—Latin, are rapidly mastering their craft under one of the most experienced teachers. The seven commissions, each presided over by a Cardinal, are pushing on their work spite of heat, malaria, or due vacations. The Pope receives a daily report of their progress. A special commission, composed of high dignitaries, are appointed quartermasters, and Rome has to find lodgings for her guests at their bidding. Nay, the inaugural sermon is already weighing on the mind of Padre Luigi da Trento, the Archbishop of Iconium, the Apostolic Preacher of the Vatican.

Nor is literature, in the widest sense of the word, idle on the subject. Articles and notices and essays and pamphlets, Liberal and Ultramontane, rabid and sensible, Catholic, Protestant, Rationalistic, and so forth, glut the papers and the book market in honour of the coming question of the hour. But mighty little is to be said of these efforts, and he who would attribute to them a higher value than that of, in the main, a catchpenny literature, would be mistaken.

When was it that the last Œcumenical Council closed? It was the Council of Trent, convoked in the throes of the German Reformation: it sat and rose and sat again from the 13th of December, 1545, to the 4th of December, 1563, and its decrees were confirmed by the Pope early in the following year. But at the beginning of it a sermon was preached in which it was likened to the Last Council, wherein Christ and the Apostles would sit in judgment over the living and the dead. And the learned and pious have ever since considered this a prophetical sermon, inasmuch as between Trent and that supreme Synod there were to be no more Councils. They were wrong, but so was the whole world. No one would have dreamt of a like revival coming to pass before our eyes. Nay, there were those who doubted long after the preparations had commenced. Perhaps our readers have forgotten the circumstances under which this Council was ushered into the world. It may be well to recapitulate.

On the 8th of December, 1864, the tenth anniversary of the "dogmatic definition of the Immaculate Conception of the Virgin Mother of God," there appeared, together with an encyclical letter, the famous Syllabus, treating in ten chapters and eighty paragraphs of the principal errors of our time. On the 6th of June, 1867, seventeen questions, chiefly on Church discipline (with regard to heretics, civil marriages, &c.), were addressed in a circular letter to all the bishops. On the 26th of that same month the Pope pronounced an allocution in the Secret Consistory, in the presence of five hundred bishops, wherein he made known to them his long-cherished desire to summon a General Council, by the means of which the Catholic Church would celebrate its highest triumph, convert her enemies, and carry the Kingdom of Christ all over the world. The bishops replied in an address that their hearts were filled with joy at this prospect of a General Council, which could not but become a source of unity, sanctity, and peace. The Pope received the address joyfully, and, in accordance with their wishes, placed the Council under the special patronage of her who

had bruised the serpent's head, and promised that wherever
it was held it should be inaugurated on the anniversary
of the proclamation of the Immaculate Conception. On
the 29th of June, 1868, the Bull of the Indiction of the
Council was duly promulgated. This was followed, on
the 8th of September of the same year, by an Apostolic
Letter addressed to all the Bishops of the Oriental rite not
in communication with Rome, inviting them to be present
at the Synod "even as their ancestors had been present at
the second Council of Lyons and that of Florence," where
they were not allowed to vote and had to sit apart. Abbate
Testa was delegated to deliver these missives personally to
the schismatic bishops or patriarchs. Finally, on the 13th
of September, that Apostolic Letter to all Protestants and
other non-Catholics was indited, which exhorts them to
"embrace the opportunity of this Council" (*occasionem
amplectantur hujus concilii*).

We remarked at the time that the effect upon the schismatic mind of the East was scarcely to be called encouraging. The Greek Patriarch would not look at the
letter, though it was handsomely bound in red morocco, and
emblazoned with gold letters bearing his own name. He
had read all about it in the newspapers, and did not see how
the Council could do aught but lead to further strife. The
peace once arrived at by the two Churches had long fallen
to the ground. His mind was perfectly easy on the subject.
And so the gorgeous volume was taken from the divan and
handed back to the delegate, who was bowed out and departed in peace. The Metropolitan of Chalcedon returned
the Encyclical, with the simple but graphic "Epistrephete,"
which might be freely rendered "Avaunt." The Bishop of
Varna did not see how he could accept what his master had
refused, and so he sent back the Encyclical. The Bishop of
Salonica had no less than five reasons for his declining, to
wit—1. What would his Patriarch say? 2. Why at Rome,
why not in the East? 3. Because the Pope wants to get us
into his grasp; 4. The Pope wears a sword, which is against
Scripture; let him put it down and disband his army; 5.

Let him give up the "*Filioque*" and there will be no more
disunion between Greeks and Latins—which last proposition,
all things considered, is very delicious. Yet there were some
exceptions, which the official Roman Press calls "consoling."
One schismatic bishop returned the letter, yet with the
promise that he would think about it for himself; and
another, the venerable Bishop of Trebizond, well stricken in
years, seems to have been quite overcome, and received the
Encyclical with the most profound tokens of reverence and
admiration, pressed it to his forehead, then to his bosom,
looked at it from all sides, for, alas! he knew not the
mystery of Latin characters, and exclaimed from time to
time, "Oh, Rome! oh, Rome! oh, Holy Peter! oh, Holy
Peter!" But, adds the official account quaintly enough, it
was utterly impossible to get anything else out of him—
notably, whether he meant to come to the Council or not.

The effect in Europe we have witnessed. That Catholic
Power which indeed is of the most vital importance in the
matter—France—has declared, through M. Baroche, the
Minister of Justice and Worship, before the Legislative
Assembly, in July, 1868, that the Government would place
no obstacles in the way of the meeting. It did not know
about sending representatives. It did not care for the
omission of a personal invitation to the Emperor. Church
and State should not be separated; but it repudiated the
Syllabus, and prohibited its promulgation from the pulpit.
It would not admit the infallibility of the Pope. It would
take its stand upon the Concordat and the Organic Articles
—that arsenal of anti-Papal weapons which forbids the publication even of any Papal emanation without the previous
authorization of the Government. In the interval Austria—
the Austria of the Hapsburgs still—has torn her Concordat
to pieces and has punished priests. Spain, that other darling
daughter of Rome, has proclaimed, in the first hour almost
of its regeneration, liberty of conscience. In Bavaria, the
Government has asked the Universities whether the Syllabus
was likely to interfere with the rights and prerogatives of
the State. The Theological Faculty of Munich has answered

within the last few days. Würzburg takes further time.
Phrase it as cautiously as they will, the Professors cannot
help declaring that the Syllabus, whether accepted "*nude et
pure*" or "*materialiter*," negatively or positively, in the
redaction of Pater Schrader—who has already undertaken
the labour of transforming the negative Syllabus into a kind
of dogmatic Magna Charta—or not, it must eventually
occasion some not unimportant changes in the relation
between Church and State.   And that State and Government of Bavaria know enough now, and they have done the
civil thing too.

And amid all these signs and tokens the 8th of December
approaches rapidly.   We may, perhaps, give the probable
programme of the beginning of the performance, as we may
gather it from previous similar occasions, notably Trent.
First of all, all Christendom will solemnly be called upon for
its prayers on behalf of the Synod.   Next, one or several
days' fast will be proclaimed.   On the day fixed, the 8th of
December, the Assembly will walk in solemn procession to
St. Peter's, where, on this occasion, the Papal throne will be
erected at the end of the transept, and the altar of the
Council in the centre, the stalls for the Fathers being
grouped around it.   The Pope or his Legate will then celebrate High Mass, and in the prayers the Holy Ghost will
be specially invoked.   To all present a full remission of
their sins will next be announced, and blessings will be invoked both on the Pope and the Assembly, the Pope chant-
ing thrice, "Ut hanc sanctam Synodum et omnes gradus
ecclesiasticos benedicere et regere digneris."   After this
the President—the Pope or his Legate—puts the question,
"Does it please you, to the honour and glory of the holy and
undivided Trinity, the Father, the Son, and the Holy Ghost,
to the increase and augmentation of the faith and the Christian religion, to the extermination of heresy, the peace and
unity of the Church, the improvement of the clergy and the
Christian people, to the suppression and extinction of the
enemies of the Christian name, to resolve and to declare that
this Council do commence and have commenced?"   The

Placet having been given, the next meeting being fixed, the Ambrosian hymn of praise is sung, and the assembly disperses. And what next?

Profound mystery shrouds the proceedings. And yet, perhaps, we may tell our readers in secret what we have learnt on very good authority. Three things will be done at the Council, which is not to last more than three weeks altogether. The three things will be the declaration of the infallibility of the Pope, which is to be proposed at the beginning of the meetings by an English prelate; the dogmatised Syllabus will be made law ; and, further, the dogma of the Assumption of the Virgin, derived from two apocryphal writings of the fifth century, will be proclaimed. We hope to return to all three.

So much for the work of the Session. This Council will in many ways be different from its predecessors. From Nicæa to Trent, they always used to be convened in order to devise means against some special enemy, be it Arius or Luther, Henry IV. or Frederick II., the Saracens or the Templars. Occasionally the Jews also were taken into consideration, as at the fourth Lateran Council the yellow patch was made canonical. Casually, also, as at the fifth Lateran Council, the fair formerly held at Lyons was transferred to Geneva, and the like important matters. But generally there was some very special and pressing emergency, some schism, some flagrant error or scandal to be met in solemn conclave convoked generally by both the secular and the spiritual powers. What is this Council convened for? The Encyclical says :—

" It is well known by how horrible a tempest the Church is now shaken. . . . By the most bitter enemies of God and men has the Catholic Church and its salutary doctrine, and venerable power, and the highest authority of this Apostolic see been assailed—trodden under foot ; all sacred things have been despised, ecclesiastical goods have been plundered, the bishops and highest ecclesiastical dignitaries and Catholic men harassed in all manners, religious orders extinguished, and all kinds of impious books and pestilential journals . . . have been spread abroad. . . . In this Œcumenical Council shall all those things be most accurately examined and determined which in these particularly hard times have particular reference to the greater glory of God, the integrity of the faith, the worthy celebration of Divine worship, and the everlasting salvation of men, the discipline and the salutary and solid instruction of the clergy, and the observance of the ecclesiastical laws, the improvement of morals, the Christian education of youth, and the common peace and concord of all. And with the most intense eagerness we must strive, with God's good help, to remove all evils, both from the Church and civil society."

"Nec credo quod Papa possit scire totum quod potest facere per potentiam suam," writes the Augustine monk Augustino Trionfo of Ancona, in his "Sum of the Power of the Church"—"I do not believe that the Pope could know all that he can do by his power." He shows in that book that the Pope has not merely power over heaven and hell, but also over purgatory, and by his indulgences could clear it at once, only he thinks that he had better not do it if he can help it. Pius IX., who, somehow or other, has contrived to lose the best part of his patrimony, to put himself in the wrong with the secular powers, with all Italy—that same Italy which once hailed him as her champion and liberator, and which now with the last remnant of pious patience awaits his death to crown herself at Rome—may do all he says. The world may fall at his feet when the Syllabus is proclaimed, when the Blessed Virgin's assumption is made into a dogma, and when he is infallible, he and every single Pope that ever lived. But, perchance, it may not. If not, he may imitate the example of Benedict XIII., who, forsaken by all Christianity, retired to his castle of Peniscola, there to pronounce his anathema over all Christendom. And when the Council of Constance had formally deposed him he pointed to his few faithful monks and said, "At Peniscola, and not at Constance, dwells the Church; even as in Noah's Ark there was whilom assembled all humanity."

And, indeed, though at Rome, and though in the midst of his prelates, about whose poor part in the whole transaction we shall yet have to speak, Pius IX. already sits in grim solitude. The last paragraph of the Syllabus declares it a damnable error to suppose that the Pope "can or ought to reconcile himself and come to an understanding (recon-

ciliare et componere) with progress, liberalism, and modern civilization." Was anything ever more precise? Never has the curse pronounced by Innocent III. upon our Magna Charta and the Barons that framed it been abrogated, but it has grown and spread since, and two worlds rest under its shadow in peace. That "disgrace to the English nation," that "thing of no account," which, in its thousand reflections and images, has now become the supreme law of nearly all civilised nations, shall they, shall we abrogate it at the Council's bidding? Or shall not the winds of Heaven carry back to Rome its own weird cry, echoed by a whole world, *Non Possumus?*

SEPTEMBER 21, 1869.

Roma locuta est. But what a difference between the answers once and now! "The only line of conduct on the part of the Government with regard to the Œcumenical Council is one of *complete inaction.*" Thus, telegraphically, Catholic Belgium, since we last wrote. And, as a matter of course, "no delegate will be sent" by that Catholic Power. By way of complement to what we said last week, the *Constitutionnel* of a few days ago gives further utterance to the official mind of France. It is all for the best of the Council that the Emperor does not mean to send a representative. The relations between Church and State in France, it says, are very well settled by the Concordat. A delegate would tempt the assembled Fathers into the erroneous belief either that the Government wished to interfere in the discussion of dogmas which do not concern it in the least, or, on the other hand, that it admitted the right of the Council to discuss "matters belonging exclusively to the secular Government." These are very hard words to bear all the harder, as they are universally admitted to represent the views of the firstborn son of the Church himself. And the answer given to them by the official Roman press is wofully deficient in strength. Governments should send their delegates, it says, in order that these may tell them "what the Council considers to be the duties of Governments towards their subjects." " But they will have to learn that lesson yet, sooner or later," it adds mysteriously.

Nor should, among the latest official utterances, that of Switzerland be omitted. These sons of the Alps have a diplomatic way of their own. Count Hohenlohe, having proposed that they should join in preventive measures against the resolutions of the Council, they reply, somewhat curtly, that they did not see any reason for doing so; they had nothing to do with any deliberations; but if the resolutions of the Council should trench upon any of the religious rights of their citizens, or in any way tend to a breach of the peace, then the clerical dignitaries were very well acquainted with the Federal Constitution and the legal means it provides against any such illegal attempts. Alas! Will no one interfere? Shall the pathetically expressed " expectations" of the general meeting of the Catholic Leagues of Germany "that both the Governments and the Princes will refrain from taking any steps which might disturb the liberty of these deliberations on the part of the Council," be so literally fulfilled? Where is the time when the position of worldly dignitaries at these Councils was matter of gravest import? And where, too, are the days when Emperors said, as did Constantine the Great with regard to the Council of Nicæa, " What has seemed good unto three hundred holy Bishops is not otherwise to be considered than the sentence of God's only Son." Time was when the question whether these Councils were divinely or humanly set was very hotly contested. Before the Fathers of Trent it was very eloquently proved how that these assemblies were the distinct counterparts of certain other Councils such as that of the angels in Job, or of the Trinity itself; not to mention those of Sichem, of " Pope " Eleazar, and Joshua, of Zadok and Abiathar, and so forth. But, by way of compromise, the middle course of styling them "apostolical" came to be adopted, because the Synod of Jerusalem, in 52 A.D., when " the Apostles and the Elders came together for to consider" a certain grave matter which had caused "no small dissension and disputation" at Antioch, is taken to be the first authoritative Council of the Church. It followed that the words used on that occasion, "for it seemed good to the Holy Ghost and to us," were with some variations adopted by those Synods that came after. Thus Cyprian writes to Pope Cornelius,—" It has pleased unto us at the suggestion of the Holy Ghost (*suggerente*)." The Synod of Arles says,—" It has, therefore, pleased unto us, in the presence of the Holy Ghost and his Angels." No wonder that Gregory the Great placed the authority of the four first Councils on the same level with the four Gospels.

Another question seems settled now. If Church historians are not agreed on the point with whom the convocation of General Synods lies—the worldly or ecclesiastical Powers—this chilling indifference on the part of the former sets that point at rest. As a matter of fact, however, the first eight Councils have been convoked by Emperors, either at the supplication of the Popes, or the Popes were asked to send their Legates. It is equally beyond dispute that in some of these Councils the Emperors presided " πρὸς εὐκοσμίαν "— " for the sake of good order "—as the documents of the fifth Council have it. Alas! neither Napoleon, nor Francis Joseph, nor Victor Emmanuel—not even Isabella of Spain, will claim precedence of seat or vote this time. Which reminds us that ecclesiastical ladies did take part in Synods, notably in England. At the Synod of Whitby in 664, where such questions as the tonsure, &c., were discussed, Abbess Hilda took her proper seat, as did somewhat later Abbess Ælfleda at the Synod held on the Neith river in Northumberland.

" Speech is silver, silence is gold," says the Eastern proverb. If the Powers offend by their reticence and discretion, two documents which have appeared in print since our last article will offend more by their utterance, though even they contain more between the lines than within them. We mean, in the first instance, the answer given by the theological faculty of Munich, the substance of which we gave last week. Secondly, the pastoral letter issued by the Bishops at Fulda assembled, previous to their departure to the Council. The theologians of Munich are already declared to have put themselves in open antagonism to the Church. They are accused of attempting to bring the worldly arm and influence of the State to bear upon the deliberations of the Church, and of standing out in appalling contrast to the unanimous declaration of the Bishops assembled in Rome in 1867. These, 500 in number, had entirely and unconditionally, and with "one mouth and one heart," agreed to everything the Pope had said, affirmative or negative; they adopted what he adopted, they rejected what he rejected; while these German professors dare to hint that Pater Schrader—he, the official exegete of the Syllabus —has not well understood certain theses of this document, because its promulgation in the shape which he gave it would be fraught with grave perils. Still worse, perhaps, is the apparently loyal declaration of the Bishops of Fulda, who, assembled at the tomb of St. Boniface, address their dioceses on the subject of the Council. "They do not," they say, "think that this Council will be a magic cure for all ills and dangers, and that it will change at once the face of the earth;" they only look upon it as a means of further opening up "the gates of Divine truth and wisdom." As regards, however, the fears that even among faithful members of the Council have found expression, they wish to remind them that—

"Never and never shall and can a General Council establish a dogma not contained in Scripture or in the Apostolical Traditions. . . . Never and never shall and can a General Council proclaim doctrines in contradiction to the principles of justice, to the right of the State and its authorities, to culture (*Gesittung*), and the true interests of science (*Wissenschaft*) or to the legitimate freedom and wellbeing of nations. . . . Neither need any one fear that the General Council will thoughtlessly and hastily frame resolutions which needlessly would put it in antagonism to existing circumstances, and to the wants of the present times; or that it would, in the manner of enthusiasts, endeavour to transplant into the present times views, customs, and institutions of times gone by."

In reply, finally, to the insinuation that there would not be the fullest liberty of debate, they say:—

"The Bishops of the Catholic Church will never and never forget at the

General Council, on this most important occasion of their office and calling, the holiest of their duties, the duty of bearing testimony to truth;
they will, remembering the Apostolic word, that he who desires to please
men is not the servant of Christ, remembering the account which they will
soon have to give before the throne of the Divine Judge, know no other
line of conduct but that dictated by their faith and their conscience."

There is a very peculiar ring in these words. This is not
the voice of the *Civiltà*, neither of that Ultramontane party
in Germany whose organ are the *Laacher-Stimmen*; neither
is it Liberal Catholic Germany which speaks through these
Bishops—that Germany which, deeply devoted to the Church
though it be, distinguishes carefully between it and Papacy,
and which finds utterance in the *Allgemeine-Zeitung*. We
wonder how these Bishops will discuss the paragraphs of the
Syllabus. But when, in another place, they innocently hold
that "the Church contains within itself the most varied
communities, corporations, and phases of religious life, that
it tolerates, nay *protects*, the differences of theoretical and
practical opinions," they seem to have forgotten much.
Shall it be ours to remind them of a certain institution
called the Index? Let us trust that the general loyal
tenour of this their pastoral letter will make the powers that
be overlook those black spots, as they did with *Eusebius's*
Chronicle and Church History, which escaped condemnation
in the very first Index ever compiled, only through the
several instructive notes contained in it.

The Index: it has been rather busy again of late, though
it does take its time, and authors dead and gone for a generation may be summoned bodily to appear and defend their
misdeeds; or they may live, like Dumas *père*, and, having
for thirty years or so been translated into all the languages
of the world, watch the effect of the interdict upon the
lending libraries. But it would really not be very difficult
to find reasons why both these aforesaid documents should
not be placed upon that list, whether on account of a *sen-*
tentia erronea, or *hæresi proxima*, of a *sententia de hæresi*
suspecta, *hæresim sapiens* (the smell of heresy!), or of one
"*male sonans*" of a sentence offensive to pious ears, or one

" *scandalosa*," " *seditiosa*," or " *temeraria* ; " for it is by these canons that the critics of the Vatican review books, and in the good old times the matter might be of some consequence even to the life and limb of their authors.

The Council of Trent had a good deal to say on this Index question, and we are not sure that the new Council may not find it among the minor work now being prepared for them by the congregations. The origin of the whole institution has been found by some in the Acts—in Paul's exorcising the spirit of divination within that certain damsel " which brought her masters much gain by soothsaying." As early as 325 the Fathers of Nicæa prohibited Arius's " Thalia," and the first prototype of all future Indices was prepared by a Council under Gelasius. True, the printed Acts of the Councils speak of this Index as dating of 494, but, considering that it contains a work by Sedulius which did not appear till 495, the last year of Gelasius must be assumed to be the right one, more especially as all other conjectures do not hold water. The decree in question, " *De libris recipiendis*," itself does by no means contain the prohibited books only. On the contrary, it first gives the Biblical canon, as first fixed at the Synod of Hippo, in 393. It next fixes the respective ranks of the Churches—to wit, Rome, Alexandria, Antioch. And the opinion held in the old and later Church that Peter and Paul had suffered on different days under Nero is declared heretical. Next come the Councils recognised by the Church, Nicæa, Ephesus, and Chalcedon. The fourth division is devoted to the enumeration of the patristic works approved or partly approved. To the latter belong the Acts of the Martyrs, which are not read in the Church because their authors are partly not known, partly heretics, and would cause offence among the ignorant and unbelievers. Origen is only partly to be read, inasmuch as he is approved by Jerome ; the rest, together with their authors, are to be disapproved (*renuenda*). Eusebius, as we mentioned above, is to be tolerated, though he has been rather lukewarm in the first book of his relation, and though he has written a book in defence of schismatic Origen. But he has made many instructive notes. The fifth division condemns un-exceptionally a number of so-called "apocryphal" books of "*opera spuria*," of "heretical" books, or books the authors of which were in the odour of heresy, certain Acts of Synods —which have thus unfortunately perished—many Acts of Apostles and Evangels, and among these not only the Pastor Hermas, but that very book upon which the dogma to be promulgated by the forthcoming Council is based—the *Liber Transitus (assumptio) S. Mariæ.* Other works condemned are the writings of Tertullian, Lactantius, Africanus, Montanus, &c., as well as the correspondence between Christ and Abgar and all phylacteries and writings of heretics from Simon Magus to Acacius of Constantinople. Many are the various readings in the different codices of this decree, and wild and hot have been and are the battles of the learned on the subject. But in the main the points at issue do not alter the facts here enumerated. On this book of the Assumption we shall speak anon. Meanwhile we will follow in its outlines the history of this censorial movement. As long as literature was a thing of clerks and scribes, who, however fast they copied, could easily be checked, the Church was safe. With the invention of printing, however, the matter began to assume a serious aspect, and though it was styled of the Devil and the "black art" in general, it throve amain. The printing presses were, therefore, placed under ecclesiastical supervision. No book was allowed to be printed without express permission of the episcopal bench, on peril of excommunication, of a fine of a hundred ducats, the public burning of the work in question, and the ruin of printer and publisher generally. But when at the time of the Reformation the number of pamphlets, and treatises, and sermons, and letters, and theses became "even as a flood," this simple control proved of no avail and proper *Indices* were printed. These contained the works prohibited, the inquisitorial decrees, the names of heretics, whether they had published anything or not, the names of printers who had once issued some heretical work, and whose future books, whatever their contents might be, were therefore

Q

prohibited once for all. Flanders, France, Spain saw the birth of the first of these productions. Gradually the thing assumed an official character, and Paul IV. is glorified as the first *summus censor librorum orbis terrarum*. Editions of this official document appeared in Rome in 1549, in 1557, in 1559, and Pius V. handed the whole matter over to the Council of Trent. The Council of Trent did not seem to care much for this business, the less as many grave voices made themselves heard in its midst—how that this was not their proper work, but belonged to a learned academy; further, since "the *Index* as it lay before them comprised both good and bad books;" and finally a committee was nominated which laid down ten rules, and from want of time —the Council sitting only about twenty years—handed the matter back to the Papal Chair. From that time dates the *Sancta Congregatio Indicis Librorum Prohibitorum*. Instituted by Paul V., it received its constitution by Sixtus V. Every now and then a new edition was published, with additions. The one published in 1664 under Alexander VII., comprises the decree of the 5th of March, 1616, condemning Copernicus, "*de revolutionibus orbium*," and that of the 23rd of August, 1634, on Galileo's Dialogue. And ever since it has continued its labours with grim rigour, in spite of Benedict XIV.'s somewhat milder regulations, and some of its latest decrees were directed against the moderate German philosopher and theologian Gunther—decrees which have hastened the crisis in Germany.

One of the questions put before the Theological Faculty of Munich turned upon the point whether a Papal *ex cathedrâ* utterance was or was not binding as such upon every Christian's conscience? And the professors confessed not to know what an *ex cathedrâ* utterance of the Pope meant. There are no criteria, they say, whereby to recognize the same. There are, they allege, no less than twenty different hypotheses on the conditions requisite for a like *ex cathedrâ* decision. "And perhaps the Council will wisely decide that point, together with the Infallibility"—they conclude. This *ex cathedrâ* has indeed been a puzzle to many within and without the Church. A distinction is made between the utterances of the Pope as " *Doctor Privatus* " and as " *Doctor Ecclesiæ*," but no one knows when he speaks as one or as the other. All that is required, or rather presupposed, by the Church is that, when speaking *ex cathedrâ*, he should have consulted some one first, should have gravely pondered over the matter in hand, should have prayed that God might enlighten him. But even if he had not done so it cannot alter his decision, for, say the ecclesiastical authorities, this would open the doors to all manner of doubt and heresy, since any decision of his might be put aside on the plea that he had not sufficiently pondered over the matter. And, as a matter of fact, the Church has put aside many an undoubted *ex cathedrâ* and " *doctor ecclesiæ* " decision, such as Innocent III.'s decree that all the ceremonial laws of the Deuteronomy are binding for the Church, since Deuteronomy means the second law, and the second law could only mean the second Church, which is Christianity; or, to go a little further back, as Vigilius' decision on another literary production, the writings of the three theologians, Theodore, Theodoretus, and Ibas, suspected of Nestorianism. In 546 he declared them to be orthodox, in 547 he pronounced them to be heterodox, and in 553 again declared them orthodox, whereby he offended the fifth Œcumenical Council at Constantinople, convoked by Justinian, which, as he defended his views by the " Constitution," broke off all Church communication with him. Whereupon he recanted personally, saying that he had hitherto in his opposition to the Council and its views been the instrument of Satan. He died, however, on his way back to Rome.

But this question belongs rather to the chapter of the " Infallibility " and its historical progress. We have only turned to it here by way of digression on the *ex cathedrâ*. And well observes an old writer, Ebermann, that, on the whole, though there may be occasionally a weak or ignorant Pope, yet his words must be considered binding in all ways, since it is not so much he who speaks, but that through him speaks He who before now has spoken through the mouth even of a she ass—"*qui novit etiam per asinam loquentem dirigere iter nostrum.*"

We shall speak now of the most innocuous of new dogmas to be inaugurated by the Council, that of the Assumption of the Virgin Mary. We have mentioned already that the fundamental work in question stands on the first Index of Gelasius. And as late as the ninth century, Usuard's "Martyrologium' says, under the heading "*Dormitio Sanctæ Dei Genitricis Mariæ,*" that although her body, that venerable temple of the Holy Ghost, was hidden by the Divine Council, yet the sobriety of the Church had preferred pious ignorance (*cum pietate nescire*) to teaching aught frivolous or apocryphal on the subject. There are a number of versions of the legend thus condemned extant in Greek, in Latin, in Arabic, in Syriac, being more or less translations of each other. The story is by no means bereft of a certain poetical fervour, though some of its features belong to other Greek and Aramaic legends, notably that cycle of sagas of the Assumption of Moses, to which Jude alludes in his Epistle. As authors of the Greek and Latin respectively are mentioned John the Apostle and Bishop Melito, of Sardis; the latter directing his version principally against one Leucius. Thorny are the critical questions which beset even this little tale; but for them we must refer our readers to the proper folios, or octavos, as the Arabic, the Syriac, the Greek, and the Latin have all been edited within the last fifteen years or so, some even for the first time. And these are the outlines of the legend.

Two years after the ascension of Christ (but even here, at the outset, we are met by discrepancies as to date in the various versions) an angel appeared to the Virgin, bearing a palm branch, saying, "Hail, Mary, full of Grace, God is with thee. On the third day from this thine assumption shall come to pass, thy Son expects thee in the midst of the angels." And she begged that all the Apostles might be summoned near her. The angel promised it and departed amid great radiance. And all of a sudden, wherever the Apostles were, even to the ends of the earth, John in

Ephesus, and Simon in Rome, and Paul in Tiberias, and
Thomas in India, and Matthew in Berytus, and Bartholomew
in Armenia, &c., they were lifted up by a cloud and brought
to the door of Mary. And when they had all prayed there
arose at the third hour of the third day a great commotion
and earthquake, and Christ descended in a cloud with hosts
of Angels, and Michael took Mary's soul into Paradise.
Next the Apostles went to bury the body, while a great
light shone around them, singing " When Israel went forth
from Egypt." But while they went to the valley of Jeho-
shaphat a certain Jew came out of the town and began to
abuse them and to take hold of the bier, whereupon his
hands clung to it and he could not remove them, suffering
great agonies, while the Angels in the clouds struck the
people with blindness. He is then converted, seeing the
miracle and having kissed the bier is healed, and the palm
branch is given to him that he might remove the blindness
from the eyes of the people, and when they had buried her
and closed the vault, Christ appeared again and asked the
Apostles what they thought he ought to do for the Virgin.
Whereupon they counselled him that as He had taken her
soul He should also take her body. And this was done.
Michael rolled the stone from the mouth of the tomb and
Mary sprang forth and blessed the Lord, and He kissed her;
and as she rose Heavenwards she threw her girdle down to
St. Thomas, who had been saying Mass in India, and who
had suddenly been transported to Mount Olivet. He kissed
it and took it to the Apostles, who were still assembled at
her now empty tomb. They would not at first believe that
he had seen her rise to Heaven, but when they saw the
girdle they were convinced. Then the same cloud which
had carried the Apostles from their different places took
them up again and transported them to their different places,
" even as Abacuc, the prophet, carried the food to Daniel in
the lions' den and was carried back to Judæa."

One MS. concludes thus, after stating that the author was
" Joseph, who placed the body of Christ in my sepulchre and
have seen and spoken with Him after His resurrection,"—

" and let every Christian know that he who has this book by him or in his house, whether he be an ecclesiastic, or a layman, or a woman, the Devil will not hurt him, his son will not be a lunatic, or a demoniac, or deaf, or blind. In his house there will be no sudden death. Whosoever shall read this sermon shall be saved."

And this is the basis of the dogma of the Assumption, to be solemnly proclaimed, if all goes well, perchance yet in this year of grace, 1869, as one of the means to restore universal peace and goodwill among men, and to remove all evils " both from the Church and the world." And still the world stands aside, silent, preferring its evils, but marvelling greatly.

October 5, 1869.

"*Eritis sicut Deus—*" "and ye shall be like unto God, knowing good and evil." . . . Here is the dogma of the Infallibility, worded very precisely. We know who first laid it down and what ensued. If we are not mistaken, it is Mephisto also who, in the guise of Faust, inscribes these words into the album of the young student.

There is a peculiar fascination to our minds in this dogma. The most repulsive, the most humiliating though it be to all human dignity, there is yet a something about it which arouses a morbid curiosity. The very boldness with which for the last five or six hundred years—for full thirteen Christian centuries no one dared even to hint at a like notion—it has ever and anon lifted up its face among men; that boldness with which, at this hour, with all that has gone before of Rome and its Popes, it claims public recognition, endows it with a weird interest. And its manifold stages as well as the means by which it grew do, indeed, form a rare chapter in the history, not merely of Rome, but of all mankind.

But we must forbear, for the present, to speak of it. We shall rather turn to the manifold signs and sounds around us, sounds not very unlike those that issue startlingly and abruptly, and not without casual admixtures of grotesqueness, from a tuning orchestra. And first of all there is that Papal despatch to "Dr. Cumming of Scotland,—Care of Archbishop Manning"—which has arrived since our last. There is a blushing coyness displayed in it with regard to this same Infallibility, even as that of a bride before the happy day. In one place it is the "opinion held by the Church as to the infallibility of its judgment;" in another, "we thereby signified that the primacy, both of honour and of jurisdiction, which was conferred upon Peter and his successors by the Founder of the Church, is placed *beyond the hazard of disputation.*" Turn we, however, to another passage of a more instructive nature in this letter. "No room can be given at the Council for the defence of errors which have already been condemned." Does this mean that Councils do not reopen questions settled by other Councils, notably questions on "errors condemned" by them? Our readers are acquainted, no doubt, with that famous work of Pseudo-Isidorus,—those hundred and odd forged decretals and synodal acts, which ever since Pope Nicolas I. have worked such terrible mischief, and which now are condemned by the Church itself. Can it be that a new history of all the Councils has been prepared by those cardinals and professors now so busy in the Vatican *in usum Delphinorum?* If not, we fail to see the force of the statement. Or does it mean that there will be no time for discussion—that there is still alive in the Vatican that fondly-cherished hope of making this Council "like unto that of Chalcedon"—*i.e.,* of three weeks' duration? Convoked by the Emperor Marcian, and subsequently approved by Leo I., that Council sat from the 8th October to the 1st of November, and the assembled prelates worked so hard approving the ready-made canons (the number of which was at once disputed) that they could have put both our Houses of Parliament, of Convocation, nay, even the Ritual Commission, to the blush. In 14 (or 13) days they held no less than about 21 sittings. But, unfortunately, of all the manifold meetings of this Œcumenical Council κατ' ἐξοχὴν, only the first six were subsequently allowed to have been œcumenical, and it has been deemed expedient to preserve a record of them alone in the oldest MSS. of the Synodal Acts. Worse still, this great prototype of the coming Council ended by the Papal Legate Lucentius uttering a protest "against what had been decided upon contrary to the canons, and he would go and tell it to his master, the Apostolic Bishop, so as to enable him to come to a decision with regard to the insult thus offered to his own chair and the breaking of the canons." And nobody cared. The protest was duly entered into the protocol, and the Commissioners adjourned the meeting, quietly remarking, "The decisions we have read the whole Synod has confirmed." The point in which the Council thus set aside the Pope and his demands was neither more nor less than the setting up of a " New Rome "—Constantinople to wit. " To the chair of the Old Rome," says the twenty-eighth Chalcedonian canon, "the Fathers have vouchsafed certain prerogatives *on account of its being an Imperial residence*, and on the same grounds have the 150 Bishops here assembled vouchsafed the same privileges to New Rome, which should, for the same reasons as the old, be exalted in ecclesiastical matters even as the elder Imperial Rome " — (" καὶ ἐν τοῖς ἐκκλησιαστικοῖς μεγαλύνεσθαι πράγμασι "). And this objectionable canon, which strikes at the root of Roman supremacy, remained in force in spite of Leo's loud and violent protest and threats, and breaking off of communications, and the rest of it. *Absit omen.* Several other vexatious things came to pass at that Council, among them that trifling mishap which occurred in the sixteenth sitting. When the Imperial Commissioners requested both the Roman and the Greek Legates to substantiate their claims, the Roman Legate, Paschasius, read out a translation of the sixth Nicæan canon, with the little addition, " *Quod Ecclesia Romana semper habuit Primatum.*" Whereupon, say the Synodal Acts, the secretary of the Consistory, Constantine, forthwith produced the Greek original, wherein not a trace of those words was to be found. And the Roman Legates were much confounded. How that passage came to be there in the Latin document "none could ever

tell." Howbeit, is it not the only sudden " various reading"
in the history of Roman documents.

No; Chalcedon was not a happy precedent to go back to.
We do not say that either Paris, or Vienna, or Madrid is
very anxious just now to play " New Rome,"—Council, Pope,
and all. We have repeatedly had to record their painful
indifference regarding all things connected with the Council;
but there were better examples to choose from, we should
have thought. Why not take, for instance, the very first
Œcumenical held at Rome, in 1123, under Sixtus II.,
whereof there are absolutely no contemporary accounts?
On that occasion there were assembled nine hundred members, that is to say, two Abbots to one Bishop, and its very
first canon starts proudly with the words :—" We prohibit by
the authority of the Apostolical See,"—the Fathers assembled being, so to say, nowhere. It was opened on the
18th of March, and on the 6th of April the Bull embodying
its work was already issued, signed by the Pope and the
Cardinals. There certainly was a little unpleasantness
mixed up with it too. The case of the Archbishop of Pisa,
to whom the Pope had first given the right of consecrating
Bishops, and whom he had subsequently deprived of it, had
been submitted to the Council by Calixtus, though, as he
said, " No mortal has a right to judge a decision of a Pope."
And when the judgment of the Council went—as a matter of
course—against the Archbishop, he threw his ring and his
crosier at the Pope's feet—" for which the Pope severely
reprimanded him." Or the very next Œcumenical, 16 years
later, the second of the Lateran, might have been taken as a
pattern. Innocent II. opened that with an extraordinary
speech, likening his own Bishops to her who had received
ring and staff from Judah (Thamar). He next proceeded,
according to Harduin, to snatch the crosiers from the hands
of the Bishops of his rival, Petrus Leonis, and to tear
with his own sainted hands the *pallia* from their shoulders.
Among the other business of the session there was also
the excommunication of King Roger of Sicily; while
Theobald of Canterbury was invested with the *pallium*, and

the founder of Fulda—whence the Bishops lately issued their manifesto—was canonized. These and a few other things settled, the assembled fathers and passive witnesses throughout were sent home. The Œcumenical which followed, in 1179, held altogether three sittings, wherein no less than 27 decrees or *capitula* were discussed. On the debates the records are absolutely silent—for the simple reason that there were none. Its official title had already become "Generale Concilium *Summi Pontificis.*" Some of its canons are, by the way, instructive.

For example, in order "to obviate the further selling of Church ornaments, for the purpose of covering the expenses caused by episcopal visitations," it was ruled that no Archbishop should henceforth go about with more than forty to fifty horses, nor any Cardinal with more than twenty-five; a bishop was not to exceed the number of from twenty to thirty, an Archdeacon from five to six, and Deans were not to have more than two: which seems hard. Neither should they bring hounds or falcons to their visitations. Another canon rules that churches, Church benefices, and the like should not be given away before they have become vacant. By a third canon ecclesiastics of a *higher* degree are to dismiss their concubines, and a cleric who frequents nunneries "more than is necessary" shall be reprimanded by his bishops, and eventually be deprived of his Church benefice. The last but one canon, the one renewed in the happy days of the Concordat in Austria, rules that neither Jew nor Saracen shall keep Christian servants, and that those who live in the same locality with a Jew or a Saracen shall be excommunicated. But if history is silent as to debates at this Council, it is a pleasure to learn, at least, that there were present two English, two Scotch, and one Irish Bishop, Laurentius, who possessed three cows, and was appointed Legate of Ireland.

We have digressed. We cannot help thinking that even the *Amen*, as it was, and still is, expected from the Bishops, may be a long-drawn-out one. Church music knows of certain compositions called *Amen fugues*, and many are the ups and downs in these same performances. To return, however, once more to the Pope's correspondence "towards" our Scotch divine. There was just one little point which we rather objected to. His Holiness had "seen from the newspapers." Now, we know that his Holiness does not disdain the noble pastime of billiards. If we may believe trustworthy authority he is not a bad hand at it either. We confess that it always gladdens our heart to think of his Holiness, against whom personally we have nothing but the tenderest feelings, beguiling an occasional hour in this gently frolicsome manner. Some of his predecessors sought their pleasures elsewhere. But "seeing from the newspapers!" He does not even say in the *Civiltà,* or in the *Tablet,* or in the *Westminster Gazette,* but newspapers! It seems to overthrow all one's notions. Holiness, Infallibility itself, skimming a column of *The Times* between two strokes. He really should not have said it. And if that Patriarch of Constantinople irreverently refused to look at the Encyclical because "it had already appeared in the public papers" his case was different. Abbate Testa did not present himself before him until many weeks after the Encyclical had been in print. But a letter to Rome, even "from Scotland," *ought* to have reached the Pope before the newspapers. But let that pass. Let his Holiness cheerfully continue to read his papers. His path is not altogether strewn with roses. Hadrian IV. used to say that "the most miserable state on earth was that of a Pope; his throne was surrounded with spikes on all sides; his happiness was bitterness, and a burden too heavy to bear, weighed his shoulders down even to the ground:"—a woful utterance echoed by Nicolas V., who added that "there was not a more miserable and unhappy creature on earth than himself," and that also "there was not a soul that would tell him the truth." More heart-rending still is that bitter cry of Marcellus II., that he did not see "how any Pope could ever be saved!"

The interval has brought us also the episode of Père Hyacinthe, the Carmelite superior, the pet of Notre Dame, who "raises his protest" with no uncertain voice. He will not be gagged. A " Son of the Saints," he will not be " one of the dumb dogs." He, too, appeals to the Council "as a Christian and a priest, against those doctrines and those practices which are called Roman, but which are not Christian." If this Council should not have freedom of deliberation, which, he says, is " the essential character of an Œcumenical Council," he will " cry aloud to God and to man to claim another, really assembled in the Holy Spirit." He withdraws from the monastery, which is changed for him into " a prison of the soul;" he " rejects the chains which he is offered;" he appeals to Christ himself, even as Huss did. " *Ad tuum, Domine Jesu, tribunal appello.*" And what is the answer? Many words of hard abuse, many sighs, many tokens also of applause, many conjectures, and " It is said that the Reverend Father will be excommunicated."

Excommunication — Inquisition — to us what do these words mean? Even to him what will they be? But there was a time when they did mean something worse than a thousand deaths. We shall take an opportunity of recalling these ghastly subjects to our readers, so that those who have forgotten may remember and never again forget. If other countries have, from " religious " motives, poured out human blood like water, they have bitterly repented, and they have as with one accord inscribed independence of religious opinion upon their banner. And Rome?—She issues the Syllabus. This Syllabus will not hurt a fly, but it proclaims aloud that Rome has not changed, will not change, and cannot change. *Non possumus.* We have already expressed our profound sympathy with Père Hyacinthe, as we would with any one who cried out from the depths of his soul. But we confess that, though we see in him a champion very different from many who have issued forth like himself in single combat against Rome, we know not yet what he means to do beyond leaving his convent. Will he arraign the authorities that bade him revoke, before the Council? But he at once declares that he will not submit if judgment goes against him. And, altogether, to talk of Hyacinthism as some French organs already do, seems to us a little too premature. Has he, beyond the wild cry caused by that long Roman hand which laid itself with an iron grip around his neck—has he a programme? How far does he object to Rome? And what is the meaning of another Council to which he will appeal? Composed of whom? How far does he renounce, if he renounces them at all, those words of his which we happen to have before us, contained in his *Conférences* of 1866?—"Nous sommes les représentants humains de la souveraineté divine sur les consciences. . . . La souveraineté de Dieu, le Royaume de Dieu, c'est l'Eglise." And again, in defining this Catholic system, he calls it, "Le règne de Dieu sur les consciences! . . . Nous sommes les représentants de Dieu. Le règne de Dieu existe ici-bas, organisé, complet, vivant—c'est l'Eglise." If the Catholic Church be "the reign of God over the consciences," we do not quite see how he can object to its decrees. Nor does he seem inclined to reject what he held before in any way. Let us wait and see. We would neither underrate the weight of his step nor expect too much. Meanwhile, we cannot help congratulating the eloquent and bold friar that he lives in the Paris of 1869—though it be the year of the Vatican Council.

And there is balm in Gilead, even in Munich. Two professors have not shared in that well-known reply given by the theological faculty of Munich. They answer by themselves. But we fear, though this answer is intended as a pre-eminently ultramontane manifesto, it will please Rome even less than the other. It is a very long document, which we have printed already, and the gist of which is best given in its own words :—

"From this detailed reply to the five questions there follows the dogmatic general result that an eventual sanctioning on the part of the next Œcumenical Council of the Syllabus as it lies before us, and a raising into a dogma of the Infallibility of the Pope as speaking *ex cathedrâ* would not alter directly (*unmittelbar*) as such the present *status quo* between Church and State, and would not carry with it as a doctrine binding upon the conscience of every Christian the dogma of a divinely instituted sovereignty of the Pope over the Monarchs and the Governments. Nor would

the further doctrine of a divine origin of the personal and real immunities
of the clergy, not merely generally, but also in detail and purely as such,
produce any transforming influence upon school teaching as far as the relations between Church and State are concerned."

If our readers should find this not over easy to comprehend, we can assure them that it was far from easy to
translate—more especially as there is not a single full stop
in the whole paragraph. We had first to uncoil many a
weary noun and adjective and participle, and what we
believe are called "auxiliary sentences." But if both our
readers and ourselves may complain of this hard task, that of
the dissenting professors was harder still. No wonder they
took time. Their answer to Count Hohenlohe goes to show
in the main that with all the Infallibility of Church *and*
Pope, the decrees of Council would, as far as their practical
bearing is concerned, be mere official waste paper ; nay, not
even would the teachers of dogmatic theology be bound
to take notice of them. More especially as regards the
supremacy of the Pope over temporal Governments, they
argue (in reply to question two), that whether this supremacy be declared a "*potestas directa*," or "*potestas indirecta
in temporalia*," it mattered absolutely nothing. Because
"such a dogma *could* not be laid down as binding to a
Christian conscience, but would ever remain matter of *free
theological opinion*,—even if it *could* be proved valid by
scientific arguments of the most profound and striking kind."
Speaking of the *ex cathedrá* utterance of the Pope, they, too,
find it difficult to decide what constitutes a like "*locutio*,"
and hope, as did the other professors, that this may be
settled by the "infallible" ecclesiastical office itself. As to
Father Schrader, the official framer of the Syllabus done
from the negative into the positive, he seems already
disavowed, thrown overboard, found wanting. There is not
one word of him. On the contrary, these two *malcontent*
professors always "assume that the paragraphs of this
Syllabus *errorum* (by a curious misprint the word *terrorum*
figures in our copy) should be rejected unchanged as they
are." But here comes a delightful piece of comfort. Even

if they be so rejected, in "Bausch und Bogen," they argue "they would not for all that be rejected as heresies, at least not *in toto*; but there would be many different degrees of censure attached to them, as, indeed, most of these paragraphs have substantially already been condemned by the Church." They would only be as a Papal letter has already styled them—"Propositions and doctrines respectively false, audacious, scandalous, erroneous, injurious to the Holy See, derogatory to its rights, subversive to the rule of the Church and its divinity, schismatical, heretical, and contrary to the Council of Trent." And, the document naively adds, has not the Council of Constance called many of Wycliff's and Huss's theses only *sententiæ erroneæ, temerariæ, seditiosæ*," and has not Martin V. himself confirmed that mild judgment, instead of calling them *heretical?* Good Pope! Most lenient Council! But did we not read somewhere that this same benevolent Council burnt that man Huss alive? And were not, only the other day, vast multitudes gathered together in that ancient city of Prague to do honour to the memory of the "Saint and Martyr," some of whose opinions had been declared "erroneous?" Let these professors beware! They are uttering many *sententias seditiosas!* Neither does it seem very likely that the Vatican will smile upon them for raking up, just at this moment, with the most innocent air in the world, memories which it fain would bury out of sight. In their German thoroughness—unless they be wolves in sheep's clothing—they go over a goodly list of decrees on the part of Popes, backed by Councils, against the temporal powers:—how Innocent deposed Frederick II. in the Council of Lyons, by virtue of the power of binding and loosing given to him by Christ—words into the original meaning and purport of which we may enter by-and-by; how his subjects were declared free of their oath of allegiance and their duty of obedience towards him both as Emperor and King, and how the *Excommunicatio latæ sententiæ* was pronounced upon all those who should give him any "advice, help, or favour." And, continue these indiscreet advocates, did not the Council of Trent excommu-

nicate all those—Emperors, Kings, Dukes, Princes, &c.—
who allowed duelling within their domain? and were not
their cities, fortresses, or places bestowed upon them by the
Church, near which a duel should happen, forfeited?—an
ecclesiastical fact which, for all things in the world, looks
very much like a special reminder to Napoleon III. and the
gallant journalists of the Second Empire. Indeed, they say,
if all those emanations against the temporal Powers, by
Gregory VII., by Urban II., by Lucius III., by Innocent III.,
by Honorius III., by Gregory IX., by Paul IV., by Pius V.,
in bulls, and decretals, and letters innumerable, have never,
even within the Church, unanimously been considered more
than "assertions" of a *theoretical* Divine right, they cannot
surely, neither they nor their like, be now made binding
either "*de fide*" or "theologically." True, the first Gallican
paragraph which authoritatively embodies that view has been
styled "heretical" or *hæresi proxima, erronea*, &c., but these
censures they hold are of a private nature, not ecclesiastically
authoritative:—even though Innocent XI. and Alexander
VIII. disapproved this Gallican constitution, and Pius VI.
called the paragraphs of it *temerarias, scandalosas, injurias.*
All this, they conclude, does not affect the teaching. There
are many different theories on the subject, and no decree
of the Council would make any difference in the interpretation and expounding of these and the like matters on the
part of Ecclesiastical Professors. Infallibility or not, *ex
cathedrá* or not, Council or not, those things must and
will ever remain subjects "of free theological opinion."

This is the voice of the two Professors of Righteousness.
We were bidden to hold our hands until we had heard this
protest. We have heard it, and we think it more damaging
than either Fulda or Hyacinthe. But the Roman Press did
not see at first, and partly pretends still not to see, what
harm there is in the Fulda Manifesto.

These Germans! Whenever they issued from their woods
they have always proved dangerous foes to Rome—from the
time of Varus to that of Luther. And now they advance
upon her, daring her with her own decretals:—those same

decretals over which, as Dante has it, the Pope and the Cardinals have forgotten Gospel the Nazarene :—

> " l' Evangelio e i Dottor magni
> Son derelitti, e solo al Decretali
> Si studia sè, che pare a' lor vigagni.
> A questo intende il Papa e i Cardinali
> Non vanno i lor pensieri a Nazzarette
> Là dove Gabbriello aperse l'ali." . . .

OCTOBER 19, 1869.

By this time Père Hyacinthe lies under the *Excommunicatio latæ sententiæ*, coupled with the "mark of infamy." Ten days the General of the Barefooted Carmelites gave him to retract, "to raise himself generously, and to repair the great scandal." He has not answered the solemn summons. But, as the *Gaulois* informs us, M. Charles Loyson, *ci-devant* Frère Hyacinthe, is about to start a newspaper, entitled *The Christian, Echo of Clerical Democracy.* Another account describes him as having departed for America.

We should, we confess, have liked to see an answer from Hyacinthe to the letter of the General, who avers that he never dreamt of prohibiting Hyacinthe from preaching, either at Notre Dame or any other church. On the contrary, he told him to confine himself exclusively to the pulpit. The strictures passed upon him referred to his speeches at the Peace League and other public places. He writes :—

"You must know, Reverend Father, that I have never forbidden you to preach, that I have never given you any order or imposed on you any restrictions with regard to your sermons. . . . If you have renounced a reappearance in the pulpit of Notre Dame it is of your own free will that you have renounced it, and not in virtue of any measures taken by me towards you."

Extremely characteristic, by the way, is the manner in which the Roman press treats the matter. In one instance, it is " the fall of a leaf towards the autumn." The wind of pride had dried it up, the frost of rebellion had chilled it long ago, and now it has become detached from the living

R

trunk, and has fluttered to the ground. And although the master of the vineyard may mourn over it, he cannot save it. It must be trodden under foot and its place will know it no more. More dried leaves have fallen in their time, and have gone to bury themselves in the mire. There was Carlo Passaglia, there was Cristoforo Bonaviso, and Eusebio Realli, a Lateran canon; there were the Liverani, Bobone, Perfetti, and dozens of others who fell away during the Italian Revolution; there were the many Frenchmen of great and little note, and among them Robert de Lamennais, of whom Hyacinthe "possesses neither the talents, nor, as yet, the sins." And whether these rebels be dead or alive, their end has been miserable beyond words, while Rome lives, and will live, and the Church passes on from generation to generation. "Is Pius IX. less great, less powerful, less formidable in consequence to his enemies? No, certainly not. All the harm has come to the leaves only."

But as if to balance these proud assertions, another "inspired" organ takes the other line—*ad misericordiam*. The Rev. Father Hyacinthe says in his letter that he intends to appeal to another Council from the decrees of the forthcoming one, which, he has reason to believe, will not be "free." And why, asks that organ, is the Council not to be free? "Who will intimidate it or bribe it?" *Pius IX., old, feeble, poor Pius IX.*, who, so far from having to give anything to his Bishops, has to rely on poor Peter's pence which they are about to bring him?" As to these poor contributions, it may be observed, in passing, that the collections are being pushed on with great vigour and enthusiasm, and that, together with the mites expected from the Bishops, the trifle of from four to five millions is hopefully and confidently looked for at Rome.

Meanwhile, M. Loyson is not quite given up yet. Santa Teresa is being particularly invoked to "stop him on the brink of the precipice." And there is hope even for the excommunicated. If they are beyond the pale, if no one may eat with them or speak to them, they may become Popes for all that. There was, *e.g.*, Formosus, Bishop of

Porto, who, though excommunicated by Pope John VII., followed Stephen V. on the Papal throne. Shall we digress again? He recalls an interesting episode in Church history, one which bears most emphatically to our minds upon the subject of Popes. It has also something to do with the "Bulgarian question."

The Bulgarians, it seems, did not embrace Christianity till the end of the ninth century, although, or because, they had been in close connexion with the Byzantines for many generations. At last they were baptized. But their king, Bogoris, soon found himself, in spite of all the instructions of his Greek missionaries, even of the Bishop who had baptized him, and given him the name of Michael, in a hopeless state of puzzle and bewilderment. Not only did his subjects object to the new faith and rise in rebellion against both it and him, but he did not know what this his new faith really consisted of. The many dogmas and ceremonies preached to him and enforced upon him by the shoals of teachers who now flocked into his dominions, each bearing new, contradictory, and even heretical tenets, became too much for him, and he despatched legates to the two religious authorities of the time—the Emperor of Germany and the Pope of Rome—to ask them for proper teachers. But long before the clerical envoys of the Emperor of Germany had reached Bulgaria, bearing vessels and garments and books, the Roman priests had already taken possession of the length and the breadth of the land. Wherefore the Germans more speedily returned than they had come. One of those special legates sent by the Pope was our Formosus, and he brought with him 106 chapters of replies to the questions raised by these new believers. Let us extract a few.

One of the first of these canons treats on the subject of trousers. The Bulgarians may wear them, it says, both they and their wives, as they please. Those who are drunk may not go to the communion, but they who have bled from their noses may. A woman may go to church on the very day of her delivery if she likes. The books taken from the

Saracens are to be destroyed. A husband is not to dismiss his wife *excepta causa fornicationis*. It is not lawful to rest from labour on Saturday; it can only be permitted on Sunday. Bathing is allowed both on Wednesday, Friday, and Sunday. The horse's tail on the top of the standard is to be replaced by a cross. Criminals may be punished *except when they are clerics*. No one is to pray for relations who have died in a state of unbelief. The three patriarchal sees founded by the Apostles are Rome, Alexandria, and Antioch. The Bishops of Constantinople and of Jerusalem, though called Patriarchs, have not the same authority, because the former was only established through princely favour (they had evidently forgotten the Chalcedonian Council at Rome), and the latter, the present Jerusalem, is no longer the old one, which has been totally destroyed. The law books which the legates have brought they have to bring back again, " because you Bulgarians would not interpret them properly. As to Christianity, about which you want to know, since, as you say, you have Christians of all kinds, Greeks, Armenians, and others, among you who teach different things—*the Roman Church has always been without any stain and possessed of the true Christianity*. My legates and your future Bishop will always tell you what is to be done in dubious cases—the last appeal lies with the Apostolic chair." These and other things—also the gifts brought by the legates—pleased King Michael so much that he, by way of symbol, caught hold of his own hair and vowed himself and his subjects the perpetual servants of the Roman Church. He then sent a second legation to Rome begging that our Formosus, who had displayed great talent in this mission, might be made Archbishop of Bulgaria. But they knew better at Rome. He was not made Archbishop of Bulgaria, under the plea that he had already a see of his own and must not change. He was excommunicated instead by Pope John VII., on account of these Bulgarian matters. But another Pope came to the throne—Marinus, and he forthwith removed his uninfallible predecessor's excommunication. He passed away and another Pope also, and when Stephen V.

died Formosus himself ascended the Holy Chair. Five years later he was murdered, and was followed by Boniface VI., who sat on the throne of St. Peter for exactly a fortnight, and made room again for Stephen VI.

But we have not done with Formosus yet. By command of the new Pope his corpse was taken from the tomb, dressed in Pontifical garments, and bodily arraigned before a special Council. A deacon was engaged for the defence, and the charge ran "that the Pope Formosus had from criminal ambition exchanged his episcopate Porto with the Chair of Rome." The defence was considered non-valid, and the dead man was solemnly condemned—the tribunal decreeing that he was not a legitimate Pope, and that all his decrees as well as all his ordinations were null and void. He was thereupon deprived of his robes, the three fingers of his right hand, wherewith the Papal blessing is given, were cut off, and the mutilated corpse was thrown naked into the Tiber. So that his former state of excommunication would have been better than his latter state. True, Pope Stephen VI. himself was dragged out of the church, thrown into a dark prison, and strangled the very next year. He was followed by Pope Romanus, who was murdered four months afterwards, and was succeeded by Theodore, "the benevolent," who was murdered twenty days afterwards, and was followed by Sergius III., who was expelled, and was followed by John IX. He held three Synods in two years, and died to make room for Benedict IV., who was murdered three years later, and was succeeded by Leo V. Four weeks afterwards he was murdered by his chaplain Cristophorus, who became Pope, and who six months later was thrown into prison and killed there, and Sergius "the Antipope" ruled in his stead. Here follows that famous epoch called the *Pornocracy*, coupled with the names of Theodora the mother, and Marozzia and Theodora her daughters: even Marozzia, the mother of Pope John XI., about whose father the ecclesiastical writers may be consulted with advantage. Sergius, "*homo vitiorum omnium servus*"—the slave of all the vices— died soon under suspicious circumstances; but he received a noble epitaph in the Vatican, on which he was styled "the good shepherd who had loved all his flock together," and visitors were informed on it that in that place they would behold the remains "both of the 'pious Sergius' and of Peter the Apostle." Next Anastasius III. came to the throne, which he held for two years, and after him Laudo, who ruled for half a year and eleven days. And after him came John X., the favourite "nephew" of Theodora the Elder. When he had been thrown into prison and murdered Leo VI. was chosen. Six months afterwards he was followed by Stephen VII. Two years later Marozzia's son, but twenty-five years old, became Pope. But Marozzia's other son imprisoned both his mother and his brother the Pope, who died in the third year of his imprisonment, and was followed by Leo VII., who died two years afterwards.

But we really must stop—only that the history of the Papacy is so very fascinating, replete on every page with matter of quite thrilling interest. It has but one drawback. There is so much blood. And its fumes mingled with those of many ghastly revels, are apt to make the brains of us poor fools of "civilization and progress" to reel and our hearts to grow sick within us. . . . . What were those words the Archbishop of Westminster spoke the other day? "I" —the Pope—"claim to be the Supreme Judge and Director of the consciences of men; I am the sole last Supreme Judge of what is right and wrong." Shall we answer this? Let that most horrible procession of murdering and murdered Popes answer. Let him go into his own chamber and answer himself. . . . . "Sole last Supreme Judge?" Did it ever strike him that Gregory the Great repudiated with horror what he called the "blasphemous and criminal" title even of "œcumenical patriarch?"

But by the side of this all the other statements made by his Eminence pale. Divorce, secular education, and religious doubts are the *foundations* of civilization. The state of Rome is the proof of the "Supernatural Society," for "piety, morality, public order, true civilization, charity, courtesy, justice, and goodwill." So be it. There is nothing like a positive statement. As regards divorce, however, would it not be wise if Dr. Manning, a theologian, were a little less scathing and scornful about it? He should remember that, after all, it is a "Divine Institution," and to be found even in the Vulgate, in spite of its many corrections and emendations of the text. But we shall not discuss these matters with the Archbishop. He knows best, no doubt, what he ought to say. Also, why it is England, of all countries in the world, which has been chosen as the special butt at this moment. We do not mean the wanton and absurd insult expressly thrown in the face of London—bad as it may be—as compared to Rome, that sink of sinks. What we mean is the way in which this supreme sovereignty of the Pope is flaunted in our face in preference to all other nations. While in Germany, for instance, the official Roman organs deny as loudly as ever they can all and any desire on the part of the Pope to set himself over worldly powers, we, in England, are told that the "Prince on the throne and the Legislature that makes laws for kingdoms"—both Queen and Parliament—stand under the jurisdiction of this "Supreme Judge." In order to prove how remote a like thought be from the Papal mind, the distinct disclaimer of Boniface VIII. himself is adduced by other official Roman writers and speakers. Nay, they go so far as to quote the words of Innocent III.'s Decretal "*Novit*," at the very outset of which he protests that "no one should think of him as wishing to diminish or disturb the jurisdiction of the King or his power—he, the Pope, who cannot sufficiently exercise his own jurisdiction, why should he wish to usurp another?"—and further, "*Cum rex superiorem in temporibus minime recognoscat.*" In their zeal those apologists have, it is true, forgotten what else is to be found in Innocent's works. That he is God's real representative in all things, *veri Dei vere Vicarius*, is a phrase which occurs up and down in his letters. And in his epistle to the Emperor of Constantinople he proves to him that the "submitting" to kings or governors which St. Peter enjoins upon all men (i. 2, 13, and 14) *does not include priests*. Furthermore, he tells him, "Thou shouldst know that God created two lights in the firmament, the sun and the moon—that means, he created two dignities, the Papal authority and the regal power. But the former, which is set over the days, *i. e.*, the spiritual things, is greater; that over the things of flesh is smaller, and there is the same difference between Popes and Kings as there is between the sun and the moon." Need we say that the scholiasts have danced a mathematical jig on this passage? The earth, they say, is seven times bigger than the moon, the sun is eight times bigger than the earth: *ergo* is the Pontificate 47 (?) times bigger than royalty. This figure, however, did not seem quite to suffice, and Laurentius amends it by another arithmetical process into exactly 1,744 times, by which the Pontifical power surpasses that of royalty. But not these and the like passages are chosen by the spokesmen abroad. We are alone, it seems, to be favoured with a barefaced and exaggerated revival of theories which elsewhere are zealously hushed into silence. These theories have before now been heard in this land of ours, and much blood and many tears have been shed through them. Are the times deemed ripe in the Vatican? Let these counsellors beware. Rome has had to rue many a too hasty step, too loud a cry, too defiant a challenge.

Converts are not always desirable acquisitions. We are told that the Jews compassed sea and land to make one proselyte. We are also told that they likened their converts to a very objectionable and irritating bodily disease, and that they did never quite trust them, even to the twenty-fifth generation. The German reformation was ripened, if not brought about, by the too zealous agitations of a Roman convert. Among ourselves we have those who have been pronounced "thorns in the side of their new mother." But Archbishop Manning, we deem, has by this oration, sincerely meant as no doubt it was, struck her a heavier blow than she has received from either Fulda or Munich, Hyacinthe or the Cabinets of Europe. Let him now go to Rome, that abode of saintliness, and move, according to the programme, the dogma of the Infallibility. Let him receive his red hat—he has well deserved it.

Regarding that first reply of the Munich Faculty—not the so-called Protest of the two Professors—there have been some very bitter words in the Bavarian Press. It appears that there has been a little shuffling. The official organ, in publishing it, did not publish it at length. It preferred to omit the very important introduction. Questioned on the subject, it took refuge in a variety of replies—first, that the introduction was of no consequence; next, that it placed the reply in a totally different light, and was, therefore, irrelevant, we presume. But the opponents were not to be appeased. They wanted the introduction *sans phrase*. It, too, has now been published. And here it is:—

"In replying to some questions put before them by the Royal Bavarian Government regarding the forthcoming Council, the undersigned did not think they were doing anything which ran counter to the good traditions of former centuries. It is well known that the legates (*oratores*) of the Catholic monarchs and States took a vivid interest in the Council of Trent. These legates were furnished with carefully-weighed instructions referring to subjects fixed or proposed for the debates of the Council, and not rarely tried on their part to advance propositions or to influence the course of the transactions and the framing of the final decisions. To this hour, it is true, the Catholic Governments have not been invited yet to take part in the Council, but it doubtless lies in the nature of the given circumstances that they, too, should endeavour in good time to get clear on the point as to what eventually should be their line of action in the face of resolutions which, not merely possibly, but scarcely otherwise than necessarily, must touch upon political ground. The history of the last Council of Trent offers manifold proofs that precisely those monarchs who were most distinguished by religious zeal and devotion towards the Church had furnished their legates with the most detailed instructions and orders. The undersigned do not feel called upon to decide whether the questions put before them by the Government are the only possible ones, or even the most prominent ones, that might be put under the given circumstances in this exalted matter. But in answering them, as they do, according to their best knowledge and conscience, they are penetrated by the vivid desire that also thereby that harmony between Church and State may be furthered which, at least as long and in as far as there exist Catholic Governments, should not be a mere ideal. As sons of the Catholic Church, the undersigned preserve with their entire heart that devotion towards the deliberating and deciding authorities of the future Council to which every disturbing interference is absolutely foreign, and only because and inasmuch as they would wish to see the Church secured also in its outer existence against the distinctive tendencies of impiety do they wish that in every respect a real and clear understanding on the limits and points of contact of the legal State with the order and task of the Church be either preserved or the way be paved towards it."

What is most important and most formidable about this procemium is the fact of these Professors suggesting more questions to be put and to be answered. They evidently like their task. But, honest, learned, and involved as they are, we think they have, on the whole, said enough for the present. Let them rest on their laurels for a while. We know their views, and so do the Bavarian Government and the Vatican; and we cannot think without a shudder of reading, translating, and inwardly digesting a few more columns like unto the former. Meanwhile the Gallican Church has sounded the war-note by no less a personage than the Bishop of Sura (where is Sura? we have heard of a Jewish Academy of this name; is there to be a new "prince-dom of the exile"?) *and* Dean of the Theological Faculty of Paris, Monseigneur Maret. He has written two volumes *On the General Council and the Public Peace*, which he submits to the Council. More are to follow, but these may suffice as to the general tendency. In a circular letter to his brother Bishops he refers them to the preface of the book, written, he says, in the exercise of an episcopal right, and inspired by love to the Church and the Holy See. He has dedicated these two volumes to the Pope himself. In the letter addressed to His Holiness he writes first to excuse himself that he cannot himself be the bearer of his work, inspired, he repeats also to him, by his episcopal duty. "At the moment of the assembling of an Œcumenical Council," he proceeds, "which is called upon to perform such great tasks, and foreseeing, as I do, the sinister consequences wherewith projects might be fraught, conceived and proclaimed by venerable men who, however, do not seem fully aware of the perils of their undertaking—it appears to me both useful and necessary to draw the picture of the constitution of the Church in its greatness and perfection, and in that unchanging character which its Divine Founder intended to impart to it." He has published this book, he says, so that all may read it—the Pope, the Bishops, the priests, the people, clerics as well as laymen. "I publish them before the Council so that they all *may have time* to read them." Briefly, the whole work, from beginning to end, is devoted to one object—to the most fervent and unsparing fight against the dogma of the Papal infallibility and to the defence of Gallicanism. "In professing all the respect due to the decisions and bulls of Sixtus IV., Alexander VIII., Clement XI., Pius IV., we adhere to doctrines which appear to us true."

If the Gallican constitution is called an arsenal, these volumes are a powder-magazine. They are learned, being the matured labour of many years; they are eloquent, they are daring. They, above all things, mean war—war to the knife. And there is a peculiarly French note of fierce sadness ringing out in the first lines, which contrasts very strikingly with both the scorn and the satisfaction of our Westminster Archbishop:—

"After eighteen centuries of Christianity, what spectacle does the intellectual and moral world offer? . . . The Christian religion is divided into hostile and rival communities. In the midst of the highest culture, of a brilliant civilization, philosophy shrinks from religion, science divorces itself from faith, politics cannot direct men any longer towards their higher destinies, the noblest aspirations of our nature remain without any fixed object, the human soul is floating at the mercy of the most contradictory doctrines and tendencies."

We 'shall have to return to this book again and again. The Council begins to bear fruit already: such as has probably not been foreseen. There will be a greater harvest still, we ween, before it is all over. And all this time those busy men of the Vatican work, work, work. And this is, according to good information, their present procedure:— The Pope, assisted by the leading Congregation of Cardinals, works out the sketch of every single canon; the Congregation of Cardinals next sends it to the Congregation of the Six Committees; the Cardinal who presides over these collects the votes, together with the *motives*, and returns them to the Cardinals' Congregation, which finally redacts the wording of the canon and sends it, together with a *précis* of the votes, to the secret press of the Quirinal. The volume thus gradually forming is not to be shown to the Bishops before the day of the Council, so that, it is said, not only the whole initiative will remain in the hands of the Pope, but the Bishops will not have too much time to prepare their eventual opposition. But the Vatican has by this time become aware also of the clouds that are gathering around, and it has in its wisdom bethought itself of a counter-blast to all those jarring, professional, episcopal, and journalistic voices. The plan of an album has been conceived. Lists are circulating among the "learned and educated" in which "any one who occupies himself with profane or sacred science" shall subscribe in advance a formula of submission to the decrees of the Council. That it should be ours to tell it! Even in Rome, that ideal representative of the "supernatural," with all her ecclesiastico-academical bodies and schools and colleges, not more than fifteen names could, as the *Correspondance Havas* informs us, be gathered for this album. So that the intended monster-folios will have to be reduced to a pocket edition, and a very minute one, which is grievous.

November 12, 1869.

The Eastern proverb says, "Woe is me when I keep silent; woe is me when I speak." So long has the Vatican been abused for apparently taking no notice of all the ominous voices and tokens around, that it has at last broken its Trappist vows. That "Moniteur of the Vatican," the "true echo of the Holy chair": even the *Civiltà*, has been authorized to give a piece of the infallible mind to the world, before the official hour has struck. But how golden was that silence—how erudite, how eloquent, how honest compared with that speech! There are in the last two numbers of that organ two emanations—Encyclicals in undress, as it were. One treats of the Bishops of Fulda, another of the positions of the Fathers in Council, and, by way of *bonne-bouche*, even the long-forgotten "Liberals of Bonn and Coblentz" are passingly mentioned. To them, of course, the answer was brief and obvious enough:—"Did they imagine the Council would be without the Holy Ghost?"—And nothing more need be said on that score. A Council cannot err; the Holy Ghost knows better than all the Prelates—than even those of Coblentz and Bonn. Or do they doubt it? If so: Anathema!—So far, so good. Next comes Fulda. Here the answer was a little more difficult. But Rome is up to the occasion. With all the hammering in St. Peter's and debating in congregations and framing of new Latin pronunciations and house-huntings for the saintly guests and laying in of stores—even cigars, if rumour speaks true—and the erection of monuments for events which have not happened, and the gathering in of pence and collecting of autographs, and all that feverish, festive bustle that keeps the powers that be at work day and night: their right hand has not forgotten its cunning. What the *Civiltà* is made (officially) to read out of that formidable Bishop's manifesto is simply—" a victorious refutation of the liberal calumnies." This Pastoral, it says, will clear up " all errors that may still be floating in the public mind with regard to the Syllabus and the Council." Do not these Bishops end with a wish for the " Unity and harmony of the Church?" And what but Liberalism produces division and schism in the Church? Has not His Holiness for this reason also condemned it in the 80th thesis of the Syllabus? *Ergo*, do the Fulda Bishops in their manifesto show themselves good and true sons of the Church by condemning so emphatically what the Pope has condemned, viz.—Liberalism!—*Q. e. d.* Is there anything in and out of the *Epistolæ Obscurorum Virorum* to be compared to this reasoning? We know it not. But what we do know is that these Bishops will give their own explanation in good time—if they can make themselves heard in Rome.

We think it was that delightful nation of the *Lalenbürger* who once built unto themselves a splendid Town-hall. And when it was quite ready, and the solemn inaugural procession was forming, it struck one of the worthy burghers that a trifle had been forgotten in that brave erection—the windows. Whereupon they were advised to collect as much sunlight as they could and carry it in in bags; which they did. Twice has the original plan of the Council-structure in St. Peter's been altered, until at last everything was most satisfactorily settled—throne, galleries, benches, curtains, and all, down to the mosaics behind the Bishops' seats—when of a sudden it occurred to an indiscreet questioner whether, as there was to be some speaking in the Council, people would be able to understand what the speakers said? And, lo! it was tried, and it was found that not one syllable would be heard; so that, instead of the Tower of Babel which was expected, there was to be a deaf and dumb asylum. And now, at the twelfth hour, it has been decided to save appearances and to accommodate the Fathers in another place. Lest, however, the enormous outlay might be supposed to be wasted, these same Fathers will solemnly be marched in to the original structure on the first day, and forthwith marched out again.

Will they say much in that other place? Or rather, will what they do say be of the slightest consequence? Also on this question — a very burning one — has the Vatican spoken by the mouth of its own infallible echo. Not directly, though,—there might be rocks ahead,—but in an "inspired" letter to the *Avenir National.* And thus says the *Civiltà* :—

"What is the Pope in relation to the Episcopate in Council assembled? As the successor of Peter, he is, according to Scripture, the corner-stone of the Church, the possessor of the keys of Heaven, the Shepherd of the flock of Christ. According to the Council of Lyons, he is the guide of the Universal Church; according to that of Florence, he is the head, the father, the master of all Christianity. . . . These are the relations between the Pope and the Church, whether the latter be considered in its isolated and special groups or as a whole, *in corpore* or in Council. What, then, tell us these relations between Pope and Church in their special groups or in Council? Supreme authority and subjection—the former vested in the Pope, the latter the part of the Assembly of the Bishops. . . . Not only have the Popes, whenever they deemed it useful and proper, fixed the term of the definitions, but they therewith combined the prohibition to discuss or in any way (*menomamento*) to alter them! . . ."

This is clear enough. Professors of Munich, Bishops of Fulda, Hyacinthe in America, Maret in Paris, Catholic world, take notice! No illusions, no compromise. The Pope has to command, the Bishops "have a right" to obey—implicitly. They may perchance be allowed to hold a conversation *sotto voce*, but as for discussing anything, how dare they!

We like this *communiqué*. It reads like an Encyclical; even with regard to its appeal to history, which it interprets as it does the Fulda Manifesto: facts being of the slightest possible consequence. And we cannot help further congratulating ourselves that leaders or *communiqués* in "Ephemerides" should begin to supersede Bulls. Here is a concession to that progress of the age which it is "a damnable error to suppose that the Pope could ever be reconciled with." However fearful and wonderful the weapons wherewith these saintly journalists fight, we prefer it greatly to the old familiar "*Excommunicamus et Anathematizamus.*"

Or have they forgotten the *Cœna Domini?* Why, indeed, use dead and rotten argument while there is a living Bull at hand? That question of the authority of a Council in relation to the Pope has been settled long, long ago:—

"In the name of Almighty God, the Father, and the Son, and the Holy Ghost, likewise through the authority of the Holy Apostles Peter and Paul, and Our Own, do we excommunicate and anathematize . . . . all and everyone, of whatever state, grade, and condition,—and even so do we lay the interdict upon all such universities, colleges, and chapters which, from our ordinances or mandates, or from those of the Roman Pope for the time being, should appeal to a forthcoming general Council. . . . ."

Thus the second paragraph of that famous Bull, which used to be read aloud, first three times, then once, a year (on Maundy-Thursday or *Cœna Domini*) by the Pope in the presence of all the Cardinals, Archbishops, and Bishops in pontifical garments, and in the presence of the vast concourse of people who, from the ends of the earth, had flocked to Rome for Apostolic absolution and blessing. After the reading, these highest dignitaries of the Church threw their burning tapers to the ground, trod them under foot, while the bells

were tolled in an irregular and funereal fashion—to indicate
that by this excommunication the light and the grace of the
Holy Ghost were extinguished in the excommunicated, and
while the believers were called to church by the regular
and clear sounds of the bells, *in pulsatione ordinata*, the
cursed ones were to be driven out and dispersed by those
vague and irregular "pulsations."   The Bull was next affixed
each time to the doors of the principal churches of Rome,
the Basilica of Peter and the Lateran Church, and most
horrible were its consequences.

It was well worth the time spent upon its composition, this
" *Bulla Cœnæ*," this famous Index of the " reserved cases"—
i.e., excommunications for crimes which only the Pope of
Rome himself could remove.   The very first of these cases
dates from the Council of Clermont in 1130, where Innocent II. reserved to himself alone the right of absolving
any one who had laid violent hands on a priest (*Percussio
Clerici*).   And by small degrees these cases increased in
number, until they reached the figure of about 110, of which
20 are embodied in this *Bulla Cœnæ*.   The framing of this
latter document took only about 300 years—from Urban V.
to Urban VIII.; but what a document it is, and how intimately it concerns us!   We gave the second paragraph
above; here is its first :—

" We Excommunicate and Anathematize, . . . all Hussites, Wycliffites,
Lutherans, Zwinglians, Calvinists, (&c.), as well as all and every heretic,
of whatsoever name or sect, as well as those who receive, protect, and
generally defend them, as well as such who knowingly read, keep, print
. . . their heretical or religious writings, . . . as well as those schismatics
who withdraw themselves from the obedience of the Pope for the time
being."

Another paragraph treats of wreckers—an occupation to
which, it seems, not only Bishops whose sees bordered on the
shore were given, but the privilege of which was regularly
bestowed upon certain monasteries.   When this amiable and
saintly practice was abrogated, a special exception was made
with regard to heretics and unbelievers, who, having escaped
the fury of the elements, were not to be spared therefore

.by the servants of God. Another paragraph enacts that no one should be prevented from going to Rome. That means that those Bishops who had hitherto been in the habit of kidnapping, imprisoning, wounding, ill-treating, and slaying such abbots, or priests, or fellow Bishops who set out to Rome for the purpose of lodging complaints against them should do so no more. Thus, *e.g.*, a wrathful Bishop of Bath locked his dissatisfied clergy up in their own church, and starved them into peaceful submission and the giving up of their travelling plans. The Bishop of Waterford seized upon the Bishop of Lismore on his way to Rome, threw him into prison and chains, and, " having well beaten him," took possession of his bishopric, even as did Archbishop Gaufrid of York with his malcontents, who were going to tell Celestine III. And while Napoleon III., that good son of the Church, places his own steamers, free of charge, at the disposal of the Bishops Romeward bound, the Emperor Frederic II. had sent his illegitimate son Enzius, in 1241, into the Pisan waters to attack the Prelates going to the Council. He made, indeed, a great haul of legates and Archbishops and Bishops and abbots on that occasion, and he carried them all in chains into Apulia. Philip IV., with much less trouble, simply confiscated the goods of all those Bishops who had gone to Rome in obedience to the call of Boniface. In the next place there are solemnly cursed those who in any way should molest ecclesiastics, or who should appeal from Rome to the worldly Powers, who cite clerics before a lay tribunal, who usurp clerical property, who levy taxes on churches or convents, and—finally—do " we excommunicate and anathematize all those who, by themselves or others, directly or indirectly, under whatsoever title or pretext, should presume to invade or occupy and hold the Holy City, the kingdom of Sicily, the islands of Sardinia and Corsica, the lands this side the Pharos, the Patrimony of Peter in Tuscia, the Duchy of Spoleto, the Counties Venaisin, Sabina, the Marches of Ancona, Avignon," and a vast variety of counties, dukedoms, provinces, cities in and out of Italy which, alas, have for many a long day since been so

invaded, occupied, and held. It has indeed had strange
fates, this pet Bull, fostered by successive generations of
Popes. There was mystery about it from its very birth.
The Patriarchs, Archbishops, and Bishops would not publicly proclaim it, some of the later Popes would not even
let it out of their hands, while the worldly Powers stamped
it out by common consent. Neither the *Avisamenta* nor
the *Centum Gravamina* of the German nation at the
Council of Constance even make mention of it. Philip II.
sent the Papal Nuncio, who came to proclaim it, out of
his empire, without hesitation. France, Portugal, and
Germany showed their contempt for it equally, and when
Clement XIII., forgetting that it was the latter half of the
18th century, excommunicated Duke Ferdinand of Parma
on the ground of this Bull, the days of Roman supremacy
were counted. France simply renewed the edict issued by
its Parliament in 1580, whereby all and any Bishops or
Archbishops who should make known this Bull would be
tried for high treason. Portugal promised to make an
example of anybody who should say a word in favour of this
Papal emanation, and that all or any judge who should as
much as mention it as a legal document should be treated
as a rebel against the King's person. A similar fate befell
it at the hands of Maria Theresa and the dukes and princes
and republics of Italy, until Clement XIV. wisely abrogated
the public reading of this Bull in church on the day after
which it was named, saying that "it was no longer a time
for Anathemas, but for Grace." Yet it has never been formally revoked, though Joseph II. made it actually disappear
from the rituals, suggesting that the blank leaf should bear
the words " *Obedientia melior quam victima.*"

The Council of Florence and the Council of Lyons, for-
sooth! Why not the Council of Chalcedon, too? For it
is but the feeble echo of that feeble organ of German Ultra-
montanism, the *Laacher-Stimmen*, which is reproduced now,
years after the original, by the learned of the Vatican. Why
have they dropped that third Council there quoted, we
wonder? And must we again freshen up their memory on

one or two little points in ecclesiastical history? Did they ever hear of the Council of Constance? It was there that we were told the other day, *à propos* of the different degrees of curse and condemnation attaching to opinions, that John Huss was so leniently treated. Not all his sayings had been accounted "heretical"—only a few. He certainly was burnt on that occasion, but that was only for a few things he held, not all.

That Council of Constance did many things. Among others, it issued, in its fifth general sitting, as " Decrees of the whole Synod," the following :—" 1. That this Synod, properly assembled in the Holy Ghost, forming a General Council of the Church Militant, derives its power directly from God, and everybody, *even the Pope*, is obliged to submit to it in that which appertains to the Faith, the eradication of schism, and the reformation of 'head and limbs' (of the Church, *scil.*). 2. Whosoever, *were it even the Pope*, persistently refuses obedience to the orders, statutes, and decrees of this Holy Synod, and every other legally assembled General Council, with regard to the above points and others related to it, is to undergo penance and to be punished accordingly, even if other (non-ecclesiastical) means should have to be resorted to."

That is explicit—is it not? More so than either Lyons or Florence, which are so grandly quoted by the Vatican advocates on the relation between Council and Pope, and which have no more to do with that question than with the man in the moon. But those Constance prelates were more explicit still. They first forced the Pope of the period, John XXIII., formally to abdicate, " on account of the great scandal caused by his great and heavy sins." He suggested two formulas of abdication, fraught with insults to the two anti-Popes of the period, Benedict XIII. and Gregory XII. But these formulas were rejected by the Council, and, finally, he not merely subscribed to another, but " swore and vowed solemnly and publicly to God and the Church, and this Holy Council, to restore peace unto the Church by laying down the Papal dignity." This he swore on the

2nd of March. On the 20th of the same month Frederick
of Austria gave a tournament, by way of entertainment to
the endless number of people who had flocked to Constance.
The clergy alone, with their servants, amounted to 18,000
persons. There were 1700 "Posaunner, Pfeiffer, Flöther,"
and there were, says honest Dacher, who had to make out
the lists, "mulieres communes, quas reperi in domibus, et
ultra et non minus, *exceptis aliis*, DCC," a number confirmed
by other list-makers. "Offen fahrend Dirnen ob 700, heim-
lich Dirnen und Curtisanen vast viel," say Reichenthal and
Justinger. And while they were all rejoicing at the tournament, ex-Pope John cancelled his resignation by abscond-
ing, in the disguise of an ostler, to Schaffhausen, whence
he informed the Council that he was very happy where
he was, "free and in fresh air." And the confusion and
the strife in Church and Council now became irreparable.
No less than seventy-two charges were drawn up by the
Council containing the crimes of which John had been
"notoriously" guilty, and of which murder, unchastity,
simony, and theft formed principal items. Eighteen of
these were subsequently struck out, "though they were
crimes well attested by witnesses—in order to save the
dignity of the Church." John had, in the interval, been made
prisoner by the Burggraf of Nuremberg, and at Radolfszell
these fifty-four dread charges were communicated to him
by legates of the Council. His reply was "that he most
deeply repented having furtively left Constance. Death
would have been better for him than this flight. He would
not defend himself. He submitted entirely to the decrees
of the Synod, as he had already previously declared. *The
Council was sacred and infallible and never would he think
of contradicting it.*" And on the twelfth general sitting of
the Council, held in the Cathedral of Constance, in the
presence of the Emperor, mass was sung by the Patriarch
of Antioch, and was followed by the Litany, with the verse,
"Now is the judgment of this world, now shall the Prince
of this world be cast out" (John xii. 31); at the end of
which Pope John XXIII, was formally deposed in terms

of most scornful contempt. All the charges against him were solemnly and briefly reiterated. He was condemned to be kept prisoner and to await further punishment. And with him were solemnly deposed Angelo Corrario and Peter da Luna—whilom Benedict XIII. and Gregory XII.—the two other infallible contemporary Popes; the one in Spain, the other in France. John's Papal Seal, or Bulla, having been publicly broken to pieces, and his Papal arms having been publicly and solemnly torn to pieces, the meeting adjourned, or rather service was at an end. When John was informed of it all he merely observed that they were perfectly right, and that he wished he had never been Pope. How he died, having bought his liberty for 30,000 florins, and having again been made Cardinal-Bishop of Tusculum by his successor, Martin V., is related in a very edifying manner in Church history. Indeed, he had but a narrow escape from being canonized. He lies buried in the famous Baptistery near the Cathedral of Florence.

One characteristic episode at the end of this wonderful Council must not be forgotten. The Emperor Sigismund, who played a very prominent part at it, had lived high at Constance, both he and his suite. But, as usual, he had no money. Whereupon the townspeople, his creditors, as he was about to leave, seized upon his dinner service. He however, equal to the occasion, addressed them in a very touching speech, exhorting them not to keep his plate, but rather certain beautifully worked coverlets and cushions, which he would take out of pawn without delay. They were much moved by this speech and kept the coverlets. But they had overlooked the little fact that these had the Imperial arms woven into them and could not in any way be sold, "which impoverished many of them of Constance to a piteous degree," says the chronicler.

The Vatican prelates do not refer to the Council of Constance, which is to the purpose. Nor do they refer to that of Basle, held under the very next Pope, Eugenius IV. For, finding the prelates assembled too much imbued with the spirit of Constance, which is equally pertinent, this Pope

closed the Council for a year and a half, to be reopened
at Bologna. But the Council peremptorily refused to be
closed. At Basle it was and at Basle it would remain, the
Pope was told, until it had done its business, which consisted
chiefly in " the amelioration of morals in the Church and
the restoration of peace," and by way of a further hint it
confirmed solemnly the decree of Constance whereby every
person, especially the Pope, has to submit to the authority
of the Council. They also begged his Holiness to favour
the assembly with his sublime presence or his representatives, " else they would feel compelled to judge him according
to the laws of the Church." The Pope, without delay,
graciously acceded to their humble wishes; which, however,.
did not prevent the Council, when he subsequently played
them false, from excommunicating his Holiness.

We repeat it : neither Lyons nor Florence, so glibly quoted
by these saintly *savans* in support of their pet doctrine of the
absolute power of the Popes over the Councils, ever touched
that question. The supremacy of Rome, in the matter of
rank, was discussed there, and in relation, not to prelates in
or out of Council, but to the *Greek Church*. And we know
how long the union arrived at on these two occasions lasted
—that one night's gourd. If the Council of Lyons had
established this same union in 1274, it was exactly in 1282
—eight years afterwards—that the Greek churches were
" plentifully sprinkled with holy water to purify them from
the taint of that union." And all its previous advocates
and wellwishers, both clerics and laymen, were laid under
penances, and the Greek Emperor, who had lent his countenance to it, was not even allowed a decent burial by his
own son. Thus much for Lyons and its achievements. Next
comes Ferrara-Florence, when the Greek Emperor, even at
the temporary price of the *Filioque*, wished the West to
relieve him from the Grand Turk, and when the Pope on
one side and the Council on the other tried to outbid each
other at Constantinople, even as two rival Cheap Jacks. One
of the principal sources for this Council is, indeed, formed
on a contemporary work called *A Truthful History of an*

Unjust Council, by Syropulos, himself a member of that
Council. Very amusing are the preliminaries to it—how
the Basle prelates and the Pope sent rival galleys for the
Greeks, and how the two nearly came to blows in the Bos-
phorus; how these Greeks were much puzzled as to which
was the proper firm—Basle or Rome; and how the Sultan
advised the Emperor Manuel (Palæologus) rather to form an
alliance with himself, against whom he sought the assistance
of these Latin rivals; what wranglings there were when the
assembly had been opened at last even on that vital question
where the rival chairs should stand; how the Pope contrived
to have a bigger and a more costly throne than either the
Patriarch or the Emperor—which made them both say bitter
things about the worldly vanity of Rome; how, further, the
rations of these Greeks were stopped the instant they
proved unmanageable, and were increased whenever they
behaved properly:—all this is very instructive reading, and
it makes one's heart ache in these days to read that the Pope
allowed His Majesty during his attendance at the Council
no less than thirty florins a month, while the Patriarch
received twenty-five, the "Despot" twenty, the "officers"
four, and the servants three florins a-piece. No less
instructive are the discussions of this Ferrara-Florence
Council themselves. The third point on the list—Purgatory
—being chosen first, great and hot disputes arose, in which
Judas Maccabæus, and St. Paul, and Lazarus, and Basil the
Great, and Gregory of Nyssa and John Damascene, and
Peter, and Abraham's bosom were freely handled by both
parties; and when, in the course of the debate, the question
was put by a Latin prelate, What was the nature of hell fire?
his Greek opponent glibly answered that the eminent Father
who had put the question would, he was sure, in good time
find out the answer by personal experience. No more could
they agree about the state of the souls of the saints, or any
other similar topic, as long as they were at Ferrara. But
when they had received two florins extra pay (and their
four months' arrear besides) for their journey from Ferrara
to Florence, whither the Council was removed in 1439,

things went on more smoothly—until that second union came to pass, which was, if possible, of even less duration than the first. The first cry of the Greek Bishops when they touched their native shore was, "We have sold our faith; we have exchanged orthodoxy for heterodoxy. May our hands which signed the unjust decree be cut off! May our tongues which have agreed with the Latins be plucked out!" And the people shunned them, and their clerical brethren would not even officiate with them. Nor was the union itself proclaimed in Constantinople, and before many years had passed it was a thing of naught. A Church Council assembled in Santa Sophia in 1450, which solemnly and unconditionally revoked, rejected, and annulled for ever the decree of the Council of Florence "as contrary to the Faith."

Such is a sample of the arguments now in preparation at the Vatican. As regards especially this Greek question and its present aspect, our readers may remember what we told them in our first paper about the reception of the Papal Legates by the Patriarchs. They may find further details as to the contemporary Greek opinions in a learned and lucid paper in the current *Edinburgh Review*.

Two more regal utterances have come to hand since we last wrote. Both Prim and Victor Emmanuel have officially declared that they will not allow the Council's eventual decrees to interfere in any way with the laws of their lands. And there are dark rumours afloat regarding the occupation question. What if Napoleon III., in order to give the Vatican absolute freedom of deliberation, should withdraw his troops just for the time being? There is something fascinating in the picture of what would happen. If Napoleon had any humour left in him, here is, indeed, an occasion. However, come what may, there is one piece of comfort left. Isabella, late of Spain, has promised to be present at the Œcumenical Council. Who can say that there is no balm in Gilead?

XII.

APOSTOLICÆ SEDIS.[1]

"*Apostolicæ Sedis Moderationi*—" it has befitted the moderation of the Apostolic See to issue, in accordance "with the
change of times and things," a new edition of Excommunications, Suspensions, and Interdicts. — Thus, briefly, the
preamble to the notorious "Constitution" promulgated by
Pius IX. at the beginning of the present Council.

We do not intend to consider the merits of that document
either from the philosopher's or the antiquary's point of
view. Neither shall we enter upon its single clauses, armed
with the Bible and the Fathers, theologically. We only
offer a few stray data towards the better understanding of
some of its details. If there be a moral in them, it shall be
the readers', not ours, to point it.

Our document contains six principal divisions. Four are
devoted to Excommunications exclusively. Of them we
have a sum total of thirty-six. Twelve of these, again, are
"especially reserved" to the Pope, while seventeen are
merely "reserved" to him. Three are left to the bishops,
or "ordinaries," and the final four are "reserved to nobody."
The fifth general division contains seven cases of Suspension
reserved to the Pope, and the whole decree winds up with
two "reserved" Interdicts. Thus the sum total amounts to
forty-five. All these cases are *Latæ Sententiæ*, which means
that such Excommunication, Suspension, or Interdict follows

---

[1] This article appeared in 'Macmillan's Magazine,' February, 1870.
Re-printed by permission.

the respective transgression without any further process—
sentence being, as it were, already pronounced: while in
what is styled *Ferendæ Sententiæ* a special investigation and
verdict are requisite. The term, like many others used in
the Church, belongs to classical Rome. In that ancient
Commonwealth it meant to give one's vote or judgment,
or rather, to *carry* (*ferre*) that vote, in the shape of a
little waxed tablet, inscribed with certain initials (*A*-bsolvo,
C-ondemno, &c.), to the *Cista* (not *sitella*) or urn. Voting
in Council, which was done *vivâ voce*, was, therefore, mostly
called *sententiam dicere*, to *speak* one's opinion.

The first and principal division consists of the old *Bulla
Cœnæ*, with certain alterations to be mentioned further on.
This "Lord's Supper Bull" derives its name from the fact
that certain anathemas which it embodies were promulgated
by the Popes—down to exactly one hundred years ago—
first three times a year; finally, only once. The day
specially fixed upon was Maundy-Thursday, as the day of
grace when Christ after supper had prayed for the unity
and concord of the Church. It was on that day, also, that
Paschal II., in 1102, excommunicated Henry IV. of Germany
as *hæreticorum caput*, and Gregory IX. did the same to the
Emperor Frederick II. in 1227: somewhat to their own
later discomfiture. And on that day, year by year, it was
the Pope's privilege, immediately after he had pronounced
the apostolic benediction over the countless multitudes, to
utter as many curses as the Bull, which always moved with
the times, contained during his pontificate. It was the office
of the cardinals, archbishops, and bishops who surrounded
him, dressed in their pontificals, to throw, when the last
word had been said, the burning tapers to the ground and to
tread them under foot. The bells, meanwhile, were set in
motion, but in a peculiar fashion, so as to make their tolling
a thing of great horror. They were rung "inordinately,"
and "*in detestationem*," viz. of those who had been cursed.
Finally, the decree was nailed to the doors of the Basilica
of St. Peter and the Church of the Lateran. Those who fell

under its provisions were forbidden to participate in all or any sacrament and to enter a church. No one was allowed " to pray with them or to speak to them, to eat with them or to drink with them, to hold communion with them in council, to kiss them or to greet them. They are not to be buried, and no bell is to be tolled where they have lived." And all this was carried out in very bitter earnest.

The *Bulla Cœnæ*, in its latest shape, which is due to Urban VIII., embodies twenty of those cases in which the Pope alone, to the exclusion of every mortal, can absolve, and which, in this sense, are "reserved" to him. This, so far from being at first considered a hardship, was pressed upon the Papal see by the Clergy itself. The very first authenticated "reserved case" established at the Council of Clermont in 1130, was, as it were, "an Act for the better protection of ecclesiastical persons," and probably owes its origin to England. The English law of the period did not, it seems, take sufficient care of the ecclesiastics in the realm, and loud and incessant were their cries against the violence they had to endure "at the hands of robbers and evil-doers, who do not sufficiently respect the Church of God and His anointed." And when Innocent II., after the death of Honorius II., had been furtively elected Pope by a minority of sixteen or seventeen cardinals—an Antipope, Pier Leone, the favourite of Rome, being proclaimed as Anaclete II. by a majority of thirty cardinals the very next day—and had been confirmed by St. Bernard amid general acclamation, one of his first acts at that Council of Clermont was the canon called *Percussio clerici.* The anathema, to be recalled only by himself, was pronounced upon any one who should lay violent hands upon any clerical person or monk. The offence, however, cannot have been of very long standing. The preamble states that " *new* medicaments must be applied to *new* vices." The anathema was renewed in the following year at the Council of Rheims, in 1134 at that of Pisa, and in 1139 at that of the Lateran ; while at a synod held in London in 1138 (at which clerics were also forbidden to carry on the trade of usurers), and at another held either at Westminster or at Winchester in 1143, this edict was, as "necessary for the time," especially and solemnly promulgated for domestic use. At the latter synod the Fathers of their own accord added another crime as "reserved" for the Pope, viz. that of breaking into churches.

The principal force of this "Reservation" lay in the fact that the culprit was compelled to make a journey to Rome, the abode of him who alone could "loose" him. Thus Innocent III. writes to the Bishop of Montreale,—"For greater security and higher reverence has the Apostolic See reserved to itself alone the right of absolution, in order that those whom neither the fear of God nor the clerical holiness (*religio*) keep in check should be restrained at least by the labour and difficulty of the road,"—an argument which may have lost some of its force since the twelfth century.

Ere we proceed, however, it behoves us to say a word about the whole theory of the "Reservation." Theoretically, every ordained priest has the power of absolving. It is given to him, during the imposition of hands, by the Holy Ghost. But with this *potestas ordinis*, it is held by some, is not also combined the *potestas jurisdictionis*, or power of jurisdiction, both of which are requisite for absolving. This second and more important power is inherent in the Church, or rather the Episcopate, and must be given *specially*. Bishops, therefore, may impart it to their subordinate priests or withhold it from them, as they see fit. The Council of Trent confirmed ancient rules embodying this view, by declaring the absolution pronounced by a priest over any one not subject to his ordinary or delegated jurisdiction, null and void. The Pope, as summit and crown of the Church, and as "holder of the keys," stands also above the Episcopate, and may therefore reserve to himself all and every sin, to the exclusion even of the bishops. He is the *Judex ordinarius*, the *Pastor pastorum*, called *in plenitudinem potestatis*, and his excommunication may be removed by none but himself, or his special *locum tenens* or delegate. Such is one ecclesiastical theory. But there is another, backed by other ecclesiastical authorities. It is this: that the Pope usurps that right, of which he also has not made use during the first Christian centuries, which alone are "normal," and the privileges of which are "ancient and divine;" whilst those of a later date, like the *Reservation*, are due in a great measure to the Isidorian Decretals, which are condemned as forgeries by the Church itself. Such rights are but "accidental and human," and therefore of no account. As long as the Pope does not abuse them, they may be left to him; if he does, they must be taken from him, even against his will. The orthodox reply to this is, that Gregory the Great and Alexander II. had *de facto* had special cases brought before them, and that these constitute an apt and proper precedent for the early centuries. It is not generally emphasized, we think, that in both cases it was simply the Papal judgment invoked and given against a bishop and an archbishop respectively. Be this, however, as it may, practically the bishops often and early enough resorted of their own free accord to the punishment of a peregrination to Rome as an apt way of getting a troublesome sinner out of the country for some time—with the chance of his never returning again. On the other hand, the good people of Rome did not object to the often noble penitents, who spent their money whilst they performed their penance. Thus went Romewards King Robert of France, and with him went the bishops who had sanctioned his incestuous marriage; thus Guarnerius, the criminal Bishop of Strasburg, "*fasting with much fatigue.*" Remedius of Lincoln sent a priest guilty of murder to Gregory VII.; Henry IV. of Germany stood at Canossa; and King Philip of France was absolved from adultery by Urban II., at Rome. Also did Archbishop Laurentius of Dublin, among others, consign no less than one hundred and fifty "licentious Irish priests" to the Holy Father in 1197, and the Bishop of Groswardein himself was ordered to go to Rome, to get absolution—if he could—for a certain sin of which he had been notoriously and repeatedly guilty.

The first reserved case having been established, it was
found expedient to make exceptions, partly in favour of the
clergy, but partly also in favour of those laymen who should
"punish" clerics "caught *in flagranti* with their wives,
mothers, daughters, or sisters," or who should defend themselves against "unjust violence" on the part of a cleric.
Occasionally also the Pope waived his right, or rather transferred it to cardinal legates or special bishops.   Thus the
Bishop of Genoa was permitted by Alexander III. to absolve
a certain canon who had beaten a sub-dean.   Another step
in the other direction, however, was to make this ban valid
without special excommunication, which at first had been
indispensable.   It was now considered pronounced *ipso facto*,
or *latæ sententiæ;* terms which are indeed not used in the
matter during the first stages.

Out of this single case there grew, in the course of a few
centuries, about one hundred and twenty, from which the
Bulla Cœnæ of Urban VIII. has selected, as mentioned
above, exactly twenty.   But it took some time—about two
centuries—before to the first was added the second, and to
the second the third case.   At the commencement of the
fourteenth century we find no more than three authenticated
reserved cases.   In 1364, however, Urban V. was already
able to issue a regular Bull with seven cases from Avignon,
among which there appears for the first time the occupation
of the Papal dominion and the hindering of Papal messengers, as well as the selling of ammunition to the enemies
of the Church.   The latter proviso was enacted with a
special view to that Pope's pet crusade, inaugurated by the
King of Cyprus and Peter Thomas, which came to so speedy
and ignominious an end.   A new and revised edition of the
Cœna was put forth by Gregory XI. in 1370, and another
by Gregory XII. in 1411, which begins in this wise:—" We
excommunicate and anathematize, in the name of God the
Father, and the Son, and the Holy Ghost, and by the authority of the Holy Apostles Peter and Paul and our own,
all heretics, 'Gazaros, Patarenos, Pauperes de Lugduno,

Arnaldistas, Speronistas et Passaginos,' and all other heretics
of whatsoever name, and'all them that favour, receive, and
defend them. Likewise do we excommunicate and anathematize," &c. &c. &c.

In 1512, Julius II. re-issued the Bull, with twelve cases,
among which figures already the curse upon falsifiers of
Papal Bulls and other sacred emanations. In 1536, Paul
III. had brought his version up to seventeen, including the
curse upon them that would make clerical persons submit to
the civil authorities, and those who abstract relics from
Roman churches. Not quite fifty years later, in 1583, under
Gregory XIII., the Bull had swollen to twenty-one cases,
among which there is the reading of Luther and all or any
heretic, and the printing or defending of such heretics'
writings. In its final shape, that due to Urban VIII., it has
lain dormant since Clement XIV., who would no longer read
it on Maundy-Thursday—"it no longer being a time for
cursing but for grace," he said. But only dormant. It has
quietly kept its place, in spite of many prohibitions, in
several modern rituals. It is now first abrogated formally
by this new " Constitution."

We have been at the pains of comparing the two documents somewhat closely, in order to see wherein the " moderation " of the Apostolic See aforementioned has manifested
itself. First of all it must be noted that our document is
considerably larger, embodying as it does a number of such
reserved cases as were left out in the ancient *Bulla Cœnæ*.
Next, that the time-honoured introduction to the special
paragraphs of the old Bull, "*Excommunicamus et anathematizamus*," has given way to special, business-like headings.
Indeed, the difference between those two papal terms of
displeasure seems to have become somewhat shadowy in
these latter days. This was not so at one time. Indeed, as
early as the ninth century the faithful knew that while " excommunication " merely meant exclusion from the Church
and all its benefits, together with public penitence and
banishment from home and society, — not to forget the

instant dismissal from all and every civil and military office or dignity: the state of those that lay under the "anathema" was far worse. They were cut off utterly and irrevocably as "putrid and desperate members" from the entire body of the Church. Unto them there is "*nulla legum, nulla morum, nulla collegii participatio*," whether they be alive or dead. Their names "shall not be remembered even among the defunct," nor shall "even in their dying hour any communication be held with them." In many other respects the text of this new "Constitution" of Pius IX. follows that of the Bull, as far as it goes, pretty closely, sometimes literally. Except, perhaps, that paragraph 1 of the latter figures now as paragraphs 1 to 3, or that the "Latinity" has undergone certain alterations. If, *e.g.*, the old edict has "ac omnes et," the new reads "et omnes ac;" for "ac iis," we have "eisque," for "et generaliter" we get "ac generaliter," and similar improvements, "in accordance with the change of times."

Yet more significant emendations, both of omission and commission, are not wanting. We have already said that clause 1 of the *Cœna* is broken up here into three, which deal respectively with "apostates and heretics," with "readers, keepers, printers, and defenders of heretical books," and "schismatics and others disobedient to the Pope." While in the first new paragraph we miss the familiar names of "Hussites, Wycliffites, Lutherans, Zwinglians, Calvinists, Huguenots, Anabaptists, Trinitarians," and so forth, we rejoice to find the second clause altered in favour of those persons whose business it is to read all the bad books which are to be placed on the Index. Hitherto, the anathema included all and every one who read such heretical writings, "from whatsoever cause; publicly or secretly; in whatsoever spirit; and under whatsoever colour." This provision is no more. Cursed are now only those who "knowingly read, keep, print, use, *without the authority of the Holy See*, the books of those apostates and heretics which propagate heresy, as well as those, by whomsoever written, which are specially prohibited by apostolic letters." So that the Fathers of the "Congregation of the Index"—here brought to public recognition—are theoretical outcasts no more. Clause 2 of the *Cœna* becomes clause 4 in our document. It excommunicates all and every one who should presume to appeal from the Pope to a future Council. The origin of this decree has again to be looked for in England, where the clergy, in the thirteenth century, ·so far from paying Innocent IV. what he demanded, dared to appeal to a future general Council instead. The same was done by the two cardinals de Colonna, Jacobus and Petrus, whom Boniface VIII. had deposed and excommunicated. Philip IV. of France appealed against the same Pope, after having publicly burnt the Bull, "Listen, O my son," directed against himself. Lewis the Bavarian appealed in 1324 against John XXII., and finally there appealed the whole College of Cardinals—except four, whom Gregory XII. had created, in spite of his solemn oath to the contrary —against that Holy Father. It was Martin V. who first sought to suppress this demurring to Papal authority by excommunication; which, however, did not prevent the University of Paris and the clergy of the diocese of Rouen from appealing against Calixtus III. Whereupon Pius II. issued the Bull "Execrabilis," which, very stringent and very pathetic as it was, was so utterly disregarded by Sigismund, Duke of Austria, that, not later than a month after its promulgation, he appealed to a future Council. Not very long afterwards, the Archbishop of Mayence, being excommunicated, followed his example in also appealing against his excommunication to a future Council. Likewise did the Venetians appeal to a Council against Julius II., and though Gregory XIII. at last placed this sin formally upon the *Cœna*, Louis XIV. again appealed against Innocent XI. Even so, a few months ago, Père Hyacinthe threatened to appeal, eventually, to a future General Council. We at first missed one passage of this clause in our new Bull, that treating of "Universities, Colleges, and Chapters," until we discovered it later on, leading off the division of "Interdicts."

T

Entirely gone are clauses 3 to 5 of the old Bull. They treat, respectively, of pirates and corsairs "in our sea, from Argentorato to Terracina, and all their abettors," further of wreckers—wrecking being a privilege granted occasionally to bishops and monasteries—and of leviers of such tolls as had not been sanctified by the Pope. Clause 6 of the old Bull reappears as number 9 of the new. It is devoted to falsifiers of Papal briefs and writs, and there is one alteration noticeable. For the old "*falso fabricantur*" we have the mild "*falso publicantur*," so that it is the propagator more than the author who must now beware. Time certainly was, when forging absolutions for all manner of sin was the source of sundry good incomes, both lay and clerical, but it is to be feared that this trade has become somewhat slack. Nor are they who sell horses, arms, and other war-materials to the Turks, Sarassins, and other heretics, any longer under the ban, or those "even if they be emperors, or kings, or clerical dignitaries," who impede the carrying of victuals to Rome, or who slay or imprison them that go to Rome to complain of their bishops—a practice once in vogue, but to which the bishops themselves often put a stop by the unghostly means here condemned. Again, clause 11 that was, has become clause 5 that is, and it is preserved scrupulously intact. It treats of all and any harm done to patriarchs, archbishops, bishops, and legates. They are not to be "killed, mutilated, wounded, beaten, captured, imprisoned, stopped, persecuted, or turned out of their dioceses, lands, territories, or dominions." Once upon a time, the Emperor Frederic II. took prisoner no less than a hundred ecclesiastics, on their way to Rome—among them three Papal legates, the Archbishops of Rouen, Auch, Bordeaux, and many bishops and abbots, some of whom died in his strongholds in Apulia. In the same spirit of irreverence the King of England caused the Papal legates to be "well beaten" and turned out of the country in 1232. Even Pope Urban IV. when, as Innocent IV.'s legate, he went to Germany, was put into prison. It was in 1311, at the Council of Vienne, that

Clement V. had this case therefore formally entered as
"reserved." When Cardinal Borromeo was shot in his own
chapel, Pius V. extended, in 1569, the curse to all those
who, having any knowledge of the perpetrator of an offence
against those Church dignitaries, should fail to betray him.
Not long after this, Henry III. of France put the Cardinal
of Lorraine to death, and Gregory XIII. not only embodied
the case in the *Cœna*, but extended the protective anathema to even the legates and messengers of the Apostolic
See.

Three more of the new paragraphs correspond, framed a
little more concisely, to those of the old document. They
refer to the supremacy of ecclesiastical jurisdiction. Cursed
is now, as was then, all and every person who recurs to the
civil courts in anything relating to the Church, or to persons
belonging to the Church : cursed is likewise every one who
makes laws contrary to the liberty of the Church, or who
impedes the progress of any ecclesiastical emanation in any
way whatsoever. This excommunication applies, in one
shape or another, to well nigh every single king, and emperor, and prince, and president, and parliament and court
of justice, and judge (except the Pope and his own advisers)
who at this moment exercise any authority whatsoever. The
origin of this "appeal from the abuse of the Apostolic Chair
(as it was called) to the secular courts," emanated from the
clergy itself, and finds its first expression in the reformatory
decrees of the Councils of Basle and Constance. This power
of appeal against, *e.g.*, the bestowal of rich benefices upon
what were considered the wrong persons, was first granted to
the French clergy by Charles VII. in 1438, but rescinded
by the Concordat of 1515. The Parliament, however, in
utter disregard of it, continued to hear cases lodged by the
clergy against the bishops, and by the bishops against the
Popes. Then it came to pass that Gregory XIII. cursed all
these appeals in the *Cœna*, as well as the so-called *placitum
regium*. By virtue of this Placet every Papal Bull or other
emanation had to be examined by the civil powers before its

promulgation was allowed. In France it was even necessary
that both Parliaments, that of Toulouse and of Paris, should
give their permit each time, one being considered insufficient. In Spain the prelates themselves claimed the right
to look into those publications before they endorsed them,
and eventually refused to take any notice of them. The
pretext to this proceeding was given by the prodigious
numbers of forged Papal letters in circulation. Only such
as they saw reason to approve, they said, did they consider
genuine : since the Pope would not issue what displeased
them. Leo X. protested, but in vain. Even so did Innocent
VIII. ; and finally Julius II. made all let or hindrance
against the publication of any of his emanations, whatever
their nature, a case in the *Cœna*.

Regarding the other portion of this enactment, that of
bringing clerical matters before lay tribunals, nothing can
be more instructive than the history of the struggle between
the Church and the State, or the clerical and lay courts, as
to the limits of their authority. The former not merely
excommunicated all those who brought their complaints in
Church matters before laymen, but actually threatened
whole countries where a like thing was to happen, with the
interdict and the refusal of burial. On the other hand, the
civil authorities punished all those who took their cases to
the Church authorities. They fined them and imprisoned
them ; them, their friends, notaries, and counsels, until they
desisted. Worse still, if any one had, with a large outlay,
at last obtained a censure from Rome against his adversary,
he was himself compelled to procure absolution for such
censure. Stronger even was the resistance against arraign-
ing ecclesiastics bodily before a lay forum ; and the Synod
of Nismes, in 1096, declared this to be nothing less than
" terrible sacrilege ;" and to clinch the matter, all judicial
acts against clerics were pronounced null and void. The
Third Lateran Council excommunicated the very attempt of
bringing a cleric to ordinary justice, and incessant were the
reiterations and protests enacted by subsequent Councils.

But little attention was paid to them until, in 1536, Paul III. embodied the matter in the *Cœna*. In 1855, Pius IX. had to yield the point in the late Austrian Concordat, but he did so under protest, and with the special clause *temporum ratione habita*. The Concordat has gone the way of many another Concordat, and the old enactment has now renewed its days.

The tenth clause of the new Bull is not found in the old Bull, though it is not new in itself. It is one of the six-score "outside cases" of which we spoke before. It prohibits clerics who have sinned against the seventh commandment from confessing and absolving the women with whom they have sinned. The frail ones must go to another and more impartial confessor; or rather, as the Council of Rheims enacted, the priest in question is to be absolved first, after which he shall absolve those women. However, the prohibition, entered and re-entered upon the Acts of Council after Council, does not seem to have been very rigorously kept. At last, however, the matter had become so flagrant, that Benedict XIV., in the "*Sacramentum Pœnitentiæ*," forbade a priest ever to absolve at the confessional a woman with whom he had notoriously broken his vows—even during a Jubilee. His absolution is, except in case of death "and if no other priest be nigh," that is, if another priest could not be called in "without great risk of infamy and scandal," declared null and void; and, adds Benedict in that decree, the guilty confessor should not persuade himself of the existence of a like risk of infamy and scandal, if there really be none such. Further, though the absolution given by a like confessor be valid, he himself remains under the excommunication for all that.

Our eleventh paragraph corresponds to the seventeenth of the *Cœna*. It prohibits usurpation and sequestration of Church property. For the old *quive . . . usurpant vel . . . sequestrant* we have the new latinity, *usurpantes aut sequestrantes*; for *fructus* we have *bona*; for the plural *jurisdictiones* we have the singular; the word *proventus* has been struck out, and also the whole sentence, "Which belong unto Us and the Apostolic See," as well as the word "monasteries." The tailpiece whereby such seizing of goods or lands was permitted, if done by order of the Pope, is also no more. It is true enough that the Church has often had to suffer from these "usurpations." She was so rich that the worldly powers, in spite of the thunders of the first, second, and third Lateran Councils, would stretch out their hands after the *res dominicæ, Deo sacratæ, τὰ τοῦ θεοῦ,* &c., as these possessions were variously styled. And not merely, as the third Lateran Council complained, "when these men want to build castles or to go to war," did they contract forced loans with the Church, but as early as the fourteenth and fifteenth centuries many princes fell into a way of secularising right and left what they deemed an encumbrance upon the Holy Church, which, they said, "was to look to the riches of heaven." Nay, not satisfied with annexing churches and chapels, they even took possession sometimes of the castles, villas, parks, and fishing and hunting grounds, of archbishops and bishops. The consequence was so wild an uproar, that the Synod of Lavaux pronounced the Anathema upon such robbers, and placed their entire domains under the Interdict. If such *comes, senescallus, baro, judex,* or *capitantus* died, his body was not to be buried—even if he had died in a state of absolution—until his heir had made restitution to the full. Further Councils deprived even those who only advised burial of such transgressors of the benefit of interment. Yet matters do not seem to have been altered much by these threats. When Louis XI. of France wished a General Council to be summoned, Sixtus IV. bitterly answered, "It would be better for the honour of some princes if a like Council did not take place, since it might otherwise reveal their usurpation of Church property." In 1512, Julius II. entered this sin duly in the old Bull. Paul III. extended its provisions still further, and Gregory III. made new additions with special regard to the Holy See and all that belonged to it.

The last paragraph of the "specially reserved" cases of the new document forms also the last paragraph of the *Bulla Cœnæ*. But a considerable shortening has taken place :—

"Likewise do we excommunicate and anathematize all those"—so reads the old—"who by themselves or by others, directly or indirectly, *under whatsoever title or colour*, do presume to invade, destroy, occupy, and detain, entirely or in part, the Holy City, the kingdom of Sicily, the islands of Sardinia and Corsica, the lands this side of the Pharos, the Patrimony of Peter in Tuscia, the Duchy of Spoleto, the counties of Venaisin, Sabina, the Marches of Ancona, Massa, Trebaria, Romandiola, Campania, and the maritime provinces, and their lands and places, and the lands of the special commission of the Arnulphs, and our cities Bologna, Cesena, Rimini, Benevento, Perugia, Avignon, Civita Castello, Trederzo, Ferrara, Comachio, and other cities, counties, and places, or rights belonging to the Roman Church itself, and subject directly or indirectly to the said Roman Church, or who presume *de facto* to usurp, disturb, retain, and in various ways to interfere with, that supreme jurisdiction over them belonging to Us and to this same Roman Church. Likewise (do we, &c. &c.) their partisans, favourers, and defenders, who give them assistance, counsel, or favour of whatsoever kind."

The present remarkably concise version runs as follows :—

"Those who invade, destroy, retain, either by themselves or by others, the cities, lands, places, or rights belonging to the Roman Church, or who usurp, disturb, and retain supreme jurisdiction over them, or who give ' *ad singula prædicta* ' help, counsel, or favour."

Ad ecclesiam Romanam pertinentia, "belonging to the Roman Church," says the new Canon. What does belong to the Roman Church now? Rome herself is "held, invaded, occupied." And it is grievous to see our clause literally pronouncing excommunication over the Pope and his Cardinals themselves. For is it not they who do "retain the supreme jurisdiction" in whatever still, apparently at least, belongs to the Church? However, the Pope may disregard even anathemas. Can he not "loose"?

Thus much for the new edition of the *Bulla Cœnæ*, which, in spite of Clement XIV. having declared it "unchristian and dangerous," in spite of Joseph II.'s order to "tear it out of the Rituals," silently kept its place for a hundred years—awaiting that resurrection which has now come. At no time, however, has it been a favourite. Many patriarchs, bishops, and archbishops would not hear of it on any account, though they were ordered to publish it in their dioceses— nay, fell under the very ban of excommunication by not doing so. Thus Archbishop Affre writes: "Quant à la Bulle 'In Cœna Domini' on ne reprochait pas au clergé de France d'avoir voulu la promulguer. Et, en effet, il n'y a jamais pensé." The Council of Trent had certainly made the "Bull" rather illusory by granting, in its twenty-fourth sitting, the power of absolving from all *secret* reserved cases, to every bishop. This privilege was, however, withdrawn by Pius V. and Gregory XIII. In the middle of the seventeenth century much wrangling again restored this right to the bishops. They now received the permission ("Quinquennial Faculties") to absolve from *all* reserved cases, open or secret, including heresy. And still the Bull was not liked, and still none would tolerate it. If previously Philip II. had turned the Nuntius who came as its bearer out of Spain; if France, Portugal, and even Rudolph II. of Germany had prohibited its publication; its end came when Clement XIII. saw fit to pronounce the anathema over Ferdinand of Parma, in 1768. Its introduction into France was nearly made a *crimen læsæ majestatis*. The same was done in Portugal, where the Crown Fiscal damned the Breve as "contrary to the Gospel, which had inculcated obedience to Cæsar." Maria Theresa followed fiercely. Ferdinand VII. of Naples banished both the Bull and the priests who presumed to take it seriously, out of his states. The Duke of Parma issued a decree which branded the Bull as a source of rebellion and useless banishments, and annulled it. The same was done by Monaco, Genoa, Venice. Maria Theresa sent a special edict to Lombardy to warn the printers and possessors of this document. The "Oekonomaljunta" were authorized to inflict upon such transgressors what punishment they pleased.

Then came Clement XIV. who abrogated it; and then—exactly a hundred years later—Pius IX. who renewed it in.

the shape now before us. We can but briefly glance at the rest of the edict, which embodies what obsolete "extra" cases it has been deemed proper thus solemnly to revive, referring such of our readers as are eager for more details to Mansi, Phillips, Hefele, Le Bret, Hausmann, Raumer, and the acts and histories of the Church generally. Cursed are, again, *e.g.* those who defend, even privately, propositions condemned by the Pope—which applies especially to the "*Syllabus.*" Cursed are they who lay violent hands, "at the instigation of the devil," on "monks of either sex,"— which is the aboriginal "*Percussio clerici,*" in the very words of 1130. Cursed are they who "perpetrate" a duel, as well as all participators and abettors thereof, and those who do not prevent them, if they can, "be they even of royal or imperial dignity." This prohibition dates, in the shape of a Bull, from Leo, in 1519, and extended even to spectators, who were mulcted in many ducats. Cursed are, further, all Freemasons and Carbonari. It was at the Council of Avignon, in 1325, that all secret societies were first condemned. But Freemasons as such, of whose existence Clement XII. "had heard a rumour," were especially anathematized by him in a Bull. And the inquisitors received strict orders to look after the orthodoxy of the supposed Brethren. Benedict XIV. renewed this "Constitution," giving six reasons for so doing, and its last Papal confirmation dates 1846, and is signed Pius IX.

Many also are the regulations re-enacted regarding ecclesiastics themselves. Such is the one which prohibits the violation of the "Clausura" by pain of reserved excommunication. Time was when women, by reason of special Papal permits, were free to enter monasteries, there to choose their own confessors: an arrangement which does not seem to have given general satisfaction to the outer world. When the scandal grew too fierce, Pius V. restricted the permission to the monasteries of the congregation of the Holy Virgin "of the Mount." Women might visit those, but only when there was a service, or procession, or a sermon, or burial, or any kind of ceremony. And there always was some kind of ceremony. In the course of the eighteenth century, however, this custom of allowing women to visit the refectories and dormitories, " in order to take part in processions and other ceremonies," had spread far beyond the original bounds;—until Benedict XIV., in 1742, issued a new and more stringent Bull. On the other hand, Gregory XIII. had restricted men, as early as 1575, from paying stray visits to nunneries—unless they possessed special licences. As for clerics who had *ipso facto* the permission of entering nunneries, these were exhorted in that Bull not to make too extensive a use of their privilege, else both they and the nuns who received them would fall under the ban.

Besides these " cases," which thus seem to have required renewing rather urgently, we meet again with the trading in indulgences, defrauding the Church by obtaining higher prices for masses, and the pilfering of alms—all very ancient institutions. Then we have also simony, of which there are three cases,—" confidential simony " among them. This is rather recent. It appears first in the sixteenth century, and means that somebody hands over his clerical office, which is a certain hindrance to him, to some one else for a life pension. Generally this pension left so little to the real *de facto* dignitaries that these came to be styled *custodini*, or even, as at the Councils of Rouen and Narbonne, *cistellarii asini*, " inasmuch as they bore the burden of office while another ate the fruits thereof." Bishops, archbishops, patriarchs, nay, cardinals themselves, casually obtained benefices in order to resign them, in favour of some one perhaps not yet born, for a consideration. This scandal, too, became at last so flagrant that Pius IV., having exhausted all his powers of exhortation, anathematized it: declaring all such benefices accepted *in confidentiam* null and void; all contracts thereto referring, waste paper; and all those who lived upon the incomes of places which other people held, bound to refund. But this Bull again had to be renewed, because flagrantly disregarded, by Pius V. and by endless provincial Councils, and was even ordered to be read out aloud every Sunday in church. In cursing this form of simony anew, Pius IX. shows that it flourishes now, as ever.

Among the "non-reserved" cases we meet the Inquisition, which is not to be "intimidated" or hurt. Curious as this proviso may seem to us, there was a time when it went hard enough with the officers of that institution. Some of them found their deaths in a surprisingly sudden manner, and the Dominicans, who were especially singled out for the function of holy espionage, at one time actually wrote to Innocent IV. begging to be excused for the future. But he would not part with them, and wrote them letters of comfort instead. Pope Pius V., when plain Michael Gislerius, had undertaken to find out something about the Bishop of Bergamo, but he only narrowly escaped being lynched instead. Remembering these things when he ascended the Papal throne, many were the protecting clauses wherewith he surrounded the Inquisition and its officers, down to the lowest menials—as well as all inquisitorial witnesses, accusers, denouncers, spies, &c. Likewise were anathematized by him all those who should touch the inquisitorial houses, properties, churches, and other goods, as well as books, letters, protocols, transactions, &c. &c. Another not reserved case of our new Bull treats of those who do not, within a certain time, denounce such confessors or priests by whom they have been instigated to certain disgraceful acts; and yet another, of those who are instrumental in giving Christian burial to notorious heretics, or such as lie under special excommunication or interdict. To the bishops, or "ordinaries," are left exactly three cases: to wit, married clerical persons of either sex, who, by marrying, not only fall under the excommunication themselves, but bring it down also upon the partners of their guilt; further, those who use forged apostolic letters; and another, which we prefer not to mention. Among the second division of the excommunications, there is also a clause threatening those who should extract relics from sacred cemeteries or the Roman catacombs; but we miss the ancient enactment

against purloining things from the Vatican. Formerly—
since Clement III.—the very porters had to take an oath
that they would "neither steal, nor allow to be stolen therefrom, relics, gold, silver, gems, pallia, ornaments, books,
papers (*chartulæ*), oil, lead, iron, brass, stones, doors, wood,
or the tables thereof." The Vatican is better guarded now,
and the oath is dispensed with.

Thus far our notes. Whether the Council now sitting
will, or will not, mark an epoch in the history of Rome—
whether this "Constitution" itself, some of whose enactments may, at one time, have been useful enough, be a mere
brutum fulmen, as alleged, or not—we do not pretend to
know. But they are both Signs of the Times as singular as
they are humiliating.

XIII.

THE ROMAN PASSION DRAMA.[1]

THE Roman "Passion Drama" increases in interest. The world at large, which has hitherto looked on with a sort of languid wonderment akin to contempt, opens its eyes and listens. Instead of rumours more or less contradictory, we have been able to present our readers in the course of the last few days with a series of documents which certainly were worth perusal. There was the petition for the Infallibility —which breathes the spirit, the learning, and the righteousness of our own Cardinal *in spe*, Monsignor Manning—signed by a nameless crowd of Italians. Then came the counterpetition, much shorter, very much to the point, full of dignity, and ominous in its bearing; and it had the signatures of Cardinal Schwarzenberg and the archbishops and bishops of Germany and Hungary. Next we had the manifesto attributed to Cardinal Rauscher, signed by the same, or nearly the same, distinguished prelates, against the Papal order of proceedings, introduced, contrary to all precedents, into this Council: an order which is meant to gag and kill that which is the first condition of a Council—free expression of opinion. Over and above these we have had the protest of "Janus" Döllinger, for which the Municipal Council of Munich have offered him the freedom of their city.

Perhaps by the time this reaches Rome the contemptuous shout will greet us : — *Consummatum est.* The Infalliblists are said to be now moving swiftly and surely towards their goal. Organized to perfection, with all and every means at

---

[1] Re-printed, by permission, from the 'Pall Mall Gazette' of Feb. 10, 1870.

their disposal, and stung to the quick by the sudden danger of losing what already seemed theirs—they have lost no time in gathering all the signatures that were to be got from the episcopal multitudes who depend upon the Papal coffers even for daily bread, and they have carried their petition to the Council. The anti-Infalliblists, broken up into at least five groups of nationalities, hemmed in at every single step, alternately bullied and flattered, believing to the last in the official assurance that the intended proclamation of that dogma was all a myth, hesitated, deliberated, waited. Nay, that very counter-petition, brief as it was, they would not issue until they had held some fifteen or sixteen meetings over it. No wonder the Infalliblists will " have it," whenever the hour comes.

That is to say, the majority will outvote the minority. Now it so happens that never since the Council of Nicæa have parties outvoted each other at a Council. Not a single dogma has ever been carried against an opposition. Every single " resolution " was passed either unanimously or not at all. Even at Trent, where, as now at the Vatican, the Council was hectored by an overwhelming number of Italians, some dogmas which Rome had tenderly at heart were, after having already passed all the preliminary stages, thrown up—simply and solely because some few bishops openly remonstrated. The worst is that—so little did that party which rules the Vatican and the Council dream of the possibility of an opposition—not longer than two years ago one of their first spokesmen, the Jesuit Father Matignon, printed these words:—" Le Concile n'imposait rien à notre foi qui n'eût obtenu à peu près *l'unanimité des votes.* L'obligation de croire est une chose si grave, le droit de lier les intelligences est un droit si auguste et si important, que les pères pensaient rien devoir user qu'avec la plus grande réserve et la plus extrême délicatesse."

We do not pretend to foresee what will happen next. The Bishops of Fulda pledged themselves before they went to Rome, saying: " Never *shall* or *can* a General Council establish a dogma not contained in Scripture or in the Apostolic traditions." They have kept their word in trying hard to prevent it. But if they do not succeed, what will be their next step? For now they will not be in a mood even to decree the bodily assumption of the Virgin Mary, or to "raise the holy Joseph out of the obscurity in which he has so long and undeservedly languished," as the petitions put it which have now reached our own country for signature.

It may be well on the eve of the new phase to take another glance at these documents before mentioned. There is, first, the petition itself, the sum and substance of all that which the Jesuits have preached from the housetops and in the secret chamber for some twenty years past, for which they have collected money and built churches, monasteries, and convents, and have founded societies and journals and schools from one end of the globe to the other. It is the *Unità*, the *Laacher-Stimmen*, Father Schrader, Monsignor Manning, all rolled in one. And what is the gist of it?— We *must* have the Infallibility. True, it is not in Scripture any more than in the Fathers. But two Councils, one of which was openly proclaimed at Trent to have been non-œcumenical, have said something which, if garbled and misquoted, might look as if they had assumed that Infallibility. Besides which, several provincial synods held within the last twenty years under our own auspices have been made to say something like it. And thus we have on our side the "ancient testimonies of the Church." But, they add, in somewhat anxious loquaciousness, had we known that these Germans were about to oppose us at the last moment we certainly should have taken different steps. There is no special reason why the dogma should be proclaimed just now, or why it should be proclaimed at all. But—we are *in* for it. To withdraw is impossible. We, you, and the Pope are all committed and compromised as deeply as ever we can be, and it *must* be passed. If you do not pass it, what will the world say of us? Think of the newspapers— will they not pretend that they have frightened us out of our dogma? Nay, the faithful themselves would look upon

us rather suspiciously, if not contemptuously, if we should
now back out of what we have inculcated so indefatigably
for all these years. Nay, other things would begin to be
called in question by them at which we dare not even hint.
Yet some say the time is not ripe. The dogma is good, but
" inopportune." It will frighten away, they fancy, or pretend to fancy, the feeble in Faith within, and the schismatics
and heretics without. Why, this is the very thing we want.
Let the traitors in the camp, those rotten leaves, drop off
openly. That will only strengthen our hands. As for
heretics and schismatics, we fancy they will be rather at-
tracted by our unshrinking boldness. They will, in the
midst of the dissensions in their own Churches, or in the
struggles of their own scepticism, take refuge in what would
appear to them to rest on such firm foundations, that which
dares all storms, and alone remains unmoved while all else
moves right or left. Therefore, it is good, and it is oppor-
tune, to make Infallibility as the crown and summit of that
proud edifice, the Roman Church. Nay, the Catholic people
have a *right* to it. Therefore sign, and sign quickly: *Peri-
culum in mora!*

We have shown in our abstract of Dr. Döllinger's protest
what mincemeat he made of that document. But for some
reason or other he still seems to have left out the most
important point when he showed that the two proofs taken
from the Councils of Lyons and Florence were rotten to the
core. At Lyons, he says, the point in question was *not*
agreed upon, as alleged, by both Greeks and Latins, but the
Pope sent a formula to the Emperor Michael Palæologus to
sign, wherein the sentence quoted was contained. The
Emperor, utterly unable to help himself, signed, but protested. The bishops had absolutely nothing to do with it,
they were not even in a position to be asked about it. All
this is true enough; but Dr. Döllinger might have pointed
out further that that formula had no more to do with
declaring the Pope infallible than with declaring him immortal, it being simply and solely intended as a recognition
of the long-contested superiority of the Roman Chair *to that*

of Constantinople. Not long ago the *Civiltà* tried on that passage as a proof that the Pope was superior to the Council. But it was very soon warned off, if we remember right, in one of that series of papers which appeared in the *Times* before the opening of the Council. It was there shown how neither Lyons nor Florence had anything to do with that question. The Infalliblists have again "cooked" their passage. They quote: "Subortas de fide controversias debere *Romani Pontificis* judicio definiri"—"Discussions on matters of faith must be settled by the judgment of the Roman Pontiff." But these two words "Roman Pontiff" *do not exist in the original.* In the "Symbol" sent by the Pope, and signed by the Emperor, to which the Infalliblists refer, and which begins, "Credimus Sanctam Trinitatem," we find the word *suo* instead, and that pronoun happens to refer not to the Pontiff, but to the *Roman Church,* "*which* before all other Churches is called to defend the truth," and "to *which,* through Peter, whose successor is the Pope, is given the plenitude of power, the primacy and supremacy over all other Churches." It is always, from beginning to end, the *Ecclesia Romana,* and not the Pope. It is she who, "though she has honoured other Churches with privileges, has yet always preserved her own prerogative, both in *General Councils* and elsewhere." Neither is there, in the oath sworn on that occasion in the name of the Emperor by the Logothetos, the slightest mention made of a Pontiff. It is the Church, and nothing but the Church herself, to which, as such, the Greeks yield the Primacy. As a matter of history, what the Council of Lyons had established in 1274 was utterly revoked by the Greeks in 1282, and the very remembrance of it was stamped out.

As to that notorious Council of Florence, "which some do not blush to babble of as non-œcumenical," Dr. Döllinger has sufficiently shown how the Infalliblists have forged and falsified the quotation taken from that. There is one "definition," however, which they might have quoted, but did not, belonging to that ill-fated Florentine Council—we mean the infallible decree of Eugenius IV., "That the souls of all

those who die in the state of original sin descend to the
infernal regions;" which means that all those untold mil-
liards of human beings who have not received baptism,
whether they have been born before that institution, or have
not been discovered by Exeter Hall, go to hell. Let us add
at once that many and sore have been the wrigglings of
theologians on this point. That religion which is love did
seem to deal a little harshly on that point. But they all
took comfort finally in this, that it was not an Œcumenical
Council which had said it, only a Pope; and it was only
both together who, according to the catechism as used to
this hour, make up Infallibility. Nous avons changé tout
cela: 'there is no chance for those poor unbaptized souls
now !

It is well known now that the two episcopal protests were
not permitted to be printed in Rome, while the original
petition was issued by the official press. That of Cardinal
Schwarzenberg lifts up its voice against the gag upon the
freedom of deliberation. It claims this freedom as guaran-
teed by the Council of Trent, and the Bishops hint—nay,
say—that if the Pope be the head they are the limbs of the
Church. Woe unto that head which is separated from its
limbs! Whether it be or be not conscious of its existence
after being separated, it certainly does not thrive much after
the separation. The other protest, Cardinal Rauscher's,
very deliberately sets its face against that pernicious and
degrading dogma, as well as against the manner in which
the bishops are being bullied into it. Not that the dogma
is particularly inopportune, but they will not have it at any
time or price. "They know the spirit and temper both of
the peoples and the Governments of their native lands," and
they raise their protest at this supreme hour to avert what
they know to be fraught with "very grave perils to the
whole Church." Besides which, they find, in looking "at
the *genuine* documents of the Church," very serious and
manifold difficulties. They trust the dogma will not be
brought before them in any shape whatsoever, for "their
soul recoils" from even discussing it. Of the new "modera-

tion" petition let us, in all charity, be silent. It gives five *raisons d'être*, and trembles all over. If we were in the habit of quoting Scripture, we would mention a certain passage which talks of things neither hot nor cold, and what happens to them. So will it happen unto that expression of opinion.

XIV.

ON SEMITIC LANGUAGES.[1]

SHEMITIC or rather Semitic languages, a term commonly applied to a certain number of cognate idioms supposed to have been spoken by the Shemites—*i.e.* the descendants of Shem. Considering, however, that the Canaanites and the Phœnicians, the Cushites and a number of Arabic tribes, all derived in the genealogical list of Genesis x. from Cham, *did* speak "Shemitic," while Elam and Lud derived from Shem did not, as far as our present information goes (Ashur has now the benefit of a strong doubt):—that designation, first advocated by Eichhorn and Schlözer, must be pronounced a complete misnomer, although it has kept its ground up to this moment for sheer want of a precise and accurate term. It has supplanted that other one, used from the Church Fathers downward, of "Oriental Languages;" a denomination perfectly satisfactory to the "linguistic consciousness" of generations that viewed Hebrew as the mother of all languages, and whose acquaintance with Eastern idioms was limited to this and an imperfect idea of Phœnico-Punic, "Chaldee"—Jewish or Christian—and Arabic. But when, towards the end of the last century, the gigantic discoveries in the realm of Eastern philology suddenly made these idioms shrink into the small proportions of a family of dialects confined for a long period to a narrow corner of the south-west of Asia; that most comprehensive name of Oriental Languages had, notwithstanding single protests, to be put aside for ever. Leibnitz's suggestion of "Arabic" being too narrow for the whole stock, "Syro-Arabic" formed

---

[1] Re-printed, by permission, from 'Kitto's Cyclopedia of Historical Literature.'

in analogy to "Indo-European," was proposed, but that too has not been found generally expressive enough, apart from the objection of its being apt to be erroneously understood in a linguistical rather than in a geographical sense. Thus, in default of a better name, the above will probably be retained for some time to come, with the distinct understanding of its being a false and merely conventional expression.

Comparative philology, although, compared with what we now understand by this term, a very embryonic one, exercised itself at an early period, and in a vague manner, in these idioms. The resemblance between them is indeed so striking at first sight—its roots being as nearly identical as can be—that it could hardly have been otherwise. It is the difference between them rather than the similarity that requires a closer scrutiny in order to be discovered at all. As it is, they do not vary among themselves to the extent even of the dialects in any single group of the Indo-European languages. Yet, as we shall further show, the idea still entertained by not a few scholars—viz. of one of the Shemitic languages standing in the relation of maternity to another—must now be utterly discarded, and all that can be granted to the speculative "Science of Language" is the possibility of some kind of extinct prototype, out of which they might have individually developed. Exactly as there is an "Idea" (in the Platonic sense) of a primeval mother of all the Indo-European tongues floating before the minds of our modern investigators.

Meanwhile, the existence of three distinct "Shemitic" dialects of independent existence, each bearing a clearly-marked individuality of its own in historical times, has been established beyond all doubt; and, as usual, different names and divisions have been proposed for them. The most widely adopted and the most rational ones are those that are taken from the abodes of the different tribes who first spoke them. Thus we have: a. The northern or north-eastern branch—i. e. that of the whole country between the Mediterranean and the Tigris, bordered by the Taurus in the north; by Phœnicia, the land of Israel, and Arabia, in the south; and embracing Syria, Mesopotamia (with its different "Arams"), and Babylonia. This is called the "Aramaic" branch. *b.* The idiom spoken by the inhabitants of Palestine: "Hebraic." And *c.* That of the south or the peninsula of Arabia—"Arabic;" the idiom confined to this part up to the time of Mohammed. Another recent division is the so-called historical, framed in accordance with the preponderance of these special branches at different periods. By this the Hebraic would assume the first place, extending from the earliest times of our knowledge of it down to the sixth century B.C., when the Aramaic begins to take the lead, and the field of Hebrew and Phœnician—the chief representatives of Hebraic—becomes more and more restricted. The Aramaic again would be followed by the Arabic period, dating from the time of Mohammed, when Islam and its conquests spread the language of the Koran, not merely over the whole Shemitic territory, but over a vast portion of the inhabited globe. But this last division is so arbitrary, not to say fallacious—for there is every reason to suppose that "Aramaic" flourished vigorously in its own sphere during, if not before the whole Hebraic period, and again that "Hebraic" (as Phœnician) kept its ground simultaneously with the later "Aramaic" period—that its own authors had to hedge it in with many and variegated restrictions. So that it is, in fact, reduced simply to a "subjective" notion or method, not further to be considered. But we further protest all the more strongly against it, as it might easily lead to the belief that the one idiom gradually merged into the other—Hebrew *into* Aramaic, Aramaic *into* Arabic, much as Latin did into the *Volgare*—which would be utterly contrary to fact. The vulgar Arabic spoken now in Palestine no more developed out of Aramaic, than the English spoken in Ireland developed out of Celtic or "Fenian."

Sinking for a moment the distinctions between these different Shemitic idioms, and viewing them as one compact Unity, more especially in comparison with that other most important family, the Indo-European languages, we are struck, as were the Church Fathers and the medieval grammarians, with more signs of primeval affinity than their mere identity of word-roots. And indeed, if this had constituted our sole proof and criterion, the circle of relationship would have had to be widened to an astonishingly large extent. One of the chief and indisputable characteristics of Shemitic has, since the days of Chajug, been held to be their triliteralness. That is, that every word consists, in the first instance, merely of three consonants, which form, so to say, the soul of the idea to be expressed by that word; while the respective special modifications are produced by certain vowels or additional letters. Some of the latter have, in a few instances, remained stationary, but even then they are always clearly distinguishable from the root, as mere casual accessories. But these very additional and only casually annexed consonants have led investigation to doubt that time-hallowed axiom of triliteralness. So far, it has been said, from this being a primeval inborn attribute of these idioms, nay, a sign of their having been handed down (especially in the Hebraic form) as nearly like their original prototype as can be: it is rather a sign of a very advanced stage of development in which they all participated, and which renders them almost as unlike their primitive type as any foreign group of languages. There must have been a time, it is contended, when not three, but two radicals with an intermediate vowel—a monosyllable in fact—formed the staple of some original "Shemitic" language. Out of this they may have sprung simultaneously, by one of those linguistic revolutions consequent upon sudden historical events —emigrations and the like. Not indeed in the sharply-outlined form in which we now find them, but predisposed to their development of linguistic individual peculiarities: one and all however bent upon the extension of their monosyllabic root into a triliteral—in a way that the consonant prefixed should express what *nuances* an advancing civilisation found it necessary to distinguish in every one of the scanty roots forming the common stock of the whole

Shemitic family. These biliterals, to which the roots thus are traced back, are nearly all of an onomatopoetical nature; that is, they are imitative sounds of a primitive kind. As long as they were used, the untold grammatical distinctions of an advanced human stage—flexions, categories, constructions—could, if they existed at all, only have existed in an embryonic state.—The authors and defenders of this ingenious conjecture—the unexpected use of which we shall presently show—fail, however, to answer the question, when and how this most extraordinary step from two to three letters could so suddenly and simultaneously have been introduced as must needs be presupposed. Not one of the monosyllabic languages known to us has ever changed its roots in this extraordinary manner, and the adduced analogy of the quadriliterals having been formed from the triliterals is not to the point.

Yet this analytical discovery of monosyllabic bases, if it does not assist us as much as was expected in the solution of the many difficult problems offered by the Shemitic idioms when compared among themselves, was made to support a much more sweeping theory—viz. that of an original affinity, nay identity, between Shemitic and Aryan, at some most remote period. A period, in fact, when Aryans and Shemites dwelt in the same homesteads; a period anterior to the final development of the roots of their—common—rudimentary language, and, of course, long anterior to grammars: and therefore also called the *antegrammatical* stage. And this theory has been advocated and warmly defended from Schlegel down to our day by some of the most eminently Aryan and Shemitic scholars. Nay, even the absurd extreme to which it has been carried by Delitzsch and Fürst did not bring its original form into discredit. These two scholars, to wit, do not stop at the affinity, but assume a downright relationship of parentage between the two groups. Their proofs and their specimens of words, however, do not sufficiently support their hypothesis. For the most part arbitrary to an immense degree, and erroneous in their application, they resolve themselves either into accidental simi-

larities or into such affinities as are easily explained by
late importations (the existence of which has never been
doubted) from one group into the other—caused by the
constant contact between the two families in prehistorical as
well as historical times.   Quite apart from that other most
unfortunate accident of their trying to prove their case by
certain Talmudical and Syriac words which bore an undeniable family-likeness to certain Greek and Latin words
of similar meanings; but which were really words taken
from Greek and Latin in late Roman times, and spelt in a
slightly disguised Shemitic fashion.

We cannot in this place further enlarge upon a point
which trenches so nearly upon those obscure problems about
the origin of language in general, that prominently occupy the
minds of scientific inquirers in these days.   Whatever be the
final issue, if ever there be one, we cannot but simply state
the fact that, grammatically, there cannot be a more radical
difference than that which exists between the two groups,
while lexically or etymologically a certain affinity between
them is perfectly incontestable even to the most critical and
unprejudiced eye.   However different the conclusions they
draw, on these points even the most extreme schools agree.
But whether, as some hold, there was once a stage where
there was no grammar at all, or whether there was a kind of
grammar which contained the two subsequently so widely
varying forms of it *in nuce;* or again whether the two races
ever did inhabit the same soil at all, and whether the phenomenon of the lexical property common to both may be
explained on the one hand by certain linguistical laws that
unchangingly rule body and soul of humanity, and produce
everywhere the same onomatopoetical sounds, the origin of
which we may or may not be able to trace in our present
stage, or on the other hand by a certain interchange of
ideas and objects at different periods of their existence :—we
shall leave undiscussed in this place, content to have shown
the different standpoints.   The most remarkable, and perhaps
the least easily-accounted-for phenomenon, is the striking
similarity of the pronouns and numerals, not only in Indo-

Germanic and Shemitic, but even in Coptic, which for this and other reasons has indeed been held by some to be both lexically and grammatically the Chamite link between the two. With what small show of reason, however, we cannot stop to explain.

Among these last-mentioned curious mutual interchanges that took place in what we may call—comparatively speaking—historical times, we find first of all certain Egyptian words that have early crept into Hebrew, partly possibly before the sojourn at Goshen. Thus we find פרעה, אור, אחו, אברך, perhaps also חרבה, תבה, and others, some of them still to be found in Coptic, and not explained by Shemitic etymology. On the other hand, certain words, chiefly designations of animals, are found in Coptic which are taken from Shemitic—גמל, נשר, איל, פיל, etc. Next stand those verbal importations from India, brought home by the trading expeditions to "Ophir"—e.g. כרכם, נרד, קוף, אהלים, and the like—which are easily traceable to Sanscrit and its dialects. [And here we would draw attention to the word יון (Yavan), the Shemitic designation for the Greeks, which seems to be the Sanscrit युवजन Yuvajana = Lat. juvenis—i.e. a younger branch (of emigrants probably).] Strangely enough, while the Greek was enriched to an extraordinary extent by the Shemitic traders, in proportion to the immense variety of articles then imported into Greek ports; the Greek idiom is generally supposed to have added next to nothing to the Shemitic before the time of Alexander. Vegetable substances, precious stones, materials for garments, the garments themselves, animals, musical instruments, weights, and last not least, the letters of the alphabet—all these, together with their native names, were imported by Shemites (Phœnicians) into the Greek territory and language, when they first emerged from their narrow West-Asiatic homes and opened up a trade with the whole world. The use of many of these words in the fragments of the most ancient Greek literature that has survived shows them to have been at the earliest period already part and parcel of that idiom to such an extent that even their origin had been completely forgotten, cf. אזוב ὕσσωπος; בשם, βάλσαμον; בוץ, βύσσος; לבנה, λίβανος; ספיר, σάπφειρος; כתנת, χιτών; כנור, κινύρα, etc. Whether, however, many of the hitherto unexplained Shemitic words may or may not be Greek, and date from exactly the same period, and their importation be owing to the same causes, we cannot here discuss.

And leaving altogether the ever-shifting quicksands of this lexical affinity between the two families, which, as we said, cannot but be accepted in the main as an established fact, we come to the more safe and easy ground of their grammatical difference. This may be summed up briefly in the above-mentioned present triliteral nature of the Shemitic roots; and in the peculiarity of the three consonants that constitute them representing the idea, and the ever-changing vowels added to them its ever-changing aspects, varieties, and modifications. The consonants of the Shemitic root form, in this wise, without the accessory vowels, an unpronounceable word, while the Indo-Germanic root or word is complete and self-sufficient. Among further most vital differences between the two, we may point to the totally different way of the declensions of their nouns (cf. the Shemitic status constructus and emphaticus), the numerous verbal modes utterly unknown to the Aryan conjugation, the absence of a definite tense in Shemitic, the inability of the latter of forming compound nouns or new *nuances* of verbs by prepositions, and the like. All of which cripples the action of the Shemitic idioms to no small extent, while the unlimited power of forming words upon words at the spur of the moment, and the marvellous flexibility of the verb and the precision of its tenses, endow the Aryan with unequalled wealth, power, and elegance.

This most fittingly leads us to the question of the respective "ages" of these two prominent families of languages. Not that to the one or to the other is to be assigned a longer, more ancient term of existence—for this notion of the direct parentage is, as we said, confined to bygone unscientific centuries, and to the Delitzsch-Fürst school: if there be one. But it may fairly be asked—and this is by

no means a barren speculation—which may have retained
its ancient stamp with greater fidelity, and which thus
reflects best the shape of its original? And there can be
but one answer. The more simple, child-like, primitive of
the two is, without any doubt, the Shemitic. Abstraction
and metaphysics, philosophy and speculation, as we find
them in the Aryan, are not easily expressed in an idiom
bereft of all real syntactic structure; bereft further of that
infinite variety of little words, particles, conjunctions, auxiliary verbs, etc., which, ready for any emergency, like so
many small living links, imperceptibly bind word to word,
phrase to phrase, and period to period: which indeed are
the very life and soul of what is called Construction. This
want of exactness and precision, moreover, naturally inherent
in idioms represented by words of dumb sounds, whose
meaning must be determined according to circumstances by
a certain limited number of shifting vowels, whose conjuga-
tions, though varied and flexible to an extraordinary degree,
yet lack a proper distinction between the past and the future
(cf. the Hebrew "perfect" and "aorist," which lend themselves to almost any tense between past and future). There
certainly is—who can doubt it?—notwithstanding all these
shortcomings, a strength, a boldness, a picturesqueness, a
delicacy of feeling and expression about these Shemitic
idioms which marks them, one and all, as the property of a
poetically, not to say "prophetically" inspired race. But
compare with this the suppleness of Aryan languages and
that boundless supply of aids that enable them to produce
the most telling combinations at the spur of the moment;
their exquisitely consummate and refined syntactical development, that can change, and shift, and alter the position
of word, and phrase, and sentence, and period, to almost any
place, so as to give force to any part of their speech. With
all these, and a thousand other faculties and capabilities,
they might certainly at first sight almost lead one to the
belief that they must have grown upon another stock—the
Shemitic—and outgrown it. But discarding this unscientific
notion, it cannot be denied that they are the "younger" of

the two. The stage of Realism, as represented by the former, must naturally have preceded that of Idealism, of which the Aryan alone is the proper type and expression. The Shemitic use of the materialistic, "sensual," term for physiological and psychological phenomena must be older than the formation and common usage of the Aryan abstract term. The name for the outward tangible impression which must have everywhere been identical originally with that of the sensation or idea connected with it, has remained identical in the Shemitic from its earliest stage to its final development. It is, in fact, this unity of idea and expression, which, above all other symptoms, forces us irresistibly to place the Shemitic into the first rank as regards " antiquity," such as we explained it; that is, of its having retained the closest likeness to some original form of human speech that preceded both the other family of language and itself.

The signs characteristic of the common Shemitic stock have been touched upon already in the foregoing paragraphs, as far as they could be brought to bear upon the questions under consideration. To these we may now add the peculiarity of there being but two genders in Shemitic, and that these are also distinguished in the second and third person of the verb; that, further, the genitive is formed by the juxtaposition merely of the two respective nouns, slightly changed in their vocalisation, while prepositions principally form the other cases, and suffixes indicate the oblique cases of pronouns.

We shall now, as summarily as possible, speak of the Shemitic idioms in their special branches, and endeavour to point out as we proceed whatever is best fit to throw a light on the many questions respecting their comparative age, development, and history, referring always for fuller details and points beyond our present task to the several articles devoted to them individually in the course of this work. The first and to the Biblical student most important of these idioms, is the middle Shemitic, Hebraic, or Hebrew, the language of the Hebrew people during the time of their

independence in Caanan. The term Hebrew (עברי) itself
has been derived by some from Eber, the father of Peleg
and Joktan; by others from the appellative עבר, scil. הנהר
—*i.e.* the other side of the river Euphrates, whence the
Abrahamites immigrated into Canaan (LXX. ὁ περάτης).
This double derivation is already mentioned in Theodoretus;
other derivations are from عبر, to explain, etc. No less
have Iberians, Arabians, and other words of similar sound
been pressed into the service. The canonical books of the
O. T. do not use that term to designate the language, which
they call variously שפת כנען language of Canaan, in contradistinction to Egyptian; and יהודית Jewish, in contradistinction to Aramaic (or Ashdodian). It first occurs in
Ecclesiasticus and Josephus, as ἑβραϊστί, γλῶττα τῶν
Ἑβραίων. In the N. T., ἑβραϊστί, ἑβραῒς διάλεκτος, means
Aramæan, in contradistinction to Greek. Philo, ignorant
of the language, calls it γλωσσὰν χαλδαϊκὴν. When
Aramaic had, after the return from the captivity, become
the popular tongue, and Hebrew was chiefly confined to
temple, synagogue and academy, it received the name
לשון הקדש holy language, or more accurately, לשן בית
קודשא, language of the sanctuary. One of the many
vexed and barren questions connected with it is that regarding its original soil—that is, whether Abraham imported it
as his own native tongue into Canaan, or whether, finding
it there, he and his descendants merely adopted it. Those
who held or hold Hebrew to be, if not the oldest of all
languages, the oldest at least of the Shemitic idioms, naturally decide for the former view, since it could not but have
remained the traditional inheritance of the chosen race. The
defenders of the latter view, on the other hand, point to the
circumstance that Abraham came from Mesopotamia, where
Aramaic was the common idiom used—*e.g.* by Laban, the
grandnephew of Abraham (Gen. xxxi. 47), as a translation
of Jacob's Hebrew; further, to its denomination "language
of Canaan," the geographical position of which country,
between the Aramæans and the Arabs, would seem exactly
to correspond to the linguistical position of their respective

tongues. Again, the close resemblance of the Phœnician to
the Hebrew, and certain proper names of Canaan, such as
מלכיצדק, אבימלך, and the like, are brought forward in
support of this second theory. Yet there is a third—viz.
that the idiom itself may first have been fully developed by
the Abrahamides in Canaan, who may have neither brought
it nor found it there, but from a fusion of their own
original "Aramaic" and the Canaanitish language spoken
in their new homes produced it and developed it.

Intimately connected with this question is the more
general one as to the age of this language itself. That it
was the aboriginal tongue from which all others have been
derived is, as we hinted before, an opinion not in accordance
with the uncontested results of modern philology. The
argument of the etymology of certain proper names in the
early documents of Genesis אדם from אדמה, earth; חוה from
חי life, etc.), was already disposed of by Grotius, who held
that Moses may have *translated* them simply into Hebrew
according to the genius of this language, and by Clericus,
who pointed out how these names were chiefly appellative
names, to a great extent given after the events had taken
place to which they point. Yet it was further argued, many
names (from Kain to Lemech principally) allow of no etymology whatsoever, therefore this must be the original
tongue of all men. Such most primitive arguments, however, disposed of, we are still left in the utmost uncertainty:
and, in the absence of documents and testimonies, we must
resign ourselves to give up all hopes of ever arriving at
more than vague theories on the subject. Much more to
the purpose, however, is the attempt to find out the relative
position of Hebrew among its sister idioms. The oldest
Shemitic documents that have survived are in Hebrew, and
in them we find this language and its structure fully developed; so fully indeed, that what progress we do perceive
in it is a downward progress: the beginning of decay. It
further bears so distinctive a character of high antiquity,
originality, simplicity, and purity—the etymology of its
grammatical forms is still at times so clearly visible in it

and it alone, while it has disappeared in the other dialects
—that if not the oldest absolutely, it is certainly the one
Shemitic tongue which seems to come nearest to the one
primitive type of the Shemitic idioms now generally assumed. With regard to its lexical and grammatical position
it occupies that mean between the Aramaic as the poorest,
and the Arabic as the richest. Its principal wealth and
strength, however, lie in its religious and ethical element.
Whatever may have been lost of its documents and the
words which they contained, that which remains is sufficient
to show the peculiar tendency and character of its voca-
bulary. There are, *e.g.*, fourteen different terms for "ask,
inquire," twenty-four for "keep the Law," nine for "trust in
God," &c. Of foreign elements we chiefly discover those
original terms for foreign objects, persons, or dignities, introduced from the Egyptian idiom during the Mosaic period,
and from the Assyrian, Babylonian, Persian, &c., at later
times. Few traces are found of dialectical differences—
although there are some of a vulgar idiom (מֵן, מה, Manna,
&c.) — while on the other hand the difference between
prosaic and poetical diction is most striking. Fuller forms
in flexions, suffixes, peculiar formations of nouns, the use of
grand epithets, and above all, rare words (mostly Aramaic),
are the distinguishing characteristic of its poetry. It loves
to draw for peculiarity of expression both upon the ancient
and partly obsolete stock of words, and upon the language
of the common people: no less than upon dialects of
idiomatic affinity. Other poetical peculiarities are the
omission of the relative or the use of the demonstrative in
its stead, the omission of the article, and the like.

There is, however insignificant the changes undergone by
the Hebrew and the Shemitic languages in general be, as
compared with those of Indo-Germanic—and the reasons for
this stability of the former are founded in their whole character and history—yet a certain change noticeable in the
Hebrew, as preserved in the O. T. Whether this be due to
the difference of the ages in which the several books were
written, or to peculiarities of the respective writers, as some

hold, seems hardly to allow of a doubt. Whatever may be owing to provincialism, or individuality, or even to the more solemn and therefore different style of poetry—and we cannot always distinguish these things as clearly as we could wish—enough remains to show a gradual and important difference between the earlier and· the later stages of the language in the earlier and later books of the O. T. Certain corresponding periods—two, three, or more—have accordingly been assumed. Thus some distinguish between the time before and that after the exile; others between Mosaic, Davidic, Solomonic periods, and the period after the exile. Yet these divisions are of a most precarious nature. It is quite true that certain words and forms which occur in the Pentateuch do not occur again until very late. That again, terms used at first in prose occur afterwards only in poetry, or have completely changed their forms and meanings. Further it is undoubtedly true that during the Davidian time, and that of his son, the influence of the schools founded by Samuel, and the influence of two such eminent kings and their brilliant literary achievement, together with the flourishing condition of the country itself, could not but make itself felt also in a generally higher and finer cultivation of style, diction, and language, throughout the writings of the period. It must also be allowed that the Assyrian invasion, and all its consequences—principally the spread of Aramæan in Palestine—corrupted the purity of the language, blunted its sense of grammatical niceties, and caused those who most desperately clung to the ancient style to introduce, instead of the living elements of former days, dead archaisms. But we doubt whether any genuine division can be instituted, as long at least as the now prevailing uncertainty as to the date of certain parts of the Scripture will last—and we fear it will not soon be removed.

Vague though our notions about the time when Hebrew was first spoken be, we have the clearest dates as to the time of its disappearance as a living language. When at the return from the exile all the ancient institutions were restored, it was found that the people no longer understood their own Scriptures in their vernacular, and a translation into Aramaic (out of which sprang the Targums) had to be added, "so that they might understand them." That Aramaic soon became, as we said, the language of the schools and of public worship almost exclusively, somewhat like the Latin in the Middle Ages.

Closely allied to the Hebrew, as already observed by Augustine, Jerome, and others, is the Phœnician, which in our own days, with the increasing number of monuments brought to light, has risen to high importance. No language of antiquity perhaps was so widely spread. The whole ancient world almost being the vantage-ground of Phœnician enterprise, the language was naturally disseminated over the widest possible space, and the natural consequence was, that gradually yielding to foreign influence it did not keep up its original purity, and became in proportion more and more divergent from the Hebrew. Characteristic to it are certain inflexions it retained, which were long obsolete in Hebrew, no less than certain words and phrases, considered archaic in Hebrew, but of common occurrence in Phœnician. Again, there is a tendency towards a darkening, so to say, of vowels—*e.g.* the Hebrew *a* becomes occasionally *o*, the *e* becomes *i* or *y*, the *i* changes into *y* or *u*, the *o* into *u*, and the like. The gutturals are at times interchanged, consonants are assimilated or omitted, &c. A grammar of this idiom has not been attempted yet, nor does the knowledge of the inflexions which we possess offer sufficient material for a systematic investigation at this present moment. A few items towards it, however, are, that the Hebrew termination of the nominative in *ah* becomes *at* in Phœnician, that the formation of the pronoun differs, that there is a greater variety of genitive forms in the Phœnician, &c. The abundance of Aramaism noticed in the language may have crept in at a late period only. The surviving remnants consist merely of inscriptions on coins and stones, chiefly discovered in their colonies. Of a written literature nothing has come down to us, save a few proper names and texts imbedded in a fearfully mutilated state in Greek and

Roman writings, and a few scraps of extracts from their writers, translated into Greek, but of extremely doubtful genuineness. From all we can gather there must have existed an immense number of Phœnician writings at a remote period of antiquity: chiefly of a theological or theogonical nature, whose authors were identified with the gods themselves. From the Phœnician is to be distinguished the Punic, a corrupted dialect of it, spoken in the western colonies up to the seventh century A.D., while the mother-tongue had completely died out on its native soil as early as the third century. There was even a translation of the Bible extant in Punic, but not a trace of it has remained.

We now turn to the northern Shemitic or "Aramaic" branch, spoken between the Mediterranean and the Tigris; north of Phœnicia, the land of the Israelites, and Arabia; and south of the Taurus; a dialect poorer both grammatically and phonetically than either of the two others. Its peculiarities, moreover, are much of the nature of provincialisms, or perhaps even point to a stage of corruption of language. Thus it is not the change of vowel which produces the passive mood, but a special prefix (את); the article does not begin but end the word; the sibilants are hardened (cf. דְּהַב, gold; טור, rock; תוב, return), etc. The earliest trace of its distinction from the Hebrew is the well-known translation of Jacob's גלעד into יגר שהדותא. A very difficult question, and one, we fear, not to be solved before further progress in our knowledge of cuneiform literature has been made, is that of the language of Babylonia. That Aramaic was spoken there is undoubted, but whether it was the only idiom prevalent, as in Syria and Mesopotamia, or whether the Chaldæans who had conquered Babylonia had brought with them another non-Shemitic (Medo-Persian) language "akin to the Assyrian," has been the subject of long discussions. But even granted that "Chaldæan" was akin to Assyrian, it need not therefore by any means have been a non-Shemitic language. It is, on the contrary, now assumed almost unanimously to be Shemitic; how far, however, it differs from the other dialects, and in particular what may have been its direct or indirect influence upon Aramaic, we cannot here investigate.

Considering the vast importance of cuneiform studies—for Shemitic in general, and for our knowledge of Aramaic or "Chaldee" in particular—we shall try briefly to sum up the results hitherto arrived at in this youngest of philological and palæographical sciences. There are three principal kinds of cuneiform—a mode of writing, be it observed by the way, principally used for monumental records: a kind of cursive being used for records of minor importance—called respectively the Persian, Median, and Assyrian. The first, which seems to have died out 370 B.C., has from thirtynine to forty-four alphabetical signs or combinations, which never consist of more than five wedges. Its words are divided by oblique strokes. The language it represents is Indo-Germanic—the mother of Zend. The second, variously called Median, Scythic, &c., and supposed to represent a Turanian dialect, is the least known and the least important. An alphabet of about one hundred syllabic combinations has been constructed out of the very scanty remains in which it appears. The third and most momentous kind, the Assyrian, seems to have spread widest. Not only in Babylon and Nineveh, on the Euphrates and Tigris, but in Egypt itself has it been found. More than four hundred combinations, phonetic, syllabic, and ideographic, have been distinguished in it, although our knowledge is limited to a proportionately small number of them. But the difficulties offered here are of the most extraordinary kind. The spelling is varied constantly, the signs occasionally represent different sounds (polyphonous), and the same sounds again are represented by different signs (homophonous). Finally, not one, but five or more dialects have been traced in them; dialects belonging to different tribes or periods. Thus it will be easily understood that many and momentous philological problems await their solution from the progress on this field; and little but conjecture is as yet allowed on the special points of our present subject. Of a primeval Babylonian literature, however, supposed to be preserved in certain

Arabic translations, of which some hopes were entertained of late years, nothing reliable has come to light—although the existence of ancient Babylonian writings on mathematics, astronomy (combined with astrology), and chronology is affirmed by ancient authors.

Turning, however, to what specimens of "Aramaic" there *are* preserved, we first of all find certain dialects represented in them which have been variously divided into "Chaldee" and "Aramaic," or into "East-Aramaic" and "West-Aramaic," or again, into "Jewish," "Heathen," and "Christian," and finally, into "Palestinian" and "Babylonian" Aramaic. Discarding the term "Chaldee" as liable to give most rise to misunderstanding—it is first found in the Alexandrines (χαλδαϊστί), and was adopted by Jerome—we may, for the sake of brevity, distinguish between Aramæan ארמית and Syriac (לשון דעבר הנהר, סורסי), which carry, at least in their present form of writing, the most unmistakable line of demarcation on their face. In the first, the Aramaic (Jewish), we have further to distinguish—*a.* The *Galilean* dialect, which seems to have been notorious for its carelessness in the use and pronunciation of its consonants and vowels. The sounds of K and Ch, P and B, &c., and above all the gutturals, were hardly distinguishable in their speech. Of so little importance, indeed, do ,these seem to have been, that they are frequently lost altogether, and entirely new sounds and compounds are formed—scarcely to be reduced to any grammatical or logical rule—by the mere vulgarity of an idiom saturated, moreover, with unconglomerated foreign elements to the last degree. *b.* The *Samaritan—i.e.* vulgar Hebrew and Aramæan mixed up together, in accordance with the genesis of the people itself. It, too, changes its gutturals, uses the *y* most extensively, and does not distinguish the mute consonants. *c.* The *Jerusalem* or *Judæan* dialect scarcely ever pronounces the final gutturals; and has besides many peculiar turns of its own, which show all the symptoms of provincialism, but it boasts of a fuller vocalisation. Its orthography, however, is one of the strangest imaginable. This last is the most important dialect of the three Aramaic ones, for in it the whole gigantic Targumic and (partly) Talmudical literature is written, while of the Samaritan there exist but few documents of a theological, liturgical, and grammatical nature, and the Galilean never had, as far as we know, any literature of its own. We need but briefly mention here the minor ("heathen") branches, such as *Zabian*—standing between Aramaic and Syriac, the language of a mystico-theosophical sect called the Mendaites (= Gnostics), which is largely mixed with Persian elements, and almost bereft of grammar; the *Palmyrene*, a kind of Syriac, written in square Hebraic characters; and the *Egypto-Aramaic*, found on some monuments (stone of Carpentras, Papyri), probably due to Babylonian Jews living in Egypt, who had adopted the religion of their new country.

All "Aramæan" literature — in contradistinction to "Syriac"—is, it need hardly be added, Jewish; from the chapters in Daniel, written in this idiom, to the last remnant penned in Palestine or Babylon (the worship in the temple and the earlier schools being, as we said, the only places for which the "Holy Language" was partly retained), this was the exclusively used popular idiom. It had, in fact, become so popular and universal that it came to be called Ἑβραϊστί (N. T. *passim*). How it grew to be so universally adopted has hardly been sufficiently explained as yet; for the Captivity alone, or even any number of successively returning batches of immigrants from Babylonia, do not quite account for the phenomenon of a seemingly poor and corrupt dialect supplanting so completely that other hallowed by the most sacred traditions, that this became a dead language in its own country. The fact, however, is undeniable, as at the time of Christ even Scripture itself was popularly only known through the medium of the Aramaic Targums. Nearly all the Shemitisms in the N. T. are Aramaic, and the same may be said with regard to those found in Josephus: cf. Matt. v. 22, ῥακά = ריקא : xvi. 17, βὰρ Ἰωνᾶ = בר יונה; xxvii. 46, ἠλὶ ἠλὶ λημὰ σαβαχθανί = אלי אלי למה שבקתני; 1 Cor. xvi. 22, μαρὰν ἀθά = מרן אתא; Joseph.

Antiq. iii. 10. 6, ’Ασαρθά = עצרתא; iii. 7. 1, οὓς Χαναίας καλοῦσι = כהניא, etc.

"*Syriac*" is the designation of an idiom used since the second Christian century in the Church, which, though written in different characters (Estrangelo), is yet so closely akin to Aramæan that up to this day the opinions are divided as to the propriety of making any difference at all between the two. As distinguishing marks between them have been adduced, principally, the "darker" vocalisation of Syriac—*o* for *a*, *au* or *ai* for *o* or *i*, etc.—its different accentuation, its ג as the prefix of the third pers. future for the Aramaic י, the formation of the Syriac infinite by מ, and its greater wealth of words, chiefly taken from the Greek; all of which, however, together with other peculiarities, are reduced by the advocates of the unity of both dialects to provincial differences and to the peculiar circumstances of the times. But here again, without entering more fully into the question, we can only venture the statement that there seems to be a great *primâ facie* probability at least for their being radically identical; only let it not be forgotten that in order to be able to form a real judgment it will be first of all necessary that carefully-prepared editions of the literatures of both should be in our hands. Something has been done for the comparatively poor Syriac branch; for the Aramaic, nothing. That, however, the present Maronite dialect, as well as those of the Jacobites, Nestorians, and other Chaldee Christians, is essentially different from both Syriac and Aramaic, is undoubted: just as the vulgar Arabic spoken in Morocco and Algeria differs from classical Arabic.

The Southern or "*Arabic*" branch presents to us the most remarkable phenomenon of one special idiom—the Arabic—suddenly, as it were, starting out of utter obscurity as the richest, most complete, and most refined among its sister idioms, at a time comparatively modern, and exactly when the two other branches seemed to have accomplished their mission, and what remained of their life was merely artificial. So exquisitely finished and so boundlessly wealthy, both

lexically and grammatically, has it been from the moment
when it first became known, that, as there was no unripe
infancy and no struggling growth observable in it, so there
was also no age, and far less a decay. It thus ranks as the
freshest and "youngest:" precisely in the same sense as the
Hebrew may be styled the "oldest" among the Shemitic
idioms—not, as we said above, on account of its having in
reality preceded the others, or still less of its having given
birth to the others, but because for some reason or other its
growth stopped at a certain period, and it seems to have
retained its ancient physiognomy, while its sister dialects
went on developing and renewing themselves as much as in
them lay and circumstances permitted. As the Arabic was
in the sixth century, so it remained almost unchanged up to
our day, except perhaps that in absorbing foreign, especially
Greek elements of culture, it did not assimilate them quite
in the same congenial manner as an Indo-Germanic idiom
would have done. But for all that this language must have
an age equal at least to that of the other two sister dialects.
There are traces of its peculiarities—peculiarities which
divide it as sharply as can be from them—to be found in
the earliest records of the O. T. We have, e.g. the article
אל (the Hebrew [הל]) in אלמדד (Gen. x. 26), and further
in words like אלאמים]א, אלטושם]א, אלקש, אלקום]א. The phenomenon, further, of a real declension by the change of the
termination of the cases, by certain "broken" plurals, &c.,
together with many forms of its conjugation, entirely and
radically unknown to Shemitic as represented by its other
dialects, proves its early and most independent existence.
That, further, the Arabs stood in great renown for wisdom,
or what we should now call literary proficiency—if this be
not a misnomer for a time when writing was unknown among
them—in the earliest historical times, seems clear enough
from the queen of Sheba's being an Arab queen, the friends
of Job being Arabs, and Solomon's own wisdom being compared to the wisdom of the Arabs. How it came to pass
that absolutely nothing should have survived of all that
literature which certainly must have been produced among

them is a phenomenon no less remarkable. Although two facts must be borne in mind always—viz. that it all was oral, and that it was in verse, or at least in a rhythmical form adapted to those early proverbial sayings and poems of which a vague Arabic tradition still speaks; and Mohammed, for reasons of his own, discouraged, nay condemned, poetry— the sole vehicle of all science, all tradition, all religion, before him, in the "time of ignorance." A comparison between the Arabic and the two other branches most strikingly shows that superabundance, lexically and grammatically, of the former over the two latter of which we spoke. No one, the Arabs hold, could, without being inspired, keep the whole wealth of their language in his memory. For not only have single words (sword, lion, serpent, etc.), hundreds and thousands of *nuances* of terms, but many a single word has untold numbers of different meanings. The number of its root and words is like three, respectively ten, to those of the Hebrew—such as the monuments of both now are in our hands. No doubt, had more survived of the Hebrew literature, the proportion would not have been quite as startling —for we now have only fragments of its religious writings to compare with the endless series of historical, poetical, philological, astronomical, and other Arabic literature; a literature which indeed does not leave a single part of science or *belles-lettres* uncultivated, and which spreads over about eight hundred years—subsequently to the time of Greece and Rome. Nor can the brilliant Hebrew literature that sprang up in the middle ages, partly through Arabic influence, be taken into account. Arabic, though its "classical" period may be closed with Mohammed, never became Neo-Arabic, while the difference between classical Hebrew and late Hebrew, which had to coin new words at every turn, is quite unmistakable. Arabic grammar shows the same ascendency over that of its sister idioms as does its dictionary. It has twice as many forms of conjugation as the Hebrew, itself richer than the Aramaic by the Hiphal, the futurum *paragog.* and *apocop.* etc. The Arabic has, besides, over both the advantage of a *comparative*, and of a *dual* in the verb. The Hebrew ל"ה verbs, which in Aramaic are hardly distinguishable from the ל"א, in Arabic split into the two distinct forms of ל"ו and ל"י; just as many a Hebrew root with more than one signification appears in Arabic as a variety of roots, by a slight change of a consonant. Nay, of these, it has five more than the Hebrew and Aramaic. It has also, through the amplitude of its vocalisation, the charm of a more sonorous, a fuller and richer tone and colour than either. But it must also be acknowledged that the harmonious flow of the more ancient idioms, their unfettered ease and freedom, together with a number of peculiar forms, like the parallelism with its exquisite natural beauty, is lost to a great extent in the Arabic, in which the work of the schools, their pedantic striving after a consummate correctness of expression, and their rhetorical "painting of the lily," is often painfully clear. But to the Arabic alone is also due the spread of Shemitic—which had been carried atomically, so to speak, by the Phœnicians to the ends of the earth, but which, with a few isolated exceptions, never really struck root anywhere—to an extent never dreamed of by any ancient or even modern language; a spread that has not ceased yet, but is enlarging its circles from year to year, together with Islam itself. It is, however, as we said, only the last century before Mohammed, that has left us a few traces of pre-Islamic literature. From the time of Mohammed it grew with exotic rapidity into one of the most widely and brilliantly cultivated. It embraced well nigh all the branches of human knowledge and research. Theology, medicine, philosophy, philology, history, mathematics, geography, astronomy, etc., are most extensively represented—though as yet only a beginning has been made in making the treasures of information these works contain as widely useful as they might be made. From the fourteenth century, however, the glory of Arabic literature began to wane.

We have here spoken only of the chief representative of the Arabic branch, the Arabic itself—still spoken now in the whole south-west of Asia, in the north and east of

Africa, in Malta, partly even in India, and everywhere in fact where Mohammedanism reigns supreme—which was originally the dialect of one tribe only, viz. the Koreish. The ancient traditions speak of Cahtanic and Ismaelitic dialects: but at present we can only make a vague distinction between those of Yemen and of Hedjaz, during the ante-Islamic times. As the Koreish in the north-west were the spokesmen, as it were, of the latter, so the Himyars or Homerites made their dialect the predominant one in the south, until the Koran swept it completely out of Arabia, and, save a few scattered quotations embedded in later writings, and some partly mutilated inscriptions of difficult reading and more difficult understanding, every trace of it in its original form has disappeared. The Ethiopic or Gheez alone, which was spoken up to the fourteenth century in Abyssinia, seemed to have come nearest to it. But considering the scantiness of its own literary remains, which are chiefly of a theological nature (partly unpublished), and as such subject to the influence of foreign (European) missionaries—who also left their imprint upon it in its exceptional writing from left to right; considering further the small progress we have as yet made in deciphering the Himyaritic, nothing but a very cautious judgment on the relation of the two can be pronounced. The Amharic, a barbarous Gheez dialect, stands, so to say, on the utmost line of the Arabic Shemite, and deserves but a passing mention. The idioms of the Gallas, Hamtonga, and a number of other tribes, however, no longer belong to the Shemitic, notwithstanding some outer resemblances which have misled former investigators.

Respecting the visible representation of the Shemitic Languages, it may be broadly observed that writing, which in no language fully expresses all the sounds in their various shades, has, in the Shemitic Languages this additional imperfection, that only the consonants—the skeleton of the word—are represented by real letters, while the vowels originally are either entirely omitted, or only the longer ones are expressed by certain consonants (matres lectionis).

It was only at a comparatively late period that also the minor vowels were added in the shape of little strokes and dots above or below the line, but this aid too is only intended for less practised readers. Arabic and Hebrew are still commonly written and printed without vowels. Another point is the direction of the Shemitic writing from right to left (of which only modern Ethiopic makes an exception), a peculiarity still inherent in the alternate line of the *Boustro-phedon* of the early Greeks. The nearest approach to the most ancient form of the Shemitic characters is found in the Phœnician, from which also all our European alphabets are derived.

XV

ON THE TARGUMS.[1]

TARGUM (תַּרְגּוּם, from תִּרְגֵּם; Arab. تَرجَم, to translate, explain); a Chaldee word of uncertain origin, variously derived from the roots רגם, רקם (comp. Arab. رقم, رقّن, &c.), and even identified with the Greek τράγημα, desert (Fr. dragées), (trop. τραγήματα τῶν λόγων, Dion. Hal. Rhet. 10, 18), which occurs often in the Talmud as מיני תרנימא, or תרניטא ("such as dates, almonds, nuts," &c. Pes. 119 b):— the general term for the CHALDEE, or, more accurately ARAMAIC VERSIONS of the Old Testament.

The injunction to "read the Book of the Law before all Israel . . . . the men, and women, and children, and the strangers," on the Feast of Tabernacles of every Sabbatical year, as a means of solemn instruction and edification, is first found in Deut. xxxi. 10–13. How far the ordinance was observed in early times we have no means of judging. It would appear, however, that such readings did take place in the days of Jeremiah. Certain it is that among the first acts undertaken by Ezra towards the restoration of the primitive religion and public worship is reported his reading "before the congregation, both of men and women" of the returned exiles, "in the Book in the Law of God" (Neh. viii. 2, 8). Aided by those men of learning and eminence with whom, according to tradition, he founded that most important religious and political body called the Great Synagogue, or Men of the Great Assembly (אנשי כנסת הגדולה, 536–167), he appears to have succeeded in so firmly establishing

---

[1] From Dr. Wm. Smith's 'Dictionary of the Bible,' vol. iii.

regular and frequent public readings in the Sacred Records, that later authorities almost unanimously trace this hallowed custom to times immemorial — nay to the time of Moses himself. Such is the statement of Josephus (*c. Ap.* ii. 17); and we read in the Acts, xv. 21, "For Moses of old time hath in every city them that preach him, being read in the synagogue every sabbath-day." So also Jer. Meg. i. 1: "Ezra has instituted for Israel that the maledictions in the Pentateuch should also be read in public," &c. Further, Meg. 31 *b*, "Ezra instituted ten things, viz., that there should be readings in the Law also in the afternoon service of Sabbath, on the Monday, and on the Thursday, &c. . . . . But was not this instituted before in the desert, as we find ' they went for three days and found no water' (water meaning the Law, as Is. lv. 1 is fancifully explained by the Haggadah), until the 'prophets among them' arranged the three weekly readings? So Ezra only reinstituted them," comp. also B. Kama, 82 *a*, &c. To these ancient readings in the Pentateuch were added, in the course of time, readings in the Prophets (in some Babylonian cities even in the Hagiographa), which were called הפטרות, *Haftaroth;* but when and how these were introduced is still matter of specu-lation. Former investigators (Abudraham, Elias Levita, Vitringa, &c.) almost unanimously trace their origin to the Syrian persecution, during which all attention to the Law was strictly prohibited, and even all the copies of it that were found were ruthlessly destroyed; so that, as a sub-stitute for the Pentateuchical Parasha, a somewhat corre-sponding portion of the Prophets was read in the synagogue, and the custom, once introduced, remained fixed. Recent scholars, on the other hand, without much show of reason, as it would appear, variously hold the *Haftarah* to have sprung from the sermon or homiletic exercise which accom-panied the reading in the Pentateuch, and took its *exordium* (as Haftarah, by an extraordinary linguistic stretch, is ex-plained by Frankel) from a prophetic passage, adapted in a manner to the Mosaic text under consideration; or, again, they imagine the *Haftarah* to have taken its rise spontaneously during the exile itself, and that Ezra retained and enforced it in Palestine.

If, however, the primitive religion was re-established, together with the second Temple, in more than its former vigour, thus enabling the small number of the returned exiles—and these, according to tradition, the lowest of the low, the poor in wealth, in knowledge, and in ancestry,[1] the very outcasts and refuse of the nation as it were [2]—to found upon the ruins of Zion one of the most important and lasting spiritual commonwealths that has ever been known, there was yet one thing which neither authority nor piety, neither academy nor synagogue, could restore to its original power and glory—the Hebrew language. Ere long it was found necessary to translate the national books, in order that the nation from whose midst they had sprung might be able to understand them. And if for the Alexandrine, or rather the whole body of Hellenistic Jews, Greek translations had to be composed, those who dwelt on the hallowed soil of their forefathers had to receive the sacred word through an Aramaic medium. The word מפורש, *Mephorash*, "explanatorily," "clearly," or, as the A. V. has it, "distinctly," used in the above-quoted passage of Neh. viii. 8, is in the Talmud explained by "Targum."[3] Thus to Ezra himself is traced the custom of adding translations in the then popular idiom —the Aramaic—to the periodical readings (Jer. Meg. 28 b; J. Ned. iv., Bab. Ned. i.; Maim. Hilch. Teph. xii. § 10, &c.),

---

[1] "Ten kinds of families went up from Babylon: Priests, Levites, Israelites, profaned (חללי, those whose fathers are priests, but whose mothers are not fit for priestly marriage); proselytes, freedmen, bastards (or rather those born in illegal wedlock); Nethinim (lowest menials of the Temple); שתוקי ('about whose lineage there is silence,' —of unknown fathers); and אסופי, 'foundlings, of unknown father and mother' " (Kidd. 4, 1).

[2] "Ezra, on leaving Babylon, made it like unto pure flour " כסולת נקייה (ib.).

[3] " 'And they read in the book of the Law of God clearly (מפורש), and gave the understanding, so that they understood the reading:'—'in the book of the Law'—this is Mikra, the original reading in the Pentateuch; 'מפורש, clearly'—this is Targum" (Meg. 3 a; Ned. 37 b). To this tradition also might be referred the otherwise rather enigmatical passage (Sanh. 21 b): "Originally," says Mar Sutra, "the Law was given to Israel in Ibri writing and the holy (Hebrew) language. It was again given to them in the days of Ezra in the Ashurith writing and the Aramaic language," &c.

Y

for which he is also reported to have fixed the Sabbaths, the
Mondays and Thursdays—the two latter the market and
law-days, when the villagers came to town—of every week
(Jer. Meg. i. 1; Baba Kama, 82 *a*). The gradual decay of
the pure Hebrew vernacular, among the multitude at least,
may be accounted for in many ways. The Midrash very
strikingly points out, among the characteristics of the long
sojourn of Israel in Egypt, that they neither changed their
language, nor their names, nor the shape of their garments,
during all that time. The bulk of their community—shut
up, as it were, in the small province of Goshen, almost
exclusively reduced to intercourse with their own race and
tribes, devoted only to the pasture of their flocks, and
perhaps to the tilling of their soil—were in a condition
infinitely more favourable for the retention of all the signs
and tokens of their nationality than were the Babylonian
captives. The latter scattered up and down the vast empire,
seem to have enjoyed everywhere full liberty of intercom-
munication with the natives—very similar in many respects
to themselves—to have been utterly unrestrained in the
exercise of every profession and trade, and even to have
risen to the highest offices of state; and thus, during the
comparatively short space, they struck root so firmly in the
land of their exile, that when opportunity served, they were,
on the whole, loth to return to the Land of Promise. What
more natural than that the immigrants under Zerubbabel, and
still more those who came with Ezra—several generations of
whose ancestors had been settled in Babel — should have
brought back with them the Aramaic, if not as their vernacular, at all events as an idiom with which they were
perfectly familiar, and which they may partly have continued to use as their colloquial language in Palestine, as, in
fact, they had had to use it in Babylon? Continuous later
immigrations from the "Captivity" did not fail to reinforce
and further to spread the use of the same tongue. All the
decrees and official communications addressed to the Jews by
their Persian masters were in Aramaic (Ezr. Neh. *passim*),
Judæa being considered only as part of the Syrian satrapy.

Nor must it be forgotten that the whole colonists in Palestine
(2 K. xvii. 24) were Samaritans, who had come from " Aram
and Babel," and who spoke Chaldee; that intermarriages
with women from Ashdod, Ammon, and Moab had been
common (Neh. xiii. 23); that Phœnicia, whose merchants
(Tyrians, Neh. xiii. 16) appear to have settled in Palestine,
and to have established commercial relations with Judæa
and Galilee, contains large elements of Chaldee in its own
idiom. Thus it came to pass that we find in the Book of
Daniel, for instance, a somewhat forced Hebrew, from which,
as it would seem, the author gladly lapses into the more
familiar Aramaic (comp. ii. 4, &c.); that oracles were
received by the High-priests Johanan [1] and Simon the Just [2]
in the Holy of Holies (during the Syrian wars) in Aramaic
(Sotah, 33 a) and that, in short, some time before the
Hasmonean period, this was the language in which were
couched not only popular sayings, proverbs, and the like
(משל הדיוט. Beresh. R. 107 d; Tanch. 17 a; Midr. Tehill.
23 d; 51 f, &c. &c.), but official and legal documents
(Mishnah Ketub. 4, 8; Toseftah Sabb. c. 8; Edujoth, 8, 4—
c. 130 B.C.), even certain prayers [3]—of Babylonian origin probably—and in which books destined for the great mass of
the people were written. [4] Thus, indeed, the Hebrew Language—the "language of Kenaan" (Is. xix. 18), or "Jehu-
dith" (2 K. xviii. 26, 28; Is. xxxvi. 11) of the Bible—
became more and more the language of the few, the learned,
the *Holy Language,* לשון הקדש or, still more exactly, לישן
בית קודשא, "Language of the Temple," set aside almost

---

[1] "The youths who went to combat
at Antiochia have been victorious."

[2] "Perished has the army which
the enemy thought to lead against the
Temple."

[3] Introduction to the Haggadah for
the Pesach (כהא לחמא): "Such was
the bread of misery which our fathers
ate in the land of Mizrajim. Whoever
is needy, he come and eat with us;
whoever is in want, he come and celebrate the Pesach. This year here,
next year in the land of Israel; this
year slaves, next year free men." The

Kaddish, to which afterwards a certain
signification as a prayer for the dead
was given, and which begins as follows: Let there be magnified and
sanctified the Great Name in the
world which He has created according
to His will, and which He rules as
His kingdom, during your life and
your days, and the life of the whole
house of Israel, speedily and in a near
time, and say ye, 'Amen: Be the
Great Name praised for ever and evermore,'" &c.

[4] Megillath Taanith, &c.

exclusively for the holy service of religion: be it the Divine
Law and the works in which this was contained (like the
Mishnah, the Boraithot, Mechilta, Sifri, Sifra, the older
Midrashim, and very many portions of the Talmud), or the
correspondence between the different academies (witness the
Hebrew letter sent from Jerusalem to Alexandria about 100
B.C., Chag. Jer. ii. 2), or be it the sacred worship itself in
temple and synagogue, which was almost entirely carried on
in pure Hebrew.

If the common people thus gradually had lost all knowledge of the tongue in which were written the books to be
read to them, it naturally followed (in order "that they
might understand them") that recourse must be had to a
translation into the idiom with which they were familiar—
the Aramaic. That further, since a bare translation could
not in all cases suffice, it was necessary to add to the translation an explanation, more particularly of the more difficult
and obscure passages. Both translation and explanation
were designated by the term *Targum*. In the course of
time there sprang up a guild, whose special office it was
to act as *interpreters* in both senses (*Meturgeman* [1]), while
formerly the learned alone volunteered their services. These
interpreters were subjected to certain bonds and regulations
as to the form and substance of their renderings. Thus
(comp. Mishnah Meg. *passim*; Mass. Sofer. xi. 1; Maimon.
Hilch. Tephill. 12, § 11 ff; Orach Chaj. 145, 1, 2), "neither
the reader nor the interpreter are to raise their voices one
above the other;" "they have to wait for each other until
each have finished his verse;" "the Meturgeman is not
to lean against a pillar or a beam, but to stand with fear and
with reverence;" "*he is not to use a written Targum*, but he
is to deliver his translation *vive voce*"—lest it might appear
that he was reading out of the Torah itself, and thus the
Scriptures be held responsible for what are *his own* dicta;
"no more than one verse in the Pentateuch, and three in

---

[1] מתורגמן, תורגמן, תורנמינא (Ar.) | *Turcimanno*; Fr. *Truchement*; Engl.
ترجمن; Arm. *Sargmaniël*; Ital. | *Dragoman*, &c.

the Prophets [a greater licence is given for the Book of Esther] shall be read and translated at a time ; " " that there should be not more than one reader and one interpreter for the Law, while for the Prophets one reader and one interpreter, or two interpreters, are allowed," &c. (comp. Cor. xiv. 21 ff; xii. 30; 27, 28). Again (Mishnah Meg. and Tosiftah, *ad loc.*), certain passages liable to give offence to the multitude are specified, which may be read in the synagogue and translated; others, which may be read but not translated; others, again, which may neither be read nor translated. To the first class [1] belong *the account of the Creation*—a subject not to be discussed publicly, on account of its most vital bearing upon the relation between the Creator and the Kosmos, and the nature of both: the deed of Lot and his two daughters (Gen. xix. 31); of Judah and Tamar (Gen. xxxviii.); the first account of the making of the golden calf (Ex. xxxii.); all the curses in the Law; the deed of Amnon and Tamar (2 Sam. xiii.); of Absalom with his father's concubines (2 Sam. xvi. 22); the story of the woman of Gibeah (Judg. xix.). These are to be read and translated—being mostly deeds which carried their own punishments with them. To be read but not translated are [2] the deed of Reuben with his father's concubine (Gen. xxv. 22); the latter portion of the story of the golden calf (Ex. xxxii.); the benediction of the priests (on account of its awful nature). And neither to be read nor translated are the deed of David and Bathsheba (2 Sam. xi. and xii.), and according to one the story of Amnon and Tamar (2 Sam. xiii.). (Both the latter stories, however, are, in Mishnah Meg. iv. 10, enumerated among those of the second class, which are to be read but not translated.)

Altogether these *Meturgemanim* do not seem to have been held generally in very high respect; one of the reasons being probably that they were paid (two *Selaim* at one time, according to Midr. R. Gen. 98), and thus made (what P.

---

[1] Comprised in the mnemonic formula, בלל תֹּה עֹקן נִשֹּׁפה (Meg. 25 a).

[2] רֹּעֲבֹּרֹי, ib.

Aboth especially inveighs against) the Torah "a spade to dig with it." "No sign of blessing," it was said, moreover, "could rest upon the profit they made by their calling, since it was money earned on the Sabbath" (Pes. 4 *b*). Persons unfit to be readers, as those whose clothes were so torn and ragged that their limbs became visible through the rents (פורח), their appearance thus not corresponding to the reverence due to the sacred word itself, or blind men, were admitted to the office of a Meturgeman; and, apart from there not being the slightest authority attached to their interpretations, they were liable to be stopped and silenced, publicly and ignominiously, whenever they seemed to overstep the bounds of discretion. At what time the regulation that they should not be under fifty years of age in odd reference to the "men of fifty," Is. iii. 3, mentioned in Juchas. 44, 2) came into use, we are not able to decide. The Mishnah certainly speaks even of a minor (under thirteen years) as being allowed both to read and to act as a Meturgeman (comp. Mishnah Meg. *passim*). Altogether they appear to have borne the character of empty-headed, bombastic fools. Thus Midr. Koh. has to Eccl. vii. 5: "'It is better to hear the rebuke of the wise:'—these are the preachers (Darshanim)—'than for a man to hear the song of fools:'—these are the Meturgemanim, who raise their voices in sing-song, (בשיר, or with empty fancies):—'that the people may hear.'" And to ix. 17: "'The words of wise men are heard in quiet'—these are the preachers (Darshanim)—'more than the cry of him that ruleth among fools'—these are the Meturgemanim who stand above the congregation." And though both passages may refer more especially to those Meturgemanim (Emoras, speakers, expounders) who at a later period stood by the side of the *Chacham*, or president of the Academy, the preacher κατ' ἐξοχήν (himself seated on a raised daïs), and repeated with a loud voice, and enlarged upon what the latter had whispered into their ear in Hebrew (חכם לוחש לו לשון עברית, comp. Matt. x. 27, "What ye hear in the ear, that preach ye upon the housetops"), yet there is an abundance of instances

to show that the Meturgeman at the side of the reader was
exposed to rebukes of a nature, and is spoken of in a manner,
not likely to be employed towards any but men low in the
social scale.

A fair notion of what was considered a proper Targum
may be gathered from the maxim preserved in the Talmud
(Kidd. 49, *a*): "Whosoever translates [as Meturgeman] a
verse in its closely exact form [without proper regard to its
real meaning] is a *liar*, and whoever adds to it is *impious and
a blasphemer*: *e.g.* the literal rendering into Chaldee of the
verse, 'They saw the God of Israel' (Ex. xxiv. 10), is as
wrong a translation as 'They saw *the angel* of God;' the
proper rendering being, 'They saw the glory of the God of
Israel.'"   Other instances are found in the Mishnah (Meg.
iv. 8); "Whosoever renders the text (Lev. xviii. 21) 'And
thou shalt not let any of thy seed pass through the fire to
Molech,' by 'Thou shalt not give thy seed to be carried over
to heathenism (or to an Aramite woman)' [*i.e.* as the Gemara
ad loc.; Jer. Sanh. 8, and Sifri on Deut. xxiii. 10, explain it,
one who marries an Aramaic woman; for although she may
become a proselyte, she is yet sure to bear enemies to him
and to God, since the mother will in the end carry his
children over to idolatrous worship]; as also he who enlarges
upon (or figuratively explains) the sections relative to incest
(Lev. xviii.)—he shall forthwith be silenced and publicly
rebuked."   Again (comp. Jer. Ber. v. 1; Meg. iv. 10),
"Those who translate 'O my people, children of Israel, as
I am merciful in heaven, so shall ye be merciful on
earth:'—'Cow or ewe, it and her young ye shall not kill
in one day' (Lev. xxii. 28)—they do not well, for they
represent the Laws of God [whose reasons no man dare
try to fathom] as mere axioms of mercy;" and, it is added,
"the short-sighted and the frivolous will say, 'Lo! to a
bird's-nest He extends His mercy, but not to yonder
miserable man . . . .'"

The same causes which, in the course of time, led to the
writing down—after many centuries of oral transmission—of
the whole body of the Traditional Law, the very name of

which (תורה שבעל פה, "oral law," in contradistinction to
תורה שבכתב, or "written law") seemed to imply that it
should never become a fixed, immutable code, engendered
also, and about the same period, as it would appear, written
Targums: for certain portions of the Bible, at least.[1]

The fear of the adulterations and mutilations which the
Divine Word—amid the troubles within and without the
Commonwealth—must undergo at the hands of incompetent
or impious exponents, broke through the rule, that the
Targum should only be *oral*, lest it might acquire undue
authority (comp. Mishnah Meg. iv. 5, 10; Tosifta, *ib.* 3; Jer.
Meg. 4, 1; Bab. Meg. 24 *a*; Sota, 39 *b*). Thus, if a Targum
of Job is mentioned (Sab. 115 *a*; Tr. Soferim, 5, 15; Tosifta
Sab. c. 14; Jer. Sabb. 16, 1) as having been highly disapproved by Gamaliel the Elder (middle of first century
A.D.), who caused it to be hidden and buried out of sight:—
we find, on the other hand, at the end of the second century,
the practice of reading the Targum generally commended,
and somewhat later Jehoshua ben Levi enjoins it as a special
duty upon his sons. The Mishnah even contains regulations
about the manner (Jad. iv. 5) in which the Targum is to be
written. But even in their written, and, as we may presume,
authoritatively approved form, the Targums were of comparatively small weight, and of no canonical value whatsoever. The Sabbath was not to be broken for their sake as it
was lawful to do for the Scripture in the original Hebrew
(Sab. 115 *a*). The Targum does not defile the hands (for
the purpose of touching consecrated food) as do the Chaldee
portions of Ezra and Nehemiah (Yad. iv. 5).

The gradual growth of the Code of the written Targum,
such as now embraces almost the whole of the O.T., and
contains, we may presume, but few snatches of the primitive
Targums, is shrouded in deep obscurity. We shall not fail

---

[1] As, according to Frankel, the
LXX. was only a partial translation
at first. Witness the confusion in the
last chapters of Exodus, which, as mere
repetitions (of chaps. xxv. and xxix.),
were originally left untranslated.
Saadia in a similar manner uses the
formulas كذلك or مثل ذلك in
repetitions.

to indicate the opinions arrived at as to the date and authorship of the individual versions in their due places; but we
must warn the reader beforehand, that no positive results
have been attained as yet, save that nearly *all the names and
dates hitherto commonly attached to them must be rejected.*
And we fear that, as long at least as the Targum shares the
fate of the LXX., the Samaritan Pentateuch, the Midrash,
the Talmud, &c.:—viz., that a really critical edition remains
a thing occasionally dreamt of, but never attempted;—so
long must we abandon the hope of getting any nearer a
final solution of this and many other still more important
questions. The utter corruption, moreover, of the Targum,
bitterly complained of already by Elias Levita—(an author,
be it observed, of very moderate attainments, but absurdly
overrated by certain of his contemporaries, and by those who
copied his usually shallow dicta without previous examination)—debars us from more than half its use. And yet
how fertile its study could be made; what light it might be
made capable of throwing upon the Bible itself, upon the
history of the earliest development of Biblical studies, versions, and upon the Midrash—both the Halachah and Haggadah—snatches of which, in their, as it were, liquid stages,
lie embedded in the Targums:—all this we need not urge
here at length.

Before, however, entering into a more detailed account, we
must first dwell for a short time on the *Midrash*[1] itself, of
which the Targum forms part.

The centre of all mental activity and religious action
among the Jewish community, after the return from Babylon,
was the Scriptural Canon collected by the Soferim, or men
of the Great Synagogue. These formed the chief authority
on the civil and religious law, and their authority was the
Pentateuch. Their office as expounders and commentators

---

[1] מדרש (Arab. مدرس), first used
in 2 Chr. xiii. 22, xxiv. 27; "Commentary," in the sense of Cæsar's
"Commentaries," enlargement, em-
bellishment, complement, &c. (A. V. story!). The compilers of Chronicles
seem to have used such promiscuous
works treating of biblical personages
and events, provided they contained
aught that served the tendency of the
book.

of the Sacred Records was twofold. They had, firstly, to
explain the exact meaning of such prohibitions and ordinances
contained in the Mosaic Books as seemed not explicit enough
for the multitude, and the precise application of which in
former days, had been forgotten during the Captivity. Thus,
e.g. general terms, like the "work" forbidden on the Sabbath,
were by them specified and particularized; not indeed according to their own arbitrary and individual views, but according
to tradition traced back to Sinai itself. Secondly, laws
neither specially contained nor even indicated in the Pentateuch were inaugurated by them according to the new wants
of the times and the ever-shifting necessities of the growing
Commonwealth (*Geseroth, Tekanoth*). Nor were the latter
in all cases given on the sole authority of the Synod; but
they were in most cases traditional, and certain special letters
or signs in the Scriptures, seemingly superfluous or out of
place where they stood, were, according to fixed hermeneutical rules, understood to indicate the inhibitions and
prohibitions (*Gedarim*, "Fences"), newly issued and fixed.
But Scripture, which had for this purpose to be studied most
minutely and unremittingly—the most careful and scru-
tinizing attention being paid even to its outward form and
semblance—was also used, and more especially in its non-
legal, prophetical parts, for homiletic purposes, as a wide
field of themes for lectures, sermons, and religious discourses,
both in and out of the Synagogue:—at every solemnity in
public and private life. This juridical and homiletical expounding and interpreting of Scripture—the germs of both
of which are found still closely intertwined and bound up
with each other in the Targum—is called *darash*, and the
avalanche of Jewish literature which began silently to gather
from the time of the return from the exile and went on rolling
uninterruptedly—however dread the events which befel the
nation—until about a thousand years after the destruction of
the second Temple, may be comprised under the general
name *Midrash*—"expounding." The two chief branches
indicated are, *Halachah* (הלך, "to go"), the rule by which
to go, = binding, authoritative law; and *Haggadah* (הגד,

" to say ") = saying, legend,—flights of fancy, darting up from
the Divine word. The *Halachah*, treating more especially
the Pentateuch as the legal part of the O. T., bears towards
this book the relation of an amplified and annotated Code;
these amplifications and annotations, be it well understood,
not being new laws, formerly unheard of, deduced in an
arbitrary and fanciful manner from Scripture, but supposed
to be simultaneous oral revelations *hinted at* in the Scripture:
in any case representing not the human but the Divine interpretation, *handed down through a named authority* (*Kabbala,
Shemata*—" something received, heard "). The *Haggadah*,
on the other hand, held especial sway over the wide field of
ethical, poetical, prophetical, and historical elements of the
O. T., but was free even to interpret its legal and historical
passages fancifully and allegorically. The whole Bible, with
all its tones and colours, belonged to the *Haggadah*, and this
whole Bible she transformed into an endless series of themes
for her most wonderful and capricious variations. " Prophetess of the Exile," she took up the hallowed verse, word
or letter, and, as the *Halachah* pointed out in it a special
ordinance, she, by a most ingenious exegetical process of her
own, showed to the wonder-struck multitude how the woeful
events under which they then groaned were hinted at in it,
and how in a manner it predicted even their future issue.
The aim of the *Haggadah* being the purely momentary one
of elevating, comforting, edifying its audience for the time
being, *it did not pretend to possess the slightest authority*. As
its method was capricious and arbitrary, so its cultivation
was open to every one whose heart prompted him. It is saga,
tale, gnome, parable, allegory,—poetry, in short, of its own
most strange kind, springing up from the sacred soil of
Scripture, wild, luxuriant, and tangled, like a primeval
tropical forest. If the *Halachah* used the Scriptural word as
a last and most awful resort, against which there was no
further appeal, the *Haggadah* used it as the golden nail on
which to hang its gorgeous tapestry: as introduction, refrain,
text, or fundamental stanza for a gloss; and if the former
was the iron bulwark around the nationality of Israel, which

every one was ready at every moment to defend to his last
breath, the latter was a maze of flowery walks within those
fortress-walls. That gradually the *Haggadah* preponderated
and became *the Midrash* κατ' ἐξοχήν *of the people*, is not surprising. We shall notice how each successive Targum
became more and more impregnated with its essence, and
from a version became a succession of short homiletics. This
difference between the two branches of Midrash is strikingly
pointed in the following Talmudical story: "R. Chia b. Abba,
a Halachist, and R. Abbahu, a Haggadist, once came
together into a city and preached. The people flocked to
the latter, while the former's discourses remained without a
hearer. Thereupon the Haggadist comforted the Halachist
with a parable. Two merchants come into a city and spread
their wares,—the one rare pearls and precious stones; the
other a ribbon, a ring, glittering trinkets: around whom will
the multitude throng? . . . Formerly, when life was not yet
bitter labour, the people had leisure for the deep word of the
Law; now it stands in need of comfortings and blessings."

The first collections of the *Halachah*—embracing the
whole field of juridico-political, religious, and practical life,
both of the individual and of the nation: the human and
Divine law to its most minute and insignificant details—were
instituted by Hillel, Akiba, and Simon B. Gamaliel; but the
final redaction of the general code, *Mishnah*,[1] to which the
later Toseftahs and Boraithas form supplements, is due to
Jehudah Hannassi in 220 A.D. Of an earlier date with
respect to the contents, but committed to writing in later
times, are the three books: *Sifra*, or *Torath Kohanim* (an
amplification of Leviticus), *Sifri* (of Numbers and Deuteronomy), and *Mechiltha* (of a portion of Exodus). The masters
of the Mishnaic period, after the Soferim, are the Tannaim,
who were followed by the Amoraim. The discussions and
further amplifications of the Mishnah by the latter, form the

---

[1] Mishnah, from *shana*, " to learn,"
" learning," not, as erroneously translated of old, and repeated ever since,
Δευτέρωσις, " repetition;" but corre-
sponding exactly with Talmud, (from *lumad*, " to learn "), and Torah (from *horeh*), " to teach:" all three terms meaning " *the study*," by way of emi-nence.

Gemara (Complement), a work extant in two redactions, viz. that of Palestine or Jerusalem (middle of 4th century), and of Babylon (5th century A.D.), which, together with the Mishnah, are comprised under the name Talmud. Here, however, though the work is ostensibly devoted to *Halachah*, an almost equal share is allowed to *Haggadah*. The Haggadistic mode of treatment was threefold: either the simple understanding of words and things (*Peshat*) or the homiletic application, holding up the mirror of Scripture to the present (*Derush*), or a mystic interpretation (*Sod*), the second of which chiefly found its way into the Targum. On its minute division into special and general, ethical, historical, esoteric, &c., Haggadah, we cannot enter here. Suffice it to add that the most extensive collections of it which have survived are Midrash Rabbah (commenced about 700, concluded about 1100 A.D.), comprising the Pentateuch and the five Megilloth, and the Pesikta (about 700 A.D.), which contains the most complete cycle of Pericopes, but the very existence of which had until lately been forgotten, surprisingly enough, through the very extracts made from it (Jalkut, Pesikta Rabbathi, Sutarta, &c.).

From this indispensable digression we return to the subject of Targum. The Targums now extant are as follows:—

I. Targum on the Pentateuch, known as that of Onkelos.

II. Targum on the first and last prophets, known as that of Jonathan ben Uzziel.

III. Targum on the Pentateuch, likewise known as that of Jonathan ben Uzziel.

IV. Targum on portions of the Pentateuch, known as Targum Jerushalmi.

V. Targums on the Hagiographa, ascribed to Joseph the Blind, viz.:—

1. Targum on Psalms, Job, Proverbs.

2. Targum on the five Megilloth (Song of Songs, Ruth, Lamentations, Esther, Ecclesiastes).

3. Two (not three, as commonly stated) other Targums to Esther: a smaller and a larger, the latter known as Targum Sheni, or Second Targum.

VI. Targum to Chronicles.

VII. Targum to Daniel, known from an unpublished Persian extract, and hitherto not received among the number.

VIII. Targum on the Apocryphal pieces of Esther.

We have hinted before that neither any of the names under which the Targums hitherto went, nor any of the dates handed down with them, have stood the test of recent scrutiny. Let it, however, not for a moment be supposed that a sceptic Wolfian school has been at work, and with hypercritical and wanton malice has tried to annihilate the hallowed names of Onkelos, Jonathan, and Joseph the Blind. It will be seen from what follows that most of these names have or may have a true historical foundation and meaning; but uncritical ages and ignorant scribes have perverted this meaning, and a succession of most extraordinary misreadings and strangest ὕστερα πρότερα—some even of a very modern date—have produced rare confusion, and a chain of assertions which dissolve before the first steady gaze. That, notwithstanding all this, the implicit belief in the old names and dates still reigns supreme will surprise no one who has been accustomed to see the most striking and undeniable results of investigation and criticism quietly ignored by contemporaries, and forgotten by generations which followed, so that the same work had to be done very many times over again before a certain fact was allowed to be such.

We shall follow the order indicated above:—

I. THE TARGUM OF ONKELOS.

It will be necessary, before we discuss this work itself, to speak of the person of its reputed author as far as it concerns us here. There are few more contested questions in the whole province of Biblical, nay general literature, than those raised on this head. Did an Onkelos ever exist? Was there more than one Onkelos? Was Onkelos the real form of his name? Did he translate the Bible at all, or part of it? And is this Targum the translation he made? Do the dates of his life and this Targum tally? &c. &c. The ancient accounts of Onkelos are avowedly of the most corrupted and confused kind: so much so that both ancient and modern investigators have failed to reconcile and amend them so as to gain general satisfaction, and opinions remain widely divergent. This being the case, we think it our duty to lay the whole—not very voluminous—evidence, collected both from the body of Talmudical and post-Talmudical (so-called Rabbinical) and patristic writings before the reader, in order that he may judge for himself how far the conclusions to which we shall point may be right.

The first mention of "Onkelos"—a name variously derived from Nicolaus (Geiger), Ὄνομα καλός [sic] (Renan), Homunculus, Avunculus, &c.—more fully "Onkelos the Proselyte," is found in the Tosiftah, a work drawn up shortly after the Mishnah. Here we learn (1) that "Onkelos the Proselyte" was so serious in his adherence to the newly-adopted (Jewish) faith, that he threw his share in his paternal inheritance into the Dead Sea (Tos. Demai, vi. 9). (2.) At the funeral of Gamaliel the Elder (1st century A.D.) he burnt more than 70 minæ worth of spices in his honour (Tos. Shabb. 8). (3.) This same story is repeated, with variations (Tos. Semach. 8). (4.) He is finally mentioned, by way of corroboration to different Halachas, in connexion with Gamaliel, in three more places, which complete our references from the Tosiftah (Tos. Mikv. 6, 1; Kelim, iii. 2, 2; Chag. 3, 1). The Babylonian Talmud, the source to which we turn our attention next, mentions the name Onkelos four times: (1.) As "Onkelos the Proselyte, the son of Kalonikos" (Callinicus? Cleonicus?), the son of Titus' sister, who, intending to become a convert, conjured up the ghosts of Titus, Balaam, and Christ [the latter name is doubtful], in order to ask them what nation was considered the first in the other world. Their answer that Israel was the favoured one decided him (Gitt. 56). (2.) As "Onkelos the son of Kalonymus" (Cleonymus?) (Aboda Sar. 11 a). It is there related of him that *the* emperor (*Kaisar*) sent three Roman cohorts to capture him, and that he converted them all. (3.) In Baba Bathra 99 *a* (Boraitha), "Onkelos the Proselyte" is quoted as an authority on the question of the form of the Cherubim. And (4) the most important passage—because on it and it alone, in the wide realm of ancient literature, has been founded the general belief that Onkelos is the author of the Targum now current under this name—is found in Meg. 3 *a*. It reads as follows: "R. Jeremiah, and, according to others, R. Chia bar Abba, said: The Targum to the Pentateuch was made by the 'Proselyte Onkelos,' from the mouth of R. Eliezer and R. Jehoshua; the Targum to the Prophets was made by Jonathan ben Uzziel from the mouth of Haggai, Zechariah, and Malachi. . . . But have we not been taught that the Targum existed from the time of Ezra? . . . Only that it was forgotten, and Onkelos restored it." No mention whatever is to be found of Onkelos either in the Jerusalem Talmud, redacted about a hundred years before the Babylonian, nor in the Church fathers—an item of negative evidence to which we shall presently draw further attention. In a Midrash collection, completed about the middle of the 12th century, we find again "Onkelos the Proselyte" asking an old man, "Whether that was all the love God bore towards a proselyte, that he promised to give him bread and a garment? Whereupon the old man replied that this was all for which the Patriarch Jacob prayed (Gen. xxviii. 20)." The Book Zohar, of late and very uncertain date, makes "Onkelos" a disciple of Hillel and Shammai. Finally, a MS., also of a very late and uncertain date, in the library of the Leipzig Senate (B. H. 17), relates of "Onkelos, the nephew of Titus," that he asked the emperor's advice as to what merchandise he thought it was profitable to trade in. The emperor told him that that should be bought which was cheap in the market, since it was sure to rise in price. Whereupon Onkelos went on his way. He repaired to Jerusalem, and studied the Law under R. Eleazar and R. Jehoshua, and his face became wan. When he returned to the court, one of the courtiers observed the pallor of his countenance, and said to Titus, "Onkelos appears to have studied the Law."

Interrogated by Titus, he admitted the fact, adding that he had done it by his advice. No nation had ever been so exalted, and none was now held cheaper among the nations than Israel: "therefore," he said, "I concluded that in the end none would be of higher price."

This is all the information to be found in ancient authorities about Onkelos and the Targum which bears his name. Surprisingly enough, the latter is well known to the Babylonian Talmud (whether to the Jerusalem Talmud is questionable) and the Midrashim, and is often quoted, but *never once as Targum Onkelos.* The quotations from it are invariably introduced with כדמתרגמינן, "As we [Babylonians] translate;" and the version itself is called (*e.g.* Kiddush. 49 a) תרגום דדן, "Our Targum," exactly as Ephraim Syrus (*Opp.* i. 380) speaks of the Peshito as " Our translation."

Yet we find on the other hand another current version invariably quoted in the Talmud by the name of its known author, viz. תרגם עקילס, "the [Greek] Version of Akilas:" a circumstance which, by showing that it was customary to quote the author by name, excites suspicion as to the relation of Onkelos to the Targum Onkelos. Still more surprising, however, is, as far as the person of Onkelos is concerned (whatever be the discrepancies in the above accounts), the similarity between the incidents related of him and those related of Akilas. The latter (אקילס, עקילס) is said, both in Sifra (Lev. xxv. 7) and the Jerusalem Talmud (Demai, xxvii. d), to have been born in Pontus, to have been a proselyte, to have thrown his paternal inheritance into an asphalt lake (T. Jer. Demai, 25 d), to have translated the Torah before R. Eliezer and R. Joshua, who praised him (קלסו, in allusion perhaps to his name, עקילס); or, according to the other accounts, before R. Akiba (comp. Jer. Kidd. 1, 1, 2, &c.; Jer. Meg. 1, 11; Babli Meg. 3 a). We learn further that he lived in the time of Hadrian (Chag. 2, 1), that he was the son of the Emperor's sister (Tanch. 28, 1), that he became a convert against the Emperor's will (ib. and Shem. Raba, 146 c), and that he consulted Eliezer and Jehoshua about his conversion (Ber. R. 78 d; comp. Midr. Koh. 102 b). First he

z

is said to have gone to the former, and to have asked him whether that was all the love God bore a proselyte, that He promised him bread and a garment (Gen. xxviii. 20). "See," he said, "what exquisite birds and other delicacies I now have: even my slaves do not care for them any longer." Whereupon R. Eliezer became wroth, and said, "Is that for which Jacob prayed, 'And give me bread to eat and a garment to wear,' so small in thine eyes?—Comes he, the proselyte, and receives these things without any trouble !"— And Akilas, dissatisfied, left the irate Master and went to R. Joshua. He pacified him, and explained to him that " Bread " meant the Divine Law, and "Garment," the Talith, or sacred garment to be worn during prayer. "And not this alone, he continued, but the Proselyte may marry his daughter to a Priest, and his offspring may become a High-Priest, and offer burnt offerings in the Sanctuary." More striking still is a Greek quotation from Onkelos, the Chaldee translator (Midr. Echa, 58 c), which in reality is found in and quoted (Midr. Shir hashir. 27 d) from Akilas, the Greek translator.

That Akilas is no other than Aquila ('Ακύλας), the well-known Greek translator of the Old Testament, we need hardly add. He is a native of Pontus (Iren. adv. Hær. 3, 24; Jer. De Vir. Ill. c. 54; Philastr. De Hær. § 90). He lived under Hadrian (Epiph. De Pond. et Mens. § 12). He is called the πενθερίδες (Chron. Alex. πενθερός) of the Emperor (ib. § 14), becomes a convert to Judaism (§ 15), whence he is called the Proselyte (Iren. ib.; Jerome to Is. viii. 14, &c.), and receives instructions from Akiba (Jer. ib.). He translated the O. T., and his Version was considered of the highest import and authority among the Jews, especially those unacquainted with the Hebrew language (Euseb. Præp. Ev. l. c.; Augustin, Civ. D. xv. 23; Philastr. Hær. 90; Justin. Novell. 146). Thirteen *distinct* quotations[1] from this Version are preserved

---

[1] *Greek quotations:*—Gen. xvii. 1, in Beresh. Rab. 51 b; Lev. xxiii. 40, Jer. Succah, 3, 5, fol. 53 d (comp. Vaj. Rab. 200 d); Is. iii. 20, Jer. Shabb. 6, 4, fol. 8 b; Ez. xvi. 10, Midr. Thren. 58 c; Ez. xxiii. 43, Vaj. Rab. 203 d; Ps. xlviii. 15 (Masor. T., xlvii. according to LXX.), Jer. Meg. 2. 3, fol. 73 b; Prov. xviii. 21, Vaj. Rab. fol. 203 b; Esth. i. 6, Midr. Esth.

in Talmud and Midrash, and they tally, for the most part, with the corresponding passages preserved in the Hexapla; and for those even which do not agree, there is no need to have recourse to corruptions. We know from Jerome (on Ezek. iii. 15) that Aquila prepared a further edition of his Version, called by the Jews κατ' ἀκρίβειαν, and there is no reason why we should not assume, cæteris paribus, that the differing passages belong to the different editions.

If then there can be no reasonable doubt as to the identity of Aquila and Akilas, we may well now go a step further, and from the threefold accounts adduced—so strikingly parallel even in their anachronisms and contortions—safely argue the identity, as of Akilas and Aquila, so of Onkelos, ' the translator,' with Akilas or Aquila. Whether in reality a proselyte of that name had been in existence at an earlier date—a circumstance which might explain part of the contradictory statements; and whether the difference of the forms is produced through the y (ng, nk), with which we find the name sometimes spelt, or the Babylonian manner, occasionally to insert an n, as in Adrianus, which we always find spelt Andrianus in the Babylonian Talmud; or whether we are to read Gamaliel II. for Gamaliel the Elder, we cannot here examine; anything connected with the person of an Onkelos no longer concerns us, since he is not the author of the Targum; that it was so, being, as we saw, only once ascribed to him in the passage of the Babylonian Talmud (Meg. 3 a), palpably corrupted from the Jerusalem Talmud (Meg. i. 9). And not before the 9th century (Pirke der. Eliezer to Gen. xlv. 27) does this mischievous mistake seem to have struck root, while even from that time three centuries elapsed, during which the Version was quoted often enough, without its authorship being ascribed to Onkelos.

From all this it follows that those who, in the face of this overwhelming mass of evidence, would fain retain Onkelos in the false position of translator of our Targum, must be

---

120 d; Dan. v. 5, Jer. Joma, 3, 8, fol. 41a.—*Hebrew quotations*, re-translated from the Greek:—Lev. xix. 20, Jer. Kid. i. 1, fol. 59 a ; Dan. viii. 13, Ber. Rab. 24c.—*Chaldee quotations:*—Prov. xxv. 11; Beresh. Rab. 104 b; Is. v. 6, Midr. Koh. 113, c, d.

ready to admit that there were two men living simultaneously of most astoundingly similar names; both proselytes to Judaism, both translators of the Bible, both disciples of R. Eliezer and R. Jehoshua; it being of both reported by the same authorities that they translated the Bible, and that they were disciples of the two last-mentioned Doctors; both supposed to be nephews of the reigning emperor who disapproved of their conversion (for this account comp. Dion lxvii. 14, and Deb. Rab. 2; where Domitian is related to have had a near relative executed for his inclining towards Judaism), and very many more palpable improbabilities of the same description.

The question now remains, why was this Targum called that of Onkelos or Akilas? It is neither a translation of it, nor is it at all done in the same spirit. All that we learn about the Greek Version shows us that its chief aim and purpose was to counteract the LXX. The latter had at that time become a mass of arbitrary corruptions—especially with respect to the Messianic passages—as well on the Christian as on the Jewish side. It was requisite that a translation, scrupulously literal should be given into the hands of those who were unable to read the original. Aquila, the disciple, according to one account, of Akiba—the same Akiba who expounded (*darash*) for Halachistic purposes the seemingly most insignificant Particles in the Scriptures (*e.g.* the את, sign of accusative; Gen. R. 1; Tos. Sheb. 1; Talm. Sheb. 26 a)—fulfilled his task according to his master's method. "Non solum verba sed et etymologias verborum transferre conatus est . . . . Quod Hebræi non solum habent ἄρθρα sed et πρόαρθρα, ille κακοζήλως et syllabas interpretetur et litteras, dictatque σὺν τὸν οὐρανὸν καὶ σὺν τὴν γῆν quod græca et latina lingua non recipit" (Jer. *de Opt. Gen. interpret.*). Targum Onkelos, on the other hand, is, if not quite a paraphrase, yet one of the very freest versions. Nor do the two translations, with rare exceptions, agree even as to the renderings of proper nouns, which each occasionally likes to transform into something else. But there *is* a reason. The Jews in possession of this most slavishly accurate Greek Bible-text, could now on the one hand successfully combat

arguments, brought against them from interpolated LXX.
passages, and on the other follow the expoundings of the
School and the Halachah, based upon the letter of the Law,
as closely as if they had understood the original itself. That
a version of this description often marred the sense, mattered
less in times anything but favourable to the literal meaning
of the Bible. It thus gradually became such a favourite with
the people, that its renderings were household words. If
the day when the LXX. was made was considered a day of
distress like the one on which the golden calf was cast, and
was actually entered among the fast days (8th Tebeth; Meg.
Taanith) — this new version, which was to dispel the mischievous influences of the older, earned for its author one of
the most delicate compliments in the manner of the time.
The verse of the Scripture (Ps. xlv. 3), "Thou art more
beautiful (*jofjefila*) than the sons of men," was applied to
him—in allusion to Gen. ix. 27, where it is said that Japhet
(*i.e.* the Greek language) should one day dwell in the tents
of Shem (*i.e.* Israel), Meg. 1, 11, 71 *b* and *c*; 9 *b*, Ber. Rab.
40 *b*.—Οὕτω γὰρ Ἀκύλας δουλεύων τῇ ἑβραϊκῇ λέξει ἐκδέδωκεν
εἰπὼν . . . φιλοτιμότερον πεπιστευμένος παρὰ Ἰουδαίοις, ἡρμε-
νευκέναι τὴν γραφήν, &c. (Orig. *ad Afric.* 2).

What, under these circumstances, is more natural than to
suppose that the new Chaldee Version—at least as excellent
in its way as the Greek—was started under the name which
had become expressive of the type and ideal of a Bible-
translation; that, in fact, it should be called a Targum done
in the manner of Aquila:—*Aquila-Targum.* Whether the
title of recommendation was, in consideration of the merits
of the work upon which it was bestowed, gladly endorsed and
retained—or, for aught we know, was not bestowed upon it
until it was generally found to be of such surpassing merit,
we need not stop to argue.

Being thus deprived of the dates which a close examination into the accounts of a translator's life might have furnished us, we must needs try to fix the time of our Targum
as approximately as we can by the circumstances under
which it took its rise, and by the quotations from it which

we meet in early works. Without unnecessarily going into detail, we shall briefly record, what we said in the introduction, that the Targum was begun to be committed to writing about the end of the 2nd century, A.D. So far, however, from its superseding the oral Targum at once, it was on the contrary strictly forbidden to read it in public (Jer. Meg. 4, 1). Nor was there any uniformity in the version. Down to the middle of the 2nd century we find the masters most materially differing from each other with respect to the Targum of certain passages (Seb. 54 a), and translations quoted not to be found in any of our Targums. The necessity must thus have pressed itself upon the attention of the spiritual leaders of the people to put a stop to the fluctuating state of a version, which, in the course of time must needs have become naturally surrounded with a halo of authority little short of that of the original itself. We shall thus not be far wrong in placing the work of collecting the different fragments with their variants, and reducing them into one—finally authorized Version—about the end of the 3rd, or the beginning of the 4th century, and in assigning Babylon to it as the birthplace. It was at Babylon, that about this time the light of learning, extinguished in the blood-stained fields of Palestine, shone with threefold vigour. The Academy at Nahardea, founded according to legend during the Babylonian exile itself, had gathered strength in the same degree as the numerous Palestinian schools began to decline, aud when in 259 A.D. that most ancient school was destroyed, there were three others simultaneously flourishing in its stead :—Tiberias, whither the college of Palestinian Jabneh had been transferred in the time of Gamaliel III. (200); Sora, founded by Chasda of Kafri (293); and Pumbadita founded by R. Jehudah b. Jecheskeel (297). And in Babylon for well nigh a thousand years "the crown of the Law" remained, and to Babylon, the seat of the "Head of the Golah" (Dispersion), all Israel, scattered to the ends of the earth, looked for its spiritual guidance. That one of the first deeds of these Schools must have been the fixing of the Targum, as soon as the fixing of it became indispensable, we may well presume; and as we see the text fluctuating down to the middle of the 2nd century, we must needs assume that the redaction took place as soon afterwards as may reasonably be supposed. Further corroborative arguments are found for Babylon as the place of its final redaction, although Palestine was the country where it grew and developed itself. Many grammatical and idiomatical signs—the substance itself, *i.e.* the words, being Palestinian—point, as far as the scanty materials in our hands permit us to draw conclusions as to the true state of language in Babylon, to that country. The Targum further exhibits a greater linguistic similarity with the Babylonian, than with the Palestinian Gemara. Again, terms are found in it which the Talmud distinctly mentions as peculiar to Babylon,[1] not to mention Persian words, which on Babylonian soil easily found their way into our work. One of the most striking hints is the unvarying translation of the Targum of the word נָהָר, "River," by Euphrates, *the* River of Babylon. Need we further point to the terms above mentioned, under which the Targum is exclusively quoted in the Talmud and the Midrashim of Babylon, viz., "*Our* Targum," "As *we* translate," or its later designation (Aruch, Rashi, Tosafoth, &c.) as the "Targum of Babel"? Were a further proof needed, it might be found in the fact that the two Babylonian Schools, which, holding different readings in various places of the Scripture, as individual traditions of their own, consequently held different readings in the Targum ever since the time of its redaction.

The opinions developed here are shared more or less by some of the most competent scholars of our day: for instance, Zunz (who now repudiates the dictum laid down in his *Gottesdienstl. Vortr.*, that the translation of Onkelos dates from about the middle of the first century, A.D.; comp. *Zeitschr.* 1843, p. 179, note 3), Grätz, Levy, Herzfeld, Geiger, Frankel, &c. The history of the investigation of the Targums, more especially that of Onkelos, presents the usual spectacle

---

[1] נערה, "a girl," is rendered by רביא; "for thus they call in Babylon a young girl," שכן קורין בבבל לינוקא רביא (Chag. 13 *a*).

of vague speculations and widely contradictory notions, held
by different investigators at different times. Suffice it to
mention that of old authorities, Reuchlin puts the date of the
Targum as far back as the time of Isaiah—notwithstanding
that the people, as we are distinctly told, did not understand
even a few Aramaic words in the time of Jeremiah. Following Asaria de Rossi and Eliah Levita (who, for reasons
now completely disposed of, assumed the Targum to have
first taken its rise in Babylon during the Captivity),
Bellarmin, Sixtus Senensis, Aldret, Bartolocci, Rich. Simon,
Hottinger, Walton, Thos. Smith, Pearson, Allix, Wharton,
Prideaux, Schickard, take the same view with individual
modifications. Pfeiffer, B. Meyer, Steph. Morinus, on the
other hand, place its date at an extremely late period, and
assign it to Palestine. Another School held that the Targum
was not written until after the time of the Talmud—so Wolf,
Havermann, partly Rich. Simon, Hornbeck, Joh. Morinus,
&c.: and their reasons are both the occurrence of "Talmudical Fables" in the Targum and the silence of the
Fathers. The former is an argument to which no reply
is needed, since we do not see what it can be meant to
prove, unless the "Rabbinus Talmud" has floated before
their eyes, who, according to 'Henricus Seynensis Capucinus'
(*Ann. Eccl.* tom. i. 261), must have written all this gigantic
literature, ranging over a thousand years, out of his own
head, in which case, indeed, every dictum on record, dating
before or after the compilation of the Talmud, and in the
least resembling a passage or story contained therein, must
be a plagiarism from its sole venerable author. The latter
argument, viz. the silence of the Fathers, more especially
of Origen, Jerome, and Epiphanius, has been answered by
Walton; and what we have said will further corroborate his
arguments to the effect, that they did not mention it, not
because it did not exist in their days, but because they either
knew nothing of it, or did not understand it. In the person
of an Onkelos, a Chaldee translator, the belief has been
general, and will remain so, as long as the ordinary Hand-
books — with rare exceptions—do not care to notice the

uncontested results of contemporary investigation. How scholars within the last century have endeavoured to reconcile the contradictory accounts about Onkelos, more particularly how they have striven to smooth over the difficulty of their tallying with those of Akilas—as far as either had come under their notice—for this and other minor points we must refer the reader to Eichhorn, Jahn, Berthold, Hävernick, &c.

We now turn to the Targum itself.

Its language is Chaldee, closely approaching in purity of idiom to that of Ezra and Daniel. It follows a sober and clear, though not a slavish exegesis, and keeps as closely and minutely to the text as is at all consistent with its purpose, viz., to be chiefly, and above all, a version for the people. Its explanations of difficult and obscure passages bear ample witness to the competence of those who gave it its final shape, and infused into it a rare unity. Even where foreign matter is introduced, or, as Berkowitz in his Hebrew work *Oteh Or* keenly observes, where it most artistically blends two translations, one literal, and one figurative, into one; it steadily keeps in view the real sense of the passage in hand. It is always concise and clear, and dignified, worthy of the grandeur of its subject. It avoids the legendary character with which all the later Targums entwine the Biblical word, as far as ever circumstances would allow. Only in the poetical passages it was compelled to yield—though reluctantly—to the popular craving for Haggadah; but even here it chooses and selects with rare taste and tact.

Generally and broadly it may be stated that alterations are never attempted, save for the sake of clearness; tropical terms are dissolved by judicious circumlocutions, for the correctness of which the authors and editors—in possession of the living tradition of a language still written, if not spoken in their day—certainly seem better judges than some modern critics, who through their own incomplete acquaintance with the idiom, injudiciously blame Onkelos. Highly characteristic is the aversion of the Targum to anthropopathies and anthropomorphisms; in fact, to any term which could in the eyes of the multitude lower the idea of the

Highest Being. Yet there are many passages retained in which human affections and qualities are attributed to Him. He speaks, He sees, He hears, He smells the odour of sacrifice, is angry, repents, &c.—the Targum thus showing itself entirely opposed to the allegorising and symbolising tendencies, which in those, and still more in later days, were prone to transform Biblical history itself into the most extraordinary legends and fairy tales with or without a moral. The Targum, however, while retaining terms like the arm of God, the right hand of God, the finger of God—for Power, Providence, &c.—replaces terms like foot, front, back of God, by the fitting figurative meaning. We must notice further its repugnance to bring the Divine Being into too close contact, as it were, with man. It erects a kind of reverential barrier, a sort of invisible medium of awful reverence between the Creator and the creature. Thus terms like "the Word" (Logos = Sansc. Om), "the Shechinah" (Holy presence of God's Majesty, "the Glory"), further, human beings talking not *to*, but "before" God, are frequent. The same care, in a minor degree, is taken of the dignity of the persons of the patriarchs, who, though the Scripture may expose their weaknesses, were not to be held up in their iniquities before the multitude whose ancestors and ideals they were. That the most curious ὕστερα πρότερα and anachronisms occur, such as Jacob studying the Torah in the academy of Shem, &c., is due to the then current typifying tendencies of the Haggadah. Some extremely cautious, withal poetical, alterations also occur when the patriarchs speak of having acquired something by violent means: as Jacob (Gen. xlviii. 22), by his "sword and bow," which two words become in the Targum, "prayers and supplications." But the points which will have to be considered chiefly when the Targum becomes a serious study—as throwing the clearest light upon its time, and the ideas then in vogue about matters connected with religious belief and exercises—are those which treat of prayer, study of the law, prophecy, angelology, and the Messiah.

The only competent investigator who, after Winer (*De*

Onkeloso, 1820), but with infinitely more minuteness and thorough knowledge of the subject, has gone fully into this matter, is Luzzatto. Considering the vast importance of this, the oldest Targum, for biblical as well as for linguistic studies in general—not to mention the advantages that might accrue from it to other branches of learning, such as geography, history, &c. : we think it advisable to give—for the first time—a brief sketch of the results of this eminent scholar. His classical, though not rigorously methodical, *Oheb Ger* (1830) is, it is true, quoted by every one, but in reality known to but an infinitely small number, although it is written in the most lucid modern Hebrew.

He divides the discrepancies between Text and Targum into four principal classes.

(A.) Where the language of the Text has been changed in the Targum, but the meaning of the former retained.

(B.) Where both language and meaning were changed.

(C.) Where the meaning was retained, but additions were introduced.

(D.) Where the meaning was changed, and additions were introduced.

He further subdivides these four into thirty-two classes, to all of which he adds, in a most thorough and accurate manner, some telling specimens. Notwithstanding the apparent pedantry of his method, and the undeniable identity which necessarily must exist between some of his classes, a glance over their whole body, aided by one or two examples in each case, will enable us to gain as clear an insight into the manner and "genius" of the Onkelos-Targum as is possible without the study of the work itself.

(A.) Discrepancies where the language of the text has been changed in the Targum, but the meaning of the former has been retained.

1. Alterations owing to the idiom: *e.g.* the singular,[1] " Let there be [*sit*] lights " (Gen. i. 14), is transformed into the plur.[2] [*sint*] in the Targum, "man and woman,"[3] as

---

[1] יהי   [2] יהון   [3] איש ואשתו

applied to the animals (Gen. vii. 2), becomes, as unsuitable in the Aramaic, "male and female."[1]

2. Alterations out of reverence towards God, more especially for the purpose of doing away with all ideas of a plurality of the Godhead: *e. g.* the terms Adonai, Elohim, are replaced by Jehovah, lest these might appear to imply more than one God. Where Elohim is applied to idolatry it is rendered "Error."[2]

3. Anthropomorphisms, where they could be misunderstood and construed into a disparagement or a lowering of the dignity of the Godhead among the common people, are expunged: *e. g.* for "And God smelled a sweet smell" (Gen. viii. 21), Onkelos has "And Jehovah received the sacrifice with grace;" for "And Jehovah went[3] down to see the city" (Gen. xi. 5), "And Jehovah *revealed*[4] Himself," a term of frequent use in the Targum for verbs of motion, such as "to go down," "to go through," &c., applied to God. "I shall pass over[5] you" (Ex. xii. 13), the Targum renders "I shall protect you."[6] Yet only anthropomorphisms which clearly stand figuratively and might give offence, are expunged, not as Maimonides, followed by nearly all commentators, holds, *all* anthropomorphisms, for words like "hand, finger, to speak, see," &c. (see above), are retained. But where the words remember, think of,[7] &c., are used of God, they always, whatever their tense in the text, stand in the Targum in the present; since a past or future would imply a temporary forgetting on the part of the Omniscient.[8] A keen distinction is here also established by Luzzatto between חזי and גלי, the former used of a real external seeing, the latter of a seeing "into the heart."

4. Expressions used of and to God by men are brought more into harmony with the idea of His dignity. Thus Abraham's question, "The Judge of the whole earth, should he not (לא) do justice?" (Gen. xviii. 25) is altered into the

---

1 דכר ונוקבא
2 טעוות עממיא
3 וירד
4 ואתגלי
5 פסחתי
6 אחוס
7 פקד ,זכר

8 Comp. Prayer for Rosh hashana, ואין שכחה וכו", "And there is no forgetting before the throne of Thy glory."

affirmative: "The Judge .... verily He will do justice." Laban, who speaks of his gods [1] in the text, is made to speak of his religion [2] only in the Targum.

5. Alterations in honour of Israel and their ancestors. Rachel "stole" [3] the Teraphim (xxxi. 19) is softened into Rachel "took;" [4] Jacob "fled" [5] from Laban (ib. 22), into "went;" [6] "The sons of Jacob answered Shechem with craftiness" [7] (xxxiv. 13), into "with wisdom." [8]

6. Short glosses introduced for the better understanding of the text; "for it is my mouth that speaks to you" (xlv. 12), Joseph said to his brethren: Targum, "in your tongue," [9] *i.e.* without an interpreter. "The people who had made the calf;" (Ex. xxxii. 35) Targum, "worshipped," [10] since not they, but Aaron made it.

7. Explanation of tropical and allegorical expressions: "Be fruitful (lit. ' creep,' from שרץ) and multiply" (Gen. i. 28), is altered into "bear children;" [11] "thy brother Aaron shall be thy *prophet*" [12] (Ex. vii. 1), into "thy interpreter" [13] (Meturgeman); "I made thee a god (Elohim) to Pharaoh" (Ex. vii. 1), into "a master;" [14] "to a head and not to a tail" (Deut. xxviii. 13), into "to a strong man and not to a weak;" [15] and finally, "Whoever says of his father and his mother, I saw them not" (Deut. xxxiii. 9), into "Whoever is not merciful [16] towards his father and his mother."

8. Tending to ennoble the language: the "washing" of Aaron and his sons is altered into "sanctifying;" [17] the "carcasses" [18] of the animals of Abraham (Gen. xv. 11) become "pieces;" [19] "anointing" [20] becomes "elevating, raising;" [21] "the wife of the bosom," [22] "wife of the covenant." [23]

9. The last of the classes where the terms are altered, but the sense is retained, is that in which a change of language takes place in order to introduce the explanations of the oral

---

[1] אלהים	[2] דחלתי	[13] מתורגמנך	[14] רב
[3] ותגנוב	[4] ונסיבת	[15] לתקיף ולא לחלש	[16] רחים
[5] בורח	[6] אזיל	[17] ויקדשון	[18] פגרים
[7] במרמה	[8] בחוכמא	[19] (בתרים) פלניא	[20] משח
[9] בלשניכון	[10] דאשתעבדו	[21] תרבי	[22] אישת חיקיך
[11] אתילידו	[12] נביאך	[23] אישת קיימך	

law and the traditions: *e.g.* Lev. xxiii. 11, "On the morrow after the Sabbath [1] (*i.e.* the feast of the unleavened bread) the priest shall wave it (the sheaf)," Onkelos for Sabbath, *feast-day*.[2] For frontlets[3] (Deut. vi. 8), Tefillin (phylacteries).[4]

(B.) Change of both the terms and the meaning.

10. To avoid phrases apparently derogatory to the dignity of the Divine Being: "Am I in God's stead?"[5] becomes in Onkelos, "Dost thou ask [children] from me?[6] from before God thou shouldst ask them" (Gen. xxx. 2).

11. In order to avoid anthropomorphisms of an objectionable kind. "With the breath of Thy nose"[7] ("blast of Thy nostrils," A. V., Ex. xv. 8), becomes "With the word of Thy mouth."[8] "And I shall spread my hand over thee"[9] (Ex. xxxiii. 22), is transformed into "I shall with my word protect thee."[10] "And thou shalt see my back parts,[11] but my face[12] shall not be seen" (Ex. xxxiii. 23): "And thou shalt see what is behind me,[13] but that which is before me[14] shall not be seen" (Deut. xxxiii. 12).

12. For the sake of religious euphemisms: *e.g.* "And ye shall be like God"[15] (Gen. iii. 5), is altered into "like princes."[16] "A laughter[17] has God made me" (Gen. xxi. 6), into "A joy[18] He gives me"—"God" being entirely omitted.

13. In honour of the nation and its ancestors: *e.g.* "Jacob was an upright man, a dweller in tents"[19] (Gen. xxv. 27), becomes "an upright man, frequenting the house of learning."[20] "One of the people[21] might have lain with thy wife" (Gen. xxvi. 10)—"One singled out among the people,"[22] *i. e.* the king. "Thy brother came and took my blessing with deceit"[23] (Gen. xxvii. 35), becomes "with wisdom."[24]

14. In order to avoid similes objectionable on æsthetical

---

[1] שבת		[14] ית דקדמי	[13] ית דבתרי
[2] יומא טבא	[3] טוטפות	[17] צחוק	[16] רברבין	[15] אלהים
[4] תפילין	[5] התחת אל׳ אנכי	[19] יושב אהלים	[18] חדוא
[6] המני את בעיא וכו׳		[20] משמש בבית אולפנא
[7] וברוח אפיך	[8] ובמימר פומך	[22] אחד העם	[21] חד דמיחד בעמא
[9] ושכותי כפי	[10] ואנין במימרי	[24] בחוכמא	[23] במרמה
[11] אחור	[12] פני		

grounds. "And he will bathe his foot in oil"[1]—"And he will have many delicacies[2] of a king" (Deut. xxxiii. 24).

15. In order to ennoble the language. "And man became a living being"[3] (Gen. ii. 7)—"And *it* became in man a speaking spirit."[4] "How good are thy *tents*,[5] O Jacob —"How good are thy *lands*,[6] O Jacob" (Num. xxiv. 5).

16. In favour of the Oral Law and the Rabbinical explanations. "And go into the land of Moriah"[7] (Gen. xxii. 2), becomes "into the land of worship" (the future place of the Temple). "Isaac went to walk[8] in the field" (Gen. xxiv. 63), is rendered "to *pray*."[9] [Comp. SAM. PENT., p. 1114 *b*]. "Thou shalt not boil a kid[10] in the milk of its mother" (Ex. xxxiv. 26) — as meat and milk,[11] according to the Halachah.

(C.) Alterations of words (circumlocutions, additions, &c.) without change of meaning.

17. On account of the difference of idiom: *e.g.* "Her father's brother"[12] (=relation), (Gen. xxix. 12), is rendered "The son of her father's sister."[13] "What God does[14] (future) he has told Pharaoh" (Gen. xli. 28)—"What God will do,"[15] &c.

18. Additions for the sake of avoiding expressions apparently derogatory to the dignity of the Divine Being, by implying polytheism and the like : "Who is like unto Thee[16] among the gods?" is rendered, "There is none like unto Thee,[17] Thou art God" (Ex. xv. 11). "And they sacrifice to demons who are no gods"[18]—"of no use"[19] (Deut. xxxii. 17).

19. In order to avoid erroneous notions implied in certain verbs and epithets used of the Divine Being: *e. g.* "And the Spirit of God[20] moved" (Gen. i. 2)—"A wind from before the Lord."[21] "And Noah built God an altar"[22] (Gen. viii.

---

[1] שמן [2] תפנוקי [3] לנפש חיה [10] נדי בחלב [11] בשר וחלב

[4] והות באדם לרוח ממללא [12] אחי [13] בר אחת

[5] אהליך [6] ארעך [14] עושה [15] עתיד למעבד

[7] מוריה [8] לשוח [16] מי כמוך [17] לית בר מנך

[9] פולחנא. [Abraham instituted, according to the Midrash, the morning-(Shaharith), Isaac the afternoon-(Minha), and Jacob the evening-prayer (Maarib).] [18] לא אלהי [19] לית בהן צרוך

[20] רוח אלהים [21] רוח מן קדם אלהים

[22] לה'

20)—"an altar before[1] the Lord." "And God[2] was with
the boy" (Gen. xxi. 20)—"And the word of God[3] was in
aid of the boy." "The mountain of God" (Ex. iii. 1)—
"The mountain upon which was revealed the glory[4] of
God." "The staff of God" (Ex. iv. 20)—"The staff with
which thou hast done the miracles before[5] God." "And I
shall see[6] what will be their end"—"It is open (revealed)
before me,"[7] &c. The Divine Being is in fact very rarely
spoken of without that spiritual medium mentioned before;
it being considered, as it were, a want of proper reverence to
speak to or of Him directly. The terms "Before" (קדם)
"Word" (Λόγος מימרא) "Glory" (יקרא) "Majesty" (שכנתיה),
are also constantly used instead of the Divine name: e. g.
"The voice of the Lord God was heard" (Gen. iii. 8)— "The
voice of the Word." "And He will dwell in the tents of
Shem" (ix. 27)—"And the Shechina [Divine Presence] will
dwell." "And the Lord went up from Abraham" (Gen.
xvii. 22)—"And the glory of God went up." "And God
came to Abimelech" (Gen. xx. 3)—"And the word from
[before] God came to Abimelech."

20. For the sake of improving seemingly irreverential
phrases in Scripture. "Who is God that I should listen
unto His voice?" (Ex. v. 2)—"The name of God has not
been revealed to me, that I should receive His word."[8]

21. In honour of the nation and its ancestors. "And
Israel said to Joseph, Now I shall gladly die"[9] (Gen. xlvi.
30), which might appear frivolous in the mouth of the patriarch, becomes "I shall be comforted[10] now." "And he led
his flock towards[11] the desert" (Ex. iii. 1)—"towards a good
spot of pasture[12] in the desert."

22. In honour of the Law and the explanation of its obscurities. "To days and years" (Gen. i. 14)—"that days and
years should be counted by them."[13] "A tree of knowledge

---

[1] קדם ה'	[2] אל'	[3] מימרא דה'
[4] יקרא	[5] מן קדם ה'	[6] נלי קדמי
[8] לא אתגלי לי דאקבל במימריה		
[9] אמותה	[10] אנחמה	
[11] אתר הם'	[12] שפר רעיה ב'	
[13] לממני בהון		

of good and evil "—" A tree, and those who eat its fruits [1] will distinguish between good and evil." "I shall not further curse for the sake of [2] man " (viii. 21)—" through the sin [3] of man." "To the ground shall not be forgiven the blood [4] shed upon it " (Num. xxv. 33)—" the *innocent* [5] blood."

23. For the sake of avoiding similes, metonymical and allegorical passages, too difficult for the comprehension of the multitude : *e.g.* "Thy seed like the dust of the earth " (Gen. xiii. 16)—" mighty [6] as the dust of the earth." "I am too small for all the benefits " (Gen. xxxii. 10)—" My good deeds [7] are small." "And the Lord thy God will circumcise thy heart "—" the folly of thy heart." [8]

24. For the sake of elucidating apparent obscurities, &c., in the written Law. "Therefore shall a man leave his father and his mother " (Gen. ii. 24)—" the home " [9] (not really his parents). "The will of Him who dwelleth in the bush "— " of Him that dwelleth in heaven [10] [whose Shechinah is in heaven], and who revealed Himself in the bush to Moses."

25. In favour of the Oral Law and the traditional explanations generally. "He punishes the sins of the parents on their children " (Ex. xx. 5), has the addition, "when the children follow the sins of their parents " (comp. Ez. xviii. 19). "The righteous and the just ye shall not kill " (Ex. xxiii. 7)—" He who has left the tribunal as innocent, thou shalt not kill him," *i.e.*, according to the Halacha, he is not to be arraigned again for the same crime. "Doorposts " (*mesusoth*) (Deut. vi. 9)—" And thou shalt write them . . . . and *affix them* upon the posts," &c.

(D.) Alteration of language and meaning.

26. In honour of the Divine Being, to avoid apparent multiplicity or a likeness. "Behold man will be like one of us, knowing good and evil" (Gen. iii. 22)—" He will be the only one in the world [11] to know good and evil." "For who

---

טפשות לבך [8]	זעירן זכוותי [7]	
בית מישכביה [9]		
דשכנתיה בשמיא [10]		
יחידא בעלמא [11]		

ואילן דאכלין פירוהי [1]	בעבור [2]
בדיל חובי [3]	לדם [4]
לדם נקי [5]	סניאין [6]

is a God in heaven and on earth who could do like Thy deeds and powers?" (Deut. iii. 24)—"Thou art God, Thy Divine Presence (Shechinah) is in heaven[1] above, and reigns on earth below, and there is none who does like unto Thy deeds," &c.

27. Alteration of epithets employed of God. "And before Thee shall I hide myself"[2] (Gen. iv. 14)—"And before Thee it is not possible to hide."[3] "This is my God and I will praise[4] Him, the God of my father and I will extol[5] Him" (Ex. xv. 2)—"This is my God, and I will build him a sanctuary;[6] the God of my fathers, and I will pray before Him."[7] "In one moment I shall go up in thy midst and annihilate thee"—"For one hour will I take away my majesty[8] from among thee" (since no evil can come from above).

28. For the ennobling of the sense. "Great is Jehovah above all gods"—"Great is God, and there is no other god beside Him." "Send through him whom thou wilt send" (Ex. iv. 13)—"through him who is worthy to be sent."

29. In honour of the nation and its ancestors. "And the souls they made[9] in Haran" (Gen. xii. 5)—"the souls they made subject to the Divine Law[10] in Haran." "And Isaac brought her into the tent of his mother Sarah" (Gen. xxiv. 67)—"And lo righteous were her works,[11] like the works of his mother Sarah." "And he bent his shoulder to bear, and he became a tributary servant" (Gen. xlix. 15)—"And he will conquer the cities of the nations and destroy their dwelling-places, and those that will remain there will serve him and pay tribute to him." "People, foolish and not wise" (Deut. xxxii. 6)—"People who has received the Law and has not become wise."[12]

30. Explanatory of tropical and metonymical phrases. "And besides thee no man shall raise his hand and his foot in the whole land of Egypt" (Gen. xli. 44)—"There shall

---

שכנתך בשמיא [1]	אסתתר [2]	אסלק שכנתי [8] אפלח קדמוהי [7]
לית אפשר לאטמרא [3]	אנוהו [4]	דישעבידו לאורייתא [10] עשו [9]
ארוממנהו [5]		ותקנין עובדהא [11]
אבני ליהזמקדש [6]		קבילו אורייתא ולא חכימו [12]

not a man raise his hand to seize a weapon, and his foot to ride on a horse."

31. To ennoble or improve the language. "Coats of skin" (Gen. iii. 21)—"Garments of honour [1] on the skin of their flesh." "Thy two daughters who are found with thee" (Gen. xix. 15)—"who were found faithful with thee." "May Reuben live and not die" (Deut. xxxiii. 6)—"May Reuben live in the everlasting life."

The foregoing examples will, we trust, be found to bear out sufficiently the judgment given above on this Targum. In spite of its many and important discrepancies, it never for one moment forgets its aim of being a clear, though free, translation *for the people*, and nothing more. Wherever it deviates from the literalness of the text, such a course, in its case, is fully justified—nay, necessitated—either by the obscurity of the passage, or the wrong construction that naturally would be put upon its wording by the multitude. The explanations given agree either with the real sense, or develop the current tradition supposed to underlie it. The specimens adduced by other investigators, however differently classified or explained, are easily brought under the foregoing heads. They one and all tend to prove that Onkelos, whatever the objections against single instances, is one of the most excellent and thoroughly competent interpreters. A few instances only—and they are very few indeed—may be adduced, where even Onkelos, as it would appear, "dormitat." Far be it from us for one moment to depreciate, as has been done, the infinitely superior knowledge both of the Hebrew and Chaldee idioms on the part of the writers and editors of our document, or to attribute their discrepancies from modern translations to ignorance. They drank from the fullness of a highly valuable traditional exegesis, as fresh and vigorous in their days as the Hebrew language itself still was in the circles of the wise, the academies and schools. But we have this advantage, that words which then were obsolete, and whose meaning was known no longer—only guessed at—are

---

[1] לְבוּשִׁין דִּיקָר

to us familiar by the numerous progeny they have produced
in cognate idioms, known to us through the mighty spread
of linguistic science in our days; and if we are not aided by
a traditional exegesis handed down within and without the
schools, perhaps ever since the days of the framing of the
document itself, neither are we prejudiced and fettered by it.
Whatever may be implied and hidden in a verse or word, we
have no reason to translate it accordingly, and, for the attain-
ing of this purpose, to overstrain the powers of the roots.
Among such small shortcomings of our translator may be
mentioned that he appears to have erroneously derived שְׁאֵת
(Gen. iv. 7) from נשא; that נוכחת (xx. 6) is by him
rendered אוכחת; אברך (Gen. xli. 43) by אבא למלכא;
אָבֵד (Deut. xxiv. 5) אָבֵד; and the like. Comp. however
the Commentators on these passages.

The bulk of the passages generally adduced as proofs of
want of knowledge on the part of Onkelos have to a great
part been shown in the course of the foregoing specimens
to be intentional deviations; many other passages not mentioned merely instance the want of knowledge on the part
of his critics.

Some places, again, exhibit that blending of two distinct
translations, of which we have spoken; the catchword being
apparently taken in two different senses. Thus Gen. xxii.
13, where he translates: "And Abraham lifted up his eyes
after these, and behold there was a ram;" he has not "in his
perplexity" mistranslated אחר for אַחַר, but he has only
placed for the sake of clearness the אַחַר after the verb (he
saw), instead of the noun (ram); and the חדא, which is
moreover wanting in some texts, has been added, not as a
translation of אחר or אַחַר, but in order to make the passage
more lucid still. A similar instance of a double translation
is found in Gen. ix. 6: "Whosoever⁚ sheds a man's blood, by
man shall his blood be shed"—rendered "Whosoever sheds
the blood of man, by witnesses through⁚ the sentence of the
judges shall his blood be shed;" בָּאָדָם, by man, being taken
first as "witness," and then as "judges."

We may further notice the occurrence of two *Messianic*

passages in this Targum: the one, Gen. xlix. 10, Shiloh; the other, Num. xxiv. 17, "sceptre:" both rendered "Messiah."

A fuller idea of the "Genius" of Onkelos as Translator and as Paraphrast, may be arrived at from the specimens subjoined in pp. 387–392.

We cannot here enter into anything like a minute account of the dialect of Onkelos or of any other Targum. Regarding the linguistic shades of the different Targums, we must confine ourselves to the general remark, that the later the version, the more corrupt and adulterated its language. Three dialects, however, are chiefly to be distinguished: as in the Aramaic idiom in general, which in contradistinction to the Syriac, or Christian Aramaic, may be called Judæo-Aramaic, so also in the different Targums; and their recognition is a material aid towards fixing the place of their origin; although we must warn the reader that this guidance is not always to be relied upon.

1. The Galilean Dialect, known and spoken of already in the Talmud as the one which most carelessly confounds its sounds, vowels as well as consonants. "The Galileans are negligent with respect to their language,[1] and care not for grammatical forms"[2] is a common saying in the Gemara. We learn that they did not distinguish properly between B and P (ב, פ), saying Tapula instead of Tabula, between Ch and K (כ and ק) saying χείριος for κύριος. Far less could they distinguish between the various gutturals, as is cleverly exemplified in the story where a Judæan asked a Galilean, when the latter wanted to buy an אמר, whether he meant עֲמַר (wool), or אִמַּר (a lamb), or חֲמַר (wine), or חֲמֹר (an ass). The next consequence of this their disregard of the gutturals was, that they threw them often off entirely at the beginning of a word per aphæresin. Again they contracted, or rather wedged together, words of the most dissimilar terminations and beginnings. By confounding the vowels like the consonants, they often created entirely new words and forms. The Mappik H (ה) became Ch

---

[1] לא הקפידו   [2] לא דייקא לשנא

(somewhat similar to the Scotch pronunciation of the initial H). As the chief reason for this Galilean confusion of tongues (for which comp. Matt. xxvi. 73; Mark xiv. 70) may be assigned the increased facility of intercourse with the neighbouring nations owing to their northern situation.

2. The Samaritan Dialect, a mixture of vulgar Hebrew and Aramean, in accordance with the origin of the people itself. Its chief characteristics are the frequent use of the *Ain* (which not only stands for other gutturals, but is even used as *mater lectionis*), the commutation of the gutturals in general, and the indiscriminate use of the mute consonants ב for ו, ק for כ, ח for ק, &c.

3. The Judæan or Jerusalem Dialect (comp. Ned. 66 *b*) scarcely ever pronounces the gutturals at the end properly, often throws them off entirely. Jeshuâ becomes Jeshu; Sheba—Shib. Many words are peculiar to this dialect alone. The appellations of "door,"[1] "light,"[2] "reward,"[3] &c., are totally different from those used in the other dialects. Altogether all the peculiarities of provincialism, shortening and lengthening of vowels, idiomatic phrases and words, also an orthography of its own, generally with a fuller and broader vocalisation, are noticeable throughout both the Targums and the Talmud of Jerusalem, which, for the further elucidation of this point as of many others have as yet not found an investigator.

The following recognised Greek words, the greater part of which also occur in the Talmud and Midrash, are found in Onkelos: Ex. xxviii. 25, [4] $\beta\acute{\eta}\rho\upsilon\lambda\lambda o\varsigma$; Ex. xxviii. 11, [5] $\gamma\lambda\upsilon\phi\acute{\eta}$; Gen. xxviii. 17, [6] $\iota\delta\iota\acute{\omega}\tau\eta\varsigma$; Lev. xi. 30, [7] $\kappa\omega\lambda\acute{\omega}\tau\eta\varsigma$; Ex. xxviii. 19, [8] $\theta\rho\acute{a}\kappa\iota\alpha\varsigma$ (Plin. xxxvii. 68); Ex. xxxix. 11, [9] $K\alpha\rho\chi\eta$-$\delta\acute{o}\nu\iota o\iota$, comp. Pes. der. Kah.' xxxii. (Carbunculi); Deut. xx. 20, [10] $\chi\alpha\rho\acute{a}\kappa\omega\mu\alpha$ (Ber. R. xcviii.); Ex. xxviii. 20, [11] $\chi\rho\hat{\omega}\mu\alpha$; Num. xv. 38, Deut. xxii. 12, [12] $\kappa\rho\acute{a}\sigma\pi\epsilon\delta o\nu$; Ex. xxx. 34,

---

[1] בבא for דשא   [2] שרגי for בוציני   [9] כרכדינא   [10] כרכום

[3] אגר for סוטר   [4] ברלא   [11] כרום (ימא) (Mich. *Lez. Syr.* 435,

[5] נלף   [6] הריוט   makes it *Persian*.)

[7] חלטתא   [8] טרקיא   [12] כרוספדא

¹ κίστος ; Gen. xxxvii. 28, ² λῆδον; Ex. xxiv. 16, ³ φάρσος ;
Ex. xxvi. 6, ⁴ πόρπη ; Gen. vi. 14, ⁵ κέδρος ; Ex. xxviii. 19,
⁶ κέγχρος (Plin. xxxvii. 4). To these may be added the un-
recognised ⁷ κεραμίς (Ex. xxi. 18), ⁸ λιβρούχης or λεβρόχη
(Gen. xxx. 14), &c.

The following short rules on the general mode of tran-
scribing the Greek letters in Aramaic and Syriac (Targum,
Talmud, Midrash, &c.), may not be out of place :—

Γ before palatals, pronounced like ν, becomes נ.

Z is rendered by ז.

H appears to have occasionally assumed the pronunciation
of a consonant (Digamma) ; and a ו is inserted.

Θ is ת, T ט. But this rule, even making allowances for
corruptions, does not always seem to have been strictly
observed.

K is ק, sometimes כ.

M, which before labials stands in lieu of a ν, becomes נ :
occasionally a נ is inserted before labials where it is not
found in the Greek word.

Ξ, generally כס, sometimes, however, נז or כצ.

Π is פ, sometimes, however, it is softened into ב.

P is sometimes altered into ל or נ.

'P becomes either רה or הר at the beginning of a word.

Σ either ס or ז.

The *spiritus asper*, which in Greek is dropped in the
middle of a word, reappears again sometimes (συνέδροι—
Sanhedrin). Even the *lenis* is represented sometimes by a ה
at the beginning of a word; sometimes, however, even the
asper is dropped.

As to the vowels no distinct rule is to be laid down, owing
principally to the original want of vowel-points in our texts.

Before double consonants at the beginning of a word an א
prostheticum is placed, so as to render the pronunciation
easier. The terminations are frequently Hebraised :—thus

¹ בשת	² לטום	⁵ קדרום	⁶ קנברי
³ פרסא	⁴ פורפא	⁷ בירמיזא	⁸ יכרוחין

οι is sometimes rendered by the termination of the Masc. Pl. ם, &c.

A curious and instructive comparison may be instituted, between this mode of transcription of the Greek letters into Hebrew, and that of the Hebrew letters into Greek, as found chiefly in the LXX.

א sometimes inaudible (*spirit. len.*) Ἀαρών; Ἐλκανά; sometimes audible (as *spirit. asper*), Ἀβραάμ, Ἠλίας.

ב = β: Ῥεβέκκα; sometimes φ: Ἰακεβζήφ, sometimes υ: Ῥααῦ, sometimes μβ: Ζερουμβαβέλ, sometimes it is completely changed into μ: Ἰαμνεῖα (2 Chr. xxvi. 6).

ג = γ: Γόμερ, sometimes κ: Δωήκ, sometimes χ: Σερούχ.

ד = δ: once = τ Ματραΐθ (Gen. xxxvi. 39).

ה = א, either *spirit. asp.* like Ὀδορρά, or *spir. len.* like Ἀβέλ.

ו = υ, not the vowel, but our *v*: Ἔυα, Λευί: thus also ου (as the Greek writers often express the Latin *v* by ου): Ἰεσσουά: sometimes = β: Σαβύ (Gen. xiv. 5); sometimes it is entirely left out, Ἀστί for Vashti.

ז = ζ, sometimes σ: Σαβουλών, Χασβί; rarely ξ: Βαύξ (Gen. xxii. 21).

ח, often entirely omitted, or represented by a *spir. len.* in the beginning, or the reduplication of the vowel in the middle or at the end of the word, sometimes = χ: Χάμ; sometimes = κ: Τάβεκ (Gen. xxii. 24).

ט = τ: Σαφάτ; sometimes = δ: Φούδ (Gen. x. 6); or θ: Ἐλιφαλάδ (2 Sam. v. 16).

י = ι: Ἰακώβ, or ι before ρ (ר): Ἰερεμίας. Between several vowels it is sometimes entirely omitted; Ἰωαδά.

כ = χ: Χαναάν; sometimes κ: Σαβαθακά (Gen. x. 7); rarely = γ: Γαφθωρειμ.

ל, נ, ר = λ, ν, ρ; but they are often found interchanged: owing perhaps to the similarity of the Greek letters. נ is sometimes also rendered μ (see above).

מ = μ, sometimes β: Νεβρώδ, Σεβλά (1 Chr. i. 47).

ש and ס = σ: Συμεών, Σηείρ, Σίν.

ע = *spir. len.*: Ἐφρών; sometimes = γ ( ) Γόμορρα; sometimes κ, Ἀρβόκ (Gen. xxiii. 2).

פ = φ: Φαλέγ, or π: Σαλπαάδ.

צ = σ: Σιδών; sometimes ζ: Οὔζ. (Gen. x. 23; Cod. Alex. Ὥς; xxii. 21: Ὤξ.)

ק = κ: Βαλάκ; sometimes χ: Χεττουρά; also γ: Χελέγ.

ת = θ: Ἰαφέθ; sometimes τ: Τοχός.

As to the Bible Text from which the Targum was prepared, we can only reiterate that we have no certainty whatever on this head, owing to the extraordinarily corrupt state of our Targum texts. Pages upon pages of Variants have been gathered by Cappellus, Kennicott, Buxtorf, De Rossi, Clericus, Luzzatto, and others, by a superficial comparison of a few copies only, and those chiefly printed ones. Whenever the very numerous MSS. shall be collated, then the learned world may possibly come to certain probable conclusions on it. It would appear, however, that broadly speaking, our present Masoretic text has been the one from which the Onk. Version was, if not made, yet edited, at all events; unless we assume that late hands have been intentionally busy in mutually assimilating text and translation. Many of the inferences drawn by De Rossi and others from the discrepancies of the version to discrepancies of the original from the Masor. Text, must needs be rejected if Onkelos's method and phraseology, as we have exhibited it, are taken into consideration. Thus, when, Ex. xxiv. 7, "before the people" is found in Onkelos, while our Hebrew text reads "in the ears," it by no means follows that Onkelos read באזני: it is simply his way of explaining the unusual phrase, to which he remains faithful throughout. Or, "Lead the people *unto the place* (A. V.) of which I have spoken" (Ex. xxxii. 34), is solely Onkelos's translation of אל אשר, scil. the place, and no מקום need be conjectured as having stood in Onkelos's copy; as also, Ex. ix. 7, his addition "From the cattle of '*the children of*' Israel" does not prove a בני to have stood in his Codex.

And this also settles (or rather leaves unsettled), the question as to the authenticity of the Targumic Texts, such as we have them. Considering that no MS. has as yet been

found older than at most 600 years, even the careful comparison of all those that do exist would not much further
our knowledge. As far as those existing are concerned, they
teem with the most palpable blunders,—not to speak of
variants, owing to sheer carelessness on the part of the
copyists;—but few are of a nature damaging the sense
materially. The circumstance that Text and Targum were
often placed side by side, column by column, must have had
no little share in the incorrectness, since it was but natural
to make the Targum resemble the Text as closely as possible,
while the nature of its material differences was often unknown
to the scribe. In fact, the accent itself was made to fit both
the Hebrew and the Chaldee wherever a larger addition did
not render it utterly impossible. Thus letters are inserted,
omitted, thrust in, blotted out, erased, in an infinite number
of places. But the difference goes still further. In some
Codices synonymous terms are used most arbitrarily as it
would appear: ארעה and אדמתא earth, אדם and אנשא man,
אורח and מהלך path, יהוה and אלהים, Jehovah and Elohim,
are found to replace each other indiscriminately. In some
instances, the Hebrew Codex itself has, to add to the confusion, been emendated from the Targum.

A Masorah has been written on Onkelos, without, however,
any authority being inherent in it, and without, we should
say, much value. It has never been printed, nor, as far as
we have been able to ascertain, is there any MS. now to be
found in this country, or in any of the public libraries abroad.
What has become of Buxtorf's copy, which he intended to
add to his never printed " Babylonia "—a book devoted to
this same subject—we do not know. Luzzatto has lately
found such a " Masorah " in a Pentateuch MS., but he only
mentions some variants contained in it. Its title must not
mislead the reader; it has nothing whatever to do with *the*
Masorah of the Bible, but is a recent work, like the *Masorah
of the Talmud*, which has nothing whatever to do with the
Talmud Text.

The MSS. of Onkelos are extant in great numbers—a
circumstance easily explained by the injunction that it should

be read every Sabbath at home, if not in the Synagogue. The Bodleian has 5, the British Museum 2, Vienna 6, Augsburg 1, Nuremberg 2, Altdorf 1, Carlsruhe 3, Stuttgart 2, Erfurt 3, Dresden 1, Leipsic 1, Jena 1, Dessau 1, Helmstadt 2, Berlin 4, Breslau 1, Brieg 1, Regensburg 1, Hamburg 7, Copenhagen 2, Upsala 1, Amsterdam 1, Paris 8, Molsheim 1, Venice 6, Turin 2, Milan 4, Leghorn 1, Sienna 1, Genoa 1, Florence 5, Bologna 2, Padua 1, Trieste 2, Parma about 40. Rome 18 more or less complete Codd. containing Onkelos.

Editio Princeps, Bologna 1482, fol. (Abr. b. Chajjim) with Hebr. Text and Rashi. Later Edd. Soria 1490, Lisbon 1491, Constantinople 1505 : from these were taken the texts in the Complutensian (1517) and the Venice (Bomberg) Polyglotts (1518, 1526, 1547–49), and Buxtorf's Rabbinical Bible (1619). This was followed by the Paris Polyglott (1645), and Walton's (1657). A recent and much emendated edition dates Wilna 1852.

Of the extraordinary similarity between Onkelos and the Samaritan version we have spoken under SAMARITAN PENTATEUCH [p. 429]. There also will be found a specimen of both, taken from the Barberini Codex. Many more points connected with Onkelos and his influence upon later Hermeneutics and Exegesis, as well as his relation to earlier or later versions, we have no space to enlarge upon, desirable as an investigation of these points might be. We have, indeed, only been induced to dwell so long upon this single Targum, because in the first instance a great deal that has been said here will, *mutatis mutandis*, hold good also for the other Targums; and further, because Onkelos is THE CHALDEE VERSION κατ' ἐξοχήν, while, from Jonathan downwards, we more and more leave the province of Version and gradually arrive from Paraphrase to Midrash-Haggadah. We shall therefore not enter at any length into these, but confine ourselves chiefly to main results.

II. TARGUM ON THE PROPHETS.

viz. Joshua, Judges, Samuel, Kings, Isaiah, Jeremiah,
Ezekiel, and the twelve Minor Prophets,—called TARGUM OF
JONATHAN BEN UZZIEL.

Next in time and importance to Onkelos on the Pentateuch
stands the Targum on the Prophets, which in our printed
Edd. and MSS.—none older, we repeat it, than about 600
years—is ascribed to Jonathan ben Uzziel, of whom the
Talmud contains the following statements:—(1.) "Eighty
disciples had Hillel the Elder, thirty of whom were worthy
that the Shechinah (Divine Majesty) should rest upon them,
as it did upon Moses our Lord; peace be upon him. Thirty
of them were worthy that the sun should stand still at their
bidding as it did at that of Joshua ben Nun. Twenty were
of intermediate worth. The greatest of them all was Jonathan
b. Uzziel, the least R. Johanan b. Saccai; and it was said of
R. Johanan b. Saccai, that he left not (uninvestigated) the
Bible, the Mishnah, the Gemara, the Halachahs, the Hag-
gadahs, the subtleties of the Law, and the subtleties of the
Soferim . . . . ; the easy things and the difficult things
[from the most awful Divine mysteries to the common
popular proverbs] . . . If this is said of the least of them,
what is to be said of the greatest, *i.e.* Jonathan b. Uzziel?"
(Bab. Bath. 134 *a*; comp. Succ. 28 *a*). (2.) A second passage (see Onkelos) referring more especially to our present
subject, reads as follows: "The Targum of Onkelos was
made by Onkelos the Proselyte from the mouth of R. Eliezer
and R. Jehoshua, and that of the Prophets by Jonathan b.
Uzziel from the mouth of Haggai, Zechariah, and Malachi.
And in that hour was the Land of Israel shaken three hundred parasangs. . . . And a voice was heard, saying, 'Who
is this who has revealed my secrets unto the sons of man?'
Up rose Jonathan ben Uzziel and said: 'It is I who have
revealed Thy secrets to the sons of man. . . . But it is known
and revealed before Thee, that not for my honour have I
done it, nor for the honour of my father's house, but for
Thine honour; that the disputes may cease in Israel.' . . .

And he further desired to reveal the Targum to the Hagiographa, when a voice was heard:—'Enough.' And why?—because the day of the Messiah is revealed therein (Meg. 3a)." Wonderful to relate, the sole and exclusive authority for the general belief in the authorship of Jonathan b. Uzziel, is this second Haggadistic passage exclusively; which, if it does mean anything, does at all events not mean our Targum, which is found mourning over the "Temple in ruins," full of invectives against Rome (Sam. xi. 5; Is. xxxiv. 9, &c. &c.), mentioning Armillus (Is. x. 4) (the Antichrist), Germania (Ez. xxxviii. 6):—not to dwell upon the thousand and one other internal and external evidences against a date anterior to the Christian era. If interpolations must be assumed,—and indeed Rashi speaks already of corruptions in his MSS. —such solitary additions are at all events a very different thing from a wholesale system of intentional and minute interpolation throughout the bulky work. But what is still more extraordinary, this belief—long and partly still upheld most reverentially against all difficulties—is completely modern: that is, not older than at most 600 years (the date of our oldest Targum MSS.), and is utterly at variance with the real and genuine sources: the Talmud, the Midrash, the Babylonian Schools, and every authority down to Hai Gaon (12th cent.). Frequently quoted as this Targum is in the ancient works, it is never once quoted as the Targum of Jonathan. But it is invariably introduced with the formula: "R. Joseph[1] (bar Chama, the Blind, euphemistically called the clear-sighted, the well-known President of Pumbaditha in Babylonia, who succeeded Rabba in 319 A.D.) says," &c. (Moed Katon 26 a, Pesach. 68 a, Sanh. 94 b). Twice even it is quoted in Joseph's name, and with the addition, "Without the Targum to this verse (due to him) we could not understand it." This is the simple state of the case: and for more than two hundred years critics have lavished all their acumen to defend what never had any real existence, or at best owed

---

[1] "Sinai," "Professor of Wheat," in allusion to his vast mastery over the traditions.

its apparent existence to a heading added by a superficial scribe.

The date which the Talmud thus in reality assigns to our Targum fully coincides with our former conclusions as to the date of written Targums in general. And if we may gather thus much from the legend that to write down the Targum to the Prophets was considered a much bolder undertaking—and one to which still more reluctantly leave was given—than a Targum on the Pentateuch, we shall not be far wrong in placing *this* Targum some time, although not long, after Onkelos, or about the middle of the fourth century;—the latter years of R. Joseph, who, it is said, occupied himself chiefly with the Targum when he had become blind. The reason given for that reluctance is, although hyperbolically expressed, perfectly clear: "The Targum on the Prophets revealed the secrets"—that is, it allowed free scope to the wildest fantasy to run riot upon the prophetic passages —tempting through their very obscurity,—and to utter explanations and interpretations relative to present events, and oracles of its own for future times, which might be fraught with grave dangers in more than one respect. The Targum on the Pentateuch (permitted to be committed to writing, Meg. 3 *a*; Kidd. 69 *a*) could not but be, even in its written form, more sober, more dignified, more within the bounds of fixed and well-known traditions, than any other Targum; since it had originally been read publicly, and been checked by the congregation as well as the authorities present;—as we have endeavoured to explain in the Introduction. There is no proof, on the other hand, of more than fragments from the Prophets having ever been read and translated in the synagogue. Whether, however, R. Joseph was more than the redactor of this the second part of the Bible-Targum, which was originated in Palestine, and was reduced to its final shape in Babylon, we cannot determine. He may perhaps have made considerable additions of his own, by filling up gaps or rejecting wrong versions of some parts. So much seems certain, that the schoolmen of his Academy were the collectors and revisers, and he gave it that stamp

of unity which it now possesses, spite of the occasional difference of style :—adapted simply to the variegated hues and
dictions of its manifold biblical originals.

But we do not mean to reject in the main either of the
Talmudical passages quoted. We believe that there was
such a man as Jonathan b. Uzziel, that he was one of the
foremost pupils of Hillel, and also that he did translate,
either privately or publicly, parts of the prophetical books;
chiefly, we should say, in a mystical manner. And so
startling were his interpretations—borne aloft by his high
fame—that who but prophets themselves could have revealed
them to him? And, going a step further, who could reveal
prophetic allegories and mysteries of *all* the prophetic books,
but those who, themselves the last in the list, had the
whole body of sacred oracles before them? This appears to
us the only rational conclusion to be drawn from the facts:
—as they stand, not as they are imagined. That nothing
save a few snatches of this *original* paraphrase or Midrash
could be embodied in our Targum, we need not urge. Yet
for these even we have no proof. Zunz, the *facile princeps*
of Targumic as well as Midrashic investigation, who, as late
as 1830 (*Gottesd. Vortr.*), still believed himself in the modern
notion of Jonathan's authorship ("first half of first century,
A.D."), now utterly rejects the notion of "our possessing
anything of Jonathan ben Uzziel" (Geiger's *Zeitschr.* 1837,
p. 250).

Less conservative than our view, however, are the views
of the modern School (Rappoport, Luzzatto, Frankel, Geiger,
Levy, Bauer, Jahn, Bertholdt, Levysohn, &c.), who not only
reject the authorship of Jonathan, but also utterly deny
that there was any ground whatsoever for assigning a Targum
to him, as is done in the Talmud. The passage, they say,
is not older, but younger than our Targum, and in fact does
apply, erroneously of course, to this, and to no other work of
a similar kind. The popular cry for a great "name, upon
which to hang"—in Talmudical phraseology—all that is
cherished and venerated, and the wish of those eager to
impart to this Version a lasting authority, found in Jonathan

the most fitting person to father it upon. Was he not the greatest of the great, "who had·been dusted with the dust of Hillel's feet?" He was the wisest of the wise, the one most imbued with knowledge human and divine, of all those eighty, the least of whom was worthy that the sun should stay its course at his bidding. Nay, such were the flames[1] that arose from his glowing spirit, says the hyperbolic Haggadah, that "when he studied in the Law, the very birds that flew over him in the air, were consumed by fire" (*nisrephu*[2]—not, as Landau, in the preface to his Aruch, apologetically translates, *became Seraphs*). At the same time we readily grant that we see no reason why the great Hillel himself, or any other much earlier and equally eminent Master of the Law, one of the Soferim perhaps, should not have been fixed upon.

Another suggestion, first broached by Drusius, and long exploded, has recently been revived under a somewhat modified form. Jonathan (Godgiven), Drusius said, was none else but Theodotion (Godgiven), the second Greek translator of the Bible after the LXX., who had become a Jewish proselyte. Considering that the latter lived under Commodus II., and the former at the time of Christ; that the latter is said to have translated the Prophets only (neither the Pentateuch, nor the Hagiographa), while the former translated the *whole* Bible; that Jonathan translated into Aramaic and Theodotion into Greek,—not to mention the fact that Theodotion was, to say the least, a not very competent translator, since "ignorance or negligence" (Montfaucon, *Pref. to Hexapla*), or both, must needs be laid at the door of a translator, who, when in difficulties, simply transcribes the hard Hebrew words into Greek characters, without troubling himself any further;[3] while the mastery over both the Hebrew and the Aramaic displayed in the Jonathanic Version are astounding:—considering all this, we need not like Walton ask caustically, why Jonathan ben

---

[1] The simile of the fire—"as the Law was given in fire on Sinai"—is a very favourite one in the Midrash.

[2] נשׂר פו.

[3] *e. g.*, Lev. vii. 18, בְּגוּל, T.

Φεγγώλ, or Φεγγούλ, by way of emendation; Lev. xiii. 6, מספחת, Μασφάα; ib. שׂאת, Σήθ; Lev. xviii. 23, תבל, θάβελ; Is. lxiv. 6, עדים, 'Εδδίμ. ·

Uzziel should not rather be identified with the Emperor
Theodosius, whose name also is "Godgiven;"—but dismiss
the suggestion as Carpzov long since dismissed it. We are,
however, told now (Luzzatto, Geiger, &c.), that as the Babylonian Targum on the Pentateuch was called a Targum
"in the manner of Aquila or Onkelos," *i.e.* of sterling value,
so also the continuation of the Babylonian Targum, which
embraced the Prophets, was called a Targum "in the manner
of Theodotion" = Jonathan ; and by a further stretch, Jona-
than-Theodotion became the Jonathan b. Uzziel. We cannot
but disagree with this hypothesis also—based on next to
nothing, and carried to more than the usual length of speculation. While Akyla is quoted continually in the Talmud,
and is deservedly one of the best known and best beloved
characters, every trait and incident of whose personal history
is told even twice over, not the slightest trace of such a
person as Theodotion is to be found anywhere in the Talmudical literature. What, again, was it that could have
acquired so transcendent a fame for his translation and
himself, that a Version put into the mouths of the very
prophets should be called after him, "in order that the
people should like it"?—a translation which was, in fact,
deservedly unknown, and, properly speaking, no translation
at all. It was, as we learn, a kind of private emendation of
some LXX. passages, objectionable to the pious Proselyte in
their then corrupted state. It was only the Book of Daniel
which was retained from Theodotion's pen, because in this
book the LXX. had become past correction. If, moreover,
the intention was "to give the people a Hebrew for a Greek
name, because the latter might sound too foreign," it was an
entirely gratuitous one. Greek names abound in the Talmud,
and even names beginning with Theo like Theodorus are to
be found there.

On the other hand, the opinion has been broached that
this Targum was a post-Talmudical production, belonging
to the 7th or 8th cent. A.D. For this point we need only
refer to the Talmudical quotations from it. And when we
further add, that Jo. Morinus, a man as conspicuous by his

2 B

want of knowledge as by his most ludicrous attacks upon
all that was "Jewish" or "Protestant" (it was he, *e.g.* who
wished to see the "forged" Masoretic Code corrected from
the Samaritan Pentateuch, *q.v.*) is the chief, and almost
only, defender of this theory, we have said enough. On the
other theory of there being more than one author to our
Targum (Eichhorn, Bertholdt, De Wette), combated fiercely
by Gesenius, Hävernick, and others, we need not further
enlarge, after what we have already said. It certainly is the
work, not of one, or of two, but of twenty, of fifty and more
Meturgemanim, Haggadists, and Halachists. The edition,
however, we repeat it advisedly, has the undeniable stamp
of one master-mind; and its individual workings, its manner
and peculiarity are indelibly impressed upon the whole labour
from the first page to the last. Such, we hold, must be the
impression upon every attentive reader; more especially, if
he judiciously distinguishes between the first and the last
prophets. That in the historical relations of the former,
the Version must be, on the whole, more accurate and close
(although here too, as we shall show, Haggadah often takes
the reins out of the Meturgeman's or editor's hands), while
in the obscurer Oracles of the latter the Midrash reigns
supreme: is exactly what the history of Targumic development leads us to expect.

And with this we have pointed out the general character
of the Targum under consideration. Gradually, perceptibly
almost, the translation becomes the τράγημα, a frame, so to
speak, of allegory, parable, myth, tale, and oddly masked
history—such as we are wont to see in Talmud and Midrash,
written under the bloody censorship of Esau-Rome; interspersed with some lyrical pieces of rare poetical value. It
becomes, in short, like the Haggadah, a whole system of
Eastern phantasmagorias whirling round the sun of the Holy
Word of the Seer. Yet, it is always aware of being a translation. It returns to its verse after long excurses, often in
next to no perceptible connexion with it. Even in the midst
of the full swing of fancy, swayed to and fro by the many
currents of thought that arise out of a single word, snatches

of the verse from which the flight was taken will suddenly
appear on the surface like a refrain or a keynote, showing
that in a reality there is a connexion, though hidden to the
uninitiated. For long periods again, it adheres most strictly
to its text and to its verse, and translates most conscientiously and closely. It may thus fairly be described as holding in point of interpretation and enlargement of the text,
the middle place between Onkelos, who only in extreme cases
deviates into paraphrase, and the subsequent Targums, whose
connexion with their texts is frequently of the most flighty
character. Sometimes indeed our Targum coincides so entirely with Onkelos,—being, in fact, of one and the same
origin and growth, and a mere continuation and completion
as it were of the former work, that this similarity has misled
critics into speculations of the priority in date of either the
one or the other. Hävernick, *e.g.* holds—against Zunz—that
Onkelos copied, plagiarised, in fact, Jonathan. We do not see,
quite apart from our placing Onkelos first, why either should
have used the other. The three passages (Judg. v. 26 and
Deut. xxii. 5; 2 K. xiv. 6 and Deut. xxiv. 16; Jer. xlviii. 45,
46 and Num. xxi. 28, 29) generally adduced, do not in the
first place exhibit that literal closeness which we are led to
expect, and which alone could be called " copying;" and in
the second place, the two last passages are not, as we also
thought we could infer from the words of the writers on
either side, extraneous paraphrastic additions, but simply
the similar translations of similar texts : while in the first
passage Jonathan only refers to an injunction contained in
the Pentateuch-verse quoted. But even had we found such
paraphrastic additions, apparently not belonging to the subject, we should have accounted for them by certain traditions
—the common property of the whole generation,—being recalled by a certain word or phrase in the Pentateuch to the
memory of the *one* translator; and by another word or
phrase in the Prophets to the memory of the *other* translator. The interpretation of Jonathan, where it adheres to
the text, is mostly very correct in a philosophical and exegetical sense, closely literal even, provided the meaning of

the original is easily to be understood by the people. When, however, similes are used, unfamiliar or obscure to the people, it unhesitatingly dissolves them and makes them easy in their mouths like household. words, by adding as much of explanation as seems fit; sometimes, it cannot be denied, less sagaciously, even incorrectly, comprehending the original meaning. Yet we must be very cautious in attributing to a Version which altogether bears the stamp of thorough competence and carefulness that which may be single corruptions or interpolations, as we find them sometimes indicated by an introductory "Says the Prophet"[1]: although, as stated above, we do not hesitate to attribute the passages displaying an acquaintance with works written down to the 4th century, and exhibiting popular notions current at that time, to the Targum in its original state. Generally speaking, and holding the difference between the nature of the Pentateuch (supposed to contain in its very letters and signs Halachistic references, and therefore only to be handled by the Meturgeman with the greatest care) and that of the Prophets (freest Homiletes themselves) steadily in view—the rules laid down above with respect to the discrepancies between Original and Targum, in Onkelos, hold good also with Jonathan. Anthropomorphisms it avoids carefully. Geographical names are, in most cases, retained as in the Original, and where translated, they are generally correct. Its partiality for Israel never goes so far that anything derogatory to the character of the people, should be willingly suppressed, although a certain reluctance against dwelling upon its iniquities and punishments longer than necessary, is visible. Where, however, that which redounds to the praise of the individual—more especially of heroes, kings, prophets—and of the community, is contained in the text, there the paraphrase lovingly tarries. Future bliss, in this world and the world to come, liberation from the oppressor, restoration of the Sanctuary on Mount Zion, of the Kingdom of Jehovah and the House of David, the re-establishment of the nation

---

[1] אֲמַר נְבִיא.

and of its full and entire independence, as well as of the
national worship, with all the primitive splendour of Priest
and Levite, singer and musician and prophet—these are the
favourite dreams of the people and of Jonathan, and no link
is overlooked by which those strains may be drawn in as
variations to the Biblical theme. Of Messianic passages,
Jonathan has pointed out those mentioned below;[1] a number
not too large, if we consider how, with the increased misery
of the people, their ardent desire to see their Deliverer
appear speedily must have tried to find as many places in
the Bible as possible, warranting His arrival. So far from
their being suppressed (as, by one of those unfortunate acci-
dents that befall sometimes a long string of *investigators*,
who are copying their information at third and fourth hand,
has been unblushingly asserted by almost everybody up to
Gesenius, who found its source in a *misunderstood sentence of
Carpzov*), they are most prominently, often almost pointedly
brought forward. And there is a decided polemical animus
inherent in them—temperate as far as appearance goes,
but containing many an unspoken word: such as a fervent
human mind pressed down by all the woes and terrors, written
and unwritten, would whisper to itself in the depths of its
despair. These passages extol most rapturously the pomp
and glory of the Messiah to come—by way of contrast to
the humble appearance of Christ: and all the places where
suffering and misery appear to be the lot forecast to the
Anointed, it is Israel, to whom the passage is referred by
the Targum.

Of further dogmatical and theological peculiarities (and
this Targum will one day prove a mine of instruction chiefly
in that direction, besides the other vast advantages inherent
in it, as in the older Targums, for linguistic, patristic, geographical, historical, and other studies) we may mention
briefly the "Stars of God" (Is. xiv. 13; comp. Dan. viii. 10,

---

[1] 1 Sam. ii. 10; 2 Sam. xxiii. 3; 1
K. iv. 33; Is. iv. 2, ix. 6, x. 27, xi.
1, 6, xv. 2, xvi. 1, 5, xxviii. 5, xlii. 1,
xliii. 10, xlv. 1, lii. 13, liii. 10; Jer.
xxiii. 5, xxx. 21, xxxiii. 13, 15; Hos.
iii. 5, xiv. 8; Mic. iv. 8, v. 2, 18;
Zech. iii. 8, iv. 7, vi. 12, x. 4.

2 Macc. ix. 10, being referred—in a similar manner—to "the people of Israel;") the doctrine of the second death (Isa. xxii. 14, lxv. 15), &c. As to the general nature of its idiom, what we have said above holds good here. Likewise our remarks on the relation between the text of the Original of Onkelos, and its own text, may stand for Jonathan, who never appears to differ from the Masoretic text without a very cogent reason. Yet, since Jonathan's MSS., though very much smaller in number, are in a still worse plight than those of Onkelos, we cannot speak with great certainty on this point. Respecting, however, the individual language and phraseology of the translation, it lacks to a certain, though small, degree, the clearness and transparency of On-kelos; and is somewhat alloyed with foreign words. Not to such a degree, however, that we cannot fully endorse Carpzov's dictum: " Cujus nitor sermonis Chaldæi et dictionis laudatur puritas, ad Onkelosum proxime accedens et parum deflectens a puro tersoque Chaldaismo biblico" (*Crit. Sacr.* p. 461), and incline to the belief of Wolf (*Bibl. Hebr.* ii. 1165): " Quæ vero, vel quod ad voces novas et barbaras, vel ad res ætate ejus inferiores, aut futilia nonnulla, quamvis pauca triplicis hujus generis exstent, ibi occurrunt, ex merito falsarii cujus-dam ingenio adscribuntur." Of the manner and style of this Targum, the few subjoined specimens will, we hope, give an approximate idea.

In conclusion, we may notice a feature of our Targum, not the least interesting perhaps, in relation to general or "human" literature: viz., that the Shemitic fairy and legendary lore, which for the last two thousand years — as far as we can trace it,—has grown up in East and West to vast glittering mountain-ranges, is to a very great extent to be found, in an embryo state, so to say, in this our Targum. When the literary history of those most wonderful circles of medieval sagas—the sole apparent fruit brought home by the crusaders from the Eastern battle-fields—shall come to be written by a competent and thorough investigator, he will have to extend his study of the sources to this despised "fabulosus" Targum Jonathan ben Uzziel. And the entire world of pious biblical legend, which Islam has said and sung in the Arabic, Persian, Turkish, and all its other tongues, to the delight of the wise and the simple for twelve centuries now, is contained almost fully developed, from beginning to end, but clearer, purer, and incomparably more poetically conceived, in our Targum-Haggadah.

The *Editio Princeps* dates Leiria, 1494. The later editions are embodied in the Antwerp, Paris, and London Polyglotts. Several single books have likewise been repeatedly edited (com. Wolff, Le Long, Rosenmüller, &c.).

JUDGES V.

AUTHORISED VERSION.	TARGUM [JONATHAN BEN UZZIEL] TO THE PROPHETS.
1 THEN sang Deborah and Barak the son of Abinoam on that day, saying,	1 AND Deborah and Barak the son of Abinoam gave praise for the miracle and the salvation which were wrought for Israel on that day, and spake :
2 Praise ye the LORD for the avenging of Israel, when the people willingly offered themselves.	2 When the children of Israel rebel against the Law, then the nations come over them and drive them out of their cities ; but when they

return to do the Law, then they are mighty over their enemies, and drive them out from the whole territory of the land of Israel. Thus has been broken Sisra and all his armies to his punishment, and to a miracle and a salvation for Israel. Then the wise returned to sit in the houses of the synagogue . . . and to teach unto the people the doctrine of the Law. Therefore praise ye and bless the Lord.

| 3 Hear, O ye kings; give ear, O ye princes; I, *even* I, will sing unto the LORD; I will sing *praise* to the LORD God of Israel. | 3 Hear, ye kings (ye who came with Sisra to the battle-array), listen, ye rulers [ye who were with Jabin the king of Kenaan: not with your armies nor with your power have ye |

conquered and become mighty over the house of Israel]—said Deborah in prophecy before God: I praise, give thanks and blessings before the Lord, the God of Israel.

| 4 LORD, when thou wentest out of Seir, when thou marchedst out of the field of Edom, the earth trembled, and the heavens dropped, the clouds also dropped water. | 4 [O Lord, Thy Law which Thou gavest to Israel, when they transgress it, then the nations rule over them : but when they return to it, then they become powerful over their enemies.] O Lord, on the day |

when Thou didst reveal Thyself to give it unto them from Seir,

AUTHORISED VERSION.	[TARGUM Jonathan ben Uzziel] TO THE PROPHETS.

Thou becamest manifest unto them in the splendour of Thy glory over the territories of Edom: the earth trembled, the heavens showered down, the clouds dropped rain.

5 The mountains melted from before the LORD, *even* that Sinai from before the LORD God of Israel.

5 The mountains trembled before the Lord, the mountains of Tabor, the mountain of Hermon, and the mountain of Carmel, spake with each other, and said one to the other : Upon me the Shechinah will rest, and to me will it come. But the Shechinah rested upon Mount Sinai, which is the weakest and smallest of all the mountains. . . . This Sinai trembled and shook, and its smoke went up as goes up the smoke of an oven : because of the glory of the God of Israel which had manifested itself upon it.

6 In the days of Shamgar the son of Anath, in the days of Jael, the highways were unoccupied, and the travellers walked through byways.

6 When they transgressed in the days of Shamgar the son of Anath in the days of Jael, ceased the wayfarers: they who had walked in well-prepared ways had again to walk in furtive paths.

7 *The inhabitants of* the villages ceased, they ceased in Israel, until that I Deborah arose, that I arose a mother in Israel.

7 Destroyed were the open cities of the land of Israel : their inhabitants were shaken off and driven about, until I, Deborah, was sent to prophesy over the house of Israel.

8 They chose new gods ; then *was* war in the gates ; was there a shield or spear seen among forty thousand in Israel ?

8 When the children of Israel went to pray unto new idols [errors], which recently had come to be worshipped, with which their fathers did not concern themselves, there came over them the nations and drove them out of their cities : but when they returned to the Law, they could not prevail against them until they made themselves strong, and Sisra went up against them, the enemy and the adversary, with forty thousand chiefs of troops, with fifty thousand holders of the sword, with sixty thousand holders of spears, with seventy thousand holders of shields, with eighty thousand throwers of arrows and slings, besides nine hundred iron chariots which he had with him, and his own chariots. All these thousands and all these hosts could not stand before Barak and the ten thousand men he had with him.

9 My heart *is* toward the governors of Israel, that offered themselves willingly among the people. Bless ye the LORD.

9 Spake Deborah in prophecy : I am sent to praise the scribes of Israel, who, while this tribulation lasted, ceased not to study in the Law : and it redounds well unto them who sat in the houses of congregation, wide open, and taught the people the doctrine of the Law, and praised and rendered thanks before the Lord.

10 Speak, ye that ride on white

10 Those who had interrupted

AUTHORISED VERSION.	TARGUM [JONATHAN BEN UZZIEL] TO THE PROPHETS.
asses, ye that sit in judgment, and walk by the way.	their occupations are riding on asses covered with many-coloured caparisons, and they ride about freely in

all the territory of Israel, and congregate to sit in judgment. They walk in their old ways, and are speaking of the power Thou hast shown in the land of Israel, &c.

JUDGES XI.

39 AND it came to pass, at the end of two months, that she returned unto her father, who did with her *according* to his vow which he had vowed: and she knew no man. And it was a custom in Israel.	39 AND it was at the end of two months, and she returned to her father, and he did unto her according to the vow which he had vowed: and she had known no man. And it became a statute in Israel, *Addition* (תוספת), that no man should offer up his son or his daugh-

ter as a burnt-offering, as Jephta the Gileadite did, who asked not Phinehas the priest. If he had asked Phinehas the priest, then he would have dissolved his vow with money [for animal sacrifices].

1 SAM. II.

1 AND Hannah prayed, and said, My heart rejoiceth in the LORD; mine horn is exalted in the LORD; my mouth is enlarged over mine enemies; because I rejoice in thy salvation.	1 AND Hannah prayed in the spirit of prophecy, and said: [Lo, my son Samuel will become a prophet over Israel; in his days they will be freed from the hand of the Philistines; and through his hands shall be done unto them wondrous

and mighty deeds: therefore] be strong my heart in the portion which God gave me. [And also Heman the son of Joel, the son of my son Samuel, shall arise, he and his fourteen sons, to say praise with nablia (harps?) and cythers, with their brethren the Levites, to sing in the house of the sanctuary: therefore] Let my horn be exalted in the gift which God granted unto me. [And also on the miraculous punishment that would befal the Philistines who would bring back the ark of the Lord in a new chariot, together with a sin-offering: therefore let the congregation of Israel say] I will open my mouth to speak great things over my enemies; because I rejoice in thy salvation.

2 *There is* none holy as the LORD: or *there is* none beside thee, neither s *there* any rock like our God.	2 [Over Sanherib the king of Ashur did she prophesy, and she said: He will arise with all his armies over Jerusalem, and a great

sign will be done with him. There shall fall the corpses of his troops: Therefore praise ye all the peoples and nations and tongues, and cry]: There is none holy but God; there is not

AUTHORISED VERSION.	TARGUM [Jonathan ben Uzziel] TO THE PROPHETS.
	beside thee; and Thy people shall say, There is none mighty but our God.
3 Talk no more so exceeding proudly; let *not* arrogancy come out of your mouth: for the Lord *is* a God of knowledge, and by him actions are weighed.	3 [Over Nebuchadnezzar the king of Babel did she prophesy and say: Ye Chaldeans, and all nations who will once rule over Israel] Do not speak grandly; let no blasphemy go out from your mouth: for God knows all, and over all his servants he extends his judgment; also from you he will take punishment of your guilt.
4 The bows of the mighty *are* broken, and they that stumbled are girded with strength.	4 [Over the kingdom Javan she prophesied and said] The bows of the mighty ones [of the Javanites] will be broken; [and those of the house of the Asmoneans] who are weak, to them will be done miracles and mighty deeds.

1 Sam. XVII.

8 And he stood and cried unto the armies of Israel, and said unto them, Why are ye come out to set *your* battle in array? *Am* not I a Philistine, and ye servants to Saul? choose you a man for you, and let him come down to me.	8 And he arose and he cried unto the armies of Israel, and said unto them: Why have you put yourselves in battle array? Am I not the Philistine, and you the servants of Saul? [I am Goliath the Philistine from Gath, who have killed the two sons of Eli, the priests

Chofna and Phinehas, and carried captive the ark of the covenant of the Lord, I who have carried it to the house of Dagon, *my Error*, and it has been there in the cities of the Philistines seven months. And in every battle which the Philistines have had I went at the head of the army, and we conquered in the battle, and we strew the killed like the dust of the earth, and until now have the Philistines not thought me worthy to become captain of a thousand over them. And you, O children of Israel, what mighty deed has Saul the son of Kish from Gibeah done for you that you made him king over you? If he is a valiant man, let him come out and do battle with me; but if he is a weak man], then choose for yourselves a man, and let him come out against me, &c.

1 Kings XIX.

11, 12 And he said, Go forth, and stand upon the mount before the Lord. And, behold, the Lord	11, 12 And he said [to Elijah], Arise and stand on the mountain before the Lord. And God revealed

AUTHORISED VERSION.	TARGUM [JONATHAN BEN UZZIEL] TO THE PROPHETS.
passed by, and a great and strong wind rent the mountains, and brake in pieces the rocks, before the LORD; *but* the LORD *was* not in the wind: and after the wind an earthquake; *but* the Lord *was* not in the earthquake: and after the earthquake a fire; *but* the LORD *was* not in the fire: and after the fire a still small voice.	himself: and before him a host of angels of the wind, cleaving the mountain and breaking the rocks before the Lord; but not in the host of angels was the Shechinah. And after the host of the angels of the wind came a host of angels of commotion; but not in the host of the angels of commotion was the Shechinah of the Lord. And after the host of the angels of commotion

came a host of angels of fire; but not in the host of the angels of fire was the Shechinah of the Lord. But after the host of the angels of the fire came voices singing in silence.

| 13 And it was *so*, when Elijah heard *it*, that he wrapped his face in his mantle, and went out, and stood in the entering in of the cave: and, behold, *there came* a voice unto him, and said, What doest thou here, Elijah? | 13 And it was when Elijah heard this, he hid his face in his mantle, and he went out and he stood at the door of the cave; and, lo! with him was a voice, saying, What doest thou here, O Elijah! &c. |

ISAIAH XXXIII.

| 22 For the LORD *is* our judge, the LORD *is* our lawgiver, the LORD *is* our king; he will save us. | 22 For the Lord is our judge, who delivered us with his power from Mizraim; the Lord is our teacher, for He has given us the |

doctrine of the Torah from Sinai; the Lord is our king: He will deliver us, and give us righteous restitution from the army of Gog.

JEREMIAH X.

| 11 THUS shall ye say unto them, The gods that have not made the heavens and the earth, *even* they shall perish from the earth, and from under these heavens. | 11 THIS is the copy of the letter which Jeremiah the prophet sent to the remaining ancient ones of the captivity in Babel: "And if the nations among whom you are will say unto you, Pray to our *Errors*:— |

O house of Israel, then you shall answer thus, and speak in this wise: The Errors unto which you pray are Errors which are of no use: they cannot rain from heaven; they cannot cause fruit to grow from the earth. They and their worshippers will perish from the earth, and will be destroyed from under these heavens."

MICAH VI.

AUTHORISED VERSION.	TARGUM [JONATHAN BEN UZZIEL] TO THE PROPHETS.
4 For I brought thee up out of the land of Egypt, and redeemed thee out of the house of servants; and I sent before thee Moses, Aaron, and Miriam.	4 For I have taken thee out from the land of Mizraim, and have released thee from the house of thy bondage; and have sent before thee three prophets: Moses, to teach thee the tradition of the ordinances; Aaron, to atone for the people; and Miriam to teach the women.

III. AND IV. TARGUM OF JONATHAN BEN UZZIEL AND JERUSHALMI-TARGUM ON THE PENTATEUCH.

Onkelos and Jonathan on the Pentateuch and Prophets, whatever be their exact date, place, authorship and editorship, are, as we have endeavoured to show, the oldest of existing Targums, and belong, in their present shape, to Babylon and the Babylonian academies flourishing between the 3rd and 4th centuries A.D. But precisely as two parallel and independent developments of the Oral Law (תֹּשׁבֹּפ) have sprung up in the Palestinian and Babylonian Talmuds respectively, so also recent investigation has proved to demonstration the existence of two distinct cycles of Targums on the Written Law (תֹּשׁבכתב)—i. e. the entire body of the Old Testament. Both are the offspring of the old, primitive institution of the public "reading and translating of the Torah," which for many hundred years had its place in the Palestinian synagogues. The one first collected, revised, and edited in Babylon, called—more especially that part of it which embraced the Pentateuch (Onkelos)—the Babylonian, *Ours*, by way of eminence, on account of the superior authority inherent in all the works of the Madinchaē (Babylonians, in. contradistinction to the Maarbae or Palestinians). The other, continuing its oral life, so to say, down to a much later period, was written and edited—less carefully, or rather with a much more faithful retention of the oldest and youngest fancies of Meturgemanim and Darshanim—on the soil of Judæa itself. On this entire cycle, however, the Pentateuch and a few other books and fragmentary pieces only have survived entire, while of most of the other books of the Bible a few detached fragments are all that is known, and this chiefly from quotations. The injunction above mentioned respecting the sabbatical reading of the Targum on the Pentateuch—nothing is said of the Prophets—explains the fact, to a certain extent, how the Pentateuch Targum has been religiously preserved, while the others have perished. This circumstance, also, is to be taken into consideration, that Palestine was in later centuries well-nigh cut off from communication with the Diaspora, while Babylon, and the gigantic literature it produced, reigned paramount over all Judaism, as, indeed, down to the 10th century, the latter continued to have a spiritual leader in the person of the Resh Gelutha (Head of the Golah), residing in Babylon. As not the least cause of the loss of the great bulk of the Palestinian Targum may also be considered the almost uninterrupted martyrdom to which those were subjected who preferred, under all circumstances, to live and die in the Land of Promise.

However this may be, the Targum on the Pentateuch has come down to us: and not in one, but in two recensions. More surprising still, the one hitherto considered a fragment, because of its embracing portions only of the individual books, has in reality never been intended to embrace any further portion, and we are thus in the possession of two Palestinian Targums, preserved in their original forms. The one, which extends from the first verse of Genesis to the last of Deuteronomy, is known under the name of Targum Jonathan (ben Uzziel) or Pseudo-Jonathan on the Pentateuch. The other, interpreting single verses, often single words only, is extant in the following proportions: a third on Genesis, a fourth on Deuteronomy, a fifth on Numbers, three-twentieths on Exodus, and about one-fourteenth on Leviticus. The latter is generally called Targum *Jerushalmi*, or, down to the 11th century (Hai Gaon, Chananel), *Targum Erets Israel*,

Targum of Jerusalem or of the land of Israel. That Jonathan
ben Uzziel, the same to whom the prophetical Targum is
ascribed, and who is reported to have lived either in the 5th–
4th century B.C., or about the time of Christ himself (see
above), could have little to do with a Targum which speaks
of Constantinople (Num. xxiv. 19, 24), describes very plainly
the breaking-up of the West-Roman Empire (Num. xxiv.
19–24), mentions the Turks (Gen. x. 2), and even Mohammed's two wives, Chadidja and Fatime (Gen. xxi. 21), and
which exhibits not only the fullest acquaintance with the
edited body of the Babylonian Talmud, by quoting entire
passages from it, but adopts its peculiar phraseology:—not
to mention the complete disparity between the style, language, and general manner of the Jonathanic Targum on the
Prophets, and those of this one on the Pentateuch, strikingly
palpable at first sight,—was recognised by early investigators
(Morinus, Pfeiffer, Walton, &c.), who soon overthrew the old
belief in Jonathan b. Uzziel's authorship, as upheld by
Menahem Rekanati, Asariah de Rossi, Gedaljah, Galatin,
Fagius, &c. But the relation in which the two Targums, so
similar and yet so dissimilar, stood to each other, how they
arose, and where and when—all these questions have for a
long time, in the terse words of Zunz, caused many of the
learned such dire misery, that whenever the "Targum
Hierosolymitanum comes up," they, instead of information
on it and its twin-brother, prefer to treat the reader to a
round volley of abuse of them. Not before the first half of
this century did the fact become fully and incontestably
established (by the simple process of an investigation of the
sources), that both Targums are in reality one—that both
were known down to the 14th century under no other name
than Targum Jerushalmi—and that some forgetful scribe
about that time must have taken the abbreviation ת"י—
'T. J.' over one of the two documents, and, instead of dis-
solving it into Targum Jerushalmi, dissolved it erroneously
into what he must till then have been engaged in copying—
viz. Targum-Jonathan, sc. ben Uzziel (on the Prophets).
This error, fostered by the natural tendency of giving a well-

known and far-famed name—without inquiring too closely
into its accuracy—to a hitherto anonymous and comparatively little known version, has been copied again and again,
until it found its way, a hundred years later, into print. Of
the intermediate stage, when only a few MSS. had received
the new designation, a curious fact, which Azariah de Rossi
(Cod. 37 b) mentions, gives evidence. "I saw," he says,
" two complete Targums on the whole Pentateuch, word for
word alike; one in Reggio, which was described in the
margin, 'Targum of Jonathan b. Uzziel;' the other in
Mantua, described at the margin as 'Targum Jerushalmi.'"
In a similar manner quotations from either in the Aruch
confound the designation. Benjamin Mussaphia (d. 1674),
the author of additions and corrections to the Aruch, has
indeed pronounced it as his personal conjecture that both
may be one and the same, and Drusius Mendelssohn, Rappoport, and others shared his opinion. Yet the difficulty of
their obvious dissimilarity, if they were identical, remained
to be accounted for. Zunz tries to solve it by assuming that
Pseudo-Jonathan is the original Targum, and that the fragmentary Jerushalmi is a collection of variants to it. The
circumstance of its also containing portions identical with the
codex, to which it is supposed to be a collection of readings,
he explains by the negligence of the transcriber. Frankel,
however, followed by Traub and Levysohn, has gone a step
further. From the very identity of a proportionately large
number of places, amounting to about thirty in each book,
and from certain palpable and consistent differences which
run through both recensions, they have arrived at a different
conclusion, which seems to carry conviction on the face of it,
viz., that Jerushalmi is a collection of emendations and
additions to single portions, phrases, and words of Onkelos,
and Pseudo-Jonathan a further emendated and completed
edition to the whole Pentateuch of Jerushalmi-Onkelos.
The chief incentive to a new Targum on the Pentateuch
(that of Onkelos being well known in Palestine), was, on the
one hand, the wish to explain such of the passages as seemed
either obscure in themselves or capable of greater adaptation

to the times; and on the other hand the great and paramount desire for legendary lore, and ethical and homiletical motives, intertwined with the very letter of Scripture, did not and could not feel satisfied with the (generally) strictly literal version of Onkelos, as soon as the time of eccentric prolix, oral Targums had finally ceased in Palestine too, and written Targums of Babylon were introduced as a substitute, once for all. Hence variants, exactly as found in Jerushalmi, not to the whole of Onkelos, but to such portions as seemed most to require "improvement" in the direction indicated. And how much this thoroughly paraphrastic version was preferred to the literal is, among other signs, plainly visible from the circumstance that it is still joined, for instance, to the reading of the Decalogue on the Feast of Weeks in the synagogue. At a later period the gaps were filled up, and the whole of the existing Jerushalmi was recast, as far again as seemed fitting and requisite. This is the Jonathan, so called for the last four hundred years only. And thus the identity in some, and the divergence in other places finds its most natural solution.

The Jerushalmi, in both its recensions, is written in the Palestinensian dialect, the peculiarities of which we have briefly characterised above. It is older than the Masora and the conquest of Western Asia by the Arabs. Syria or Palestine must be its birthplace, the second half of the 7th century its date, since the instances above given will not allow of any earlier time. Its chief aim and purpose is, especially in its second edition, to form an entertaining compendium of all the Halachah and Haggadah, which refers to the Pentateuch, and takes its stand upon it. And in this lies its chief use to us. There is hardly a single allegory, parable, mystic digression, or tale in it which is not found in the other Haggadistic writings—Mishnah, Talmud, Mechilta, Sifra, Sifri, &c.; and both Winer and Petermann, not to mention the older authorities, have wrongly charged it with inventing its interpretations. Even where no source can be indicated, the author has surely only given utterance to the leading notions and ideas of his times, extravagant and abstruse as they may oftentimes appear to our modern Western minds. Little value is inherent in its critical emendations on the exegesis of Onkelos. It sometimes endeavours either to find an entirely new signification for a word, and then it often falls into grave errors, or it restores interpretations rejected by Onkelos; but it must never be forgotten that translation is quite a secondary object with Jerushalmi. It adheres, however, to the general method followed by Onkelos and Jonathan. It dissolves similes and widens too concise diction. Geographical names it alters into those current in its own day. It avoids anthropomorphisms as well as anthropopathisms. The strict distinction between the Divine Being and man is kept up, and the word קְדָם "before" is put as a kind of medium between the former and the latter, no less than the other—"Shechinah," "Word," "Glory," &c. It never uses Elohim where the Scripture applies it to man or idols. The same care is taken to extol the good deeds of the people and its ancestors, and to slur over and excuse the evil ones, &c.:—all this, however, in a much more decided and exaggerated form than either in Onkelos or Jonathan. Its language and grammar are very corrupt; it abounds—chiefly in its larger edition, the Pseudo-Jonathan—in Greek, Latin, Persian, and Arabic words; and even making allowances for the many blunders of ignorant scribes, enough will remain to pronounce the diction ungrammatical in very many places.

Thus much briefly of the Jerushalmi as one and the same work. We shall now endeavour to point out a few characteristics belonging to its two recensions respectively. The first, Jerushalmi κατ' ἐξοχήν, knows very little of angels; Michael is the only one ever occurring: in Jonathan, on the other hand, angelology flourishes in great vigour: to the Biblical Michael, Gabriel, Uriel, are added the Angel of Death, Samael, Sagnugael, Shachassai, Usiel; seventy angels descend with God to see the building of the Babylonian tower; nine hundred millions of punishing angels go through Egypt during the night of the Exodus, &c. Jerushalmi makes use but rarely of Halachah and Haggadah, while

2 c

Jonathan sees the text as it were only through the medium of Haggadah: to him the chief end. Hence Jonathan has many Midrashim not found in Jerushalmi, while he does not omit a single one contained in the latter. There are no direct historical dates in Jerushalmi, but many are found in Jonathan, and since all other signs indicate that but a short space of time intervenes between the two, the late origin of either is to a great extent made manifest by these dates. The most striking difference between them, however, and the one which is most characteristic of either, is this, that while Jerushalmi adheres more closely to the language of the Mishnah, Jonathan has greater affinity to that of the Talmud. Of either we subjoin short specimens, which, for the purpose of easier comparison and reference, we have placed side by side with Onkelos. The Targum Jerushalmi was first printed in Bomberg's Bible, Venice, 1518, ff., and was reprinted in Bomberg's edd., and in Walton, vol. iv. Jonathan to the Pentateuch, a MS. of which was first discovered by Ashur Purinz in the Library of the family of the Puahs in Venice, was printed for the first time in 1590, as "Targum Jonathan ben Uzziel," at Venice, reprinted at Hanau, 1618, Amsterdam, 1640, Prague, 1646, Walton, vol. iv., &c.

GENESIS III. 17–24.

AUTHORISED VERSION.	ONKELOS.	TARGUM JERUSHALMI. First Recension.	TARGUM [JONATHAN BEN UZZIEL] JERUSHALMI. Second Recension.
17 AND unto Adam he said, Because thou hast hearkened unto the voice of thy wife, and hast eaten of the tree, of which I commanded thee, saying, Thou shalt not eat of it: cursed *is* the ground for thy sake; in sorrow shalt thou eat *of* it all the days of thy life;	17 AND to Adam he said, For that thou hast accepted the word of thy wife, and hast eaten from the tree of which I have commanded unto thee, and said, Thou shalt not eat from it: cursed shall the earth be for thy sake; with trouble shalt thou eat of it all the days of thy life;	—	17 AND to Adam he said, Because thou hast received the word of thy wife, and hast eaten from the fruit of the tree, of which I commanded thee, Thou shalt not eat from it: cursed be the earth, because it has not shown unto thee thy fault; in sorrow shalt thou eat of it all the days of thy life;
18 Thorns also and thistles shall it bring forth to thee; and thou shalt eat the herb of the field;	18 And thorns and thistles it shall grow for thee; and thou shalt eat the grass of the field;	18 And thorns and thistles shall it multiply for thee; and thou shalt eat the grass that is on the face of the earth. Then began Adam and said, I pray, through the mercy that is before Thee, Jehovah, let us not to accounted before Thee as the beasts that eat the grass on the face of the field: may we be permitted to arise and toil with the toil of our hands, and eat food from the fruits of the earth; and thus may there be a diffe-	18 And thorns and thistles shall grow and multiply for thy sake; and thou shalt eat the grass that is on the face of the field. Adam answered and said, I pray, by the Mercy that is before Thee, Jehovah, that we may not be deemed like unto the beasts, that we should eat the grass that is on the face of the field; may we be allowed to arise and toil with the toiling of our hands, and eat food from the food of the earth, and thus may

2 c 2

AUTHORISED VERSION.	ONKELOS.	TARGUM JERUSHALMI. First Recension.	TARGUM [JONATHAN BEN UZZIEL] JERUSHALMI. Second Recension.
		rence before Thee between the sons of man and the offspring of cattle.	there be a distinction now before Thee, between the sons of men and the offspring of cattle.
19 In the sweat of thy face shalt thou eat bread, till thou return unto the ground; for out of it wast thou taken; for dust thou *art*, and unto dust shalt thou return.	19 In the sweat of thy face shalt thou eat bread, until thou returnest unto the earth from which thou art created; for dust art thou, and to dust shalt thou return.		19 . . In the toil of the palm of thy hand shalt thou eat food, until thou returnest unto the dust from which thou wert created: for dust art thou, and to dust shalt thou return: for from the dust thou wilt once rise to give judgment and account for all that thou hast done, on the day of the great Judgment.
20 And Adam called his wife's name Eve; because she was the mother of all living.	20 And Adam called the name of his wife Chavah; for that she was the mother of all sons of man.		20 And Adam called the name of his wife Chavah; for she is the mother of all the sons of man.
21 Unto Adam also and to his wife did the LORD God make coats of skins, and clothed them.	21 And Jehovah Elohim made unto Adam and his wife garments of glory, on the skin of their flesh, and clothed them.		21 And Jehovah Elohim made unto Adam and his wife garments of honour, from the skin of the serpent which he had cast out of it, on the skin of their flesh, instead of their beauty which they had cast off; and he clothed them.
22 And the LORD God said, Behold, the man is become as	22 And Jehovah Elohim said, Behold Adam is the only one	22 And the Word of Jehovah Elohim said, Lo! man, whom I	22 And Jehovah Elohim said to the angels that were minister-

one of us, to know good and evil: and now, lest he put forth his hand, and take also of the tree of life, and eat, and live for ever:

23 Therefore the LORD God sent him forth from the garden of Eden, to till the ground from whence he was taken.

24 So he drove out the man; and he placed at the east of the garden of Eden Cherubims, [?] and a flaming sword which turned every way, to keep the way of the tree of life.

---

in the world knowing good and evil: perchance now he might stretch forth his hand and take also from the tree of life, and eat, and live for evermore.

23 And Jehovah Elohim sent him from the garden of Eden, to till the earth whence he was created.

24 And he drove out Adam; and he placed before the garden of Eden the Cherubim and the sharp sword, which turns to guard the way to the tree of life.

---

created, is alone in this world, as I am alone in the highest Heavens: mighty nations will spring from him; from him also will arise a people that will know to distinguish between good and evil: now it is better to expel him from the garden of Eden, before he stretch out his hand and take also from the fruits of the tree of life, and eat, and live for ever.

24 And He exelled Adam, and caused to reside the splendour of His Shechinah from the beginning at the east of the garden of Eden, above the two Cherubim. Two thousand years before the world was created, he created the Law, and prepared

---

ing before him, Lo! there is Adam alone on the earth, as I am alone in the highest Heavens, and there will spring from him those who know to distinguish between good and evil: if he had kept the commandment I commanded, he would have been living and lasting, like the tree of life, for evermore. Now since he has not kept what I commanded, We decree against him and expel him from the garden of Eden before he may stretch out his hand and take from the fruits of the tree of life; for if he ate therefrom he would live and remain for ever.

23 And Jehovah Elohim expelled him from the garden of Eden, and he went and he settled on the Mount of Moriah, to till the earth of which he was created.

24 And He drove out Adam from where He had made to reside the glory of His Shechinah from the beginning between the two Cherubim. Before he created the world He has created the Law: He has prepared the garden of Eden for the Righteous,

AUTHORISED VERSION.	ONKELOS.	TARGUM JERUSHALMI. *First Recension.*	TARGUM [Jonathan ben Uzziel] JERUSHALMI. *Second Recension.*
		Gehinnom [Hell] and Gan Eden [Paradise]: He prepared Gan Eden for the Righteous, that they may eat and delight in the fruits of the tree, because they kept the commandments of the Law in this world: and prepared Gehinnom for the wicked, for it is like unto a sharp sword that eats from both sides; He has prepared within it sparks of light and coals which consume the wicked, to punish them in the future world for their not having kept the commandments of the Law. For the tree of life that is the Law; whosoever keeps it in this world, he will live and last like the tree of life: good is the Law to whosoever keeps it in this world, like the fruit of the tree of life in the world to come.	that they shall eat and delight in the fruits of the tree, because they have acted during their life according to the doctrine of the Law in this world, and have kept its commandments: He has prepared the Gehinnom for the wicked, which is likened unto a sharp sword that eats from two sides: He prepared within it sparks of light and coals of fire to judge with them the wicked who rebelled in their lives against the doctrine of the Law. Better is this Law to him who acts according to it than the fruits of the tree of life, for the Word of Jehovah has prepared for him who keeps it, that he shall live and walk in the paths of the way of the life of the future world.

THE LAST CHAPTER OF DEUTERONOMY, v. 1-8.

AUTHORISED VERSION.	ONKELOS.	TARGUM JERUSHALMI. *First Recension.*	TARGUM [JOSATHAN BEN UZZIEL] JERUSHALMI. *Second Recension.*
1 And Moses went up from the plains of Moab unto the mountain of Nebo, to the top of Pisgah, that is over against Jericho. And the LORD showed him all the land of Gilead, unto Dan,	1 And Moses ascended from the encampment of Moab to the mountain of Nebo: the head of the height that is opposite Jericho. And Jehovah showed him all the land of Gilead unto Dan.	1 And Moses ascended from the plain of Moab to the mountain of Nebo, the summit of the hill which is opposite Jericho. And God showed him the whole land: Gilead unto Dan of Cæsarea.	1 And Moses ascended from the plains of Moab to the mountain of Nebo, the summit of the height which is over against Jericho, and the word of Jehovah showed him all the mighty ones of the land: the powerful deeds which Jephtha from Gilead would do, and the victories of Samson the son of Manoah, from the tribe of Dan.
2 And all Naphtali, and the land of Ephraim, and Manasseh, and all the land of Judah, unto the utmost sea,	2 And all Naphtali and the land of Ephraim and Manasseh, and all the land of Judah to the hindmost sea.	2 And all the land of Naphtali, and the land of Ephraim and Manasseh, and the whole land of Judah, to the hindmost sea.	2 And the thousand princes from the house of Naphtali who joined issue with Balak, and the kings whom Joshua the son of Nun from the tribe of Efraim, would kill, and the power of Gideon the son of Joash from the tribe of Manasseh, and all the kings of Israel, and the kingdom of the house of Judah who would rule in the land until the second Sanctuary would be laid low.
			3 And the king of the south

AUTHORISED VERSION.	ONKELOS.	TARGUM JERUSHALMI. *First Recension.*	TARGUM [JONATHAN BEN UZZIEL] JERUSHALMI *Second Recension.*
3 And the south, and the plain of the valley of Jericho, the city of palm trees, unto Zoar.	3 And the west and the plain of the valley of Jericho the city of the palms, unto Zoar.	3 And west, and the plain of the valley of Jericho the city which produces the palms, that is Zeĕr.	who would join the king of the north to destroy the inhabitants of the land, and the Ammonites and Moabites, the inhabitants of the valleys who would oppress Israel, and the exile of the disciples of Elija who would be driven out from the plain of Jericho, and the exile of the disciples of Elisha who would be driven out from the city of palms by their brethren, the house of Israel; two hundred thousand men. And the woes of each generation and the punishment of *Armalgus* [Armillus] the evil one and the battle-array of Gog. And in this great misery Michael will arise with the sword: to save, &c.

V. TARGUMS OF "JOSEPH THE BLIND" ON THE HAGIOGRAPHA.

"When Jonathan ben Uzziel began to paraphrase the Cethubim " (Hagiographa), we read in the Talmudical passage before quoted, "a mysterious voice was heard saying: It is enough. Thou hast revealed the secrets of the Prophets—why wouldst thou also reveal those of the Holy Ghost?" It would thus appear, that a Targum to these books (Job excepted) was entirely unknown up to a very late period. Those Targums on the Hagiographa which we now possess have been attributed vaguely to different authors, it being assumed in the first instance that they were the work of one man. Now it was Akylas the Greek translator, mentioned in Bereshith Rabba (see above); now Onkelos, the Chaldee translator of the Pentateuch, his mythical double; now Jonathan b. Uzziel, or Joseph (Jose) the Blind (see above). But the diversity in the different parts of the work warring too palpably against the unity of authorship, the blindness of the last-named authority seemed to show the easiest way out of the difficulty. Joseph was supposed to have dictated it to different disciples at different periods, and somehow every one of the amanuenses infused part of his own individuality into his share of the work. Popular belief thus fastened upon this Joseph the Blind, since a name the work must needs have, and to him in most of the editions, the Targum is affiliated. Yet, if ever he did translate the Hagiographa, certain it is that those which we possess are not by his or his disciples' hands—that is, of the time of the fourth century. Writers of the thirteenth century already refuted this notion of Joseph's authorship, for the assumption of which there never was any other ground than that he was mentioned in the Talmud, like Onkelos-Akylas and Jonathan, in connection with Targum; and, as we saw, there is indeed reason to believe that he had a share in the redaction of "Jonathan" to the Prophets, which falls in his time. Between him and our hagiographical Targums, however, many centuries must have

elapsed. Yet we do not even venture to assign to them
more than an approximate round date, about 1000 A.D.
Besides the Targums to the Pentateuch and the Prophets,
those now extant range over Psalms, Proverbs, Job, the five
Megilloth, *i. e.* Song of Songs, Ruth, Lamentations, Esther,
Ecclesiastes; the Chronicles and Daniel. Ezra and Nehemiah alone are left without a Targum at present; yet we
can hardly help believing that ere long one will also be
found to the latter, as the despaired-of Chronicles was found
in the seventeenth century, and Daniel—a sure trace of it at
least, so recently, that as yet nobody has considered it worth
his while to take any notice of it. We shall divide these
Targums into four groups: Proverbs, Job, Psalms;—Megilloth;—Chronicles;—and Daniel.

1. TARGUM ON PSALMS, JOB, PROVERBS.

Certain linguistic and other characteristics [1] exhibited by
these three Targums, lead to the conclusion that they are
nearly contemporaneous productions, and that their birthplace is, most likely, Syria. While the two former, however, are mere paraphrases, the Targum on Proverbs comes
nearer to our idea of a version than almost any Targum,
except perhaps that of Onkelos. It adheres as closely to
the original text as possible. The most remarkable feature
about it, however, and one which has given rise to endless
speculations and discussions, is its extraordinary similarity
to the Syriac Version. It would indeed sometimes seem as
if they had copied each other—an opinion warmly advocated
by Dathe, who endeavoured to prove that the Chaldee had
copied or adapted the Syrian, there being passages in the
Targum which could, he assumed, only be accounted for by

---

[1] *e. g.* The use of the word אַנְגְּלֵי
for angel in Targ. Ps. and Job, the
ב, affixed to the 3rd p. plur. præf. Peal, the infin. with præf. מ, besides
several more or less unusual Greek and
Syriac words common to all three.

a misunderstanding of the Syriac translation.[1] It has, on the other hand, been argued that there are a greater number of important passages which distinctly show that the Targumist had used an original Hebrew text, varying from that of the Syriac, and had also made use of the LXX. against the latter.[2] The Syriasms would easily be accounted for by the Aramaic idiom itself, the forms of which vary but little from, and easily merge into, the sister dialect of Syria. Indeed nearly all of them are found in the Talmud, a strictly Aramaic work. It has been supposed by others that neither of these versions, as they are now in our hands, exhibit their original form. A late editor, as it were, of the (mutilated) Targum, might have derived his emendations from that version which came nearest to it, both in language and in close adherence to the Hebrew text—viz., the Syriac; and there is certainly every reason to conclude from the woefully faulty state in which this Targum is found (Luzzatto counts several hundred corrupt readings in it), that many and clumsy hands must have been at work upon the later Codices. The most likely solution of the difficulty, however, seems to be. that indicated by Frankel—viz., that the LXX. is the common source of both versions, but in such a manner that the Aramaic has also made use of the Hebrew and the Greek—of the latter, however, through the Syriac medium. As a specimen of the curious similarity of both versions, the following two verses from the beginning of the book may find a place here :—

---

[1] e.g., ch. xxix. 5, the Heb. word קִרְיָה, "a city," is rendered ܩܰܪܬܳܐ, "city," in Syr. Targum translates כדבא, "a lie," which is only to be accounted for by a misunderstanding or misreading of the Syriac ܟܰܕܒܳܐ, where for the second c the Chaldee translator read a b, ܟܰܕܒܳܐ.

[2] Prov. xxvi. 10, the Masoretic text reads: רַב מְחוֹלֵל כֹּל וְשֹׂכֵר כְּסִיל;

LXX. πολλὰ χειμάζεται σὰρξ ἀφρόνων (= בְּשַׂר כְּסִיל); Targ. סני חיש בשרא דסיכלא; thus adopting exactly the reading of the LXX. against the received text: xxix. 21, מפנק מנער עבדו, quoted in the same manner in Talm. Succah. 52 b; LXX. ὃς κατασπαταλᾷ ἐκ παιδὸς οἰκέτης ἔσται; evidently reading עבד יהיה = Targ. לעברא נהוי. Comp. also xxvii. 16, xxx. 30, &c.

CHAP. I. 2–3.

TARGUM (Ver. 2).

למדע חכמתא ומרדותא
לאתבין אמרי ביונתא·

Ver. 3.

למקבלא מרדותא דשוכלא
וצדקתא ודינא ותריצותא·

SYR. (Ver. 2).

ܠܡܕܥ ܚܟܡܬܐ ܘܡܪܕܘܬܐ
ܘܠܡܣܬܟܠܘ ܡܠܠ ܘܒܘܢܐ

Ver. 3.

ܘܠܡܩܒܠܘ ܡܪܕܘܬܐ ܘܣܟܠܘ
ܘܙܕܩܬܐ ܘܕܝܢܐ ܘܬܪܝܨܘܬܐ.

Compare also vers. 5, 6, 8, 10, 12, 13 ; ch. ii. vers. 9, 10, 13–15 ; iii. 2–9, &c.

We must not omit to observe that no early Jewish commentator — Rashi, Ibn Ezra, &c. — mentions the Targum either to Proverbs, or to Job and Psalms. Nathan ben Jechiel (twelfth century) is the first who quotes it.

Respecting the two latter Targums of this group, Psalms and Job, it is to be observed that they are, more or less, mere collections of fragments. That there must have existed paraphrases to Job at a very early period follows from the Talmudical passages which we quoted in the introduction— nay, we almost feel inclined to assume that this book, considered by the learned as a mere allegory (" Job never was, and never was created," is the dictum found in the Talmud, Baba Bathra, 15 a: i.e. he never had any real existence, but is a poetical, though sacred, invention), opened the list of written paraphrases. How much of the primitive version is embodied in the one which we possess it is of course next to impossible to determine, more especially in the state of infancy in which the investigation of the Targums as yet remains. So much, however, is palpable, that the Targums

of both Psalms and Job in their present shape contain relics
of different authors in different times: some paraphrasts,
some strictly translators. Very frequently a second version
of the same passage is introduced by the formula תרגום אחר,
"another Targum," and varies most widely from its predecessor; while, more especially in the Psalms, a long series
of chapters translated literally, is followed by another series
translated in the wildest and most fanciful character. The
Cod. Erpen. still exhibits these various readings, as such,
side by side, on its margin; thence, however, they have in
our printed editions found their way into the text. How
much of these variants, or of the entire text, belongs to the
Palestinian Cycles, which may well have embraced the
whole Torah:—or whether they are to be considered exclusively the growth of later times, and have thus but a very
slender connection with either the original Babylonian or
the Palestinian Targum-works, future investigation must
determine.

The most useful in this group is naturally the Targum on
Proverbs, it being the one which translates most closely, or
rather the only one which does *translate* at all. Besides the
explanation it gives of difficult passages in the text, its
peculiar affinity to the Syriac Version naturally throws some
light upon both, and allows of emendations in and through
either. As to Job and Psalms, their chief use lies in their
showing the gradual dying stages of the idiom in which
they are written, and also in their being in a manner guides
to the determination of the date of certain stages of Haggadah.

2, 3. TARGUMS ON THE FIVE MEGILLOTH.

These Targums are likewise not mentioned before the
twelfth century, when the Aruch quotes them severally:—
although Esther must have been translated at a very early
period, since the Talmud already mentions a Targum on it.
Of this, we need hardly add, no trace is found in our present
Targum. The freedom of a "version" can go no further

than it does in these Targums on the Megilloth.   They are,
in fact, mere Haggadah, and bear the most striking resemblance to the Midrash on the respective books.   Curiously
enough, the gradual preponderance of the Paraphrase over
the text is noticeable in the following order: Ruth, Lamentations, Ecclesiastes, Esther, Song of Songs.   The latter is
fullest to overflowing of those "*nugæ atque frivolitates,*"
which have so sorely tried the temper of the wise and grave.
Starting from the almost comical notion that all they found
in the books of Mohammedanism and of Judaism, of Rome
and of Greece, if it seemed to have any reference to "Religio," however unsupported, and however plainly bearing
the stamp of poetry—good or bad—on its face, must needs
be a religious creed, and the creed forced upon every single
believer :—they could not but get angry with mere "day-
dreams" being interspersed with the sacred literature of the
Bible.   Delitzsch, a scholar of our generation, says of the
Targums in general that "history becomes in them most
charming, most instructive poetry; but this poetry is not
the invention, the phantasma of the writer, but the old and
popular venerable tradition or legend . . . . the Targums
are poetical, both as to their contents and form" (*Gesch. d.
Jüd. Poesie,* p. 27): and further, "The wealth of legend in
its gushing fullness did not suffer any formal bounds; legend
bursts upon legend, like wave upon wave, not to be dammed
in even by any poetical forms.   Thus the Jerusalem Targum in its double Recensions [to the Pentateuch], and the
Targums on the five Megilloth are the most beautiful
national works of art, through which there runs the golden
thread of Scripture, and which are held together only by
the unity of the idea" (p. 135).   Although we do not share
Delitzsch's enthusiasm to the full extent, yet we cannot but
agree with him that there are, together with stones and
dust, many pearls of precious price to be gathered from
these much despised, because hardly known, books.

The dialect of these books occupies the mean between the
East and West Aramæan, and there is a certain unity of
style and design about all the five books, which fully justifies

the supposition that they are, one and all, the work of one author. It may be that, taken in an inverted series, they mark the successive stages of a poet's life; glowing, rapturous, overflowing in the first; stately, sober, prosy in the last. As to the time of its writing or editing, we have again to repeat, that it is most uncertain, but unquestionably belongs to a period much later than the Talmud. The Book of Esther, enjoying both through its story-like form and the early injunction of its being read or heard by every one on the feast of Purim, a great circulation and popularity, has been targumised many times, and besides the one embodied in the five Megilloth, there are two more extant (*not three*, as generally stated: the so-called third being only an abbreviation of the first), which are called respectively the first: a short one without digressions, and the second— (*Targum sheni*): a larger one, belonging to the Palestinian Cycle. The latter Targum is a collection of Eastern romances, broken up and arranged to the single verses: of gorgeous hues and extravagant imagination, such as are to be met with in the Adshaib or Chamis, or any Eastern collection of legends and tales.

VI. TARGUM ON THE BOOK OF CHRONICLES.

This Targum was unknown, as we said before, up to a very recent period. In 1680, it was edited for the first time from an Erfurt MS. by M. F. Beck, and in 1715 from a more complete as well as correct MS. at Cambridge, by D. Wilkins. The name of Hungary occurring in it, and its frequent use of the Jerusalem-Targum to the Pentateuch, amounting sometimes to simple copying (comp. the Genealogical Table in chap. i., &c.), show sufficiently that its author is neither "Jonathan b. Uzziel" nor "Joseph the Blind," as has been suggested. But the language, style, and the Haggadah with which it abounds, point to a late period and to Palestine as the place where it was written. Its use must be limited to philological, historical, and geographical studies; the science of exegesis will profit little by it. The first edition appeared under the title *Paraphrasis Chaldaica libr. Chronicorum*, cura M. F. Beckii, 2 tom. Aug. Vind. 1680–83, 4to; the second by D. Wilkins, *Paraphrasis . . . . auctore R. Josepho*, &c. Amst. 1715, 4to. The first edition has the advantage of a large number of very learned notes, the second that of a comparatively more correct and complete text.

VII. THE TARGUM TO DANIEL.

It is for the first time that this Targum, for the non-existence of which many and weighty reasons were given (that the date of the Messiah's arrival was hidden in it, among others), is here formally introduced into the regular rank and file of Targums, although it has been known for now more than five-and-twenty years. Munk found it, not indeed in the Original Aramaic, but in what appears to him to be an extract of it written in Persian. The MS. (Anc. Fond, No. 45, Imp. Library) is inscribed "History of Daniel," and has retained only the first words of the Original, which it translates likewise into Persian. This language is then retained throughout.

After several legends known from other Targums, follows a long prophecy of Daniel, from which the book is shown to have been written after the first Crusade. Mohammed and his successors are mentioned, also a king who coming from Europe (אז רומיאן) will go to Damascus, and kill the Ishmaelitic (Mohammedan) kings and princes; he will break down the minarets (מנארה), destroy the mosques (מסגדהא), and no one will after that dare to pronounce the name of the Profane (פסול = Mohammed). The Jews will also have to suffer great misfortunes (as indeed the knightly Crusaders won their spurs by dastardly murdering the helpless masses, men, women, and children, in the Ghettos along the Rhine and elsewhere, before they started to deliver the Holy tomb). By a sudden transition the Prophet then passes on to the "Messiah, the Son of Joseph," Gog and Magog, and to the "true Messiah, the Son of David." Munk rightly concludes that the book must have been composed in the twelfth century, when Christian kings reigned for a brief period over Jerusalem (*Notice sur Saadia*, Par. 1838).

VIII. There is also a Chaldee translation extant of the apocryphal pieces of Esther, which, entirely lying apart from our task, we confine ourselves to mention without further entering into the subject. De Rossi has published them with Notes and Dissertations. Tübingen, 1783, 8vo.

FURTHER FRAGMENTS OF THE PALESTINIAN TARGUM.

Besides the complete books belonging to the Palestinian Cycle of Targum which we have mentioned, and the portions of it intersected as "Another Reading," "Another Targum," into the Babylonian Versions, there are extant several independent fragments of it. Nor need we as yet despair of finding still further portions, perhaps one day to see it restored entirely. There is all the more hope for this, as the Targum has not been lost very long yet. Abudraham quotes the Targum Jerushalmi to *Samuel* (i. 9, 13). Kimchi has preserved several passages from it to *Judges* (xi. 1, consisting of 47 words); to *Samuel* (i. 17, 18: 106 words); and *Kings* (i. 22, 21: 68 words; ii. 4, 1: 174 words; iv. 6: 55 words; iv. 7: 72 words; xiii. 21: 9 words), under the simple name of Toseftah, *i.e.* Addition, or Additional Targum. Luzzatto has also lately found fragments of the same, under the names "Targum of Palestine," "Targum of Jerushalmi," "Another Reading," &c., in an African Codex written 5247 A.M. = 1487 A.D., viz. to 1 Sam. xviii. 19; 2 Sam. xii. 12; 1 Kings v. 9, v. 11, v. 13, x. 18, x. 26, xiv. 13; to Hosea i. 1; Obad. i. 1.—To Isaiah, Rashi (*Isaaki*, not as people still persist in calling him, *Jarchi*), Abudraham and Farissol quote it: and a fragment of the Targum to this prophet is extant in Cod. Urbin. Vatican No. 1, containing about 120 words, and beginning: "Prophecy of Isaiah, which he prophesied at the end of his prophecy in the days of Manasseh the Son of Hezekiah the King of the Tribe of the House of Judah on the 17th of Tamuz in the hour when Manasseh set up an idol in the Temple," &c. Isaiah predicts in this his own violent death. Parts of this Targum are also found in Hebrew, in Pesiktah Rabbathi 6 *a*, and Yalkut Isa. 58 *d*. A Jerusalem Targum to Jeremiah is mentioned by Kimchi; to Ezekiel by R. Simeon, Nathan (Aruch), and likewise by Kimchi, who also speaks of a further additional Targum to Jonathan for this Book. A "Targum-Jerushalmi" to Micah is known to Rashi, and of Zechariah a fragment has been published in Bruns (Repert. pt. 15, p. 174) from a Reuchlinian MS. (Cod. 354, Kennic. 25), written 1106. The passage, found as a marginal gloss to Zech. xii. 10, reads as follows:—

"Targum Jerushalmi. And I shall pour out upon the House of David and the inhabitants of Jerusalem the spirit of prophecy and of prayer for truth. And after this shall go forth Messiah the Son of Efraim to wage war against Gog. And Gog will kill him before the city of Jerushalaim. They will look up to me and they will ask me wherefore the heathens have killed Messiah the Son of Efraim. They will then mourn over him as mourn father and mother over an only son, and they will wail over him as one wails over a firstborn."— A Targum Jerushalmi to the third chapter of *Habakkuk*, quoted by Rashi, is mentioned by de Rossi (Cod. 265 and 405, both thirteenth century). It has been suggested that a Targum Jerushalmi on the Prophets only existed to the Haftarahs, which had at one time been translated perhaps, like the portion from the Law, in public; but we have seen that entire books, not to mention single chapters, possessed a Palestinian Targum, which never were intended or used for the purpose of Haftarah. And there is no reason to doubt that the origin of this Targum to the Prophets is precisely similar to, and perhaps contemporaneous with, that which we traced to that portion which embraces the Pentateuch. The Babylonian Version, the "Jonathan" Targum, though paraphrastic, did not satisfy the apparently more imaginative Palestinian public. Thus

from heaped-up additions and marginal glosses, the step to
a total re-writing of the entire Codex in the manner and
taste of the later times and the different locality, was easy
enough. From a critique of the work as such, however, we
must naturally keep aloof, as long as we have only the few
specimens named to judge from. But its general spirit and
tendency are clear enough. So is also the advantage to
which even the minimum that has survived may some day
be put by the student of Midrashic literature, as we have
briefly indicated above.

We cannot conclude without expressing the hope—probably a vain one—that linguistic studies may soon turn in
the direction of that vast and most interesting, as well as
important, Aramaic literature, of which the Targums form
but a small item.

The writer finally begs to observe that the translations of
all the passages quoted from Talmud and Midrash, as well
as the specimens from the Targum, have been made by him
directly from the respective originals.

XVI.

ON THE SAMARITAN PENTATEUCH.[1]

THE Samaritan Pentateuch, a Recension of the commonly received Hebrew Text of the Mosaic Law, in use with the Samaritans, was written in the ancient Hebrew (*Ibri*), or so-called Samaritan character.[2] This recension is found vaguely quoted by some of the early Fathers of the Church, under the name of " Παλαιότατον Ἐβραϊκὸν τὸ παρὰ Σαμαρείταις," in contradistinction to the "Ἐβραϊκὸν τὸ παρὰ Ἰουδαίοις;". further, as "Samaritanorum Volumina," &c. Thus Origen on Num. xiii. 1, ... "ἃ καὶ αὐτὰ ἐκ τούτων Σαμαρειτῶν Ἐβραϊκοῦ μετεβάλομεν;" and on Num. xxi. 13, . . . "ἃ ἐν μόνοις τῶν Σαμαρειτῶν εὕρομεν," &c. Jerome, Prol. to Kings: "Samaritani etiam Pentateuchum Moysis *totidem*" (? 22, like the "Hebrews, Syrians and Chaldæans") "litteris habent, figuris tantum et apicibus discrepantes." Also on Gal. iii. 10, "quam ob causam"—(viz. Ἐπικατάρατος πᾶς ὃς οὐκ ἐμμένει ἐν πᾶσι τοῖς γεγραμμένοις, being quoted there from Deut. xxvii. 26, where the Masoretic text has only ארור אשר לא יקים את דברי התורה הזאת—"cursed be he that confirmeth not[3] the words of this Law to do them;" while the LXX. reads πᾶς ἄνθρωπος . . . πᾶσι τοῖς λόγοις)—"quam ob causam Samaritanorum Hebræa volumina relegens inveni כל scriptum esse;" and he forthwith charges the Jews with having deliberately taken out the כל , because they did not

---

[1] From Dr. Wm. Smith's 'Dictionary of the Bible,' Vol. II.

[2] כתב עברית, רעץ, ליבונאה, as distinguished from כתב אשורית, עזרא. Comp. Synh. 21 *b*, Jer. Meg. 5, 2; Tosifta Synh. 4; Synhedr. 22 *a*, Meg. Jer. 1, 9, Sota Jer. 7, 2, sq.

[3] The A. V., following the LXX., and perhaps Luther, has inserted the word *all*.

wish to be bound *individually* to *all* the ordinances: forgetting at the same time that this same כל occurs in the
very next chapter of the Masoretic text (Deut. xxviii. 15):—
"*All* his commandments and his statutes." Eusebius of
Cæsarea observes that the LXX. and the Sam. Pent. agree
against the Received Text in the number of years from the
Deluge to Abraham. Cyril of Alexandria speaks of certain
words (Gen. iv. 8), wanting in the Hebrew, but found in the
Samaritan. The same remark is made by Procopius of Gaza
with respect to Deut. i. 6; Num. x. 10, x. 9, &c. Other passages are noticed by Diodorus, the Greek Scholiast, &c. The
Talmud, on the other hand, mentions the Sam. Pent. distinctly and contemptuously as a clumsily forged record:
"*You have falsified*[1] *your Pentateuch*," said R. Eliezer b.
Shimon to the Samaritan scribes, with reference to a passage
in Deut. xi. 30, where the well-understood word Shechem
was gratuitously inserted after " the plains of Moreh,"—" and
you have not profited aught by it" (comp. *Jer. Sotah* 21 *b*,
cf. 17; *Babli* 33 *b*). On another occasion they are ridiculed
on account of their ignorance of one of the simplest rules of
Hebrew grammar, displayed in their Pentateuch; viz. the
use of the ה locale (unknown, however, according to *Jer.
Meg.* 6, 2, also to the people of Jerusalem). "*Who has caused
you to blunder?*" said R. Shimon b. Eliezer to them; referring
to their abolition of the Mosaic ordinance of marrying the
deceased brother's wife (Deut. xxv. 5 ff.),—through a mis-
interpretation of the passage in question, which enjoins that
the wife of the dead man shall not be " without " to a stranger,
but that the brother should marry her: they, however, taking
החוצה (= לחוץ) to be an epithet of אשת, "wife," translated
"the *outer wife*," i. e. the *betrothed* only (*Jer. Jebam.* 3; 2,
Ber. R., &c.).

Down to within the last two hundred and fifty years, however, no copy of this divergent Code of Laws had reached
Europe, and it began to be pronounced a fiction, and the
plain words of the Church-Fathers—the better known autho-

---

[1] זייפתם.

rities—who quoted it, were subjected to subtle interpretations.
Suddenly, in 1616, Pietro della Valle, one of the first dis-
coverers also of the Cuneiform inscriptions, acquired a complete Codex from the Samaritans in Damascus. In 1623 it
was presented by Achille Harley de Sancy to the Library of
the Oratory in Paris, and in 1628 there appeared a brief
description of it by J. Morinus in his preface to the Roman
text of the LXX. Three years later, shortly before it was
published in the Paris Polyglott,—whence it was copied,
with few emendations from other codices, by Walton—
Morinus, the first editor, wrote his *Exercitationes Ecclesiasticæ
in utrumque Samaritanorum Pentateuchum*, in which he pronounced the newly found Codex, with all its innumerable
Variants from the Masoretic text, to be infinitely superior to
the latter: in fact, the unconditional and speedy emendation
of the Received Text thereby was urged most authoritatively.
And now the impulse was given to one of the fiercest and
most barren literary and theological controversies: of which
more anon. Between 1620 and 1630 six additional copies,
partly complete, partly incomplete, were acquired by Ussher:
five of which he deposited in English libraries, while one
was sent to De Dieu, and has disappeared mysteriously.
Another Codex, now in the Ambrosian Library at Milan,
was brought to Italy in 1621. Peiresc procured two more,
one of which was placed in the Royal Library of Paris, and
one in the Barberini at Rome. Thus the number of MSS.
in Europe gradually grew to sixteen. During the present
century another, but very fragmentary copy, was acquired
by the Gotha Library. A copy of the entire (?) Pentateuch,
with Targum (? Sam. Version), in parallel columns, 4to, on
parchment, was brought from *Náblus* by Mr. Grove in 1861,
for the Count of Paris, in whose library it is. Single portions
of the Sam. Pent., in a more or less defective state, are now
of no rare occurrence in Europe.

Respecting the external condition of these MSS., it may
be observed that their sizes vary from 12mo to folio, and
that no scroll, such as the Jews and the Samaritans use in
their synagogues, is to be found among them. The letters,

which are of a size corresponding to that of the book, exhibit none of those varieties of shape so frequent in the Masor. Text; such as majuscules, minuscules, suspended, inverted letters, &c. Their material is vellum or cotton-paper; the ink used is black in all cases save the scroll used by the Samaritans at *Náblus*, the letters of which are in gold. There are neither vowels, accents, nor diacritical points. The individual words are separated from each other by a dot. Greater or smaller divisions of the text are marked by two dots placed one above the other, and by an asterisk. A small line above a consonant indicates a peculiar meaning of the word, an unusual form, a passive, and the like : it is, in fact, a contrivance to bespeak attention.[1] The whole Pentateuch is divided into nine hundred and sixty-four paragraphs, or *Kazzin*, the termination of which is indicated by these figures, $=$ $\therefore$ or $<$. At the end of each book the number of its divisions is stated thus :—

(250)	הזה ספר הראשון: קצין מאתים ונ				[Masoret. Cod., 12 Sidras (Parshioth), 50 Chapters].				
(200)	מאתים	„	השני	„	„	[	„ 11 „	40	„]
(130)	מאה ושלושים	„	השלישי	„	„	[	„ 10 „	27	„]
(218)	ר . ויח	„	הרביעי	„	„	[	„ 10 „	36	„]
(166)	ק . וסו	„	החמישי	„	„	[	„ 11 „	34	„]

The Sam. Pentateuch is halved in Lev. vii. 15 (viii. 8, in Hebrew Text), where the words "Middle of the Thorah"[2] are found. At the end of each MS. the year of the copying, the name of the scribe, and also that of the proprietor, are usually stated. Yet their dates are not always trustworthy when given, and very difficult to be conjectured when entirely omitted, since the Samaritan letters afford no internal evidence of the period in which they were written. To none of the MSS., however, which have as yet reached Europe, can be assigned a higher date than the 10th Christian century. The scroll used in *Náblus* bears—so the Samaritans pretend—the following inscription :—"I, Abisha, son of Pinehas, son of Eleazar, son of Aaron the Priest,—upon them be the

---

[1] דָּבָר. עַד and עַד and הִנֵּה. הִנֵּה and דְּבַר. אֵל and אַל. יָאכַל and יָאכֵל, and יִקְרָא. שֶׁ and שְׁ, the suffixes יִקְרָא and קְרָא at the end of a word, the ה without a dagesh, &c., are thus pointed out to the reader.

[2] פלנא דארהותא.

Grace of Jehovah! To His honour have I written this Holy
Law at the entrance of the Tabernacle of Testimony on the
Mount Gerizim, Beth El, in the thirteenth year of the taking
possession of the Land of Canaan, and all its boundaries
around it, by the Children of Israel. I praise Jehovah."
(Letter of Meshalmah b. Ab Sechuah, Cod. 19,791, Add.
MSS. Brit. Mus. Comp. *Epist. Sam. Sichemitarum ad Jobum
Ludolphum*, Cizæ, 1688; *Antiq. Eccl. Orient.* p. 123; Hunt-
ingtoni *Epist.* pp. 49, 56; Eichhorn's *Repertorium f. bibl. und
morg. Lit.*, tom. ix., &c.) But no European[1] has ever succeeded in finding it in this scroll, however great the pains
bestowed upon the search (comp. Eichhorn, *Einleit.* ii. 132);
and even if it had been found, it would not have deserved the
slightest credence.

We have briefly stated above that the *Exercitationes* of
Morinus, which placed the Samaritan Pentateuch far above
the Received Text in point of genuineness,—partly on
account of its agreeing in many places with the Septuagint,
and partly on account of its superior "lucidity and harmony,"
—excited and kept up for nearly two hundred years one of
the most extraordinary controversies on record. Characteristically enough, however, this was set at rest once for all
by the very first systematic investigation of the point at
issue. It would now appear as if the unquestioning rapture
with which every new literary discovery was formerly hailed,
the innate animosity against the Masoretic (Jewish) Text,
the general preference for the LXX., the defective state of
Semitic studies,—as if, we say, all these put together were
not sufficient to account for the phenomenon that men of any
critical acumen could for one moment not only place the

---

[1] It would appear, however (see
Archdeacon Tattam's notice in the
Parthenon, No. 4, May 24, 1862) that
Mr. Levysohn, a person lately attached
to the Russian staff in Jerusalem, *has*
found the inscription in question
"going through the middle of the body
of the Text of the Decalogue, and
extending through three columns."
Considering that the Samaritans themselves told Huntington, "that this inscription had been in their scroll once,
but must have been erased by some
wicked hand," this startling piece of
information must be received with
extreme caution:—no less so than the
other more or less vague statements
with respect to the labours and pretended discoveries of Mr. Levysohn.
See note, p. 426.

Sam. Pent. on a par with the Masoretic Text, but even raise
it, unconditionally, far above it. There was indeed another
cause at work, especially in the first period of the dispute:
it was a controversial spirit which prompted Morinus and
his followers, Cappellus and others, to prove to the Reformers
what kind of value was to be attached to *their* authority:
the received form of the Bible, upon which and which alone
they professed to take their stand;—it was now evident that
nothing short of the Divine Spirit, under the influence and
inspiration of which the Scriptures were interpreted and
expounded by the Roman Church, could be relied upon. On
the other hand, most of the "*Antimorinians*"—De Muys,
Hottinger, St. Morinus, Buxtorf, Fuller, Leusden, Pfeiffer,
&c.—instead of patiently and critically examining the subject and refuting their adversaries by arguments which were
within their reach, as they are within ours, directed their
attacks against the persons of the Morinians, and thus their
misguided zeal left the question of the superiority of the New
Document over the Old where they found it. Of higher
value were, it is true, the labours of Simon, Le Clerc, Walton,
&c., at a later period, who proceeded eclectically, rejecting
many readings, and adopting others which seemed preferable
to those of the Old Text. Houbigant, however, with unexampled ignorance and obstinacy, returned to Morinus's first
notion—already generally abandoned—of the unquestionable
and thorough superiority. He, again, was followed more or
less closely by Kennicott, Al. a St. Aquilino, Lobstein,
Geddes, and others. The discussion was taken up once more
on the other side, chiefly by Ravius, who succeeded in finally
disposing of this point of the superiority (*Exercitt. Phil. in
Houbig. Prol.* Lugd. Bat. 1755). It was from his day forward allowed, almost on all hands, that the Masoretic Text
was the genuine one, but that in doubtful cases, when the
Samaritan had an "unquestionably clearer" reading, this
was to be adopted, since a certain amount of value, however
limited, did attach to it. Michaelis, Eichhorn, Bertholdt,
Jahn, and the majority of modern critics, adhered to this
opinion. Here the matter rested until 1815, when Gesenius

(De Pent. Sam. Origine, Indole et Auctoritate) abolished the
remnant of the authority of the Sam. Pent. So masterly,
lucid, and clear are his arguments and his proofs, that there
has been and will be no further question as to the absence of
all value in this Recension, and in its pretended emendations.
In fact, a glance at the systematic arrangement of the
variants, of which he first of all bethought himself, is quite
sufficient to convince the reader at once that they are for the
most part mere blunders, arising from an imperfect knowledge of the first elements of grammar and exegesis; and that
others owe their existence to a studied design of conforming
certain passages to the Samaritan mode of thought, speech,
and faith—more especially to show that the Mount Gerizim,
upon which their temple stood, was *the* spot chosen and
indicated by God to Moses as the one upon which He desired
to be worshipped.[1]   Finally, that others are due to a tendency
towards removing, as well as linguistic shortcomings would
allow, all that seemed obscure or in any way doubtful, and
towards filling up all apparent imperfections:—either by
repetitions or by means of newly-invented and badly-fitting
words and phrases.   It must, however, be premised that,
except two alterations (Ex. xiii. 7, where the Sam. reads
"*Six* days shalt thou eat unleavened bread," instead of the
received "*Seven* days," and the change of the word תהיה,
"There shall not *be*," into תחיה, "*live*," Deut. xxiii. 18), the
Mosaic laws and ordinances themselves are nowhere tampered
with.

We will now proceed to lay specimens of these once so
highly prized variants before the reader, in order that he
may judge for himself.   We shall follow in this the commonly
received arrangement of Gesenius, who divides all these
readings into eight classes; to which, as we shall afterwards
show, Frankel has suggested the addition of two or three
others, while Kirchheim (in his Hebrew work כרמי שומרון)
enumerates thirteen,[2] which we will name hereafter.

---

[1] For יבחר, "He *will* elect" (the spot), the Sam. always puts בחר, "He
has elected" (viz. Gerizim).   See below.

[2] יב" שערים must be a misprint.

1. The *first* class, then, consists of readings by which emendations of a grammatical nature have been attempted.

(*a.*) The quiescent letters, or so-called *matres lectionis*, are supplied.[1]

(*b.*) The more poetical forms of the pronouns, probably less known to the Sam., are altered into the more common ones.[2]

(*c.*) The same propensity for completing apparently incomplete forms is noticeable in the flexion of the verbs. The apocopated or short future is altered into the regular future.[3]

(*d.*) On the other hand the paragogical letters ן and י at the end of nouns, are almost universally struck out by the Sam. corrector;[4] and, in the ignorance of the existence of nouns of a common gender, he has given them genders according to his fancy.[5]

(*e.*) The infin. absol. is, in the quaintest manner possible, reduced to the form of the finite verb.[6]

For obsolete or rare forms, the modern and more common ones have been substituted in a great number of places.[7]

---

[1] Thus יָם is found in the Samar. for סֹ־ of the Masoretic T.; ות for ־ת; מאורות for אֵלֶהֶם; יו for ־ן; אֲלֵיהֶם for מָאֹרֹת, &c.; sometimes a ו is put even where the Heb. T. has, in accordance with the grammatical rules, only a short vowel or a sheva:—חופַנִיו is found for חָפְנָיו; אָנִיוֹת for אֳנִיּוֹת.

[2] אֲנַחְנוּ, הָאֵל, הֵם, נַחְנוּ, become הָאֵלֶּה, חֵמָּה.

[3] וַתֵּגַד becomes וַתַּגִּיד; וַיָּמָת is emendated into וַיָּמוּת; יְרֵא (verb ל״ה) into יִרְאֶה; the final ן—of the 3rd pers. fem. plur. fut. into נָה. שׁוֹכֻוֹי is shortened into חִיתוּ, שׁוּכֵן into חַיִת.

[4] Masculine are made the words לֶחֶם (Gen. xlix. 20), שַׁעַר (Deut. xv. 7, &c.), מַהֲנֶה (Gen. xxxii. 9); feminine the words אֶרֶץ (Gen. xiii. 6), דֶּרֶךְ (Deut. xxviii. 25), נֶפֶשׁ (Gen. xlvi. 25, &c.); wherever the word נַעַר occurs in the sense of "girl," a ה is added at the end (Gen. xxiv. 14, &c.).

[5] וַיָּשֻׁבוּ הָלוֹךְ וָשׁוֹב, "the waters returned *continually*," is transformed into וַיָּשׁוּבוּ הָלְכוּ וַיָּשֻׁבוּ, "they returned, they went and they returned" (Gen. viii. 3). Where the infin. is used as an adverb. *e. g.* הַרְחֵק (Gen. xxi. 16), "far off," it is altered into הַרְחִיקָה, "she went far away," which renders the passage almost unintelligible.

[6] עָרוֹם for עֵירֹם (Gen. iii. 10, 11); וַלֵּד for יֶלֶד (xi. 30); צְפוֹרִים for the collective צִפּוֹר (xv. 10); אָמוֹת, "female servants," for אֲמָהוֹת (xx. 18); וַיֵרֶא מְנֻחָה כִּי־טוֹבָה for the adverbial טוֹב (xlix. 15); בְּרִיחִים for בְּרִיחִם (Ex. xxvi. 26, making it depend from עֵץ); מִשָּׁם, in the unusual sense of "from it" (comp. 1 K. xvii. 13), is altered into מִפֶּנָּה (Lev. ii. 2); חָיָה is wrongly put for חַי (3rd p. s. m. of חָיַי = حٓيّ); עַר, the obsolete form, is replaced by the more recent עִיר (Num. xxi. 15); the unusual fem. termination ־י (comp. אֲבִיגַיִל אֲבִיטַל) is elongated into ־ית; שֻׁהוּ is the emendation for שֵׁיוּ (Deut. xxii. 1); הַרְרֵי for הַרְרֵי (Deut. xxxiii. 15, &c.)

2. The *second* class of variants consists of glosses and interpretations received into the text: glosses, moreover, in which the Sam. not unfrequently coincides with the LXX., and which are in many cases evidently derived by both from some ancient Targum.[1]

3. The *third* class exhibits conjectural emendations—sometimes far from happy—of real or imaginary difficulties in the Masoretic text.[2]

---

[1] אִישׁ וְאִשָּׁה, "man and woman," used by Gen. vii. 2, of animals, is changed into זָכָר וּנְקֵבָה, "male and female;" (Gen. xxiv. 60), "his haters," becomes שֹׂנְאָיו, "his enemies;" for מָה (indefin.) is substituted יִרְאֶה, "he will see, choose," is amplified by a לוֹ, "for himself;" הַגֵּר הַגָּר is transformed into הַגֵּר יָגוּר (Lev. xvii. 10); וַיִּקָּר אֱלֹה אֶל בִּלְעָם (Num. xxiii. 4), "And God met Bileam," becomes with the Sam. וַיִּמְצָא מַלְאַךְ אֱלֹ' אֶת בִּ', "And an *Angel of the Lord found* Bileam;" עַל הָאִשָּׁה (Gen. xx. 3), "for the woman," is amplified into עַל אֹדֹת הָאִשָּׁה, "for the sake of the woman;" for וְלִנְכָדַי, from נכר (obsol., comp. نكا), is put לְנֶגְדִּי, "those that are before me," in contradistinction to "those who will come after me;" וַתְּעַר, "and she emptied" (her pitcher into the trough, Gen. xxiv. 20), has made room for וַתּוֹרֶד, "and she took down;" נוֹעַדְתִּי שָׁמָּה, "I will meet there" (A. V., Ex. xxix. 43), is made גֵרַשְׁתִּי שָׁם, "I shall be [searched] found there;" Num. xxxi. 15, before words הַחִיִּיתֶם כָּל נְקֵבָה, "Have you spared the life of every female?" a לָמָּה, "Why," is inserted (LXX.); for כִּי שֵׁם יְהוָה אֶקְרָא (Deut. xxxii. 3), "If I call the name of Jehovah," the Sam. has בְּשֵׁם, "In the name," &c.

[2] The elliptic use of ילד, frequent both in Hebrew and Arabic, being evidently unknown to the emendator, he alters the הַלְּבֶן מֵאָה שָׁנָה יִוָּלֵד (Gen. xvii. 17), "shall a *child* be born unto him that is a hundred years old?"

into אוֹלִיד, "shall I beget?" Gen. xxiv. 62, בָּא מִבּוֹא, "he came from going" (A. V. "from the way") to the well of Lahai-roi, the Sam. alters into בָּא בַמִּדְבָּר, "in or through the desert" (LXX., διὰ τῆς ἐρήμου). In Gen. xxx. 34, הֵן לוּ יְהִי כִדְבָרֶיךָ, "Behold, may it be according to thy word," the לוּ (Arab. لو) is transformed into לֹא, "and if not—let it be like thy word." Gen. xli. 32, וְעַל הִשָּׁנוֹת הַחֲלוֹם, "And for that the dream was doubled," becomes וַעֲלֶה שֵׁנִית ח', "The dream rose a second time," which is both un-Hebrew, and diametrically opposed to the sense and construction of the passage. Better is the emendation Gen. xlix. 10, מִבֵּין רַגְלָיו "from between his feet," into "from among his banners," מִבֵּין דְּגָלָיו. Ex. xv. 18, all but five of the Sam. Codd. read לְעוֹלָם וָעֹד, "for ever *and longer*," instead of וָעֶד, the common form, "evermore." Ex. xxxiv. 7, וְנַקֵּה לֹא יְנַקֶּה, "that will by no means clear *the sin*," becomes וְנַקֵּה לוֹ יְנַקֶּה, and the innocent *to him* shall be innocent," against both the parallel passages and the obvious sense. The somewhat difficult וְלֹא יָסָפוּ, "and they did not cease" (A. V., Num. xi. 25), reappears as a still more obscure conjectural יֵאָסֵפוּ, which we would venture to translate, "they were not gathered in," in the sense of "killed;" instead of either the אכנשו, "congregated," of the Sam. Vers., or Castell's "continuerunt," or Houbigant's and Dathe's

4. The *fourth* class exhibits readings in which apparent deficiencies have been corrected or supplied from parallel passages in the common text. Gen. xviii. 29, 30, for " I shall not do it," [1] " I shall not destroy " [2] is substituted from Gen. xviii. 28, 31, 32. Gen. xxxvii. 4, אֶחָיו, " his brethren," is replaced by בָּנָיו, " his sons," from the former verse. One of the most curious specimens of the endeavours of the Samaritan Codex to render the readings as smooth and consistent as possible, is its uniform spelling of proper nouns like יתרו, Jethro, occasionally spelt יתר in the Hebrew text, Moses' father-in-law—a man who, according to the Midrash (*Sifri*), had no less than *seven* names ; יהושע (Jehoshua), into which form it corrects the shorter הושע (Hoshea) when it occurs in the Masoretic Codex. More frequent still are the additions of single words and short phrases inserted from parallel passages, where the Hebrew text appeared too concise : [3]—unnecessary, often excessively absurd interpolations.

" convenerant." Num. xxi. 28, the עָר, " Ar " (Moab), is emendated into עַד, " as far as," a perfectly meaningless reading ; only that the עָר, " city," as we saw above, was a word unknown to the Sam. The somewhat uncommon words (Num. xi. 32), וַיִּשְׁטְחוּ לָהֶם שָׁמוֹחַ, " and they (the people) spread them all abroad," are transposed into וַיִּשְׁחֲמוּ לָהֶם שְׁחוֹטָה, " and they slaughtered for themselves a slaughter." Deut. xxviii. 37, the word לִשַׁמָּה, " an astonishment " (A. V.), very rarely used in this sense (Jer. xix. 8, xxv. 9), becomes לְשֵׁם, " to a name," *i. e.*, a bad name. Deut. xxxiii. 6, וִיהִי מְתָיו מִסְפָּר, " May his *men* be a multitude," the Sam., with its characteristic aversion to, or rather ignorance of, the use of poetical diction, reads וִיהִי מֵאִתּוֹ מִסְפָּר, " May there be *from him* a multitude," thereby trying perhaps to encounter also the apparent difficulty of the word מִסְפָּר, standing for " a great number." Anything more absurd than the מֵאִתּוֹ in this place could

hardly be imagined. A few verses further on, the uncommon use of מִן in the phrase מִן יְקוּמוּן (Deut. xxxiii. 11), as " lest," " not," caused the no less unfortunate alteration מִי יְקִימֶנּוּ, so that the latter part of the passage, " smite through the loins of them that rise against him, and of them that hate him, *that they rise not again*," becomes " *who will raise them ?*"—barren alike of meaning and of poetry. For the unusual and poetical דְּבָאֶךָ (Deut. xxxiii. 25; A. V. " thy strength"), בְּיִךָ is suggested ; a word about the significance of which the commentators are at a greater loss even than about that of the original.

[1] לֹא אֶעֱשֶׂה.   [2] לֹא אַשְׁחִית.

[3] Thus in Gen. i. 14, the words לְהָאִיר עַל הָאָרֶץ, " to give light upon the earth," are inserted from ver. 17 ; Gen. xi. 8, the word וּמִגְדָּל, " and a tower," is added from ver. 4 ; Gen. xxiv. 22, עַל אַפֵּהּ, " on her face " (nose), is added from ver. 47, so that the former verse reads " And the man took (וַיִּקַּח for וַיָּשֶׂם) a golden ring ' upon her face.'"

5. The *fifth* class is an extension of the one immediately preceding, and comprises larger phrases, additions, and repetitions from parallel passages. Whenever anything is mentioned as having been done or said previously by Moses, or where a command of God is related. as being executed, the whole speech bearing upon it is repeated again at full length. These tedious and always superfluous repetitions are most frequent in Exodus, both in the record of the plagues and in the many interpolations from Deuteronomy.

6. To the *sixth* class belong those " emendations " of passages and words of the Hebrew text which contain something objectionable in the eyes of the Samaritans, on account either of historical improbability or apparent want of dignity in the terms applied to the Creator. Thus in the Sam. Pent. no one, in the antediluvian times, begets his first son after he has lived 150 years : but one hundred years are, where necessary, subtracted before, and added after the birth of the first son. Thus Jared, according to the Hebrew Text, begot at 162 years, lived afterwards 800 years, and "all his years were 962 years;" according to the Sam. he begot when only 62 years old, lived afterwards 785 years, "and all his years were 847." After the Deluge the opposite method is followed. A hundred or fifty years are added before and subtracted after the begetting : *E.g.* Arphaxad, who in the Common Text is 35 years old when he begets Shelah, and lived afterwards 403 years : in all 438—is by the Sam. made 135 years old when he begets Shelah, and lives only 303 years afterwards = 438. (The LXX. has, according to its own peculiar psychological and chronological notions, altered the Text in the opposite manner.) An exceedingly important and often discussed emendation of this class is the passage in Ex. xii. 40, which in our text reads, "Now the sojourning of the children of Israel who dwelt in Egypt was four hundred and thirty years." The Samaritan (supported by LXX. Cod. Al.) has " The sojourning of the children of Israel, [*and their fathers who dwelt in the land of Canaan and in the land of Egypt*—ἐν γῇ Αἰγύπτῳ καὶ ἐν γῇ Καναάν] was four hundred and thirty years :" an

interpolation of very late date indeed. Again, in Gen. ii. 2, "And God [? had] finished (ויכל, ? pluperf.) on the seventh day," השביעי is altered into הששי, "the *sixth*," lest God's rest on the Sabbath-day might seem incomplete (LXX.). In Gen. xxix. 3, 8, " We cannot, until all the flocks be gathered together, and till they roll the stone from the mouth of the well," עדרים, "flocks," is replaced by רועים, "shepherds," since the flocks *could* not roll the stone from the well : the corrector not being apparently aware that in common parlance in Hebrew, as in other languages, "they" occasionally refer to certain not particularly specified persons. Well may Gesenius ask what this corrector would have made of Is. xxxvii. [not xxxvi.] 36 : "And when *they* arose in the morning, behold *they* were all dead corpses." The surpassing reverence of the Samaritan is shown in passages like Ex. xxiv. 10, "and they beheld God,"[1] which is transmuted into " and they held by, clung to God "[2]—a reading certainly less in harmony with the following—" and they ate and drank."

7. The *seventh* class comprises what we might briefly call Samaritanisms, *i.e.*, certain Hebrew forms, translated into the idiomatic Samaritan; and here the Sam. Codices vary considerably among themselves,—as far as the very imperfect collation of them has hitherto shown—some having retained the Hebrew in many places where the others have adopted the new equivalents.[3]

---

[1] ויחזו את אלהים. [2] ויאחזו.

[3] The gutturals and *Ahevi*-letters are frequently changed;— הררט becomes אררט (Gen. viii. 4); באי is altered into בעי (xxiii. 18); שבה into שבע (xxvii. 19); זחלי stands for זחלי (Deut. xxxii. 24); the ה is changed into ח in words like נהג נגבהים, which become נבחים נחג; ח is altered into ע—חמר becomes עמר. The י is frequently doubled (? as a mater lectionis); הייטיב is substituted for הוטיב; פיי for פי; איירא for אירא. Many words are joined together:— מרדרור stands for מר דרור (Ex. xxx. 23); כהנאן for כהן אן (Gen. xli. 45); הרנריים is always הר נריים. The pronouns אתֽ and אֽתֽן, 2nd p. fem.

sing. and plur., are changed into אתין, אתי (the obsolete Heb. forms) respectively; the suff. ך into אך; ךֽ into ךי; the termination of the 2nd p. s. fem. præt., תֽ, becomes תי, like the first p.; the verbal form Aphel is used for the Hiphil; אזכרתי for הזכרתי; the medial letter of the verb ע"י is sometimes retained as א or י, instead of being dropped as in the Heb. Again, verbs of the form ל"ה have the י frequently at the end of the infin. fut. and part., instead of the ה. Nouns of the *schema* קטל (אבל, &c.) are often spelt קטיל, into which the form קטול is likewise occasionally transformed. Of distinctly Samaritan words may

8. The *eighth* and last class contains alterations made in favour or on behalf of Samaritan theology, hermeneutics, and domestic worship. Thus the word *Elohim*, four times construed with the plural verb in the Hebrew Pentateuch, is in the Samaritan Pent. joined to the singular verb (Gen. xx. 13, xxxi. 53, xxxv. 7; Ex. xxii. 9); and further, both anthropomorphisms as well as anthropopathisms are carefully expunged—a practice very common in later times.[1] The last and perhaps most momentous of all intentional alterations is the constant change of all the יבחר, "God will choose a spot," into בחר, "He has chosen," viz. Gerizim, and the well-known substitution of Gerizim for Ebal in Deut. xxvii. 4 (A. V. 5):—"It shall be when ye be gone over Jordan, that ye shall set up these stones which I command you this day on Mount Ebal (Sam. *Gerizim*), and there shalt thou build an altar unto the Lord thy God," &c. This passage gains a certain interest from Whiston and Kennicott having charged the *Jews* with corrupting it from Gerizim into Ebal. This supposition, however, was met by Rutherford, Parry, Tychsen, Lobstein, Verschuir, and others, and

---

be mentioned : הַךְ (Gen. xxxiv. 31)= חֵיךְ, אֵיךְ (Chald.), "like;" חתים, for Heb. חותם, "seal;" בְּפֹרחת, "as though it budded," becomes כאפרחת = Targ. כר אפרחת; חכם, "wise," reads עד, חכום; עֲדִי, "spoil," יְפוֹת, "days," יוֹמַת.

[1] איש מלחמה, "man of war," an expression used of God (Ex. xv. 3), becomes גבור מ', "hero of war," the former apparently of irreverent import to the Samaritan ear; for יעשן אף ה' (Deut. xxix. 19, A. V. 20), lit. "And the wrath (nose) of the Lord shall smoke," יחר אף ה', "the wrath of the Lord will be kindled," is substituted; צור מחוללך (Deut. xxxii. 18), "the rock (God) which begat thee," is changed into צור מהללך, "the rock which glorifies thee;" Gen. xix. 12, האנשים, "the men," used of the angels, has been replaced by המלאכים, "the angels." Extreme reverence for the patriarchs changed ארור, "Cursed be their (Simeon and Levi's) anger," into אדיר, "brilliant is their anger" (Gen. xlix. 7). A flagrant falsification is the alteration, in an opposite sense, which they ventured in the passage ידיד ה' ישכן לבטח, "The beloved of God [Benjamin, the founder of the Judæo-Davidian empire, hateful to the Samaritans] shall dwell securely," transformed by them into the almost senseless יד יד ה' ישכן לבטח, "*The hand, the hand* of God will rest [if Hiph.: יְשַׁכֵּן, 'will cause to rest'] securely" (Deut. xxxiii. 12). Reverence for the Law and the Sacred Records gives rise to more emendations:—במבשיו (Deut. xxv. 12, A. V. 11), "by his secrets," becomes בבשרו, "by his flesh;" ישגלנה, "coibit cum ea" (Deut. xxviii. 12), ישכב עמה, "concumbet cum ea;" לכלב תשליכון, "to the dog shall ye throw it" (Ex. xxii. 30), תשלך הישלך, "ye shall indeed throw it [away]."

we need only add that it is completely given up by modern
Biblical scholars, although it cannot be denied that there is
some *primâ facie* ground for a doubt upon the subject.   To
this class also belong more especially interpolations of really
existing passages, dragged out of their context for a special
purpose.   In Exodus as well as in Deuteronomy the Sam.
has, immediately after the Ten Commandments, the following insertions from Deut. xxvii. 2–7 and xi. 30: "And it
shall be on the day when ye shall pass over Jordan . . . ye
shall set up these stones . . . on Mount *Gerizim* . . . and
there shalt thou build an altar . . . ' *That mountain* ' on the
other side Jordan by the way where the sun goeth down . . .
in the champaign over against Gilgal, beside the plains
of Moreh, ' *over against Shechem* :' "—this last superfluous
addition, which is also found in Deut. xi. 30 of the Sam.
Pent., being ridiculed in the Talmud, as we have seen
above.

From the immense number of these worse than worthless
variants Gesenius has singled out four, which he thinks
preferable on the whole to those of the Masoretic Text.   We
will confine ourselves to mentioning them, and refer the
reader to the recent commentaries upon them: he will find
that they too have since been, all but unanimously, rejected.[1]
(1.) After the words, "And Cain spoke (ויאמר) to his
brother Abel" (Gen. iv. 8), the Sam. adds, "let us go into
the field,"[2] in ignorance of the absol. use of אמר, "to say,
speak" (comp. Ex. xix. 25; 2 Chr. ii. 10, xxxii. 34), and the
absol. וינד (Gen. ix. 21).   (2.) For אחר (Gen. xxii. 13) the
Sam. reads אחד, *i.e.* instead of "behind him a ram," "one
ram."   (3.) For חמור גרם (Gen. xlix. 14), "an ass of bone "
i.e. a strong ass, the Sam. has חמור גרים (Targ. גְּרַם, Syr.
ܓܪܡ).   And (4) for וירק (Gen. xiv. 14), "he led forth
his trained servants," the Sam. reads וידק, "he numbered."

We must briefly state, in concluding this portion of the

---

[1] Keil, in the latest edition of his
Introd. p. 590, note 7, says, "Even the
few variants, which Gesenius tries to | prove genuine, fall to the ground on
closer examination."

[2] נלכה השדה.

subject, that we did not choose this classification of Gesenius
because it appeared to us to be either systematic (Gesenius
says himself: "Ceterum facile perspicitur complures in his
esse lectiones quarum singulas alius ad aliud genus referre
forsitan malit . . . in una vel altera lectione ad aliam
classem referenda haud difficiles erimus . . .") or exhaustive,
or even because the illustrations themselves are unassailable
in point of the reason he assigns for them; but because,
deficient as it is, it has at once and for ever silenced the
utterly unfounded though time-hallowed claims of the
Samaritan Pentateuch. It was only necessary, as we said
before, to collect a great number of variations (or to take
them from Walton), to compare them with the old text and
with each other, to place them in some kind of order before
the reader and let them tell their own tale. That this was
not done during the two hundred years of the contest by
a single one of the combatants is certainly rather strange :—
albeit not the only instance of the kind.

Important additions to this list have, as we hinted before,
been made by Frankel, such as the Samaritans' preference
of the imperat. for the 3rd pers.;[1] ignorance of the use
of the abl. absol.;[2] Galileanisms,—to which also belongs the
permutation of the letters *Ahevi*[3] (comp. *Erub.* 53, חמר, עמר,
אמר), in the Samaritan Cod.; the occasional softening down
of the פ into ב,[4] of כ into ג, צ into ז, &c., and chiefly the
presence of words and phrases in the Sam. which are *not*
interpolated from parallel passages, but are entirely wanting
in our text.[5] Frankel derives from these passages chiefly
the conclusion that the Sam. Pent. was, partly at least,

---

[1] *E. g.* הקרב for יקרב (Ex. xii. 48); יבא ועשה (Ex. xxxv. 10).
[2] *E. g.* זכרו for זכור (Ex. xiii. 13); רנמי for רנום (Num. xv. 35).
[3] *E. g.* והרף for וחרף (Gen. viii. 22); חוץ for עוץ (Gen. xxxvi. 28); השאף for השחף (Lev. xi. 16), &c.
[4] ויחבש for ויחפש (Gen. xxxi. 35); נשבת for נשפת (Ex. xv. 10).
[5] Gen. xxiii. 2, after בקרית הארבע the words אל עמק are added; xxvii.

27, after השדה the word מלא is found (LXX.); xliii. 28, the phrase ברוך האיש ההוא לאלהים is inserted after the Ethnach; xlvii. 21, העביד לעבדים, and Ex. xxxii. 32, אם תשא חטא תם ישא is read. An exceedingly difficult and un-Hebrew passage is found in Ex. xxiii. 19, reading בי עשה זאת כזבח שכח ועברה הוא לאלהי יעקב.

emendated from the LXX., Onkelos, and other very late
sources. (See below.)

We now subjoin, for the sake of completeness, the before-
mentioned thirteen classes of Kirchheim, in the original, to
which we have added the translation :—

1. תוספות ושנויים למעלת הר גריזים. [Additions and
alterations in the Samaritan Pentateuch in favour of Mount
Gerizim.]

2. תוספות למלאות. [Additions for the purpose of completion.]

3. באור. [Commentary, glosses.]

4. חלוף הפעלים והבנינים. [Change of verbs and moods.

5. חלוף השמות. [Change of nouns.]

6. השואה. [Emendation of seeming irregularities by
assimilating forms, &c.]

7. תמורת האותיות. [Permutation of letters.]

8. כנויים. [Pronouns.]

9. מין. [Gender.]

10. אותיות הנוספות. [Letters added.]

11. אותיות היחם. [Addition of prepositions, conjunctions,
articles, &c.]

12. קבוץ ופרוד. [Junction of separated, and separation of
joined words.]

13. ימות עולם, [Chronological alterations.]

It may, perhaps, not be quite superfluous to observe, before
we proceed any further, that, since up to this moment no
critical edition of the Sam. Pent., or even an examination of
the Codices since Kennicott—who can only be said to have
begun the work—has been thought of, the treatment of the
whole subject remains a most precarious task, and beset with
unexampled difficulties at every step ; and also that, under
these circumstances, a more or less scientific arrangement of
isolated or common Samaritan mistakes and falsifications
appears to us to be a subject of very small consequence
indeed.

It is, however, this same rudimentary state of investigation—after two centuries and a half of fierce discussion—

which has left the other and much more important question
of the *Age and Origin* of the Sam. Pent. as unsettled to-day
as it was when it first came under the notice of European
scholars. For our own part we cannot but think that as
long as—(1) the history of the Samaritans remains involved
in the obscurities of which a former article will have given
an account; (2) we are restricted to a small number of
comparatively recent Codices; (3) neither these codices
themselves have, as has just been observed, been thoroughly
collated and recollated, nor (4) more than a feeble beginning
has been made with anything like a collation between the
various readings of the Sam. Pent. and the LXX. (Walton
omitted the greatest number, "cum nullum sensus varie-
tatem constituant");—so long must we have a variety of the
most divergent opinions, all based on "probabilities," which
are designated on the other side as "false reasonings" and
"individual crotchets," and which, moreover, not unfrequently start from flagrantly false premises.

We shall, under these circumstances, confine ourselves to
a simple enumeration of the leading opinions, and the chief
reasons and arguments alleged for and against them :—

(1.) The Samaritan Pentateuch came into the hands of
the Samaritans as an inheritance from the ten tribes whom
they succeeded—so the popular notion runs. Of this
opinion are J. Morinus, Walton, Cappellus, Kennicott,
Michaelis, Eichhorn, Bauer, Jahn, Bertholdt, Steudel,
Mazade, Stuart, Davidson, and others. Their reasons for it
may be thus briefly summed up :—

(*a.*) It seems improbable that the Samaritans should have
accepted their code at the hands of the Jews after the Exile,
as supposed by some critics, since there existed an intense
hatred between the two nationalities.

(*b.*) The Samaritan Canon has only the Pentateuch in
common with the Hebrew Canon: had that book been
received at the period when the Hagiographa and the
Prophets were in the Jews' hands, it would be surprising
if they had not also received those.

(*c.*) The Sam. Letters, avowedly the more ancient, are

found in the Sam. Cod.: therefore it was written before the
alteration of the character into the square Hebrew—which
dates from the end of the Exile—took place.

[We cannot omit briefly to draw attention here to a most
keen-eyed suggestion of S. D. Luzzatto, contained in a letter
to R. Kirchheim (*Carme Shomron*, p. 106, &c.), by the
adoption of which many readings in the Heb. Codex, now
almost unintelligible, appear perfectly clear. He assumes
that the copyist who at some time or other after Ezra transcribed the Bible into the modern square Hebrew character,
from the ancient copies written in so-called Samaritan,
occasionally mistook Samaritan letters of similar form.[1]
And since our Sam. Pent. has those difficult readings in
common with the Mas. Text, that other moot point, whether
it was copied from a Hebrew or Samaritan Codex, would
thus appear to be solved. Its constant changes of ר and ד,
י and ו, ה and ח —letters which are similar in Hebrew,
but *not* in Samaritan—have been long used as a powerful
argument for the Samaritans having received the Pent. at a
very late period indeed.]

Since the above opinion—that the Pent. came into the
hands of the Samaritans from the Ten Tribes—is the most
popular one, we will now adduce some of the chief reasons
brought against it, and the reader will see by the somewhat
feeble nature of the arguments on either side, that the last
word has not yet been spoken in the matter.

(*a*.) There existed no *religious* animosity whatsoever
between Judah and Israel when they separated. The ten
tribes could not therefore have bequeathed such an animosity

---

[1] *E. g.*, Is. xi. 15, בעים instead of
בעצם (adopted by Gesenius in *Thes.*
p. 1017 *a*, without a mention of its
source, which he, however, distinctly
avowed to Rosenmüller—comp. כ"ש,
p. 107, note א); Jer. iii. 8, ואראָ
instead of ותראָ; 1 Sam. xxiv. 11;
ותחם for ואחם; Ezr. vi. 4; הדת
for הדא; Ez. xxii. 20, והנחתי for
והפחתי; Judg. xv. 20; עשרים
Samson's reign during the time of the
Philistines being given as *twenty*
years instead of *forty* (comp. *Jer. Sot.*
1), accounted for by the מ (numerical
letter for forty) in the original being
mistaken for כ (twenty). Again, 2
Chr. xxii. 2, *forty* is put instead of
twenty (comp. 2 K. viii. 26); 2 K. xxii.
4, ויתם for ויתך; Ez. iii. 12, ברוך for
ברום, &c.;—all these letters—𝍔 and
𝍔, Λ and Λ, ℶ and ℶ, צ and ℵ
—resembling each other very closely.

to those who succeeded them, and who, we may add, probably cared as little originally for the disputes between
Judah and Israel, as colonists from far-off countries, belonging to utterly different races, are likely to care for the
quarrels of the aborigines who formerly inhabited the
country.   On the contrary, the contest between the slowly
judaized Samaritans and the Jews, only dates from the
moment when the latter refused to recognise the claims
of the former, as belonging to the people of God, and rejected
their aid in building the Temple : why then, it is said, should
they not first have received the one book which would bring
them into still closer conformity with the returned exiles, at
their hands ?   That the Jews should yet have refused to
receive them as equals is no more surprising than that the
Samaritans from that time forward took their stand upon
this very Law—altered according to their circumstances ;
and proved from it that they and they alone were the
Jews κατ’ ἐξοχήν.

(b.) Their not possessing any other book of the Hebrew
Canon is not to be accounted for by the circumstance that
there was no other book in existence at the time of the
schism, because many psalms of David, writings of Solomon,
&c., must have been circulating among the people.   But the
jealousy with which the Samaritans regarded Jerusalem,
and the intense hatred which they naturally conceived
against the post-Mosaic writers of national Jewish history,
would sufficiently account for their rejecting the other
books, in all of which, save Joshua, Judges, and Job, either
Jerusalem, as the centre of worship, or David and his House,
are extolled.   If, however, Loewe has really found with
them, as he reports in the *Allgem. Zeitung d. Judenth.* April
18th, 1839, our Book of Kings and Solomon’s Song of
songs, — which they certainly would not have received
subsequently,—all these arguments are perfectly gratuitous.

(c.) The present Hebrew character was *not* introduced by
Ezra after the return from the Exile, but came into use at a
much later period.   The Samaritans might therefore have
received the Pentateuch at the hands of the returned exiles,

who, according to the Talmud, *afterwards* changed their writing, and in the Pentateuch only, so as to distinguish it from the Samaritan. "Originally," says Mar Sutra (*Sanhedr.* xxi. *b*), "the Pentateuch was given to Israel in *Ibri* writing and the Holy (Hebrew) language: it was again given to them in the days of Ezra in the *Ashurith* writing and *Aramaic* language. Israel then selected the Ashurith writing and the Holy language, and left to the Hediotes ('Ιδιῶται) the Ibri writing and the Aramaic language. Who are the Hediotes? The Cuthim (Samaritans). What is Ibri writing? The Libonaah (Samaritan)." It is well known also that the Maccabean coins bear Samaritan inscriptions: so that "Hediotes" would point to the common use of the Samaritan character for ordinary purposes, down to a very late period.

(2.) The second leading opinion on the age and origin of the Sam. Pent. is that it was introduced by Manasseh (comp. Josephus, *Ant.* xi. 8, § 2, 4) at the time of the foundation of the Samaritan Sanctuary on Mount Gerizim (Ant. van Dale, R. Simon, Prideaux, Fulda, Hasse, De Wette, Gesenius, Hupfeld, Hengstenberg, Keil, &c.). In support of this opinion are alleged, the idolatry of the Samaritans before they received a Jewish priest through Esarhaddon 2 K. xvii. 24–33), and the immense number of readings common to the LXX. and this Code, against the Masoretic Text.

(3.) Other, but very isolated notions, are those of Morin, Le Clerc, Poncet, &c., that the Israelitish priest sent by the king of Assyria to instruct the new inhabitants in the religion of the country brought the Pentateuch with him. Further, that the Samaritan Pentateuch was the production of an impostor, Dositheus (דוסתאי in Talmud), who lived during the time of the Apostles, and who falsified the sacred records in order to prove that he was the Messiah (Ussher). Against which there is only this to be observed, that there is not the slightest alteration of such a nature to be found. Finally, that it is a very late and faulty recension, with additions and corruptions of the Masoretic Text (6th century after Christ), into which glosses from the LXX. had been

received (Frankel). Many other suggestions have been
made, but we cannot here dwell upon them: suffice it to
have mentioned those to which a certain popularity and
authority attaches.

Another question has been raised :—Have all the variants
which we find in our copies been introduced at once, or are
they the work of many generations? From the number of
vague opinions on that point, we have only room here to
adduce that of Azariah de Rossi, who traces many of the
glosses (Class 2) both in the Sam. and in the LXX. to an
ancient Targum in the hands of the people at the time of
Ezra, and refers to the Talmudical passage of *Nedar.* 37 :
"And he read in the Book of the Law of God—this is
Mikra, the Pentateuch; מפורש explanatory, this is *Targum.*"
Considering that no Masorah fixed the letters and signs of
the Samar. Codex, and that, as we have noticed, the principal object was to make it read as smoothly as possible, it
is not easily seen why each succeeding century should not
have added its own emendations. But, here too, investigation still wanders about in the mazes of speculation.

The chief opinions with respect to the agreement of the
numerous and as yet uninvestigated — even uncounted —
readings of the LXX. (of which likewise no critical edition
exists as yet), and the Sam. Pent. are :—

1. That the LXX. have translated from the Sam. (De
Dieu, Selden, Hottinger, Hassencamp, Eichhorn, &c.).

2. That mutual interpolations have taken place (Grotius,
Ussher, Ravius, &c.).

3. That both Versions were formed from Hebrew Codices,
which differed among themselves as well as from the one which
afterwards obtained public authority in Palestine; that however very many wilful corruptions and interpolations have
crept in in later times (Gesenius).

4. That the Samar. has, in the main, been altered from the
LXX. (Frankel).

It must, on the other hand, be stated also, that the Sam.
and LXX. quite as often disagree with each other, and follow
each the Masor. Text. Also, that the quotations in the N. T.,

from the LXX., where they coincide with the Sam. against the Hebr. Text, are so small in number and of so unimportant a nature that they cannot be adduced as any argument whatsoever.

The following is a list of the MSS. of the Sam. Pent. now in European Libraries [Kennicott] :—

No. 1. Oxford (Ussher) Bodl., fol., No. 3127. Perfect, except the 20 first and 9 last verses.

No. 2. Oxford (Ussher) Bodl., 4to., No. 3128, with an Arabic version in Sam. characters. Imperfect. Wanting the whole of Leviticus and many portions of the other books.

No. 3. Oxford (Ussher) Bodl., 4to., No. 3129. Wanting many portions in each book.

No. 4. Oxford (Ussher, Laud) Bodl., 4to., No. 624. Defective in parts of Deut.

No. 5. Oxford (Marsh) Bodl., 12mo., No. 15. Wanting some verses in the beginning ; 21 chapters obliterated.

No. 6. Oxford (Pocock) Bodl., 24mo., No. 5328. Parts of leaves lost; otherwise perfect.

No. 7. London (Ussher) Br. Mus. Claud. B. 8. Vellum. Complete. 254 leaves.

No. 8. Paris (Peiresc) Imp. Libr., Sam. No. 1. Recent MS. containing the Hebr. and Sam. Texts, with an Arab. Vers. in the Sam. character. Wanting the first 34 chapters, and very defective in many places.

No. 9. Paris (Peiresc) Imp. Libr., Sam. No. 2. Ancient MS., wanting first 17 chapters of Gen.; and all Deut. from the 7th chapter. Houbigant, however, quotes from Gen. x. 11 of this Codex, a rather puzzling circumstance.

No. 10. Paris (Harl. de Sancy) Oratory, No. 1. The famous MS. of P. della Valle.

No. 11. Paris (Dom. Nolin) Oratory, No. 2. Made-up copy.

No. 12. Paris (Libr. St. Genev.). Of little value.

No. 13. Rome (Peir. and Barber.) Vatican, No. 106. Hebr. and Sam. texts, with Arab. Vers. in Sam. character. Very defective and recent. Dated the 7th century (?).

No. 14. Rome (Card. Cobellutius), Vatican. Also supposed to be of the 7th century, but very doubtful.

No. 15. Milan (Ambrosian Libr.) Said to be very ancient; not collated.

No. 16. Leyden (Golius MS.), fol., No. 1. Said to be complete.

No. 17. Gotha (Ducal Libr.). A fragment only.

No. 18. London, Count of Paris' Library. With Version.

Printed editions are contained in the Paris and Walton Polyglots; and a separate reprint from the latter was made by Blayney, Oxford, 1790. A Facsimile of the 20th chapter of Exodus, from one of the *Náblus* MSS., has been edited, with portions of the corresponding Masoretic text, and a Russian Translation and Introduction, by Levysohn, Jerusalem 1860.[1]

II. Versions.

1. *Samaritan.*—The origin, author, and age of the Samaritan Version of the Five Books of Moses, has hitherto—so Eichhorn quaintly observes—"always been a golden apple to the investigators, and will very probably remain so, until people leave off venturing decisive judgments upon historical subjects which no one has recorded in antiquity." And, indeed, modern investigators, keen as they have been, have done little towards the elucidation of the subject. According to the Samaritans themselves (De Sacy *Mem.* 3; Paulus; Winer), their high-priest Nathaniel, who died about 20 B.C., is its author. Gesenius puts its date a few years after Christ. Juynboll thinks that it had long been in use in the second post-Christian century. Frankel places it in the post-Mohammedan time. Other investigators date it from the time of Esarhaddon's priest (Schwarz), or either shortly before or after the foundation of the temple on Mount Gerizim. It seems certain, however, that it was composed

---

[1] The original intention of the Russian Government to publish the whole Codex in the same manner seems to have been given up for the present. We can only hope that, if the work is ever taken up again, it will fall into more competent hands. | Mr. Levysohn's Introduction, brief as it is, shows him to be utterly wanting both in scholarship and critical acumen, and to be, moreover, entirely unacquainted with the fact that his new discoveries have been disposed of some hundred and fifty years since.

before the destruction of the second temple; and being
intended, like the Targums, for the use of the people exclusively, it was written in the popular Samaritan idiom, a
mixture of Hebrew, Aramaic, and Syriac.

In this version the original has been followed, with a very
few exceptions, in a slavish and sometimes perfectly childish
manner, the sense evidently being of minor consideration.
As a very striking instance of this may be adduced the
translation of Deut. iii. 9: "The Zidonians call Hermon
שָׂרִין (Shirion), and the Amorites call it שְׂנִיר (Shenir)."
The translator deriving שׂרין from שׂר "prince, master,"
renders it רבן "masters;" and finding the letters reversed in
the appellation of the Amorites as שׂניר, reverses also the
sense in his version, and translates it by "slaves" משׁעברון!
In other cases, where no Samaritan equivalent could be found
for a Hebrew word, the translator, instead of paraphrasing it,
simply transposes its letters, so as to make it *look* Samaritan.
Occasionally he is misled by the orthography of the original:
אם כן אפוא, "If so, where . . . . ?" he renders אם כן ארגזה,
"If so, I shall be wrath:" mistaking אפוא for אפו, from אף
"anger." On the whole it may be considered a very valuable
aid towards the study of the Samar. Text, on account of its
very close verbal adherence. A few cases, however, may be
brought forward, where the Version has departed from the
Text, either under the influence of popular religious notions,
or for the sake of explanation. "We pray"—so they write
to Scaliger—"every day in the morning and in the evening,
as it is said, the one lamb shalt thou prepare in the morning
and the second in the evening; we bow to the ground and
worship God." Accordingly, we find the translator rendering
the passage, "And Isaac went to 'walk' (לשׂוח) in the field,"
by—"and Isaac went to pray (למצלאה) in the field." "And
Abraham rose in the morning (בבוקר)," is rendered בצלי,
"in the prayer," &c. Anthropomorphisms are avoided. "The
image (תמונת) of God" is rendered נעימת, "the glory."
פי יהוה, "the mouth of Jehovah," is transformed into מימר
יהוה, "the word of Jehovah." For אלהים, "God," מלאכיה,
"Angel" is frequently found, &c. A great difficulty is

offered by the proper names which this version often substitutes, they being, in many cases, less intelligible than the
original ones.[1] The similarity it has with Onkelos occasionally amounts to complete identity, for instance—

Onkelos in *Polyglott.*—Num. vi. 1, 2.

ומלל יהוה עם מושה למימר : מלל עם בני־ישראל
ותימר להון גבר או אתתא ארי יפריש למדר נדר
נזירא למזר קדם יהוה : מחמר חדת ועתיק יזר חי
דחמר חדת וחל דחמר עתיק לא ישתי וכל מתרוה
ענבין לא ישתי ועובין רטיבין וביבשין לא ייכול׃

Sam. Vers. in *Barberini Triglott.*—Num. vi. 1, 2.

ומלל יהוה עם מושה למימר : מלל עם בני ישראל
ותימר להון גבר או אתה כד יפרש למדר נדר
נזיר למתנזורה ליהוה : מן חמר ורחמ יזיר חמי
דחמר וחמי דרחמ לא ישתא וכל מור שורת ענבין
לא ישתה וענבין רטיבין וביבשין לא ייכל׃

---

[1] A list of the more remarkable of
these, in the case of geographical
names, is subjoined :—
Gen. viii. 4, for Ararat, Sarendib,
סרנדיב.
x. 10, „ Shinar, Tsofah,
צופה (? Zobah).
11, „ Asshur, Astun,
עסטון.
— „ Rehoboth, Satean,
סטכן (? Sitta-
cene).
— „ Calah, Laksab,
לכסה.
12, „ Resen, Asfah. עספה.
30, „ Mesha, Mesbal,
מסבל.
xi. 9, „ Babel, Lilak, לילק.
xiii. 3, „ Ai, Cefrah, כפרה (?
Cephirah, Josh.
ix. 17).
xiv. 5, „ Ashteroth Karnaim,
A finith Karniah,
עפינית קרניה.
— „ Ham, Lishah, לישה.
— 6, „ El Paran, Pe'ishah,
&c., פרום פלשה
לפלוג.
— 14, „ Dan, Banias, כניאס.
— 15, „ Hobah, Fogah, פוגה.

Gen. xiv. 17, for Shaveh, Mifneh,
מפנה.
xv. 8, „ Euphrates,Shalmah,
שלמאה.
— 20, „ Rephaim, Chasah,
חסאה.
xx. 1, „ Gerar, Askelun,
עסקלון.
xxvi. 2, „ Mitsraim, Nefik,
נפיק (? Exodus).
xxxvi. 8, 9, &c. „ Seir, Gablah, גבלה
(Jebal).
37, „ Rehoboth, Fathi,
פתי.
Num. xxi. 33, „ Bashan, Bathnin,
בתנין (Batanœa).
xxxiv. 10, „ Shepham,'Abamiah,
עבמיה (Apa-
mœa).
11, „ Shepham,'Afamiah,
עפמיה.
Deut. ii. 9, „ Ar (ער), Arshah,
ארשה.
iii. 4, „ Argob, Rigobaah,
ריגובאה (Ραγαβα).
— 17, „ Chinnereth, Ge-
nesar, גנסר.
iv. 48, „ Sion, Tûr Telga,
טור תלגא (Jebel
et Telj).

But no safe conclusion as to the respective relation of the two versions can be drawn from this.

This Version has likewise, in passing through the hands of copyists and commentators, suffered many interpolations and corruptions. The first copy of it was brought to Europe by De la Valle, together with the Sam. Text, in 1616. Joh. Nedrinus first published it together with a faulty Latin translation in the Paris Polyglott, whence it was, with a few emendations, reprinted in Walton, with some notes by Castellus. Single portions of it appeared in Halle, ed. by Cellarius, 1705, and by Uhlemann, Leipz., 1837. Compare Gesenius, *De Pent. Sam. Origine*, &c., and Winer's monograph, *De Versionis Pent. Sam. Indole*, &c., Leipzig, 1817.

2. Τὸ Σαμαρειτικόν. The hatred between the Samaritans and the Jews is supposed to have caused the former to prepare a Greek translation of their Pent. in opposition to the LXX. of the Jews. In this way at least the existence of certain fragments of a Greek Version of the Sam. Pent., preserved in some MSS. of the LXX., together with portions of Aquila, Symmachus, Theodotion, &c., is accounted for. These fragments are supposed to be alluded to by the Greek Fathers under the name Σαμαρειτικόν. It is doubtful however whether it ever existed (as Gesenius, Winer, Juynboll, suppose) in the shape of a complete ˌtranslation, or only designated (as Castellus, Voss, Herbst hold) a certain number of scholia translated from the Sam. Version. Other critics again (Hävernick, Hengstenberg, &c.) see in it only a corrected edition of certain passages of the LXX.

3. In 1070 an *Arabic* Version of the Sam. Pent. was made by Abu Said in Egypt, on the basis of the Arabic translation of Saadjah haggaon. Like the original Samaritan it avoids Anthropomorphisms and Anthropopathisms, replacing the latter by Euphemisms, besides occasionally making some slight alterations, more especially in proper nouns. It is extant in several MS. copies in European libraries, and is now in course of being edited by Kuenen, Leyden, 1850–54, &c. It appears to have been drawn up from the Sam. Text, not from the Sam. Version; the Hebrew words occasionally

remaining unaltered in the translation.[1] Often also it
renders the original differently from the Samar. Version.[2]
Principally noticeable is its excessive dread of assigning
to God anything like human attributes, physical or mental.
For יהוה אלהים, " God," we find (as in Saadiah sometimes)
ملاك الله, " the Angel of God ; " for " the eyes of God " we
have (Deut. ix. 12) ملاحطه الله, " the Beholding of God."
For " Bread of God :" لازم, " the necessary," &c. Again, it
occasionally adds honourable epithets where the Scripture
seems to have omitted them, &c. Its language is far from
elegant or even correct ; and its use must likewise be confined to the critical study of the Sam. Text.

4. To this Arabic version Abu Barachat, a Syrian, wrote
in 1208 a somewhat paraphrastic commentary, which has by
degrees come to be looked upon as a new Version—the
Syriac, in contradistinction to the *Arabic,* and which is often
confounded with it in the MSS. On both Recensions see
Eichhorn, Gesenius, Juynboll, &c.

III. SAMARITAN LITERATURE.

It may perhaps not be superfluous to add here a concise
account of the Samaritan literature in general, since to a
certain degree it bears upon our subject.

1. *Chronicon Samaritanum.*—Of the Pentateuch and its
Versions we have spoken. We have also mentioned that
the Samaritans have no other book of our Received Canon.
" There is no Prophet but Moses " is one of their chief
dogmas, and fierce are the invectives in which they indulge
against men like Samuel, " a Magician and an Infidel," كفر [3]

---

[1] *E. g.* Ex. xiii. 12, כל פטר רחם
(Sam. Ver. כל פתוחי רחם) remains
كل فاطر : xxi. 3, בעל אשה (Sam.
Ver. מסחן אתה) is given بعل امرأ.
[2] Thus עירה, Gen. xlix. 11 (Sam.
Ver. קרתה, "his city"), the Arab.

renders عيرة ; Gen. xli. 43, אברך
(Sam. Ver. כרוז = κῆρυξ), the Arab.
translates אב רך = الشغوق الاب.
[3] A word, it may be observed by
the way, taken by the Mohammedans
from the Rabbinical כופר (בעיקר).

(*Chron. Sam.*); Eli; Solomon, "Shiloh" (Gen. xlix. 10),
"*i.e.* the man who shall *spoil* the Law and whom many
nations will follow because of their own licentiousness" (De
Sacy, *Mem.* 4); Ezra "cursed for ever" (*Lett. to Huntington,*
&c.). Joshua alone, partly on account of his being an Ephrai-
mite, partly because Shechem was selected by him as the
scene of his solemn valedictory address, seems to have found
favour in their eyes; but the *Book of Joshua*, which they
perhaps possessed in its original form, gradually came to
form only the groundwork of a fictitious national Samaritan
history, overgrown with the most fantastic and anachronistic
legends. This is the so-called "Samaritan Joshua," or
Chronicon Samaritanum (سفر يهشع بن نون), sent to Scaliger
by the Samaritans of Cairo in 1584. It was edited by Juynboll (Leyden 1848), and his acute investigations have shown
that it was redacted into its present form about A.D. 1300,
out of four special documents, three of which were Arabic,
and one Hebrew (*i. e.* Samaritan). The Leyden MS. in two
parts, which Gesenius, *De Sam. Theol.* p. 8. n. 18, thinks
unique, is dated A.H. 764–919 (A.D. 1362–1513);—the Cod.
in the Brit. Museum, lately acquired, dates A.H. 908 (A.D.
1502). The chronicle embraces the time from Joshua to
about A.D. 350, and was originally written in, or subsequently
translated into, Arabic. After eight chapters of introductory
matter begins the early history of "Israel" under "*King*
Joshua," who, among other deeds of arms, wages war, with
300,000 mounted men—"half Israel"—against two kings of
Persia. The last of his five "royal" successors is Shimshon
(Samson), the handsomest and most powerful of them all.
These reigned for the space of 250 years, and were followed
by five high-priests, the last of whom was Usi (?—Uzzi, Ezr.
vii. 4). With the history of Eli, "the seducer," which then
follows, and Samuel "a sorcerer", the account by a sudden
transition runs off to Nebuchadnezzar (ch. 45), Alexander
(ch. 46), and Hadrian (47), and closes suddenly at the time
of Julian the Apostate.

We shall only adduce here a single specimen out of the

45th chapter of the Book, which treats of the subject of the Pentateuch :—

Nebuchadnezzar was king of Persia (Mossul), and conquered the whole world, also the kings of Syria. In the thirteenth year of their subjugation they rebelled, together with the kings of Jerusalem (Kodsh). Whereupon the Samaritans, to escape from the vengeance of their pursuer, fled, and Persian colonists took their place. A curse, however, rested upon the land, and the new immigrants died from eating of its fruits (Joseph. *Ant.* ix. 14. § 3). The chiefs of Israel (*i.e.* Samaritans), being asked the reason of this by the king, explained it by the abolition of the worship of God. The king upon this permitted them to return and to erect a temple, in which work he promised to aid them, and he gave them a letter to all their dispersed brethren. The whole Dispersion now assembled, and the Jews said, " We will now go up into the Holy City (Jerusalem) and live there in unity." But the sons of Harûn (Aaron) and of Joseph (*i.e.* the priests and the Samaritans) insisted upon going to the " Mount of Blessing," Gerizim. The dispute was referred to the king, and while the Samaritans proved their case from the books of Moses, the Jews grounded their preference for Jerusalem on the post-Mosaic books. The superior force of the Samaritan argument was fully recognised by the king. But as each side—by the mouth of their spokesmen, Sanballat and Zerubbabel respectively—charged the other with basing its claims on a forged document, the sacred books of each party were subjected to the ordeal of fire. The Jewish Record was immediately consumed, while the Samaritan leaped three times from the flames into the king's lap: the third time, however, a portion of the scroll, upon which the king had spat, was found to have been consumed. Thirty-six Jews were immediately beheaded, and the Samaritans, to the number of 300,000, wept, and all Israel worshipped henceforth upon Mount Gerizim—" and so we will ask our help from the grace of God, who has in His mercy granted all these things, and in Him we will confide."

2. From this work chiefly has been compiled another

Chronicle written in the 14th century (1355), by Abu'l Fatah.[1] This comprises the history of the Jews and Samaritans from Adam to A.H. 756 and 798 (A.D. 1355 and 1397) respectively (the forty-two years must have been added by a later historiographer). It is of equally low historical value; its only remarkable feature being its adoption of certain Talmudical legends, which it took at second hand from Josippon ben Gorion. According to this chronicle, the Deluge did not cover Gerizim, in the same manner as the Midrash (*Ber. Rab.*) exempts the whole of Palestine from it. A specimen, likewise on the subject of the Pentateuch, may not be out of place :—

In the year of the world 4150, and in the 10th year of Philadelphus, this king wished to learn the difference between the Law of the Samaritans, and that of the Jews. He therefore bade both send him some of their elders. The Samaritans delegated Ahron, Sumla, and Hudmaka: the Jews, Eleazar only. The king assigned houses to them, and gave them each an adept of the Greek language, in order that he might assist them in their translation. The Samaritans rendered only their Pentateuch into the language of the land, while Eleazar produced a translation of the whole Canon. The king, perceiving variations in the respective Pentateuchs, asked the Samaritans the reason of it. Whereupon they replied that these differences chiefly turned upon two points. (1.) God *had* chosen the Mount of Gerizim: and if the Jews were right, why was there no mention of it in their Thora ? (2.) The Samaritans read, Deut. xxxii. 35, ליום נקם, " to the *day* of vengeance and reward "—the Jews לי נקם, "*Mine* is vengeance and reward "—which left it uncertain whether that reward was to be given here or in the world to come. The king then asked what was their opinion about the Jewish prophets and their writings, and they replied, "Either they must have said and contained what

---

[1] ابو الفتح ابن ابو الحسن
السامرى الدنغى الموسوى (Bodl.;

Imp. Library, Paris). Two copies in Berlin Library (Petermann, Rosen) recently acquired.

2 F

stood in the Pentateuch, and then their saying it again was
superfluous; or more; or less;[1] either of which was again
distinctly prohibited in the Thora; or finally they must
have *changed* the Laws, and these were unchangeable." A
Greek who stood near, observed that Laws must be adapted
to different times, and altered accordingly; whereupon the
Samaritan proved that this was only the case with human,
not with Divine Laws: moreover, the seventy Elders had
left them the explicit command not to accept a word beside
the Thora. The king now fully approved of their translation,
and gave them rich presents. But to the Jews he strictly
enjoined, not even to approach Mount Gerizim. There can
be no doubt that there is a certain historical fact, however
contorted, at the bottom of this (comp. the Talmudical and
other accounts of the LXX.), but we cannot now further
pursue the subject. A lengthened extract from this chronicle
—the original text with a German translation—is given by
Schnurrer in Paulus' *Neue Repertorium*, 1790, 117–159.

3. Another " historical" work is the كتاب الاسطير on the
history and genealogy of the patriarchs, from Adam to
Moses, attributed to Moses himself; perhaps the same which
Petermann saw at *Nâblus*, and which consisted of sixteen
vellum leaves (supposed, however, to contain the history of
the world down to the end). An anonymous recent commentary on it, A.H. 1200, A.D. 1784, is in the Brit. Mus. (No.
1140, Add.).

4. Of other Samaritan works, chiefly in Arabic—their Samaritan and Hebrew literature having mostly been destroyed
by the Emperor Commodus—may be briefly mentioned Commentaries upon the whole or parts of their Pentateuch, by
Zadaka b. Manga b. Zadaka;[2] further, by Maddib Eddin
Jussuf b. Abi Said b. Khalef; by Ghazal Ibn Abu-l-Surur
Al-Safawi Al-Ghazzi[3] (A.H. 1167–8, A.D. 1753–4, Brit. Mus.),
&c. Theological works chiefly in Arabic, mixed with Sama-

---

[1] Compare the well-known *dictum*
of Omar on the Alexandrian Library
(Gibbon, ch. 51).

[2] شرح السفر الاول (13th century,

[3] Under the title كاشف الغياهب
عن اسرار المواهب

Bodl.).

ritanisms, by Abul Hassan of Tyre, *On the religious Manners and Customs of the Samaritans and the World to come;* by Mowaffek Eddin Zadaka el Israili, *A Compendium of Religion, on the Nature of the Divine Being, on Man, on the Worship of God;* by Amin Eddin Abu'l Baracat, *On the Ten Commandments;* by Abu'l Hassan Ibn El Markum Gonajem ben Abulfaraj' Ibn Chatár, *On Penance;* by Muhaddib Eddin Jussuf Ibn Salamah Ibn Jussuf Al Askari, *An Exposition of the Mosaic Laws,* &c. &c. Some grammatical works may be further mentioned, by Abu Ishak Ibrahim, *On the Hebrew Language;* by Abu Said, *On reading the Hebrew Text* قوانين المغرا. This grammar begins in the following characteristic manner :—

" Thus said the Sheikh, rich in good works and knowledge, the model, the abstemious, the well-guided Abu Said, to whom God be merciful and compassionate.

" Praise be unto God for His help, and I ask for His guidance towards a clear exposition. I have resolved to lay down a few rules for the proper manner of reading the Holy Writ, on account of the difference which I found, with respect to it, among our co-religionists—whom may God make numerous and inspire to obedience unto Him !—and in such a manner that I shall bring proofs for my assertions, from which the wise could in no way differ. But God knows best!

" Rule 1 : With all their discrepancies about dogmas or religious views, yet all the confessors of the Hebrew religion agree in this, that the ת of the first pers. (sing. perf.) is always pronounced with Kasra, and that a י follows it, provided it has no suffix. It is the same, when the suffix of the plural ם is added to it, according to the unanimous testimony of the MSS., &c."

The treatise concludes, at the end of the 12th Canon or Rule :—

" Often also the perfect is used in the form of the imperative. Thus it is reported of a man of the best reputation, that he had used the form of the imperative in the passage (Ex. iii. 13), ואמרו לי מה שמו—' And they shall say to me, What is his name?' He who reported this to me, is a man of very high standing, against whose truthfulness nothing can be brought forward. But God knows best!

"There are now a few more words to be treated, of which, however, we will treat *vivâ voce*. And blessed be His name for evermore."

5. Their Liturgical literature is more extensive, and not without a certain poetical value. It consists chiefly of hymns (Defter, Durrân) and prayers for Sabbath and Feast-days, and of occasional prayers at nuptials, circumcisions, burials, and the like. We subjoin a few specimens from MSS. in the British Museum, transcribed into Hebrew characters.

The following is part of a Litany for the dead:—

אדני · יהוה · אלהים · ברחמיך · ובך · ובשמך ·
ובכבודך · ובאדונינן · אברהם · ויצחק · ויעקב ·
ואדונינן · משה · וכו'

Lord Jehovah, Elohim, for Thy mercy, and for Thine own sake, and for Thy name, and for Thy glory, and for the sake of our Lords Abraham, and Isaac, and Jacob, and our Lords Moses and Aaron, and Eleazar, and Ithamar, and Pinehas, and Joshua, and Caleb, and the Holy Angels, and the seventy Elders, and the holy mountain of Gerizim, Beth El. If Thou acceptest [תשים] this prayer [מקרא] = reading], may there go forth from before Thy holy countenance a gift sent to protect the spirit of Thy servant, فلان ابن فلان [N. the son of N.], of the sons of [——], daughter [——] from the sons of [——]. O Lord Jehovah, in Thy mercy have compassion on him (او [or] have compassion on her), and rest his (her) soul in the garden of Eden; and forgive him (او [or] her), and all the congregation of Israel who flock to Mount Gerizim Beth El. Amen. Through Moses the trusty. Amen, Amen, Amen.

The next is part of a hymn (see Kirchheim's *Carme Shomron*, emendations on Gesenius, *Carm. Sam.* iii.):—

1.

לית אלה אלא אחר
אלהים קעימה
דקעים עד לעלם
אלה.על.כל חילין
וממי כן לעלם

There is no God but one,
The everlasting God,
Who liveth for ever;
God above all powers,
And who thus remaineth for ever.

2.

בחילך רבה נתרחץ	In Thy great power shall we trust,
דאת הו מרן	For Thou art our Lord;
באלהותך ראגדית	In Thy Godhead; for Thou hast conducted
עלמה מן רישה	The world from beginning.

3.

גבורתך כסיה	Thy power was hidden,
וטהרך ורחמיך	And Thy glory and mercy.
גלין גליאתה וכסאתה	Revealed are both the things that are revealed, and those that are unrevealed
בשלטן אלהותך וכו'	Before the reign of Thy Godhead, &c. &c.

IV. We shall only briefly touch here, in conclusion, upon the strangely contradictory rabbinical laws framed for the regulation of the intercourse between the two rival nationalities of Jews and Samaritans in religious and ritual matters; discrepancies due partly to the ever-shifting phases of their mutual relations, partly to the modifications brought about in the Samaritan creed, and partly to the now less now greater acquiescence of the Jews in the religious state of the Samaritans. Thus we find the older Talmudical authorities disputing whether the Cuthim (Samaritans) are to be considered as "Real Converts" גירי אמת, or only converts through fear—"Lion Converts" / גירי אריות—in allusion to the incident related in 2 K. xvii. 25 (*Baba K.* 38; *Kidush.* 75, &c.). One Rabbi holds כותי כגוי, "A Samaritan is to be considered as a heathen;" while R. Simon b. Gamaliel—the same whose opinion on the Sam. Pent. we had occasion to quote before—pronounces that they are "to be treated in every respect like Israelites" (*Dem. Jer.* ix. 2; *Ketub.* 11, &c.). It would appear that notwithstanding their rejection of all but the Pentateuch, they had adopted many traditional religious practices from the Jews—principally such as were derived direct from the Books of Moses. It was acknowledged that they kept these ordinances with even greater rigour than those from whom they adopted them. The utmost confidence was therefore placed in them for their ritually slaughtering animals, even fowls (*Chul.* 4 a); their

wells are pronounced to be conformed to all the conditions.
prescribed by the Mishnah (*Toseph. Mikw.* 6; comp. *Mikw.*
8, 1). See, however *Abodah Zarah* (Jer. v. 4). Their unleavened bread for the Passover is commended (*Git.* 10;
Chul. 4); their cheese (*Mas. Cuth.* 2); and even their whole
food is allowed to the Jews (*Ab. Zar.* Jer. v. 4). Compare
John iv. 8, where the disciples are reported to have gone
into the city of Samaria to buy food. Their testimony was
valued in that most stringent matter of the letter of divorce
(*Mas. Cuth.* ii.). They were admitted to the office of circum-
cising Jewish boys (*Mas. Cuth.* i.)—against R. Jehudah, who
asserts that they circumcise " in the name of Mount Gerizim "
(*Abodah Zarah,* 43). The criminal law makes no difference
whatever between them and the Jews (*Mas. Cuth.* 2; *Makk.*
8); and a Samaritan who strictly adheres to his own special
creed is honoured with the title of a Cuthi-Chaber (*Gittin,*
10 *b*; *Middah,* 33 *b*). By degrees, however, inhibitions began
to be laid upon the use of their wine, vinegar, bread (*Mas.
Cuth.* 2; *Toseph.* 77, 5), &c. This intermediate stage of
uncertain and inconsistent treatment, which must have lasted
for nearly two centuries, is best characterized by the small
rabbinical treatise quoted above—*Massecheth Cuthim* (2nd
cent. A.D.)—first edited by Kirchheim (שבע מס' קטנות
ירושלמי) Francf. 1851,—the beginning of which reads:—
" The ways (treatment) of the Cuthim (Samaritans), *sometimes* like Goyim (heathens) *sometimes* like Israel." No less
striking is its conclusion:

" And why are the Cuthim not permitted to come into the
midst of the Jews? Because they have mixed with the
priests of the heights" (idolaters). R. Ismael says: "They
were *at first* pious converts (גירי צדק = real Israelites), and
why is the intercourse with them prohibited? Because of
their illegally begotten children,[1] and because they do not
fulfil the duties of יבם (marrying the deceased brother's
wife);" a law which they understand, as we saw above, to
apply to the betrothed only.

---

[1] The briefest rendering of ממזרים which we can give—a full explanation
of the term would exceed our limits.

"At what period are they to be received (into the Community)?" "When they abjure the Mount Gerizim, recognise Jerusalem (viz., its superior claims), and believe in the Resurrection."[1]

We hear of their exclusion by R. Meïr (*Chul.* 6) in the third generation of the Tanaim, and later again under R. Abbuha, the Amora, at the time of Diocletian; this time the exclusion was unconditional and final (*Jer. Abodah Zarah,* 5, &c.). Partaking of their bread[2] was considered a transgression, to be punished like eating the flesh of swine (*Zeb.* 8, 6). The intensity of their mutual hatred, at a later period, is best shown by dicta like that in *Meg.* 28, 6. "May it never happen to me that I behold a Cuthi." "Whoever receives a Samaritan hospitably in his house, deserves that his children go into exile" (*Synh.* 104, 1). In Matt. x. 5 Samaritans and Gentiles are already mentioned together; and in Luke xvii. 18 the Samaritan is called "a stranger" (ἀλλογενής). The reason for this exclusion is variously given. They are said by some to have used and sold the wine of heathens for sacrificial purposes (*Jer.* ib.); by others they were charged with worshipping the dove sacred to Venus; an imputation over the correctness of which hangs, up to this moment, a certain mysterious doubt. It has, at all events, never been brought home to them, that they really worshipped this image, although it was certainly seen with them, even by recent travellers.

---

[1] On this subject the Pent. contains nothing explicit. They at first rejected that dogma, but adopted it at a later period, perhaps since Dositheus; comp. the sayings of Jehudda-hadassi and Massudi, that one of the two Samaritan sects believes in the Resurrection; Epiphanius Leontius, Gregory the Great, testify unanimously to their former unbelief in this article of their *present* faith.

[2] פת, Lightfoot "bucclla" (?).

XVII.

THE BOOK OF JASHER.[1]

A VERY instructive work might be written on the "Lost Books of the Bible." The number of "biblical" writings that perished must be very considerable indeed. Distinct traces of a great many have survived in our Canon. There is, *e.g.*, the "Book of the Wars of Jehovah," in Numbers. In Kings the "Book of the History of Solomon" is referred to. In Chronicles we are told of histories by Samuel, Nathan the Prophet, Gad the Seer, as sources for the life of David. In the same work there are references for the further history of Solomon to the "Prophecy of the Silonite Ahia," the "Vision of the Seer Jedai (Iddo) on Jeroboam." The Books of the Kings adduce (more than thirty times) certain Annals both of the kings of Judah and of Israel as separate works, speaking of them moreover, under different titles, so as to further favour the belief of the existence of several contemporary historical compilations. Isajah in his turn is mentioned as historiographer in Chronicles, where, further, the writings of Shemajah, of Jehu, of Hosai, &c., are spoken of. Of all these productions, great or small, there is no living trace now. They seem, indeed, to have dropped out of man's memory at a very early period. If they gave rise to some moderate discussions it was principally with regard to the possible identity of some of the differently named works. There is, however, one book mentioned in the Bible which people seemed and seem unable ever to forget. And this is the so-called "Book of Jasher." The discussions and vexations, the labours, swindles, and never-ending confusions to which this book has given rise, from the days of the

---

[1] Re-printed, by permission, from the 'Pall Mall Gazette,' August 7, 1868.

Talmud to the most recent *Times*, invest it with an importance which possibly would not have been allotted to it had it survived complete from the first letter to the last.

To begin with, the name "Book of Jasher" (or Jashar) is, at best, a misnomer. Jashar is not, as far as we know, a proper name. But if it were, it could not be one in this special connection, from grammatical reasons. It is a simple adjective (or noun), and means "upright," "just." Twice this work is distinctly quoted in the Bible : once in Joshua, on the occasion of the battle of Gibeon, and once in Samuel, at the death of Jonathan. On the first occasion it is quoted as containing Joshua's song of victory ; on the second it is referred to for David's dirge. The only reasonable inference to be drawn from both passages seems this, that the book alluded to was a collection of songs composed upon certain events important in national history. Whether it contained, also, a running prose narrative which illustrated these poetical portions is at least doubtful. That it must have existed before the "Redaction" of the Book of Joshua in its present form: and, further, that it was not completed before the time of David, seems obvious. Also that it must have disappeared at an early period. But it is very strange to see how people of old could not be brought to believe in its loss, in the face of the perfectly recognized fact that innumerable literary treasures had perished before and during the captivity: in the face even of the narrow escape which books like Ezekiel, Proverbs, the Song of Songs, Ecclesiastes, had had from being placed on the Index by the first compilers of the Canon. The Talmud, in answer to the question, "What is the Book Hayyashar?" contains many and strange conjectures proffered by the various Doctors. The passages plainly quoted in the Bible from that book are not even taken as quotations: but, in accordance with some ingeniously found similarities or allusions, it is variously pronounced to mean either Genesis, *i.e.* the book of "Abraham, Isaac, and Jacob—the Upright Ones," or Deuteronomy, or Judges. The Aramaic version (Targum) translates both times, vaguely, "Book of the Law," which may mean the Pentateuch or the

entire Old Testament. The Vulgate, following the first-
named Talmudical opinion (which is also adopted in the
" Midrash of Genesis" and by some later authorities), has:
the upright ones—" Liber Justorum." The Syriac Version
is at variance with itself. By a small orthographical contrivance the questionable word may be transformed, both in
Hebrew and in Syriac, into " song," a word which would be
particularly fitting to the probable contents of the book.
And so, while in the one passage the Peshito renders Yashar
by Ashir, it substitutes in the other a distinct and different
term, viz. " Hymns of Praise."

Those that came after, the scholiasts and the commentators and the critics, found the feast ready prepared. They
fell upon these different opinions, appropriated them, modified
them, expounded them, played upon them. Whether the
word was to be taken in the singular or the plural sense,
whether it meant righteous or song, when and by whom the
Book was composed, what it contained, whether it was an
independent work at all, whether it was intended to designate
any, and which, of the twenty-four canonical books—from
Genesis to the Minor Prophets—these questions have been
ventilated both in the church and in the synagogue with
a zeal which is both astounding and instructive.

It was about the thirteenth century that the opinion
began to get whispered abroad among Jewish scholars that
the whole quarrel was, as the German proverb has it, about
" the Emperor's beard." There was once such a book, some
boldly began to pronounce, but that book was lost. And not
long after this there appeared, one after the other, no less
than three " Books of Jashar" in the field. Let us add at
once that only *one* of these seemed to lay claim (we have
failed to discover that it really did so) to the honour of
being that long lost work itself. Written in correct, even
in elegant Hebrew, this particular book, well known now,
contained the story from the creation of Adam to the time of
the Judges. The pre-Mosaic period fills about three-fourths
of it, the Mosaic period one-fifth, and a few pages are devoted to the rest. The Song of Joshua—a mere mosaic of

biblical passages—is given in full ; that of David, however,
is not found there. Legends, as well as dates and genea-
logies, abound in it, and many an obscure passage in Scripture is explained skilfully. To add to the interest, a cleverly
written preface recounted how the book was found by one of
Titus's generals, (" bishops," as the Judæo-German version
has it), in the possession of an old man who at the siege of
Jerusalem had hidden himself in some cunningly contrived
little secret edifice. He had known, he told the general,
that the destruction was impending, and he had endeavoured
thus to place himself out of harm's reach. He had not only
taken with him "*brave*" eating and drinking, but books
rare and precious to while away his time. Need it be said
that the general instantly took a fancy to that old man and
his books—among which there was this wondrous document
—and brought him home to *Sevilla*, where he built him a
house, " which is to be seen there unto this day " ?

The book became immensely popular, and it richly deserved its popularity. But, to the grief of the biblio-
graphers, it became known, apart from its own famous title,
under two other names, which, again, in their turn, belonged
to distinct other works. Worse still, when it was first translated (into Judæo-German), a fourth title was given to it—
with a special purpose. No one, however, seems to have
doubted its authenticity : that is, its being that lost treasure
to which Joshua and Samuel referred. Until modern criticism looked into the matter and found—shall it be said ?—
that it was a clever compilation from the Talmud, from
various Midrashim, from Pseudo-Josephus (Josippon), and
many popular Jewish and Arabic legends, that it made suspicious mention of such words as Abdallah, Ali, Mohammed,.
Abu Jussuf, Emir, Khalif, &c. : all of which things put
together led to the irresistible conclusion that it was one of
the latest offshoots (the latest, perhaps) of the legendary
development known as Midrash, that it arose between the
twelfth and thirteenth century A.D., and that its birthplace
was Spain.

But we spoke of three books of that name. Of the two

others one appeared under the name of its author, Jacob, called "Tham," of Rameru, who died in 1171, and who was the most celebrated of the three grandsons of the celebrated Rashi (still falsely called Jarchi). This contains merely legal matters, or rather Talmudical discussions, and could not, one would have thought, have given rise to any confusion. Yet it did. A third book which appeared about one hundred and fifty years later, under the same title, was, again, hopelessly mixed up with it. This was a book of ethics, treating, in eighteen chapters, of topics for pious reflections, such as the creation, worship, faith, repentance, prayer, abstinence, the world to come, death, &c. And, intentionally or not, it was ascribed to the author of the foregoing work: upon whom was then also, intentionally we believe, fathered a certain connection with the above legendary book. Here again modern criticism had to do its work. That last-named ethical work is, there can no longer be any doubt, due to one Zerachiah, "the Greek," and was composed before the end of the fourteenth century.

So far we have to deal with Hebrew works, every one of which, though a *crux* to the bibliographer, is of real value and use for the student, as not unworthily representing three great branches of Hebrew literature—the legal, the ethical, and the legendary.

Three "Books of Jasher," however, were not deemed sufficient, it seems. There appeared in the year 1751 a book in London under the title "The Book of Jasher, with testimonies and notes explanatory of the text, to which is [sic] prefixed various readings. Translated into English from Hebrew by Alcuin of Britain, who went a pilgrimage into the Holy Land." A note by Wickliffe is appended, wherein he states that he approves of the book, but does not want it to be made part of the Canon. In the introduction it is related how the book came to England. "I, Alcuin of Britain," it begins, "was minded to travel into the Holy Land and into the Province of Persia in search of Holy things, and to see the wonders of the East, and I took unto me two companions, who learned with me in the

University of Oxford all those languages which the people of the East speak, namely, Thomas of Malmesbury and John of Huntingdon; and though we went as pilgrims, yet we took with us silver and gold and riches. And when we came unto Bristol we went into a ship bound for Rome, where we tarried six months, and learned more perfectly the Persic language." It goes on to relate how they heard of the existence of that long-lost book, and how they came, after many vicissitudes, to the city of Gazna, and then, after endless troubles and bribings (always with " wedges of gold "), they contrived to see the precious manuscript, which was in width " 2 foot 3 inches and in length about 9 foot." It was written in a large, clear, and beautiful hand. When, after long and vain attempts on their part, the final permission for the translation was given to them, every precaution had to be used. The three men worked at it for one year and six months (some sixty pages), and, when they had finished, new gold wedges had to be used for the permission of taking away their copy. At last, after an absence of seven years, they returned by way of Ispahan and Rome to Bristol city. While in Rome, Alcuin says, he went to see the Pope, who was then ninety-five years of age, and he showed him this book. The Pope had never heard of it. Then, turning to the places in the Bible which referred to it, he cried out, " I have lived to the age of forgetfulness." " Some years after my arrival," the preface concludes, "I related this adventure to several, and showed them this work, who advised me not to suffer a copy of it to fall into the hands of the stationer lest I should incur the displeasure of the purple. Being now grown old and infirm, I have left it among other papers to a clergyman in Yorkshire."

Nothing, indeed, could exceed the utter craziness of this production, which, with its variants, its marginal glosses, its references to and extracts from, works of " Hur " (who again quotes the "Book of Aron"), Phinehas, Othniel, Jazer, Jezer, Zadok, Tobias, and the rest (much in the style of the

maddest Gnostic tracts), imposed not merely upon the
populace, but upon divines and men of learning.   In vain
did the *Monthly Review* of December of that same year,
1751, expose it.   "The whole," it concludes its criticism,
"is so full of blunders, inconsistencies, and absurdities that
we think it beneath further notice."   In vain was it urged
that Gazna was not in Persia; that Alcuin never left
Europe; that in the ninth century people did not write
modern English; that the Authorised Version, from which
that book was to a great extent almost literally taken, did
not exist at the time of Alcuin; that stationers were not
known at that time any more than the "paper on which it
is wrote" could have had any existence 300 years before its
invention; that the University of Oxford, where Alcuin had
learnt "all the Eastern languages," was not founded till
eighty-two years after his death.   In vain, also, was it
proved by irrefutable evidence that that whole trash was
due to one Ilive, a half-insane London printer, who in 1733
had published an "oration" in which he proved "the plurality of worlds," and further asserted that earth was hell,
that the souls of men were apostate angels, and that the fire
on the day of judgment would be immaterial; who after
this became a public preacher on "infidelity," and hired
Carpenters' Hall for his orations, chiefly taken from Tindal.
Nay, even the confession of his assistant in the composition
of this work, viz. that "they had laboured at it in dead
secret," that "the forms were worked off in the night time
in a private press-room after the men of the printing-house
had left their work," did not prevail.   People believed in
the book, and here is a specimen of it :—

"1. Whilst it was the beginning, darkness overspread the
face of nature.   2. And the æther moved: upon the surface
of the chaos.   3. And it came to pass that a great light
shone forth from the firmament: and enlightened the abyss.
4. And the abyss fled before the face of light, and divided
between the light and the darkness.   5. So that the face of
nature was formed : a second time. . . . 13. And it came to

pass in the process of time that the *man conceived* and brought forth Cain," &c. &c.

Marginal explanations furnished the original " Hebrew "— in English, of course. Thus for " beginning " the Hebrew had, it was stated, " the prime;" for nature, " the desert;" for æther, the "atoms;" for chaos, " confused mass of matter."

Well, this " chaos," or confused mass of matter, written according to Alcuin-Ilive *by* Jasher, the son of Caleb, was reprinted at Bristol (apparently in two editions) in 1829. Nearly one thousand of the most " literary characters," prelates, dignitaries, public establishments, the prospectus to the second edition stated, had subscribed to it; and while unpractical Ilive had sold his " Editio Princeps " for the modest sum of half-a-crown, his " Bristol pirate " fixed the price at ten shillings, from which it rose to a sovereign. The alterations made in the new issue—the editor of which, of course, had never heard of the first publication, though he copied it almost literally from beginning to end—were very characteristic. The translation here was stated to have been made in *Anglo-Saxon*, and to crown the unexampled impudence, reference is made to Alcuin's published works, in which he himself is stated to have spoken of this translation, and where, of course, not one syllable regarding it is to be found. This, no doubt, is the work mentioned by some of the *Times'* recent correspondents.

The list is not exhausted yet. . There is still the " Book of Jasher" by Dr. Donaldson. Of this we would speak,— though, in common with most critics, we are utterly at variance with the ingenious theories propounded in this book,—with very high respect. The attempt has been made here, as our readers probably are aware, to reconstruct Jashar —mosaically, as it were—out of various portions and passages in the Bible. The book, that investigator held, was compiled during the reign of David, as " the first offspring of the prophetic schools," and contained, as it were, the marrow of the Old Testament. But on this we shall not enlarge.

Thus much of the "Book of Jasher." In the face of the unceasing flow of ingenious correspondence regarding this book, which an accident has again brought into prominence, we have deemed it our duty to enter somewhat fully into the strange vicissitudes of its story.

In the face of this same correspondence also we thought it better patiently to abide our time till now.

XVIII.

EARLY ARABIC POETRY.[1]

THE traces which have come down to our times of the lite-rature that Arabia possessed during the long period prece-ding the Mohammedan era are of the scantiest description. Yet, as far back as the golden epoch of Hebrew literature, fully sixteen hundred years before the birth of the Prophet, Arab culture must have stood in very high renown. Solo-mon's own transcendent wisdom is likened unto the wisdom of the Arabs; the Queen of Sheba is an Arab Queen, and Job's wise friends are Arabs. But Islam so completely blotted out all that went before it, that the past with all its mental labour became in reality a "time of ignorance" for succeeding generations. Nothing palpable, nothing reliable at least, has survived that could be ascribed to a period anterior to the fifth century of our own era; save perhaps a few Himyaritic votive tablets, which there are few to read and fewer still to understand. Nor are the surviving relics in the real "Ishmaelite" Arabic like those of Assyria and Babylon, in which are found treatises on history, astronomy, theology, grammar, poetry, and all the arts and sciences that refined man is heir to. All we have recovered, and are still re-covering, consists of an infinitesimal number of complete poems, and a comparatively larger number of poetical chips, imbedded as quotations in the various writings of the en-lightened ages that followed.

Small as is their whole sum and substance, they yet prove unmistakably that, brilliant as were the periods of Arabic

---

[1] *Beiträge zur Kenntniss der Poesie der alten Araber.* Von Theodor Nöl-deke. Hannover: Rümpler. Re- printed by permission from the 'Satur-day Review,' June 17, 1865.

literature known to us, none were so brilliant as that of which we have so little knowledge—that immediately preceding Mohammed. Poetry at that time formed the chief glory of an Arab's life. If a poet arose in the midst of a tribe, the other tribes sent embassies of congratulation. There was feasting and dancing, exactly as on those two other proudest occasions of the birth of a young prince or the foaling of a noble mare. Mecca, and afterwards Okhad, were the Arabic Olympias where the poets held their contests under the eyes of all the nation. How it was that poetry declined at the very moment when it ought to have lifted up its head more proudly than ever—that an ancient, vast, and glorious literature was irredeemably lost among a people not conquered, but conquering, not dying, but renewing their strength like the eagle—we cannot here explain. It is essential, however, to bear in mind that all ancient Arabic literature was oral ; that, further, it was all in verse ; and that, finally, the prophet did not like poetry, save his own. And this poetry of his, except in a few instances where it rises to genuine inspiration, is of a mediocre, flat, and wearisome kind. It was very natural that Mohammed, who appealed to its superiority as a sign and proof of his divine mission, should hate rivals of his craft, particularly such rivals as might excel or even attack him. And the poets were wont to vex his soul. They wrote the most popular and heart-rending dirges upon those who had fallen fighting against him at Badr. They were occasionally personal, calling him a humbug, a madcap, a ridiculous pretender. They laughed at the people of Medina for listening to a mere runaway foreigner. There was particularly one old Jewish lady who wrote squibs on him that cut him to the quick. " By Him in whose hands my soul is," he said to Câab Ibn Malek, " these satires wound me more than arrows." He caused counter-satires to be written, but they failed. Even the "sudden visitation" by which some of the worst offenders, men and women, young and old, were found struck to death, did not stop the "press." At last he had a revelation on the subject. "Shall I declare unto you," he asks in the Surah called "the Poets," "upon whom the devils descend? They descend upon every lying and wicked person. . . . most of them are liars. And those who err follow the steps of the Poets. Seest thou not how they rove as bereft of their senses through every valley?" Poetry, in short, as the sole vehicle of all science, all tradition, all religion of the old *régime*, could not be countenanced by the prophet, except in the one instance of the Book that had lain "hidden under the Divine Throne" until the times were ripe.

That an ancient literature was wilfully destroyed by fanatical hands, as has often been asserted, we do not believe; for nothing can be destroyed wilfully but what exists palpably. Nothing being written down, it could not be torn, burnt, buried out of sight. But, at the same time, tradition is of a delicate nature. Unless constantly tended, watched over carefully, and incessantly repeated, it is apt to be quickly forgotten. Add to this that the Arabs, apart from the interdict, had better things to do for a time than to repeat the older strains of love and revenge, the tent and desert idyls, the "superstitions" or the stirring deeds of old. A new life more brilliant, more dazzling, than any they had ever dreamed of opened to them. From conquest to conquest, from glory to glory, they went onwards, and the green flag waving aloft, seized upon the golden lands of the Orient. But when to the stormy times of the acquisition under the Ommayads the peaceful times of possession under the Abassides succeeded— when the Caliphs dwelt in fairy palaces, and the rough and simple sons of the desert had exchanged their linen tents for cool and vast marble halls, and the shock of battles was followed by the rich and lazy ease of city life—the hearts of both rulers and ruled began to yearn for the sweet voice of the minstrel. Suddenly, at that juncture, traditions till then unknown came to light, which albeit oral, were considered as genuine as the Koran, the written word itself. "Teach your children the art of poetry," the prophet had said, according to the Sunnah, "for it opens the understanding and maketh valour hereditary." However, the golden time of poetry was not to be recalled by apocryphal traditions any more than by royal edicts and court patronage. Besides, the old Kasida, the only received normal form of poetry, no longer befitted the circumstances. It invariably commenced with a sorrowful remembrance of the poet's lady-love, who had gone none knew whither, and the very traces of whose tent, but yesterday gleaming afar in the wide desert-sands, had been effaced over-night. It then drifted off into the praises of the darling camel, the horse, and the sword, by whose aid he would take sure and swift revenge on all his enemies; and into similar strains, little suited for peaceful dwellers in towns and hamlets, in gardens and by rivers. New forms, however, were but of slow growth. Thus both rulers and ruled, the golden period having fled, had to put up with the next best thing, the silver period—well enough in its way, but wanting to a great extent in the old simplicity of conception, the genuine, honest sentiment, the whole tone and colour of the grand desert-songs of yore. With it, however, we have no concern here.

The golden period, then, of which we have spoken, and in the latter days of which Mohammed lived and died, stretches as far as we can ascertain, over about two hundred years. But slight are the changes which poetry underwent in it both as regards matter and form. As to the additional remnants found, and here published for the first time from MSS. in Leyden, Gotha, and Berlin, by Dr. Nöldeke, the greater part of them belongs to the latter, the most important to the earlier, section of that period. The author, so far from merely publishing and editing them, has re-imbedded them in a series of most instructive and readable essays, to which, as a kind of introduction, he has prefixed an interesting chapter on the history of criticism of ancient Arabic poetry. He here dwells chiefly on the difficulties met even by the most experienced investigator on this widely-remote field, where everything looks so wondrous strange. Monotonous as is the life of these old Bedouins, so, at first, appears their poetry. The same string of thought recurs often in the self-same order in the different poets; a circumstance which has misled some critics into the belief of their being utterly wanting in individuality. Another drawback is that woefully piecemeal state in which these fragments have come down to us; a single popular line or stanza being often the sole remnant of long poems. Irrespectively of this, the "Faith" had a hand in them, remodelling or destroying as was deemed fit. There were also some who, aided by the boundless wealth of the Arabic language, deliberately changed words and phrases because they preferred certain others of their own fancy. Thus the outraged Dûrrumma swears at people who quietly change a word, the finding of which has cost him sleepless nights, for another which is commonplace and of a different quantity; and he strongly recommends writing as a remedy for this evil. A further cause of mischief was the manifold number of versions of single favourite poems; particularly when the schools tried to put them to rights by eliminating what were often the most valuable variations. What had not the *imprimatur* of the *savans* and the pious was cast aside, and no more heard of. We may add that forgeries in the manner of Ossian were not unusual. Wholesale fatherings upon primeval authorities of productions good, bad, and worse are recorded. The wise men of Kufa, the place of the Koran-scribes which also gave its name to the ancient Kufic character, are recorded to have once sat in full conclave to decide upon the question which ancient authority should be declared the author of a poem they had just heard from a Bedouin. All these difficulties, combined with the absence of vowels and the frequent lack or incorrectness of the diacritical points —not to speak of the crying want of satisfactory works of reference—render this study by no means light and agreeable at first sight. Yet it has its reward. These fragments may be broken, defaced, dimmed, and obscured by fanaticism, ignorance, and neglect, but out of them there arises anew all the freshness, bloom, and glory of desert-song, as out of Homer's epics rise the glowing springtime of humanity and the deep blue heavens of Hellas. It is not a transcendental poetry, rich in deep and thoughtful legend and lore, or glittering in the many-coloured prisms of fancy, but a poetry the chief task of which is to paint life and nature as they really are; and within its narrow bounds it is magnificent. It is chiefly and characteristically full of manliness, of vigour, and of a chivalrous spirit, doubly striking when compared with the spirit of abjectness and slavery found in some other Asiatic nations. It is wild and vast and monotonous as the yellow seas of its desert solitudes; it is daring and noble, tender and true.

One of the most interesting chapters of the book is formed by Ibn Kuteiba's "Introduction to the Poets," hitherto un-edited. This Introduction not only contains many hitherto unknown "chips," introduced by way of specimens, together with a number of shrewd, naïve, and often caustic remarks of his own, but it evinces also a rough-and-ready kind of eman-cipation on the part of the Arabic *littérateur* from prejudice and authority, and a quaint soundness of æsthetical judgment in general. He cares not for the time in which the poet lived. "What is in chronology?" he asks. "God made every ancient writer young in his day, and every great man was, by His decree, once a very small man and a mere beginner." As may be expected from this spirit of impar-tiality, he excludes many of those nonentities who somehow have scrambled into a shady nook of Parnassus. Everybody, he argues, has written a poem once in a way. Among the "motive causes" which speed the poet he enumerates Drink-ing, Joy, Wrath, and Love. "They said to Kutayir—How do you manage when writing poetry becomes difficult to you? He said, 'I walk through the deserted habitations and through the blooming greenswards; then the most perfect songs become easy, and the most beautiful ones flow natu-rally.'" But when the poet's nature has been grieved by bad food or sorrow, everything goes wrong. Alfarazdak said, "I am, according to the judgment of the Tamimites, the best poet among them; yet sometimes an hour comes over me when I could rather have a tooth pulled out than make a verse."

Another of Dr. Nöldeke's essays treats of the poems of the Jews in Arabia. How important every fragment relating to the history of Judaism in Arabia—the principal albeit sadly troubled source of Mohammedanism—must be to the historian of Islam need not be urged. Yet there is not much to be recovered. Dr. Nöldeke is of opinion, and we entirely agree with him, that a great Jewish immigration into Arabia cannot well have taken place before the destruction of Jerusalem by Titus or Hadrian. The poetry of the Arab Jews, as far as we know it, exhibits, strangely enough, scarcely any special national traits. Not even Biblical or Haggadistic reminiscences are to be met with in their stanzas. They are Arabic *pur sang*, in style, tone, and contents. They are characterized throughout, according to Dr. Nöldeke, by a grand, noble, manly, honest spirit. Assamaual Suba, Aarabi, Garîd, are some of the foremost stars of song, not to mention Kab ben Alasraf, one of Mohammed's bitterest enemies.

Of all the remnants of primitive Arabic poetry none are more striking, more everlastingly beautiful than the elegies. There is a depth and a simplicity of pathos in the laments of Mutammim on the death of his brother Mâlik, who, a relapsed convert from Mohammedanism, was cruelly slaughtered by Châlid, Abu Bekr's general, not often met with. Alchansa, 'the most celebrated Arabic poetess, also shines exclusively in elegiac poetry. Her laments over her two murdered brothers, Muâwya and Sachr, are most pathetic, tender and passionate; yet no translation could ever convey the fulness of their beauty; to be appreciated they must be read in the majestic, soft sonorous words of the original.

Not the least curious chapter in the book is the last, on the "Bedouins cheating their creditors," containing a number of mocking-verses on usurers, overreached in cunning by the simple dwellers of the desert. It seems as if all the latent fun of these healthily constituted Arab minds had burst out here. There is a recklessness of humour, and an utter absence of "Philistine" notions of honesty—an absence which Dr. Nöldeke endeavours to excuse as best he can—about them, that administer many a shock to our received idea of the permanent gravity and piety of these ancients, but are most essential to the general truthfulness and rounding-off of the picture.

So much for the expression given, by the earliest poets known to us among the ancient Arabs, to the comedy and tragedy of their lives. The strains collected together here are but scanty, faint, and broken ; but we recognise in them the full accents of human joy and sorrow, of love and of valour, of passion and of truth. Our best thanks are due to Dr. Nöldeke for having undertaken this by no means easy task, and for having performed it with his wonted erudition and industry.

XIX.

ARABIC POETRY IN SPAIN AND SICILY.[1]

PERHAPS the most interesting period of Arabic history and literature, and the one which has most directly influenced European culture, belongs to the time of the Moorish possession of Spain. It is well known how the almost demoniacal power which, in scarcely two generations after Mohammed, had carried his flag from the Chinese mountains to the Atlantic began to collapse shortly after these gigantic conquests were achieved. The Empire of the Chalifs, more colossal than either the Roman Empire before or the Mongolian after it, broke down almost simultaneously at its two extreme ends. While in the far-away East, in the hollows of Paropamisus, the primeval banner of Iran was lifted up anew by the Tahirites, the Sheikhs of " Andalus," as all Spain was called, refused to be ruled any longer by the arbitrary governors sent to them from distant Arabia. At the same time, a change of dynasty took place in the heart of the Empire — a change sealed by one of the most dastardly massacres known even in Eastern history. Abu'l Abbas, the first of the new Abbasside rulers, not satisfied with having completely superseded the Omayyads, resolved to stamp them out even to their last trace. Abdallah, the Governor of Damascus, received the order to invite all the scions of the unhappy house of Omayya to a feast of reconciliation

[1] " Poesie und Kunst der Araber in Spanien und Sicilien." Von A. F. von Schack. Berlin: Hertz. Reprinted by permission from the 'Saturday Review,' November 17, 1866.

and goodwill. At that feast, the recital of an appropriate poem having given the signal, they were all, about ninety in number, suddenly fallen upon and murdered. Carpets were drawn over the dying victims, and louder waxed the revel while the hall swam in their blood. Nor did this hecatomb satisfy the enthusiasts of the new era. The royal tombs were opened, and their ashes were given to the winds.

But the star of the Omayyads that had gone down in the East shone forth anew in the West. Abdarrahman, a grandson of Hisham, had escaped. Of his many and strange adventures during his flight the Arab legend sings and says. At last, in the depths of the African desert, the Andalusian Sheikhs discovered him, and offered him the crown of Spain. In August, 755, he crossed the Straits, and was received in triumph by his new lieges. What internal and external foes there were, he swiftly subdued, and when Roland had broken his good sword Durenda at Roncevel, and the forlorn wails of his horn had died away, the last danger that threatened the independence of the realm seemed passed for ever. Soon the new Empire began to outshine all contemporary Europe in power and glory. Cordova, the city chosen as the capital by Abdarrahman, became the crown of Europe. The fame of its greatness and splendour, its hundreds of thousands of marble houses, its three thousand mosques, its twenty-eight suburbs, all thronged with the richest and happiest population under the sun, spread to the end of the world— even to the convent of Gandersheim in Saxony, to Hroswitha the poetess. In the midst of her lay of the martyrdom of St. Pelagius, she bursts forth into a rhapsody about this heathen city, "the brightest splendour of the world."

If the Abbassides made Bagdad "the Athens of the East," the Omayyads made Cordova the centre of all the science and art of the West. Apart from the capital, schools and academies arose through the length and the breadth of the Peninsula, and students from all parts of the world came to sit at the feet of the great masters of philosophy, mathematics, history, medicine, and the rest, who had taken up their abode in that blissful land. The literature that sprang up from such an almost unprecedented movement of mind was enormous. No less than four hundred thousand books, mostly the works of Spanish authors, are recorded to have formed the library of Hakem, one of the later Omayyads, when it was partly destroyed by the Berbers. Six months were required to dispose of those literary treasures that had not perished in the assault. Yet while all branches of literature seem to have been cultivated with nearly equal assiduity and genius, the centre and flower of all was poetry. Abdarrahman I. himself cultivated the art of song. His stanzas to the palm-tree—which, it is said, he was the first to introduce into Europe, "the land of his exile"—are full of melody and feeling. In the course of centuries the guild of Moorish singers grew to such an extent that the mere names of the most renowned among them would fill volumes. It had in fact come to this, that from the highest to the lowest in the land everybody more or less spoke the language of poetry. Al-Kazwini mentions some place where every peasant possessed the talent of improvisation, and a work still in existence treats specially of the poetically gifted kings and nobles of Andalusia. The women in the harems, the officials at their desks, the chroniclers in the bewildering midst of their dates and names, the merchants in their business correspondence—all introduced some poetical scrap or other in their spoken or written speech, if they did not indeed burst out into an independent stanza or two. Poetry was the all-pervading element, without which there seemed to be neither light nor life for these Moors. Nor was it to be feared that the literature of Spain should become one-sided and mannered, or its language corrupted by provincialisms, as would have been the case had there been no living contact with the lands of the East, where the well of Arabic flowed pure and undefiled. Not more surely do the literary productions of our day fly from one corner of civilization to the other than did those works of learning or poetry which had seen the light at the foot of the Sierra Morena or in the valleys of the Indian Caucasus reach the extreme ends of the

Islamic dominions, carried thither by pious pilgrims or well-equipped caravans.

We have endeavoured[1] to indicate the peculiar character and tone of the poetry before Mohammed, as principally represented in the *Kasida*, the true offspring of the desert. Wild, vague, monotonous, but emphatically tender and passionate, it almost invariably commences with a plaint for the lost love whose tent had been broken up and carried away during the night, then lovingly dwells upon the revenge to be taken by the aid of the swiftest of camels, most valiant of swords, and furthest-reaching 'of lances, and concludes with maxims of wisdom, expressive of the fleeting nature of life which comes and goes like a dwelling in the desert, while the skies are eternal and the stars will rise and set for ever and ever. Well adapted as were these and similar strains for Beduins, they began to assume a strange incongruousness when these same roving shepherds and robbers had become the kings of the world, dwelling in marble palaces which lay by cool streams, in palm and orange groves. When, therefore, the poets, living in the midst of the most refined and luxurious society of the Europe of the day, regardless of altered circumstances, kept on singing in the orthodox strains of the primitive Muallakat or Hamasa, they were swiftly reminded of the reality of things. The " oft-wept ruins of Chaula's dwelling-place in the yellow sands," Ibn Bessan, a writer of the period, declares to have become rather oppressive. Nor does he believe that much effect will be given to the too frequent summons, " Here let us halt, O friends, that we may weep." And as regards the question, " Is this the trace of Umm Aufa ? " nobody really could imagine, he says, that the busy winds would have kept the traces of that young lady intact for these many centuries. On the other hand, he suggests that there may be some poetical fields yet unexplored by the ancients, many a graceful thought and pleasing image that

---

[1] See page 452.

belongs to present springs and summers, preferable perhaps even to those strains which seemed universally accepted chiefly because their authors were long dead and gone. And, slowly but surely, a change did come over Andalusian poetry. Piously embodying many of the old traditions of Beduin thoughts and similes, there was yet a newness of sentiment, a sweet melodiousness, and an almost modern variety pervading it which had been utterly unknown to the olden days. The former passionate outbursts in praise of nature, of love, of hatred, of arms, of animals, become chastened and softened. In the religious strains of this period there is, together with a fervour which at times verges on fanaticism, also perceptible that vague undefinable yearning after the Infinite which is almost a trait of our own day. The elegies and the drinking-songs of those times, their love-strains and their epigrams, are all more or less characteristic of the change. They sing, as was never sung in Arabic before, of nightly boatings by torchlight, of the moon's rays trembling on the waves, of sweet meetings in the depths of rose-gardens, of the Pleiades, of the young cup-bearer, of the King's prowess and generosity, of Spain's glorious cities and rivers, mosques and villas, statuettes and vases, and of the far-away burning desert whence their fathers came. The most successful of these poetical compositions are generally the brief songs which embody the inspiration of the moment. The longer poems lack, to our Western minds, that unity of plan and execution to which classical models have accustomed us. It is surprising how the Arabs—to whom and to the Jews we owe the preservation of the great bulk of antique philosophy and science—should not have profited aught from Greek and Roman poets, with whose works they must surely have come in contact. Their ignorance of them is indeed surprising. Ibn Chaldun, that most learned and accomplished littérateur, mentions, in support of his assertion that the Persians and Greeks too had great poets, the fact of Aristotle praising Homer, whom he himself only knew from hearsay. The great philosopher, Ibn Roshd's, notion of Greek literature

may be gathered from the fact that he defines Tragedy as
"the art of approving," and Comedy as "the art of blaming."

And here we are led to a highly intricate question to
which attention has repeatedly been drawn of late—namely,
the influence of the East and its literature, oral or otherwise,
upon mediæval European literature. Arthur and his whole
Round Table have been traced to the Persian legends of the
Court of Kai Khosru or Nushirwan; the prototype of the
Graal is found in the cup of Djemjid; and whether or not
these and similar strikingly parallel sagas have arisen independently of each other, there can be no doubt about many
of the choicest gems of European folk-lore being originally
Arabic. Yet nothing can be more absurd than the notions
which contemporaneous Europe held about Moorish Spain.
Mohammed is to Turpin a golden idol, guarded by demons,
to whom human sacrifices are offered at Cadiz. The old
French "Roman de Mahomet" represents him as a baron
surrounded by his vassals, possessing the choicest forests,
orchards, rivers, and meadows — in the neighbourhood of
Mecca! Wolfram von Eschenbach, the Minnesinger of
Wartburg memory, relates how one Flegetanis, who knew
the coming and going of the stars and their dread influence
upon man, had first written the story of the Graal in heathen
(Arabic) characters. Gerbert, afterwards Pope Sylvester II.,
who had studied in Seville, became the hero of a mythic
cycle. He had learnt from the Mohammedans what the
flight and the singing of the birds betokened, how the dead
were to be raised, and where lay the hidden treasures of
the earth. Very differently, however, matters stood in the
country itself, where, especially towards the end of the
Arabic rule, a close connection between Arabs and Christians
and their respective civilizations arose—at first in the North
—chiefly through the influence of the "Mozarabic" Christians and the Jews. It was the latter principally who, under
the auspices of the Arabic dominion, not only produced
a brilliant philosophical, astronomical, grammatical, and
poetical literature of their own, but also acted as the chief
mediators between the antique and the modern, the Eastern

and Western, civilizations. It is, above all, Toledo which, after its capture by Alphonso IV., became the centre of Orient and Occident, and which therefore figures in the books of the twelfth and thirteenth centuries as the seat of necromancy and magic arts.   It was there that young Germans learned the black art under Cæsarius of Heisterbach; there Gherardo of Cremona, Michael Scott, and a host of others, subsequently suspected of all manners of devil's lore, went to study Avicenna, Averroës, and Aristotle done into Arabic.   Arabic learning became the common property of the learned world, even as Arabic poetry had long been the common and cherished property of the non-Mohammedan people of Spain, Provence, and even Italy, and remained so down to the terrible fall of Granada—a fall ever to be wept over in the history of Spain, if not of humanity.

Whether, however, Arabic influence on the contents and form of the romance poetry of Spain, such as we know it, was quite as direct as the author of the work before us thinks —whether, in particular, the two most popular stanzas of Spanish-Arabic poetry, the "Muwashaha" and the "Zad-shal," were grafted, unchanged almost, upon Spanish and Provençal poetry—we shall not here discuss.   But there can be no doubt of the existence of most striking reminiscences of Arabic poetry in Perez de Hita's historical romance of the civil wars of Granada, in the cycle of the Cid, and in the different Cancioneros, however similar or dissimilar their metres and the arrangement of their rhymes.   Nor is its influence less apparent in early Italian poetry.   Jacopo da Todi uses the same form for his Christian hymns which the Arabs used for the praise of Allah.   Not a few of the "canzone," "canzonette," and even the "ballatas" of Dante, Petrarca, Boccaccio, exhibit peculiarities of rhyme and metre belonging to the favourite Arabic lyrics.

Next to Spain, Sicily, which had been subdued by the Arabs after hard and protracted fights at the beginning of the ninth century, claims our attention.   But not before the middle of the tenth century, when Palermo became the seat of the Fatimide Governors, do the fruits of the enlightened

Moorish rule become apparent. It was then first that over the plains which in mythical times had listened to Daphne's shepherd songs, and which afterwards echoed the verses of Stesichoros, Theocritos, and Bion, Semitic poetry lifted up its voice. Grave Emirs who had never heard of the name of Æschylus rejoiced in panegyrical Kasidas in the same groves where formerly Prometheus or the Oresteia had moved Hellenic hearts, and where Theron of Akragas and his white team, victorious in the hot race, had been immortalised by Pindar. The golden days of Hiero of Syracuse seemed to have arisen once more, and the voice of song was heard in the palace and in the fields. Even when the Moslem power was broken, Roger and his Norman knights tried to perpetuate the culture of the conquered race. Their arts and sciences, their manners and customs, became the coveted inheritance of the conquerors. The kings of the House of Hauteville copied their pageants and the ceremonial of their whole royal household from the Arabs. Arabic were their coins, Arabic was their era, Arabic, nay Koranic, the mottoes and devices which they publicly adopted. Their palaces were not inaugurated in the name of the Trinity, but in that of Allah, the Merciful, the Compassionate. William the Good was, outwardly at least, much more of a Mohammedan than a Christian; and of Roger of Sicily, Monk Eadmer, his contemporary, relates that he never allowed a Moslem to embrace Christianity—"from what reason I know not, but God will judge him." Regarding Sicilian poetry, there is nothing specially characteristic in what has remained to distinguish it from the Spanish poetry of which we have spoken; except perhaps that to us, upon whom classical reminiscences would come crowding at every step, the utter absence of the slightest allusion to Proserpina, to Polyphemus, to Arethusa, and the rest, is somewhat strange, as strange as the constant allusions to gazelles and camels in Sicily, which never harboured any. There is, however, one unmistakable trait in most of these songs—namely, a certain voluptuous softness which seems indigenous to the island itself.

Of these and other topics connected with the Arabic rule in Europe the work before us pleasantly, though somewhat too rapturously, discourses. Its chief merit, however, seems to us to lie in the translations of the poems with which it is richly studded. The whole history of Spanish-Arabic poetry has hitherto lain fallow, and this first attempt bodily to transplant some of its half-Eastern, half-Western, flowers into German soil deserves to be heartily encouraged. Herr von Schack has in many instances been peculiarly happy in the execution of his task. The whole tone and texture of these strange songs is often reproduced with a faithfulness reminding us of Rückert himself. In the face of the copious modern literature on the subject there seemed to be less occasion for the essays on Moorish art contained in the book, but they too give ample evidence of careful study, worthy of the author and his labour of love.

www.ingramcontent.com/pod-product-compliance
Lightning Source LLC
Chambersburg PA
CBHW032021110726
47901CB00004B/1154